a CHANCE *to* BREATHE

a CHANCE *to* BREATHE

Stories from a 1918 Road Trip

JAMES GARDNER

A Chance to Breathe

First Edition

ISBN: 979-8-9884957-0-3

One of the gifts of being a writer is that it gives you an excuse to do things, to go places and explore. Another is that writing motivates you to look closely at life, at life as it lurches by and tramps around.

—Anne Lamott, Author of *bird by bird*

To the woods and fields or to the hilltops, there to breathe their beauty like the very air: To be not a spectator of, but a participate in, it all!

—John Burroughs, *Our Vacation Days of 1918*

For Judi, Daniel, and Claire,
and in loving memory of my father

An Author's Note

When I began this journey, my goal was to learn more about a 1918 camping trip taken by a group of famous friends. My first inclination, as a lawyer and amateur historian, was to research the trip to a point where I could make more sense of a box of documents collected from a university archive. That way I might be able to talk about it somewhat intelligently. You never know what might come up at a cocktail party. Perhaps, in retrospect, it was simply my attempt to continue something I had started with my father. Perhaps I could recapture a dialogue started years before when sharing time together at the office, or maybe I just needed a grand distraction. Whatever the reasoning, I immersed myself in all things 1918, particularly World War I and the Spanish Flu. I was curious about how Thomas Edison, Henry Ford, Harvey Firestone, and John Burroughs had become friends. Like many, I'm fascinated by stories of collected genius, whether it be painters and writers in Paris or Oxford, or John Adams, Ben Franklin, and Thomas Jefferson cloistered together in a room with instruction to write a declaration of independence. How does this happen? The camping trips, and the unlikely friendships between these four men, jut out like another branch of this curious historical phenomenon. Another more modern historical phenomenon is the need for someone, famous or not, to take time away from normal routines even in a crazy year like 1918. Exploration can always use, well, exploration.

Somewhere along the way, my personal research and travel, morphed into an idea for a book. The world can always use another book on a 1918 camping trip, right? Although the accounts in this book are meant to be historically accurate, it must be noted that they are also based in part on my own observations and experiences. Whether it be meandering the halls of an inn, gazing upon a display, or talking to a tour guide in a museum, much was personally learned by doing, seeing and listening. Retracing the 1918 trip turned out to be the greatest surprise, and, in the end, is a major part of this writing. It felt like the stories of the region and those encountered along the 1918 camping trip should find a role in this play. I hope they have.

A Gift from Polsky's

On an autumn day in 2014, my father and I entered an elevator in a downtown building in Akron, Ohio. Neither of us had any idea what to expect. For the occasion, I packed a few notepads, some pencils, and a pen. I also brought my iPhone™, wallet, and, of course, my ID. As for my dad, he brought what he always carried—his boundless optimism and, as instructed, his wallet and ID. The Art Deco building, had at one time, housed a major department store on Main Street, and was aptly named the Polsky Building in honor of Abraham Polsky and his store. After the company closed the store in 1978, the property was ultimately acquired by the University of Akron and is now home to classrooms, a bookstore, and several fast-food joints. On its lower level, below the Main Street entrance—where it once carried fine jewelry, a men's grooming bar and a delicacy shop—it was known as the Polsky Budget Store. Today, that space, is home to archives managed by the University of Akron. In 2014 these archives included the Firestone collection. As the elevator doors shut, I pressed the button for this lower level, and we glanced at each other in anticipation.

After disembarking the elevator, we followed a short hallway to a thick glass door where we were buzzed in and welcomed by several university archivists. After some brief introductions, and a friendly reminder to leave my pen in my pocket as only pencils were welcomed, we were seated at a rectangular table roughly the size of one found in any typical American dining room. The room itself was no larger than a modern–day family room. The walls were painted white, with a drop ceiling and beige carpeting. Sitting nearby, at their own tables, and in complete silence beyond anything imagined at a typical library, sat other individuals methodically combing through unknown documents. The youngest, perhaps a grad student, donned a pair of headphones and even managed to, somehow, *silently* tap his pencil along his note pad. Several bookshelves, towering near the ceiling, and standing straight in the middle of the room, initially blocked my view of a rear door which, undoubtedly, led to a massive storage area. As we waited, I glanced around the room and then back at my dad. He, in turn, was pointing to the corner of the room. There, along the floor, leaning against a table, was an address plaque that read: *Harbel Manor.* This Firestone mansion, not to be confused with Harvey Junior's former estate also referred to locally as "the Firestone mansion," was built in 1912 along 60 acres in West Hill in what was then the outskirts of town. Torn down decades before our visit to the Polsky Building, it was here that Harvey Firestone had entertained guests, including his friends Thomas Edison, Henry Ford, and John Burroughs. For a moment I became lost in thought. How could such a grand and storied mansion be reduced to a plaque leaning against a basement table? As I contemplated such an architectural loss, the back door suddenly popped open, and the silence was interrupted by the sound of squeaky wheels. From around the corner bookshelves emerged a cart carrying reams of folders and binders. As the archivist wheeled the cart up to the side of our table, I could clearly see, printed on labels and written in black ink along the folders, the words "camping trips."

Several weeks before I ever entered that elevator, or gazed upon this cart, I found myself sitting in my dad's office—a relatively common occurrence, as his office was just down the hall from mine. I'm a lawyer. He was a preeminent engineer. We shared a building, and plenty of coffee. We also shared stories, and sometimes those stories were about Akron—past and present. Many of our conversations naturally veered into talk of the tire companies and their historical dominance on all things local. My dad, and his dad, were "Firestone Men." My brother and I went to Firestone High School. If that didn't make us "Firestone Men," we were at least "Firestone Graduates." Other families have generations of "Goodyear Men," "Goodrich Men," or "General Men." It's an Akron thing, or at least it was an Akron thing. My grandparents, who shared many stories of Akron past, were proud to call this home. The city, which peaked in population at just over 290,000 in 1960 (five years before I was born), has struggled like many Midwestern cities to find a new identity or path back from lost prominence. Pictures, all in black and white, adorning the walls of my dad's office, showed a very different place. The streets were packed. The photos reflect a noticeable hustle and a bustle that confirms my grandparents' tales. When Albert Polsky ran his department store, it was, indeed, a vibrant place to call home. People came here from far and wide to find work, and with a booming economy, fortunes were made. Stately mansions, once filled with executives and their families, line the streets of older neighborhoods, standing as relics of a bygone era. A few ornate palaces also remain, left as reminders of the Rubber Barons and the grip they once held over the landscape.

Taking a sip of coffee, my dad got up from his seat, walked over to his bookshelf, grabbed an old hardback book and handed it to me. "If you ever want to read any of these, be my guest," he said. Looking at the cover of Alfred Lief's, *The Firestone Story*, I opened the book and went instantly to the middle section filled with pictures. On one page was a photograph of President William Howard Taft and Harvey S. Firestone. However, it was a picture, set horizontally on the opposite page that caught my fancy. Turning the book sideways I could clearly make out the image of Thomas Edison standing on the far left with a group of other men. What I saw, quite frankly, caught me completely off guard. The picture, dated as "August 21, 1918," showed Edison, along with Harvey S. Firestone, Jr., John Burroughs, Henry Ford and Harvey S. Firestone, Sr. posing atop an old grist mill in the West Virginia mountains. The picture, which also showed another individual identified as "R.J.H. de Loach," is further identified as a "Camping trip." I knew that these guys all knew each other, but somehow, I was unaware they were such good friends, and I most certainly was not aware that they were camping buddies. Although I admittedly knew much less about John Burroughs, it also struck me as odd that a group of industrialists would be hanging out with, for lack of a better name, an environmentalist. "Dad, did you know Thomas Edison, Harvey Firestone, and Henry Ford went on camping trips together?" I blurted out. As I shared the picture with him, we both chuckled at the fact that these men were all wearing suits in the middle of the woods in August, and we had to remind ourselves that things might have been a little different in 1918. The date, August 21, 1918, also caught my attention. By my rough calculations, the picture was taken when World War I was winding down, but before the Spanish Flu had begun in earnest. "What a fascinating time to take a camping trip!" I thought.

It has been said that a picture is worth a thousand words. In my case, as it would turn out, a picture can also result in over 100,000 written words and thousands of miles traveled. The next day, after having read much of the book, I approached my father and told him I'd love to know more about these camping trips, especially the 1918 trip. This was by design. Presenting an idea to my dad was literally like lighting a fuse. Once lit, it would not stop burning until the desired detonation. Ask anyone who knew him. My dad was a man of action, whose problem-solving prowess remains legendary to friends and colleagues alike. As it turned out, my father was not only a man of action but also a Firestone Man, and he knew the former Firestone archivist, and although the archivist was retired and their whereabouts were unknown, he would start by making a few calls. Several weeks later, after learning the records had been moved from Firestone to the University of Akron for safe keeping, we found ourselves at a table on the lower level of the Polsky Building with a cart full of camping trip pictures, receipts, notes, articles, and newspaper clippings.

At first, I did not know what to do. It was all a little overwhelming. In the end, I decided the safest bet was to try to look at everything on the cart. After all, I really had no idea what I was looking for, or why I was even looking at these documents. Having never lifted my pencil, my notepads were left blank, and although with permission I did manage to take a few pictures of certain documents, I mostly browsed in simple curiosity. In truth my initial excitement turned to fatigue and a touch of disappointment. What I initially viewed as a treasure chest, much like Lief's work on Firestone, failed to provide the requisite abundance of specifics about the camping trips. If I were seeking instant gratification, there was none to be found. However, over the coming weeks and months, after making several more trips to the lower level of the Polsky Building (with and without my dad), I managed to fill those notepads with a few thoughts and observations. I also happened upon a typed brief itinerary from the 1918 trip. It had been prepared by Harvey Firestone himself. These items, along with a few other books purchased on the internet and others sourced through a local bookstore, ultimately found themselves in a box, in the corner of my office, leaning against a table. The box remained unopened for four years.

Those chats with my dad continued. However, in time, they turned further and further away from all things Akron and the tire industry. In time, I spoke less and listened more, and our discussions slowly moved from the office to my childhood home. Our chats also became much more philosophical. We more often found ourselves talking about life, family and nature. Every story seemed to contain a life lesson. Sometimes we dipped our feet in discussions about God, religion, and an afterlife. Sometimes we sipped our coffee in silence. A terminal cancer diagnosis will do that.

My dad remained optimistic and happy throughout his ordeal. He was fond of telling the entire family that he had lived a fairytale life, having been born in America, having come of age in the 1950s, having married the most beautiful woman in the world–my mom, and having had children and grandchildren. After seeing the movie *Star Wars: The Last Jedi*, in December of 2017, he told everyone at dinner he could not believe he had even outlived Luke Skywalker. By early April, before the snow had fully melted, our chats had mostly stopped. Cancer's initial sting had been replaced by the excruciating reality of hospice. In those final few days, although I did all the talking, he most certainly did all the teaching.

A few weeks after my dad's passing, while sitting in my office, I found myself staring out the window lost in thought. I really hurt. I felt numb. For whatever reason, I thought as a grown man, things would be easier. For whatever reason, things were not. As I sat in silence, I scanned the walls of my office and, by chance, my gaze fell upon a box in the corner of the room, leaning against a table. When I opened the box, I recalled our visit to the Polsky Building and how my father had arranged for our review of the Firestone documents. We had both learned a few things from a century past, but that was where it had ended, left in another box. As I looked at my scribblings and the copied documents, I felt like it should have gone further. The story we had stumbled upon, remained largely untold. The 1918 camping trip was trapped in a box in the corner of my office, and much like the *Harbel Manor* address plaque, it was left where no one could see it. And that is when, oddly enough, I found myself humming music scored by John Williams. It wasn't *Star Wars* but was instead the theme music from another George Lucas creation: *Raiders of the Lost Ark.* Indiana Jones, the globe-trotting archaeologist, was another favorite character in my family. When not battling Nazis, or dealing with a chamber full of poisonous snakes, Jones was a bit of a crusty professor who might be found at a library buried in books, or silently combing through documents in an archive. Every adventure began with a trip to the Polsky Building, or at least a place like it. Jones, after all, was an obtainer of rare antiquities. While he unearthed buried treasure, he also unearthed stories along the way. That is what I would do. I would further unearth the 1918 camping trip, and perhaps along the way, I would unearth other unknown treasures.

For the first time in a long time, I felt an acute sense of excitement flowing through me and within a few days I set out my plan of action. It occurred to me that any hope I had in properly telling this tale, would require me to learn as much as possible about the campers themselves. I would start with Firestone, exploring Akron and nearby Columbiana, Ohio, and a trip to Dearborn, Michigan and Greenfield Village seemed like a logical place to start for Henry Ford. Of course, a trip to the Catskills in New York and West Orange, New Jersey, would, I hoped, fill in some gaps about John Burroughs and Thomas Edison. For good measure I later planned a quick trip to Fort Myers, Florida to visit the vacation homes of Thomas Edison and Henry Ford. As a native Ohioan, this was, of course, ultimately penciled in for February.

I would need to immerse myself in all things 1918, which, would also require travel. Trips to far off libraries and trips via the internet from my own dining room table. Lastly, after I had learned as much as I could about these famous campers and that fateful year, I would retrace the 1918 camping trip as best I could. The Firestone itinerary, coupled with a copy of *There to Breathe the Beauty*—a beautiful book, written by Norman Brauer in 1995, outlining all vacations collectively taken by the "Vagabonds" between 1915 and 1924—would serve as my general compass.

It is written in the Gospels: "he who seeks finds." For me this proved to be exponentially true. My search would, indeed, reveal much about a bygone era and a camping trip, taken by a group of friends, more than one-hundred years ago. Perhaps more importantly, however, I would discover much more along the way. Stories not anticipated awaited around every mountain bend, and often took me to unexpected places. Whether setting out to willfully explore, or simply to take a break from my ordinary life, I discovered I was not alone. Countless others want, have wanted, or will want, a chance to breathe. I took my dad along with me in spirit as I set out on my road trips across the country. I also made sure our box of documents from the original trip to the Polsky Building was packed right alongside my suitcase. Together we would obtain our own rare antiquities, by learning and sharing stories from a 1918 road trip.

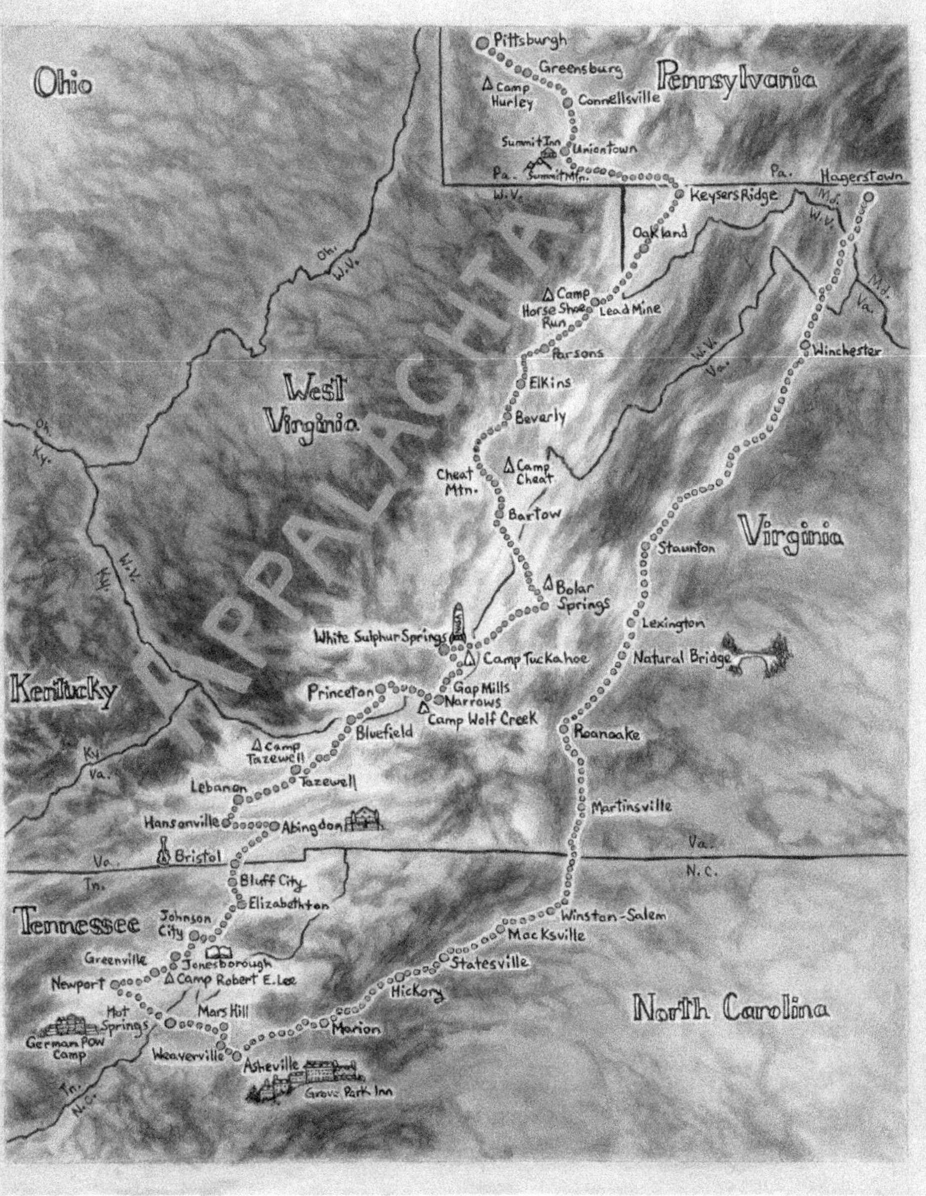
Ohio
Pennsylvania
West Virginia
Virginia
Kentucky
Tennessee
North Carolina
APPALACHIA
Pittsburgh
Greensburg
Δ Camp Hurley
Connellsville
Summit Inn
Uniontown
Summit Mtn.
Pa.
W.V.
Md.
Va.
Oh.
Ky.
Tn.
N.C.
Hagerstown
Keysers Ridge
Oakland
Δ Camp Horse Shoe Run
Lead Mine
Parsons
Winchester
Elkins
Beverly
Cheat Mtn.
Δ Camp Cheat
Bartow
Staunton
Δ Bolar Springs
Lexington
White Sulphur Springs
Camp Tuckahoe
Natural Bridge
Princeton
Gap Mills
Narrows
Camp Wolf Creek
Bluefield
Roanoake
Δ Camp Tazewell
Tazewell
Lebanon
Martinsville
Hansonville
Abingdon
Bristol
Bluff City
Elizabethton
Johnson City
Winston-Salem
Mocksville
Greenville
Jonesborough
Statesville
Newport
Δ Camp Robert E. Lee
Hickory
Mars Hill
Hot Springs
German POW Camp
Marion
Weaverville
Asheville
Grove Park Inn

I.

THE BIG NIGHT

CHAPTER 1

August 18, 1918

On a late Sunday afternoon, just outside of Pittsburgh, six vehicles raced down a dusty highway in Western Pennsylvania. The caravan consisted of two heavy Packard automobiles and two flivvers (Ford Model Ts), followed by two large upright trucks resembling mechanical covered wagons. The first of these trucks was loaded with tents, cots, lights and chairs, while the second was fitted like a grocery shop with shelves and drawers for food supplies and space for burner stoves and gas ovens. However, the large, round folding table equipped with a Lazy Susan in the center, and which could sit a total of twenty people, was not yet part of the yearly summer sojourn. It would be added soon enough. Accompanying this impressive display of supplies and equipment, was a seven-man crew, which included a Mr. R.V. Kline, who would take shifts as a driver, reporter, and photographer. Kline had also packed his gun, and decided, if need be, he would play the role of bodyguard. Another crew member was Harold Sato, a Japanese American, who would serve as a part time photographer, expense accountant, and, most importantly, chef. The only things Sato had packed, besides his clothes and bedding, were food and condiments.

It was the 230th day of 1918, a monumentally pivotal year in which breathtaking news stories came with such speed and relentlessness that it was all but impossible to fully comprehend. The next 135 days of this same year would be no different, and, in the end, it would take generations to unpack all that would happen. As the caravan moved east from Pittsburgh towards Greensburg, Pennsylvania, before turning south again, they passed scores of Army trucks, traveling in procession, loaded with young "Doughboys," weapons, and equipment en route to Europe and their date with destiny—and the Kaiser. On Saturday, one day earlier, the French Tenth Army had attacked the German held town of Noyon, France in an early offensive prior to the main Allied attack at Albert four days later on Wednesday, August 21st. Simultaneously, an allied offensive to control the entire Absheron Peninsula of Azerbaijan had ended in failure. As the war waged on, it hardly seemed possible that it had only been a month since the Romanov family had been executed. The Russian Imperial family, including Emperor Nicholas II, his wife Empress Alexandra, and their five children, including the Grand Duchess Anastasia, had been shot and bayoneted to death by Bolshevik revolutionaries, with their bodies stripped and ultimately mutilated. Nobody had even heard of a "Bolshevik" at the start of the year, now the word was on the lips of most Americans.

World War I, largely a slow grinding affair in prior years had drastically changed in 1918, taking on more of the characteristics of a mad sprint to the finish line. It seemed to the world that the trenches were literally caving in on all sides. In retrospect, there is little wonder why the tiniest of flu viruses, not visible to the human eye, received such little attention from anyone in the Spring of 1918. Although this unknown flu was followed by an alarming rate of pneumonia, it seemed to have left quietly by the Summer. A little over 100 years ago, as the caravan motored through the rolling hills in Western Pennsylvania, nobody had any idea that the virus was still there, lying in wait, and was about to create its greatest carnage in the weeks that lay ahead.

In the front seat of the dust covered Packard, on the passenger side, sat the world's greatest inventor. His suit was wrinkled, as it (almost) always was, and he wore a crooked bow tie with a vest fully buttoned to the top. Clutching a map and compass, he gave little concern to the August heat. Folded along the floor of the car, beside his dress shoes, black socks, and white ankles, were multiple newspapers, including a copy of the *New York Times*, which he would devour from top to bottom at some point before the day was through. His thinning white hair blew in the wind, and despite the ruckus the caravan made, he hardly heard a thing. Thomas Edison was seventy-one years old, had not shaven, and was hoping to get a few good miles down the road before pulling over for the night.

Another passenger, who had traveled nearly four-hundred miles with Edison from Orange, New Jersey just two days before, looked ahead and down the road with his bright twinkling eyes. A long white beard could not hide his friendly face and gentle disposition. He carried newspapers as well, along with stacks and stacks of books. Dressed in a suit and white shirt, the famous writer and environmentalist clutched his hat in his hands, hoping the drivers would find the smoothest path to soothe his aching bones, even as he surveyed the Pennsylvania countryside. At eighty-one, John Burroughs was nearly a decade older than Thomas Edison, and as the octogenarian and senior member of the party, he would be afforded "guest of honor" status.

In the front seat of the second Packard, another passenger wiggled about in his light grey double-breasted suit and necktie. His thin athletic body literally oozed a nervous energy, making it impossible for him to sit still. His hair, which had turned mostly white, was the only clue as to his age. Although he carried no newspapers, and had failed to pack any books, he was acutely aware of every supply the trucks carried. He also knew where every tool could be located should the caravan face mechanical difficulties. Henry Ford was fifty-five years old, was the chief financier of this journey, and was by far the wealthiest person in the group. His mind, when not searching the side of the road for rivers and streams, already wandered ahead to creating new contraptions for future trips, which would later be described by Burroughs as a "Waldorf-Astoria on wheels."

As the caravan motored further away from the Steel City, a father sat in the back seat of the second Packard, while his twenty-year-old son had volunteered to drive. Like Ford, he too wore a light-colored suit, but instead opted for a bow tie which was more neatly tied than Edison's. In fact, with his peppered hair parted slightly off-center, and his carefully groomed mustache, he was the most dapper of the group. He, too, clutched his hat, mostly in fear of his son's driving. At fifty years old, Harvey Firestone had been largely responsible for planning and coordinating the journey. The youngest of the famous passengers, Firestone had not only brought his son, Harvey Jr., but had also brought along diaries and notepads to chronical the journey. He had also informally arranged for the press to follow the caravan as it meandered southward during the middle part of August. The remaining two passengers were Edward N. Hurley and Professor R.J.H. DeLoach. Like the other passengers, Hurley wore a suit and tie, and carried a hat. With the darkest hair of the bunch, he also wore the thickest coat of the lot and carried a serious demeaner befitting of the commissioner of the U.S. Shipping Board. Along for the ride, however short it might be, he knew he would soon be peppered with inquiries about The War. The final passenger, the Georgia-born Professor, was dressed in a three-button suit, and wore his hair tightly cropped, especially on the sides. He had also made the nearly four-hundred-mile trip along with Edison and Burroughs. As a close friend and confidant to John Burroughs, who had been invited along for the ride, he was just happy to be a part of whatever happened next.

Earlier that day, Henry Ford, Harvey Firestone, and Harvey Jr. had departed Firestone's homestead in Columbiana, Ohio, a little over sixty miles from Pittsburgh. Ford, who had traveled from Michigan, had stayed at the homestead the night before and was the guest of honor of the Ladies' Aid Society of the Grace Reformed Church for a dinner, with chicken and cherry pie, given to Firestone's superintendents and foremen. As the three traveled across the Ohio-Pennsylvania border, Burroughs, Edison, Hurley and DeLoach, lunched at the home of Mr. Hitchcock-Edison's brother-in-law. Edison's group had lodged at the William Penn Hotel the night before, and while in the hotel lobby, Edison, who was clearly in a talkative mood, leaked details of the upcoming camping excursion. When a reporter for the *Pittsburgh Dispatch*, asked the inventor about the reasons for such a trip, Edison, reportedly said, "Ford needs a rest," followed by something along the lines of "nerves, nerves, nerves." When asked about his own nerves, Edison brushed aside such assertions by commenting, "I haven't any; I am feeling very good and hope to enjoy the little trip every moment." Had his wife been present, she might have taken exception.

Thomas Edison, who the press described as looking tan and with a penchant for smiling, was also anxious to talk about a new school to educate women to assume places vacated by men fighting in the war. The inventor was happy to relay that the school had already graduated more than 300 women in various skilled trades, and offered, "Indeed, I think the women will replace the men in every way with the proper skilled teaching." Edison, already on a roll, further dipped his toes into a discussion with the reporter about the war, commenting, "The Germans never anticipated this, or they could not have engaged the United States in war. With all their pretended knowledge and keenness, they were stupid; they were ignorant of America. Now they see what they have done! This current is going to overwhelm them." Although not asked a single question by the press, John Burroughs had found himself nodding in approval.

Had the press asked Thomas Edison, they might have learned the idea of wandering unshaven through the countryside was Edison's own, writing Firestone and Ford that he was ready to go roughing it. The inventor had hatched the idea, several years before in 1915, after enjoying the freedom of a motor trip along the California coast. *Edison Day* was to be observed at the Panama-Pacific Exposition in San Francisco in the fall of 1915, celebrating the incandescent lamp's birthday. Henry Ford and Harvey Firestone had joined the famous inventor in California for the celebrations which included bands, parades, and throngs of admiring crowds. In the end, the whole affair had greatly tired Edison, making him more than happy to take a little ride through the bystreets with his wife and in the company of Mr. and Mrs. Firestone. With another upcoming exposition planned for San Diego, Firestone suggested that they go by auto taking several cars with the tops down creating a leisurely and scenic trek along the Pacific Ocean on a new state highway. After a full day of festivities in San Diego, capped by a dinner given by Firestone, Edison mentioned the idea of finding a way to get together again. The result was yet another Edison invention: a gypsy jaunt by car for summer vacations, with or without spouses or other family members.

Later that year, when writing his friends, Edison made it clear that any such trips should also include John Burroughs to serve as the party's nature guide. Burroughs would be good company and could talk flowers with the inventor and talk birds with Ford. Ford had met Burroughs in Fort Myers one winter before, and following an acquaintance by correspondence, the two had developed a strong friendship. Thomas Edison also insisted the camping trips be gentlemen only, at least until they got the hang of what they were doing. Harvey Firestone, looking to spend time with eldest son, Harvey Jr., jumped at the opportunity for such a trip and offered to supply helpers and a good cook. Edison would ready a truck with tents, floorboards, folding tables and chairs, as well as, charging batteries, lamps and wiring. Their first excursion would take them to New York and the Adirondacks, described by John Burroughs as mighty mountains "holding their heads so high." As this 1916 journey began, Firestone was visibly anxious about the whereabouts of Henry Ford until a telegram caught up with the expedition, indicating that Ford would not be able to join them as he had encountered an unexpected obligation. Although initially disheartened by this news, everyone enjoyed the trip and agreed it should be done again, the next time *with* Ford.

The following year, John Burroughs visited Firestone at a rented house at Lemon City, outside of Miami, Florida. It was February, and the nature writer from New York was quite happy to smell fresh grass during the dead of winter. He also took the opportunity to get to know Mrs. Firestone and the children, finding "a beautiful family, a happy home." Firestone and Burroughs spent hours discussing possible spots for their upcoming summer excursion. Unfortunately, 1917 found America knee deep in war production, making it impossible for Ford or Firestone to get away. Any trip would have to wait another year.

CHAPTER 2

Flivvers and Silent Movies

Around 2:30 PM, on August 18, 1918, the two parties converged outside the William Penn Hotel in Pittsburgh, where pictures were taken, and the final bags and supplies were packed and loaded. It had been years in the making, but finally they had the full gang re-assembled: Edison, Firestone, Burroughs *and* Ford. Together, on this second Edison-inspired journey, they would take a summer road trip, with the inventor orchestrating the routes, and with only one destination in mind: Asheville, North Carolina. How and when they got there nobody really cared. And while they were largely men of power and self-created privilege, they set out, as best they knew how or could remember, to rough it. What they sought was a chance to "breath the beauty" and to escape for a bit from their regular stress-filled lives and from the frantic happenings of 1918. On a warm August day, along a dusty highway just outside of Pittsburgh, the Vagabonds were born. In many ways, so was the beloved American road trip.

The two flivvers in the convoy made for a common site in 1918, as of the six million cars in the United States, roughly 665,000 were Model Ts. (Today, by comparison, there are nearly 260 million registered vehicles in the country.) It was a period of prosperity. A time when Americans had more money and leisure time than any generation before them. It was also a period of fundamental change in America. The 20th century had ushered in rapid migration of people and money from rural areas to cities. As urban populations began to swell, many stories were written about the potential hardships of city life. One such popular movie, *A Dog's Life*, with a running time of only thirty-three minutes, was released in April of 1918 and not only captivated the public's imagination but also further solidified Charlie Chaplin as a household name.

Thirty years after Thomas Edison had embarked on "experimenting upon an instrument which does for the eye what the phonograph does for the ear," motion pictures had taken root in America. Chaplin starred or directed in four movies in 1918 alone. Another movie, which may not have caught the initial attention of the famous travelers, was *The Power and the Glory*, directed by Lawrence Windom and based on the popular novel published in 1910 by Grace MacGowen Cooke. The story follows Johnnie Consadine, a mountain girl and cotton mill worker, who is the antithesis of a hillbilly. This protagonist, well-spoken and smart, walks out of the mountains and into the horrific working conditions of the mills where she leads a charge for change. Although only a character brought to life from a novel to the big screen, Johnnie Consadine offered a glimpse into the people and places that awaited just beyond the horizon.

When the Vagabonds embarked on the 1918 road trip, they had forty-eight states to choose from. New Mexico had become the 47th State on January 6, 1912, followed by Arizona on February 14, 1912. These newest states, added a little over six years earlier, followed Idaho and Wyoming which became states in 1890 followed by Utah in 1896. The United States would not get the 49th and 50th stars on its flag until 1959, when Alaska became the 49th state in January of that year and Hawaii the 50th in August. The population of the country sat at 103 million people, or a little less than one-third of the population today. That same year the population of the United States did the unthinkable: it decreased by an estimated 60,000 people, while at the same time, life expectancy decreased by a whopping twelve years. For women life expectancy sat at 42.2 and for men the average life expectancy was a meager 36.6. The War and the Flu would leave a permanent mark.

In 1918, Americans walked nearly everywhere, typically lived in three generation homes, and often spent Friday nights dancing or playing the piano. They rode horses and trains, and electricity and indoor plumbing were still luxuries. However, life was rapidly changing with Ford's Model T and the Wright Brothers first flight just fifteen years before. The first passenger flight technically occurred in 1908 when Wilbur Wright took an employee for a ride, and it should be noted that the Burgess Company had become the first licensed commercial aircraft manufacturer in 1911.

On May 15, 1918, the National Air Mail Service was inaugurated, with a flight between New York and Washington D.C. Within a decade commercial flight would take hold as another piece of the roaring 1920s. In 1918 Americans were also earning more and wages were generally on the rise. Bricklayers might earn .81 cents an hour; carpenters .69 cents an hour; painters .63 cents an hour; and plumbers might pull in .75 cents an hour, while the American farm eked out a paltry $37.50 a month. Unemployment stood at 2%, with no minimum wage. The United States Treasury hauled in $1,127,721.83 in income tax from a little less than 4.5 million personal returns that year. Income tax, which started under Abraham Lincoln during the Civil War—and which had been further entrenched as a part of life with the ratification of the Sixteenth Amendment to the Constitution just five years before, was also on the rise. Another war meant the need for more funding. Surprisingly, in 1918, the average federal income tax paid per filer was $254.85 which represented a tax rate of only 7%.

When Americans flocked to see Charlie Chaplin, or other silent movie icons, it cost them .7 cents to see the movie. Round steak was .37 cents a pound; eggs .48 cents a dozen; milk .56 cents a gallon; bread .10 cents a loaf; and coffee hovered around .30 cents a pound. Nearly one-third of household income was spent on food. Woodrow Wilson was President, Thomas R. Marshall was Vice President, and Champ Clark, a democrat from Missouri, was Speaker of the House. A beer might cost .15 cents a quart and spirits could run as much as $1.39 a quart. In a year like 1918, when the entire world collectively needed a stiff drink, the United States was well on the way to prohibition with a slew of temporary bans meant to preserve grain for producing foods during wartime. Although not yet ratified, the eighteenth amendment of the constitution which would prohibit the manufacturing, sale, and transportation of intoxicating liquors, continued to pick up steam. In two short years the country would ostensibly be dry.

In 1918, the average American family had three children, a majority of whom were born at home and not in a hospital. Tragically 10% of infants died within the first year, whereas today that number approaches only one in two hundred. Divorce was rare, children lived with their parents until marriage, and widows almost always moved in with their adult children. In 1918, 50% of American families still lived in small towns or rural areas, and roughly half of the people living in the United States were under the age of twenty-five. Those living on farms used horses and mules in the fields, with 1915 seeing the century high in what now seems an antiquated farming method. In time the tractor would gradually replace these animals. The term "teenager" did not exist in 1918, and only 20% of youth between the age of fifteen and eighteen attended secondary school. Of those, only 9% graduated.

The tallest structure in the world was the Eiffel Tower standing proud for France at 984 feet. It would not be replaced as the tallest structure until the Chrysler Building was completed in 1930. The granddaddy of all skyscrapers, The Empire State Building, was not yet even imagined. Any structures built toward the sky, offered a counterbalance to the holes dug below the earth's surface. The Boston Subway had opened a little over twenty years before, and the inaugural subway run in New York City had occurred at 2:30 in the afternoon on October 27*th*, 1904. Streetcars were peaking in 1918, with the Brooklyn Grays baseball team being recently nicknamed the Brooklyn Trolley Dodgers, and later the Brooklyn Dodgers, as a tribute or perhaps in deference to their fans, who in order to catch a game of baseball, had to avoid speeding trolley cars through a maze of trolley lines crisscrossing the city.

Roughly 30% of the country had a telephone, but less than 20% of households had a non-wood burning stove. Almost nobody had a radio, and homes with air conditioning were rare. In 1918 there were no washing machines, dryers, televisions or computers. However, everyone wanted a toaster. Mass production of food was still in its infancy, but by 1918, a glance around any kitchen or pantry might reveal Cornflakes, Oreos, Coca Cola or Moon Pies. Catalogues were also quite the rage, and with a Sears Roebuck copy in hand, one could purchase just about anything—including a house.

As for fashion, it was also experiencing a pivotal moment. American women typically wore day dresses, and much like their French counterparts, color was finally being splashed into the wardrobe. With leather and wool scarcer during wartime, cotton, silk and fur were used more frequently. Corsets, which were typically worn at the outset of the war, had been replaced by light boned camisoles, a precursor to today's bra. An overall loosening in fashion could be detected, with the flapper look just around the corner. As for men, they typically wore suits, ties and coats, but color remained elusive with black and grey still dominating any busy street corner. Everyone—men and women alike—wore a hat.

While prohibition picked up momentum in 1918, women's suffrage continued to stumble in 1918. After the House of Representatives quickly passed the 19th Amendment, it failed by just two votes in the United States Senate. The Amendment would fail again in February of the following year by just one vote. Originally introduced to congress in 1878, the Amendment, or some reincarnation thereof, had been left to languish for forty years. The suffrage movement itself had seen multiple victories and defeats, yet the national prize remained elusive. Susan B. Anthony, who had voted in the 1872 election in Rochester, New York and was subsequently arrested and convicted for "knowingly, wrongfully and unlawfully voting for a representative for congress," had become a martyr in the worthy cause. Two years before, in 1870, Louisa Swain had cast a lawful and historic ballot for the general election in Laramie, Wyoming thanks to a law giving women the right to vote and hold office in that territory. By 1917 women's suffrage had gathered undeniable strength on a national level, culminating with picketing at the White House. When women were arrested and jailed for doing nothing more than exercising their first amendment rights, many engaged in hunger strikes, and the courts ultimately dropped all charges. On August 18, 1920, two years to the day that the Vagabonds raced across the Pennsylvania countryside, the 19*th* Amendment crossed the finish line when Tennessee became the required thirty-sixth state to ratify the amendment. One struggle behind, but with many to follow.

The year 1918 is now forever set in time, sharing a space with no other. Before the Hindenburg disaster, but after the Titanic. Wedged in at the tail-end of World War I, and before World War II. Adolf Hitler was twenty-nine years old; Winston Churchill was thirty-four; and Franklin Delano Roosevelt, the oldest of the bunch, was thirty-six and still had full use of his legs. It was after the Rose Bowl, but before the Super Bowl. Ohio State had been added to the Big Ten Conference, and Michigan had rejoined as well. However, Michigan State was not yet part of the conference and the University of Chicago had not yet dropped out after eliminating its football program.

For fans of *Downton Abbey*, Episode 5 in Season 2, takes place, precisely, in August of 1918. The first fine-dining restaurant in America had opened in New York nearly one-hundred years before. However, in 1918, there were no fast-food restaurants, as White Castle would not open in Wichita, Kansas for another three years. There were plenty of inns, but no known hotels. Although Conrad Hilton bought the Mobley Hotel in Cisco, Texas, in 1919, the first Hilton Hotel was not built until 1925, and was joined by Howard Johnson's Restaurant that same decade.

U.S. Highways did not yet exist. Gas stations were rare with the first one built just thirteen years before in St. Louis, Missouri. The second one, a Chevron station, was not built for another two years. In 1918 one in thirteen families owned a car. By 1929 four out five would have one. It was before welfare, Medicare, and Medicaid, but after the IRS was established. There was a State Department and a Justice Department, but no Energy Department, Education Department or Department of Homeland Security. Nineteen-eighteen was after the establishment of the Federal Drug Administration (FDA), but before the creation of the Centers for Disease Control and Prevention (CDC). Radio was new, and television did not yet exist. Movies, which were almost always in black and white, were all without sound.

Still before the invention of the electronic calculator, 1918 came *after* the invention of the typewriter. It also followed railroads, telegraphs, the Trail of Tears, baseball, the California Gold Rush, the Civil War, dynamite, the Statue of Liberty, the telephone, the Panama Canal, basketball and football. However, 1918 came before the roaring 20s, jazz, flappers, the Charleston, and *The Spirit of St. Louis* and Charles Lindberg's famous transatlantic flight. It was also before the Great Depression, the Dust Bowl, Pearl Harbor, the Atomic Bomb, and the Cold War. In 1918, Ronald Reagan was a long way from being President of the United States, as he was just an eight-year-old kid. It was also before the Presidencies of Truman, Eisenhower and Kennedy. However, gone were Presidents Washington, Adams, Jefferson, Polk, Lincoln, Garfield, Grant and McKinley. The former President of Princeton University was midway through his second term as the 28*th* President of the United States. To add some strangeness of this pivotal year, and for whatever reason, daylight savings time went into effect on March 31, 1918. The debates, and general head scratching of this decision, continue to this day.

In many ways, 1918 was also the year of cancellation and abbreviation, at least on the world's sports stage. The War caused the following cancellations: all professional football (soccer) league matches in Europe; the Tour de France cycling championship; all major golf championships; all rugby leagues and matches in England; the Australian Open tennis championship; the French Open tennis championship; and the

Wimbledon tennis championship. Even the famous rowing boat race between archrivals, Oxford, and Cambridge, went without contest due to the war. America's geographical isolation, and later entry in the war, spared complete cancellations but did result in noticeable abbreviations in football and baseball, whereas other sports went relatively untouched due to their earlier schedules in 1918. The Toronto Arenas defeated the Montreal Canadians 10-7 in a wild shootout to win the Stanley Cup in the inaugural season of the National Hockey League (NHL), and in an all-American final at the only Grand Slam event of the year, Robert Lindley Murray defeated Bill Tilden on what was once grass courts at the U.S. Open. As for the women, Molla Bjurstedt, a Norwegian-born, naturalized American, bested American Eleanor Goss in straight sets to win one of her record eight amateur singles titles at the U.S. Open.

In 1918, *Exterminator* (a work horse nicknamed "the goat") had not raced competitively for nearly a year, and was only entered into the Kentucky Derby after *Sun Briar*, originally entered to run, had suddenly developed a joint disorder (ringbone), leaving the owner with no other horse for entry in the prestigious race. In a pouring rain, with the track deep in mud, *Exterminator* started the race towards the back. At 30-1 odds, the horse ridden by Willie Knapp, who just a short time before, thought he would be riding a different horse, passed the heavily favored *War Cloud* and the race leader, *Escobar*, to win the 44*th* Kentucky derby. Knapp was an instant convert to the tall chestnut Gelding, and while *Exterminator* lost the Belmont Stakes by three lengths to *Johren*, the jockey remained convinced he could ride the horse to victory against the legendary *Man O'War*. Although efforts were made to arrange a match between the two horses, the race never materialized.

Approximately 350 miles east of our road trippers, on a stretch of West Twenty-eighth Street in Manhattan, between Fifth and Sixth Avenues, sat a horde of music publishing offices. Better known as Tin Pan Alley—in actuality more a solid block, rather than a single alley—this was the cradle of the music industry in 1918. Here, at any given time, multiple songs, from multiple pianos, created a less than desirable noise that some likened to children banging on tin pans. Perhaps this is why the place came to be known as Tin Pan Alley. Regardless of the name, this single block in Manhattan is where publishers and songwriters shaped much of American culture in the early part of the 20th century. In 1918, publishing houses bought the rights to songs, often peddled by the songwriters themselves. With a piano on hand, songs were banged out for consideration by these "pluggers." The publishing houses also wrote their own songs, and could crank out as many as three of four a day. A stroll along twenty-eighth street revealed signs on every block proclaiming song available for order. As a result, most news stories of the time were instantly made into a song, whether it be the sinking of a ship, the latest political scandal or The War and America's overwhelming dislike of the Kaiser.

One song writer from Tin Pan Alley, George M. Cohan, would publish more than three hundred songs including a song penned while he was riding a train in the Spring of 1917. The song, *Over There*, with its catchy lyrics that invite anyone to chime in and sing along, was a smash hit throughout the time, and many rightfully believe it is the greatest American war song ever written. Anyone who has ever been to a Memorial Day parade in the last one-hundred years has knowingly, or unknowingly, hummed along to this masterful song. In July, just a month before the famous travelers posed for pictures outside the William Penn Hotel, Enrico Caruso, an Italian Opera tenor, released *Over There* on Victor records, with parts sung in both English and French. The other top music that year, which would no doubt have been known to the famous travelers, included *Tiger Rag* by the Original Dixieland Jazz Band; *Rock A Bye Baby* by Al Jolson; and *I'm Always Chasing Rainbows* by Charles Harmon—songs which live on to this day.

It had been three years since Thomas Edison's comments appeared in the *New York Times*, outlining his thoughts on American military preparedness and his ideas for the establishment of a "great research laboratory jointly under military and naval and civilian control" to develop weapons and systems of war. Growing tired of his "retirement" from a few years before, and feeling neglected, if not forgotten by society, Thomas Edison had felt he was on a long goodbye tour for the last decade.

It was reported that when Edison's (second) wife, Mina, visited her husband at a hotel in Washington, she wrote back to her son, Theodore, that his dad had a suit with spots, wore a dirty shirt, his socks had holes, his glasses were broken, and his suitcase was not even unpacked. She also described the hotel room as looking like it had been struck by a cyclone. The "Man Who Defeated Darkness," seemed himself to be defeated. For all practical purposes, Edison appeared depressed. Of course, Washington D.C. can do that to a person. The "Dean of Inventors" had also struck a wall of sorts with his ideas. The Telescribe (a predecessor to the pager), synthetic carbolic acid, and cement (with pre-cast buildings), were just not as flashy as the phonograph, the electric light bulb, and the motion picture. His adoring public might seem grateful, but the instinctive showman knew they were not impressed. For the first time in his life, Edison felt a creeping hesitation or timidity. With age comes wisdom, but it also tends to make one less risk adverse. The Wizard of Menlo Park was beginning to show his age.

When the Secretary of the Navy approached Edison and asked him if he would be willing, as a service to his country, to act as an advisor of a new Naval Consulting Board, Edison stepped forward without hesitation. Soon he was devoting nearly all his time to experiments for the Navy, devising some forty-five inventions and plans, including methods for detecting submarines, guns, torpedoes and airplanes. However, none of these inventions or ideas were adopted by the Navy. While in the nation's capital, Edison was given a firsthand lesson in government "red tape," misguided spending, intolerable delays, and political compromises. His discouragement was matched only by his frustration, and ultimately, he moved his family to Key West, Florida to continue his work with the hope of creating a place of rapid product development that might truly assist the Navy. By the Spring of 1918, he realized it was all in vain. Whether or not Thomas Edison was clinically depressed, he was most certainly in need of a vacation when August rolled around.

John Burroughs was no stranger to roughing it, having been a wilderness traveler for decades. He also had a knack for traveling with famous friends. The prolific writer and environmentalist had joined President Theodore Roosevelt on a camping trip to Yellowstone National Park in 1903 and the two men had very much enjoyed each other's company. Roosevelt had discovered Burroughs writings when traveling in England, later telling the author that his descriptions of the New York mountains had made him homesick. In his book *Outdoor Pastimes of an American Hunter*, Roosevelt reflected that "no bird escaped John Burrough's eye; no bird note escaped his ear." Burroughs did indeed know a thing or two about birds, having penned a biography on John James Audubon the year before his trip with the President.

Another famous Burroughs traveling buddy is best known for being a proponent for those same national parks. He is also considered a father figure in the conservation movement. Burroughs first met John Muir in 1893, and the two initially developed a strained friendship which at times spilled into rivalry. Although born in Wisconsin, Muir was the confirmed man of the West, whereas Burroughs was an Easterner through and through. Both sought authoritative status on all things concerning the environment. The two men, along with a hundred or so others, were part of a journey from Seattle to Alaska on a refitted steamship in 1899. When Muir led this party to a place he had previously named "Howling Valley" in honor of the bears and wolves he'd encountered, no such predator ever appeared. Burroughs later cracked, "There might not be any bears in Howling Valley after all Muirs' imagination may have done all the howling." However, in time, the two came to genuinely appreciate each other even as they bickered like long lost brothers. In 1909 Muir invited Burroughs to visit Arizona and California, where they rode mules to the bottom of the Grand Canyon and explored the Petrified Forest and Yosemite Valley. Although the aging writer had more than a few miles under his belt, he wrote the following in his journal at the beginning of 1918: "The New Year finds me in pretty good health, writing in the morning, and sawing and splitting wood nearly an hour in the afternoon. More easily tired than one year ago, but my interest in the War, in Nature, and books, as keen as ever. Weigh about 132. Sight and hearing good, memory a little uncertain. Appetite as good as ever."

Henry Ford was a busy man in 1918 and, at the start of the trip, he was just a little over a week away from both winning and losing the Michigan primary for the U.S. Senate. Several months before, primarily at the urging of President Wilson, he reluctantly agreed to run for political office. Wilson, a Democrat, liked the idea of Ford as an ally in a predominantly Republican state and managed to plant the seed in Ford that it was his patriotic duty to make a Senate run. Although he reluctantly threw his hat in the ring, Ford refused to campaign in the traditional sense, even refusing to give speeches or make personal appearances. He also did what today might be considered unimaginable in that he entered both the Republican and Democrat primaries. Henry Ford, who gathered support from workers and farmers alike, would come in second in the Republican primary, while winning an overwhelming victory in the Democratic primary. The manufacturer, who had previously written that, "If the people of Michigan chose to elect me to that office I would accept it, but I will not lift a finger to bring it about" would be deep in the mountains of North Carolina when the votes were tallied declaring him a winner *and* a loser.

The last few years had been a whirlwind of emotion for the car maker. As a self- proclaimed "modern industrialist" he viewed war as wasteful folly, destroying economies, resources and lives. However, by August of 1918, Ford Motor had not only built tractors shipped to England, but along with fellow automakers, mass-produced Liberty motors for Allied aircraft. The flivver king, who had just several years before sworn that he would rather burn down his factory than turn it over to war production, was knee deep in the production of thousands of ambulances, cars, trucks, patrol boats, and small tanks. Ford Motor Company was also aggressively participating in drives for Liberty Loans and the Red Cross. As an American and a "modern industrialist," Henry Ford soon realized that the war could not be stopped, and instead must be won. It was the only way to end the destruction and bloodshed.

By the late Summer of 1918, Ford was also knee deep in change, not only in his business, but also on the home front. Sensing his role as a populist reformer, and with an intoxicating success that had perhaps gone to his head, Ford had previously written an article condemning the war in October of 1915 for the company publication, the *Ford Times*. It would be one of many opinion pieces attributed to Henry Ford. Many were long forgotten, and others would be used by Ford's opponent in the November 1918 election for the Senate. Still, some would haunt the legacy of Henry Ford for generations to come. In July of 1917, just a little over a year before his journey with his friends, Henry Ford & Son was incorporated and took the place of Henry Ford & Co. This company, fully owned by Henry, his wife Clara, and his son Edsel, was separate from the Ford Motor Company and would focus on producing tractors and other related farm equipment. After years of renting homes and apartments, Henry and Clara Ford had also recently moved into a 1,300-acre estate called *Fair Lane*. Thomas Edison had laid the cornerstone to the Powerhouse of the estate, and in time Edison, Firestone and Burroughs would be frequent guests, with John Burroughs even receiving a dedicated wildlife shrine named "Burroughs Grotto." Having completed his estate, and having restructured his business, Ford joined his companions with an eye on his next big move. His Senate run might have grabbed the headlines, but Henry Ford was about to reinvent car-making by moving from his original factory at Highland Park to an entirely new concept at Rouge River.

When the motorists set out for North Carolina, Harvey Firestone was at the top of his game. In 1916 Firestone had made Akron "Ohio's eight-hour town" when he instituted an eight-hour workday in Akron Rubber factories. As a result, thousands of workers from West Virginia and Kentucky drifted into Northeast Ohio. Having secured a strong relationship with Henry Ford and the Ford Motor Company, business was booming. In 1917 Firestone cranked out 3.75 million tires. The entire industry had made only 2.4 million tires just a few years before. Harvey Firestone had also set aside 1,000 acres in an area in South Akron designated as "Firestone Park" to be used as a residential community for workers. Harvey had become a national figure not only by building schools and churches, but by offering financial assistance to employees to buy homes. He also offered stock to his 10,000 employees to purchase over time at a discounted rate, stating, "every employee a stockholder, is the object of the stock distribution plan of the Firestone Company."

Much like Ford, Firestone was also knee deep in the war effort. However, unlike Ford, he had jumped in at the outset when offering to President Wilson "the use of the factory organization and all facilities in any way than can be of service to the government at war." Firestone, along with other tire manufacturers, produced gas masks, observation balloons, hip boots, short boots and gaiters. They also produced steel bases used on government trucks and the company supplied one-third of the steel tires used on artillery in the challenging mud and muck encountered on the French battlefields. Back on the home front, Firestone had also overseen the digging up of unoccupied land for hundreds of war gardens—a patriotic household garden filled with a variety of vegetables grown by citizens and designed to feed a family thereby ensuring more food reached troops. Although Firestone engineers were still two years away from perfecting a method of "gum dipping" cords, the search for increasing tire strength using fabric plies was largely successful in the years leading up to 1918. These developments pleased Firestone. He also found himself a proud father, reveling in the success of Harvey Jr., who had recently returned home from Asheville, North Carolina where he had finished at the head of his class. His son, with whom he kept in close contact through regular correspondence, had enrolled at Princeton University and served as a naval aviator in the war efforts. Much like the Fords, the Firestones had recently built a new home. Set atop 60 acres on a hill West of downtown Akron, *Harbel Manor* rivaled F.A. Seiberling's (the co founder of the Goodyear Tire and Rubber Company) *Stan Hywet*.

CHAPTER 3

Wizardry and Stagecraft

A short train ride from New York City, Menlo Park was originally where a real estate developer's dreams had gone belly up. Connected by a boardwalk and dirt roads, there were 30 or so large homes set on large lots. Homes that did not sell as anticipated. Too far from the city in a world before suburbs. Besides a saloon, and a station stop consisting of a wooden platform, there wasn't much else in this rural New Jersey location and that is precisely what Edison liked about it. Close enough to the money and investors in New York, it was also far enough away to be left alone. Here Edison could work without city distractions, annoying visitors, and those pesky investors wanting an update on his progress. It was quiet. He could think, and sleep, and build, and experiment. And, then he could do it all again the very next day.

Edison had taken the realty sales office at the corner of Lincoln Highway and Christie Street and converted it to his family home. Edison's father built the main laboratory nearby at a cost of $2,700. The lab was a plain white building, two stories, with an old apple tree behind it—usually found surrounded by barrels and machines. Twelve telegraph lines went from the nearby rail station to the second story which was essentially one long room made up of a half- dozen tables and machines. The lab also had plenty of windows, twenty to be exact, to allow in natural light. Along the walls was shelving for glass bottles and beakers holding countless chemicals and materials for experiments. Experiments that would make Edison a famous inventor and in November of 1877 when he uttered the first words ever recorded, "Mary had a Little Lamb" he quite literally crossed from inventor to wizardry becoming "The Wizard of Menlo Park."

Passengers on the Pennsylvania Railroad passed right by Menlo Park and stories began to circulate from those travelers passing through in the early Winter evenings. People spoke of seeing brilliant light gleaming through the countless windows of the Menlo laboratory. The secret was quickly getting out and so it was that Edison planned to make his light bulb formally known to the world. It would be done with great fanfare, with a public display set for New Year's Eve, 1879. He was almost too late in controlling the narrative of his great invention. Several splash headlines in the press announced Edison's breakthrough, and soon flocks of sightseers descended upon Menlo Park. They not only filled up the Pennsylvania Railroad trains, but also showed up in carriages and wagons with some even braving the December nights on foot. On these dark snowy nights in the New Jersey countryside, visitors were sometimes treated to very little making for the long trek. On other nights, visitors might be treated to a magnificent, almost magical, light escaping every crack and window from the wizard's lab.

On occasion the famous inventor would venture into the nearby metropolis of New York City to catch a boxing match or the theatre and in a world before television he was occasionally able to stroll the streets incognito. At 5'10 he was no giant, but for those who might recognize the man, he was larger than life. Edison had many fans and received stacks of letters from people hoping to meet him, and others simply offering their advice. One such fan was Sarah Bernhardt. The French actress and singer was a bonified star in her time. Strong willed and opinionated, she welcomed her celebrity and had mastered the art of getting noticed everywhere she went. In December of that same year, she was performing *La Dame aux Camelias* and decided to pay a visit to Menlo Park. However, after multiple curtain calls, throngs of autograph seekers, and a slow-moving entourage, Bernhardt did not arrive until 2 AM. She was met by a rather irritated Edison who was waiting up along with Mrs. Edison and a bouquet of flowers. Never one to accept defeat, the French star worked quickly to charm the sleep deprived couple and by all accounts did so despite her late arrival. Perhaps it helped that she came to call Edison "This King of Light." In some ways, Bernhardt's visit was a perfect dress rehearsal for turning Edison's lab into a public theatre and was a harbinger that science and entertainment were on a collision course with destiny.

It was estimated that three thousand souls streamed into Menlo Park on New Year's Eve not only to say goodbye to the 1870s, but to also usher in a new decade and perhaps catch a glimpse of a new world. By all accounts, the evening was a smashing success. Edison had "hit it out of the park" so to speak. Not only had he promised to bring light to the world, but he had also delivered on his promise. Dressed in a simple suit, with an almost disheveled appearance, he spoke plainly as he showcased his illuminated laboratory. The thirty-two-year-old Edison had even distributed electric lamps to the outside marking a clear path to his lab and into American folklore.

Had things played out differently Edison might very well have ended up as a Canadian. As early settlers in Western Upper Canada, the Edison family had arrived there from Nova Scotia in 1811. Edison's grandfather, John, had been a loyalist during the American Revolution, and along with other loyalists, had moved from New Jersey to Canada. The provincial government had encouraged settlement in the area around the northern shore of Lake Erie known as the Talbot settlement which was touted as having a mild climate and fertile land. John, with his wife Sarah and their seven children (along with their spouses and children), settled in the village of Vienna where they primarily engaged in farming and lumbering. Edison's father, Samuel, was an innkeeper with a revolutionary streak, and several years before Edison was born, his father backed an insurrection against the Canadian provincial government. When the uprising was squashed, Samuel fled to the United States fearing for his life, leaving his family behind. Indicted for high treason in Canada, he crossed the border to Detroit and set out for a new beginning as a carpenter. Edison's father wound up in Milan, Ohio, a small town near Lake Erie, where in time his family ultimately rejoined him.

Thomas Alva Edison, known as "Al" as a child, was born in the buckeye state on the snowy early morning of February 11, 1847. He was the last of seven children born, but only three of his six siblings had survived beyond the age of six which was unfortunately common for the time. His three surviving siblings were all teenagers when Al arrived, making him the only child at his parent's house for many years. By all accounts, Tom Edison was a sickly boy, often plagued with infections requiring him to spend a considerable amount of time in bed. The boy's home, built by his father with redbrick and white trim, sat at the highest point of a bluff overlooking the Huron River Valley. As a small boy often finding himself housebound, he could gaze upon Milan's canal basin with its lake schooners sailing down river, wondering about their final destinations.

Replaced by rails, canal towns, including Milan, quickly faded from the American landscape. When Thomas Edison was seven years old, his father having sensed the coming decline moved the family to the frontier town of Port Huron, Michigan. The lake port town boasted a thriving lumber business, and Edison's father laid out $2,800 on a four thousand square foot, double-story white frame house with a ten-acre grove. The home's spacious cellar would informally serve as the boy's first laboratory, and the town would serve as the backdrop for Edison's passage from boyhood to early manhood.

Whether Edison received formal education as a child remains largely unknown. His mother Nancy was a former schoolteacher, and but for two known stints at local schools, she would provide him the homeschooling that constituted the bulk of his entire education. When the famous inventor was middle-aged, he would recall, "My mother was the making of me. She was so true, so sure of me; and I felt that I had someone to live for, someone I must not disappoint." Edison would also recall, "My mother taught me to how to read good books quickly and correctly, and as this opened up a great world in literature, I have always been thankful for this early training." His father further encouraged a perusal of books from the Enlightenment including Gibbon and Hume, and the revolutionary writings from Thomas Paine.

Two specific books that quenched the lad's thirst for knowledge were Richard Parker's *Natural Philosophy* and an English translation of a textbook authored by the German chemist Carl Fresenius. *Natural Philosophy*, more commonly referred to today as physics, drew upon standard scientific works of the day including discussions of telegraphy and illustrations of the electric telegraph and steam and locomotive engines. Thomas Edison would later share with Henry Ford that Parker's work was "the first book on science I read when a boy nine years old." Fresenius was a prominent chemist whose textbooks were standards in the field, and Edison kept the translated book on hand in the cellar laboratory that came to include an array of two hundred bottles containing various powders and liquids. His mother fretted that her son might catch the house on fire or inadvertently cause an explosion with his chemical experiments. Apparently, her worries were well founded, as along with his friend, Joseph Clancy, he managed to blow out the corner of an old telegraph office downtown, burning himself, Clancy and several other boys in the explosion. The Clancy residence, well over a mile away, was ultimately connected with the Edison laboratory by lengths of stovepipe wire, jars, nails, zinc, insulated copper coil, and an assortment of other odds and ends, allowing for Morse code between the two young potential arsonists.

Although Edison would be questioned about his business sense as a grown man, he clearly developed an entrepreneurial spirit at a young age. When he was just twelve years old, he convinced his mother to let him take a position as a newsboy on a train that ran from Port Huron to Detroit. Every morning at eight, Al would board the Chicago, Detroit & Grand Trunk Junction Railroad outfitted with goodies, including candy, nuts and popcorn, to sell during the three-hour journey to what would become the Motor City. Every afternoon he picked up hundreds of copies of the *Detroit Free Press* to also sell on his return journey along with his snacks. Once in the big city, he realized he could buy items cheaply, bring them back to Port Huron, and sell them at a nice mark-up. In time, his business expanded to include grocery items including fruits and vegetables, setting up several stands, and employing several other boys. He also learned certain costs of doing business, as he was able to deter the railroad from frowning upon his activities, by providing to the wives of engineers and trainmen, blackberries and other grocery items at wholesale price.

By 1862 Edison had become a regular on the railroad, and with news of the Civil War heating up, he focused more on selling news than on selling food. After purchasing a small secondhand press, young Al set up a printing shop in the front part of a baggage car that although poorly ventilated, contained plenty of unused space. His onboard newspaper, *The Weekly Herald*, debuted on February 3, was offered for a subscription of eight cents monthly, and readers were even promised to be featured in future stories. At one point, the double-sided paper, complete with an image of a puffing locomotive, boasted a circulation of more than four hundred copies a week. So impressed was one British traveler, that he bought the entire run of newspapers as souvenirs infatuated with the idea of owning copies of a newspaper printed on a train in motion. Edison, who spent more and more time in the baggage car, ultimately set up a traveling chemistry laboratory to go along with his printing press. The youngster was not aware that flammable chemicals might not travel well, and his mom, who may have been able to warn him of such dangers, was often hundreds of miles away. It is believed that a phosphorus stick fell to the floor, set the baggage car on fire, and may very well have cost Edison his hearing. Thomas Edison later recalled that the baggage master who put out the fire "got a bad burn and boxed my ears so severely that I got somewhat deaf...." However, it is unclear if this is correct as at another time Edison recalled another episode when a conductor "took me by the ears and lifted me (onto the train). I felt something snap inside my head, and my deafness started from that time ...." Both recollections make it clear that Edison first noticed his hearing loss while working on the train, and later in life a treating physician believed his deafness may very well have been brought on by an early trauma. Edison would embrace this perceived handicap even claiming that his partial deafness was an advantage as it reduced distractions allowing him to become lost in concentration. However, his private secretary in the later years of his life, commented that although Edison handled his hearing loss with remarkable grace, there were moments when he seemed alone especially in gatherings where stories or jokes were being shared.

Between the stacks of newsprint, grocery crates, swarming fruit flies, and the countless tubes and beacons filled with chemicals, railroad personnel had become increasingly agitated with Al Edison. The burned baggage car was simply too much, and the teenage newsboy found himself ejected by a Grand Trunk conductor onto the platform at Mount Clemens along with what was left of his printing press and chemistry set. As luck would have it, Edison literally fell into the next chapter of his life. A station agent, James MacKenzie, felt a certain debt to Edison for previously rescuing MacKenzie's young son who had been playing on the tracks when an uncoupled freight car rolled toward the lad. By chance Edison had glanced out a window and was able to run out and scoop up the boy before any harm had come to him. MacKenzie's mother, who had perhaps also sensed the impending danger, arrived just in time to see Edison swoop up her son. Mrs. MacKenzie apparently fainted which tends to imply that it was indeed a close call, and from that point on Edison was given hero status in the MacKenzie household. The Mount Clemens operator was a highly skilled telegraph operator and felt obliged to teach young Edison his craft. The two undertook an intense apprenticeship lasting months and Edison later recalled that MacKenzie had taken "considerable pains to teach me." Edison often worked 18 hours a day practicing Morse code, exhibiting the bursts of energy and singularity of purpose for which he would one day be made famous.

Tom Edison had dabbled with Morse code when communicating with the makeshift line built between his basement lab and his friend James Clancy's home. However, it was while working for the railroad that he began to fully understand the importance of the telegraph for sending and receiving information. Edison would spend the mornings and afternoons with MacKenzie, returning on the evening train for solitary practice at night. He also used the facilities of a city gun shop to make his own set of instruments. During this time, the fifteen-year-old persuaded the Detroit Young Men's Society to allow him early membership thereby granting him access to its prized reading room. In the winter of 1863, Al went to work as a trainee operator at Walker's jewelry and stationery store, where he not only had access to books but also tools and other gear mechanisms used in clock repair. The small telegraph office on the premises received press dispatches overnight for a local newspaper, and Edison would often take copy until three in the morning allowing him to work in a sort of nocturnal solitude that again would become one of the inventor's signature work habits. The afternoon naps that followed the next day would also be an Edison trademark.

In the spring of 1863 Edison was hired as a night operator with the Grand Trunk Railway at Stratford Junction, just across the Canadian border in Ontario. Sam Edison's son had returned to Canada to monitor the movements of trains by means of telegraph messages exchanged with other stations along the line. He would be paid twenty-five dollars a week. Like his father, Al quickly found himself at odds with Canadian officials when the sixteen-year-old failed to stop a train to let another one through. The young man had been asked to contact a signalman, but by the time he left the telegraph office to find him the wrong train had roared through the station. Edison ran back into the office to wire, "I couldn't hold her," only to receive a succinct return message from the next station— "Hell." Fortunately, a direct collision was avoided as the tracks were straight and the two engineers were able to break in time. The following morning Edison, along with the Stratford agent, was ordered to the general superintendent's office in Toronto to explain what had happened and why a sixteen-year-old had been given such responsibility especially at night. Tom Edison was told he could be charged with criminal negligence and sent to Kingston States Prison. Taking a page from his father, Al managed to sneak out of the meeting when three unexpected English visitors were greeted by handshakes and back slaps from the superintendent. After finding the nearest door, and silently descending a staircase to the lower freight station, Edison hopped into the caboose on a freight train where he "kept secluded until (he) landed a boy free from fear in the U.S. of America."

Like hundreds of other young men, Edison became a "tramp" telegraph operator riding the rails in the latter days of the Civil War. He was part of a fraternity of operators, young and usually single, seldom meeting in person but knowing each other instead by their distinctive tapping styles. For the next few years, Al found work in Fort Wayne, Indianapolis, Cincinnati, Memphis and Louisville. Initially recognized for his ability to accurately receive messages, Edison worked tirelessly to improve his sending skills as well. Usually dressed in jeans far too short, a secondhand jacket, and a wide-brimmed hat torn on one side, one might never guess he had become one of the top operators around. It was during this time, that Edison also turned his attention to improving the equipment in his industry. Tinkering with telegraph apparatus, he sought to find ways to increase the speed in sending and receiving messages, and he compiled lists of books to devour to increase his knowledge of electricity. Unlike many of his fellow tramp operators, Edison never drank alcohol insisting it was a distraction from his greater pursuits of tinkering, reading, and thinking. He also would forget to eat, lost in his world of problem solving, and further played the role of tramp as he was always short on money. His colleagues nicknamed him "Luny Edison" or "Victor Hugo" because of his fondness for French novels. What many could not realize is that Al spent nearly every bit of his decent salary on the purchase of equipment and supplies.

In January of 1868, after he had briefly returned to Port Huron, Edison submitted an article to *The Telegrapher* for a double transmitter design that he had most likely designed and installed on a Grand Trunk Railway telegraph cable under the river between Fort Gratiot and Port Edward, Canada. Splashed on the front page of the journal, this would become Edison's first technical publication and was well received in the industry. By the time the article appeared, Edison had landed a spot as the night shift operator at a major branch for Western Union Telegraph in Boston, Massachusetts. Second only to New York City as a telegraph center in the country, and rich in an entrepreneurial spirit, Boston would provide the fertile environment for Thomas Edison to begin his career as an inventor. The city also presented plenty of money. Edison's boss, George Millikin, was also an inventor and gave Al and fellow operators permission to tinker during their free time.

By April of that same year, Edison, along with several other co-workers, began work on a stock-price printer, a fire alarm that used telegraph technology, and an electric vote recorder for Congress and state legislatures. The latter idea was filed as the first of Edison's many patent applications and was approved as U.S. Patent 90,646 issued on June 1, 1869. In all, Edison would tally 1,093 patents during his lifetime. Accompanied with a $15 fee and a model and measured drawing, the invention of a legislative vote recorder sought to shorten the tabulation of votes by hours. As each legislator voted a "Yes" or "No" the electrochemical recorder made the vote totals known almost immediately to the chamber's speaker. However, as the young inventor quickly learned, his potential customers-politicians, were in no hurry to cast their votes as it essentially eliminated the roll call and the chance to lobby for votes and curry favor. Al's first patented invention was a bust. Luckily for him, he was only twenty-one years old.

On January 30, 1869, Edison placed an announcement in *The Telegrapher*, announcing that he had resigned his position at Western Union, and would be devoting his time to creating his own inventions. Al had officially turned the page from a telegraph operator to inventor, while simultaneously fulfilling his desire for more autonomy. Just eighteen days later, Edison submitted his second patent application for a stockbroker printing instrument. He had intended to stay in Boston, but by the spring he had set his sights on New York. With no sizable inheritance or family money, Edison was dependent on finding partners who had capital. When he finally arrived in New York, he only had enough money for a cup of coffee and subsisted on plates of apple dumplings from Smith & McNell's restaurant on Washington Street. After several days of slumming it, Tom stumbled upon Samuel Law's Gold & Stock Reporting Telegraph Company on Broadway only to find the joint in an uproar over a jammed transmitter. Edison, who was able to fix the machine in less than two hours and thereby end the office panic, was hired on the spot. It was not ideal, but Edison justified it as an opportunity to get settled in the big apple and within several months Laws appointed him superintendent of the company's operating plant. When the firm later expanded by merger to become the Gold & Stock Telegraph Company, Edison found himself back on the street. However, now he was a known commodity in New York.

Edison, who was approaching mid-twenties, was now known in the city as a bona fide inventor appearing in additional trade publications. His former boss at Law's, Franklin Pope, was also let go in the merger and together with James Ashley, the editor of the *Telegrapher*, the three formed the electrical engineering firm of Pope, Edison & Company. With an office downtown at 78-80 Broadway, Edison and Pope went to work immediately on a new printing telegraph while Ashley focused more on getting the word out about their new firm. By December of 1869, the trio formed the Financial and Commercial Telegraph Company and began to provide gold quotations and stock prices to merchants who wished to avoid the more costly instruments used by brokers on Wall Street. Edison, who was paying rent at a home in Elizabeth owned by Pope's mother, searched out and located laboratory space two stops down on the Pennsylvania Railroad in Jersey City. It was here that he went to work in earnest, often catching the train back to Elizabeth in the wee hours of the night.

Backed by George Harrington, a former assistant secretary of the treasury under Abraham Lincoln, and Daniel H. Craig, a founding director of the Associated Press, Thomas Edison opened the doors of The American Telegraph Works in the fall of 1870. Capitalized by a whopping $13 million dollars, Edison's newest factory would focus on Edison's design of a shunted automatic transmitter. He brought with him machinists John Ott and William Unger. Thomas Edison would share many business ventures with Unger and found a lifelong friend and teammate in John Ott, working with him more than half of a century. By January of 1871, Edison was drowning in work with many clients biting at his heels hoping for his attention. Furthermore, his knowledge made him the best electro-mechanician in the country and an asset for Gold & Stock, especially in their negotiations of a merger with Western Union Telegraph Company. During this whirlwind of a year, Edison would return to Port Huron to bury his beloved mother, Nancy, the only person to this point of his life who really understood him. She was sixty-three.

Later that spring, a pouring rain would change the young inventor's life. Three Newark schoolgirls took shelter in the hallway of Edison's factory on Ward Street, invited inside by an employee who knew them. Once inside, Mary Stilwell, who was not quite sixteen, came upon Edison who was working on a stock ticker. Feeling emboldened she struck up a conversation with Al, and after it was decided that two of the girls should be escorted back outside by the mutual friend under cover of an umbrella, Mary found herself alone with Edison under his pulled overcoat. The daughter of a lawyer and sometime inventor, the slender, pensive looking Ms. Stilwell was hired in the fall to work for The News Reporting Telegraph Company, another Edison venture.

She was sixteen. The young Ms. Stilwell would have a second recorded encounter with her twenty-four-year-old employer, when she told him, "Mr. Edison, I can always tell when you are behind or near me." Seemingly absorbed in work, he responded, "How do you account for that?" She answered, "I seem to feel when you are near." By all accounts, what followed was a hurried courtship. One night when walking Mary home, the twenty-four-year-old inquired as to if she wished to marry him, giving her a few days to decide on a wedding date. This, of course, was contingent on her parents' approval, which he indicated he would seek the following night. Perhaps hesitate given her young age, Mary took a week to ponder the direct, if not awkward, proposal before she said "yes."

Thomas Edison wed Mary Stilwell on Christmas day 1871. After honeymooning in Boston, the newlyweds moved into a house at 53 Wright Street in Newark, New Jersey which had been purchased by Edison in November for $5,500. Located in a lovely residential neighborhood and near a trolley line, Edison made certain that his bride was given $2,000 for new furnishings, including a piano. Mrs. Edison was also able to afford domestic servants and money for an entirely new wardrobe. Edison was flush with cash and meant to spend it on creating a happy wife and a beautiful home. Sharing his newfound wealth, he also made investments in his father's and older brother's businesses back in Port Huron. In these early days of marriage, Edison executed thirty-nine patents, discovered his wife ("Popsy Wopsy") couldn't invent worth a darn, and became a father. The couple's first child, Marion, who Edison nicknamed "Dot," was born in 1873. Mother and child saw little of Edison that winter, as he often dined and slept at work. Focusing his work on an automatic telegraphy, he focused on dramatically increasing the carrying capacity of the telegraph network and sought to largely eliminate the need for skilled operators.

Edison had continued to work feverishly on both duplex and automatic telegraphy, realizing that the breakthrough in his professional field would come by being able to send multiple messages from a single telegraph line. He was soon joined by a fresh face to help him. Charles Batchelor was a British-born textile mechanic, who had come to the United States as an immigrant in 1870 to assist in the installation of thread equipment in Newark. With no specific experience in electrical technology, the modest, hardworking Batchelor, did bring skills as an experimental machinist and draftsman. The dark-bearded mechanic was especially gifted in conducting precise and delicate operations, and having been given the nickname "Batch," he became Edison's chief experimental assistant in the summer of 1873 and would serve as his right-hand man for the next twenty years.

On July 8, 1874, Edison successfully demonstrated a quadruplex telegraph between New York and Philadelphia for William Orton, the commanding ruler of Western Union. The system featured two terminal stations, each receiving and sending two transmissions simultaneously. Two days later, *The New York Times* announced the breakthrough to the world, thereby corroborating Edison's hunch that he was at last sitting on an invention potentially worth millions of dollars. Perhaps he might be able to at last turn his full attention to his own laboratory. After sitting down with Charles Batchelor, Edison drew up a list of new products to pursue to support his own shop.

One initial idea was to create a stencil of sorts, using a pen with a sharp point. As a precursor to a photocopier, this invention represented Edison's first breakthrough outside of telegraphy. Calling his invention an "electric motograph," a pen would pass over a stencil with an inked roller, puncturing the roller thereby transferring the ink onto sheets of paper below. Thomas Edison was at a loss as to how to successfully utilize such a device. However, along the way, Tom and Batch also managed to create a handheld, battery powered electric pen. This invention, which was not only cumbersome, but also required considerable skill to master, would sell over sixty thousand units throughout the next decade. Interestingly, this device, originally designed to create multiple copies of a single document, would revolutionize the tattoo industry. In 1891, a New York City tattoo artist named Samuel F. O'Reilly, took Edison's original design replacing the pen tip with a needle that would push the ink into the skin. This allowed for a faster and more precise application of ink to the skin, shortening a painful process, and creating better body art. Tattoos, previously used on slaves and prisoners, and popular only amongst the upper class as markings for status, became more popular with the masses. Whether or not Edison would have found pleasure in playing such a role in the rise in popularity in tattoos, seems unlikely. What is known, is that the electric pen gave Charles Batchelor a crash course in electricity and in late-night experimental sessions. In writing his brother back in England, Batchelor described the scenes in the laboratory at the time, "we work all night experimenting & sleep till noon in the day...we have got 54 things on the carpet." Batch further heaped praise upon his boss, writing, "he stands today the foremost inventor & electrician in this country by far," and "Edison is an indefatigable worker & there is no kind of failure however disastrous affects him."

In time, Edison lost interest in the multiplex and automatic aspects of telegraphy, turning his attention to the "acoustic" or "harmonic" telegraph and the works of Elisha Gray and Alexander Graham Bell. The science of sound was exciting and certainly riches awaited anyone who could pack more messages on a telegraph line. Edison also sensed that his Quadruplex could soon be replaced by these other methods. While conducting a series of acoustic telegraph experiments for Western Union, the laboratory team noticed a bizarre side effect when using a vibrator magnet. A spark leaped from the core of the magnet. A spark that was stronger than expected, and more forceful than anything caused by induction. Further experimentation revealed sparking when the vibrator was attached to a piece of iron and that the larger the piece of iron the larger the spark. They even connected the apparatus to gas pipes and were able to create a cascade of sparking throughout the laboratory. Noticeably excited nobody knew exactly what they had discovered. Thomas Edison, after discovering that it failed to register on a galvanometer and seemingly had no taste, believed that "the cause of the spark is a *true unknown force.*" This magic, glimpsed by Edison and colleagues, would later be revealed as high-frequency electromagnetic waves with the instruments in his lab acting much like a radio antenna.

With money in his pocket, and a few new inventions under his belt, Edison set out to do a little shopping for himself. What he sought was a new site for a laboratory of his own. The man, who was nearly deaf, ironically searched for a spot that would provide him "peace and quiet." At the start of 1876, Edison had found the perfect spot at Menlo Park and set out to build an "Invention Factory" with the goal of cranking out a minor invention every ten days and a major invention every six months. Edison purchased two tracts for $5,200, the smaller of which had a show house on it that would easily accommodate the Edison family, along with visitors and friends. The larger tract, an open field basked in sunlight, sat atop a steep, muddy boardwalk otherwise known as Christie Street. It was here that he would create a new model that would help transform American invention, and it was here that he would literally transform himself. The laboratory he built at Menlo Park was the largest private laboratory in the United States. The laboratory building, while unassuming from the outside, would soon be teeming with talented young experimenters and mechanics.

By the spring of 1876, Edison had moved the entire family to Menlo Park, including his second child, Thomas Alva Edison, Jr., born just a few months before. Junior was nicknamed "Dash" to match his older sister "Dot." Meanwhile Thomas Edison christened his new lab by setting out to tackle the new science of telephony. In many ways, the inventor was at a serious disadvantage in such a field as his issues with diminished hearing had led him to become a compulsive scribbler, who was at a loss without pencil and notebook. Messaging through sound represented a foreign frontier. The year before, Alexander Graham Bell and his assistant, Thomas Watson, while experimenting with acoustic telegraphy, had discovered that the instruments could convey any form of sound. In June of 1876, they followed this up with quite a splash, demonstrating the first working telephone at a Centennial Celebration in Philadelphia before a private audience that included

Elisha Gray—who had also developed his own telephone prototype. Legend has it that on February 14, 1876, Gray had filed with the U.S. Patent Office a caveat regarding his intentions to invent a telephone, but Bell had filed a patent application that same day, just two hours prior. Turns out Alexander Graham Bell also knew a thing or two about the deaf as his father had created an instructional method for the speechless deaf and Bell, himself, was also a teacher of the hearing impaired. While Gray may have been bitter, Edison, who was also at the celebration to exhibit his electric pen and automatic telegraph, was left flummoxed. Edison's team was on the cusp of developing a working telephone, but Bell, without an "invention factory," had gotten there first. Now, the race, in earnest, would be to improve upon the device.

One weakness in the Bell telephone was its transmitter, hampered by a weak current. This limited the distance over which it could be used. Team Edison focused on this component and set out to make improvements by conducting a series of experiments in transmission so that the telephone (speaking telegraph) could be used on longer lines. Edison also set out to improve voice quality and did so with a carbon transmitter that captured the human voice far better than Bell's magnetic design. Along the way, Thomas Edison also devised an entirely new receiver based off his electric motograph, which although it employed a rather impractical hand crank, was also capable of producing music clearly and at a volume an audience might enjoy. By 1877, Edison, Bell and Gray had emerged as direct competitors in this new technology and took this rivalry on tour by hosting a series of telephone concerts: lectures in exhibition halls. Although none of these men were natural showmen, nor naturally inclined pitchmen, Edison did have a bit more understanding of marketing than the other two. Afterall, he had already wet the imagination of any prospective audience with the creation of his invention factory. He was also smart enough to use a proxy: Edward Johnson, a former telegrapher turned salesman. In July of 1877, before an audience of nearly 4,000 people in Philadelphia, Johnson successfully conducted a telephone concert, much to the delight of everyone, including himself. The sound was crisp, and the volume excellent, as songs were played from performers some five miles away. The Edison telephone offered the opportunity to listen to live music from a distance, yet the great inventor and his team failed to fully understand the magnitude of this possibility. Why gather at a concert hall to hear music from a distance, when you might be able to do it from the comfort of your own home?

It has been said that Bell invented the telephone while tinkering with the telegraph and that Edison invented the phonograph while tinkering with the telephone. Thomas Edison, who by background naturally thought in terms of telegraphy, understood that if a messenger transmitted a message verbally, as opposed to using Morse code, that it was illogical, if not constricting, to have that same message transcribed manually at the receiving end by a human operator. The breakthrough in this technology might be found in recording the message mechanically. This would not only require the usual battery of experiments, at his lab, with his trusted team, but would also require Edison to rely on the better hearing of his assistants.

In the summer of 1877, Menlo Park played host to many late work sessions, including a few all-night affairs. So long were the working hours, that Edison established a tradition of providing a midnight dinner, often brought up by the night watchman, and used as a natural break before the team plowed back into another round of experiments before sunrise. It was during one of these midnight dinners, when guards were down and banter up, that Edison came upon an idea as he entertained himself by speaking into a rubber diaphragm for a telephone. As he did so, he noticed the vibrations on his fingers, and casually remarked, "Batch, if we had a point on this, we could make a record on some material which we could afterwards pull under the point, and it would give us speech back." The brilliance of Edison's idea was lost on no one. His words barely had a moment to swirl in the evening air—the utterance halted by the sound of workers as they scrambled from their chairs to rig up a test. After huddling over an Edison sketch, Batch grabbed some wax paper and cut them into strips while John Krueis, the laboratory's chief machinist, soldered a needle to the middle of a diaphragm and attached it to a stand. An hour later, Thomas Edison sat down, leaned forward toward the mouthpiece, and while Charles Batchelor pulled the paper through, spoke the following words: "Mary had a little lamb." These words, previously used and decided upon as a stock phrase for the lab, could literally be seen on the paper as a pattern of irregular marks. However, when the paper was reinserted and pulled through without voice, out came "ary ad ell am." Not exactly Shakespeare, the garbled words were still enough to spark an uncharacteristic celebration. By morning, as the sun peaked out over the eastern tree line, the team had succeeded in getting a clearly articulated recording from waxed paper: "Mary had a little lamb."

Menlo Park was not a paradise for everyone. While Thomas Edison described it as "the prettiest spot in New Jersey," and Charles Batchelor referred to it as "a beautiful country place," Mary Edison was not so smitten with it. Far from the city, and many of her friends, Mary felt a sense of isolation in the New Jersey countryside. Aside from Rosanna Batchelor, and John Kruesi's wife, who shared a nearby home with their husbands, the neighborhood was made up almost entirely by men. The factory, which on any given evening might resemble a local tavern, was the punctuation of masculinity, with a brass band organized by employees and a young black bear kept as a pet. In other words, it was not a place for women or children. To make matters worse, her husband essentially lived at the laboratory, only returning home for the briefest of time. With two young children, and two smaller sized canines, Mary is said to have slept many nights with a revolver under her pillow. The big Newfoundland, another family dog, did little to ease her nerves. When Mary visited friends in Newark, or had them out to visit, Edison rarely broke away from his laboratory and even when he did so, the inventor often managed to escape back up the hill at some point during the evening. Sensing his wife's isolation, Edison welcomed Mary's sister Alice to live at the house, and to add more female companionship, he invited the recently widowed Sarah Jordan and her thirteen-year-old daughter Ida to Menlo Park. Sarah ("Aunt Sally") was Mary's father's stepdaughter from his first marriage, and ultimately set up a boarding house of sorts for the single men at Menlo Park. However, the couple did manage to find some time together, as the Edison's had their third child, William Leslie, in October of 1878.

On December 8, 1877, *Scientific American,* scooped quite the story, describing how Thomas Edison had come to their office, placed a machine on a desk, turned a crank, and this same machine had enquired as to their health, asked how we liked the phonograph, informed them that it was very well, and bid all a cordial good night. The fifteen-hundred-word article imagined how the device might allow singers to continue to sing long after they had lost their voice and died, or how children of the rich might hear proof of "Papa's" determination and soundness of mind when deeding all to his mistress. Hard as they might, the authors could hardly contemplate the magnitude of the contraption gazed upon. With the breakthrough in creating the phonograph, Edison's lab slowly lost its status as a secluded retreat as groups of scientists, journalists and sightseers descended upon Menlo Park. The following spring, on April 18, 1878, when Edison accepted an invitation to present the phonograph to the National Academy of Science during an assembly at the Smithsonian Institution in Washington, the inventor morphed from novelty to celebrity. From that point on, privacy was a luxury and obscurity forever fleeting. The *New York Daily Graphic's*, William Croffut made certain of this new reality as he extoled Edison's genius and coined his new nickname: "the Wizard of Menlo Park." Edison did his part as well in September of that same year, telling a reporter from the *New York Sun*, that he had invented the first practical incandescent light bulb, one where a wire inside the glass bulb glowed brilliantly as electricity flowed through it.

CHAPTER 4

Camp Hurley

The first camp was two miles east of Greensburg, Pa. with tents pitched about a half mile off the roadway on the farm of a Mr. H.A. Miller, in what Harvey Firestone described as a "very beautiful grove of trees." It was named "Camp Hurley" in honor of their guest, the Commissioner of the U.S. Shipping Board. August 18*th* was a chilly night. The eighty-one-year-old Burroughs found it hard to sleep, and after tossing and turning, he got up at 4 AM to sit near the fire. He blamed the folding camp cots for not conserving one's bodily warmth and insisted that without extra blankets "sleep enters your tent very reluctantly." Burroughs, who had described the camp as an ideal place, with "large open oak groves on a gentle eminence well carpeted with grass, with wood and water in abundance," later remarked that with the cold evening he got "more of the bitter than the sweet." After replenishing the fire, the oldest member of the party pulled up a camp chair and pondered many things about life all while the rest of the camping party soundly slept.

It was a different scene, earlier that evening, as the campers gathered around a big fire (apparently made, in part, by a huge stump which required the united efforts of four members of the party including Mr. Edison) sharing good food and good stories with a dose of good banter. With their work and city life finally behind them, the flickering light and shadows cast a fine spell of comradery on their first night together in the world nature made. At some point, the party began talking about what everyone across the country was talking about: War. With Commissioner Hurley present and the knowledge that he might be leaving the party any day, they had a man with firsthand knowledge of the War. It was their chance to find out as much as they could while they could. How could they win the War? Would they win the War? When would it end? What would the world be like after the Great War? Much of what was said and heard was not to be repeated, but it appears that their curiosity was turned to great comfort as the United States was, indeed, changing the tide. At one point, Edison declared "The Huns are boneheads." Not surprisingly, Ford, who was the previously self-proclaimed pacifist of the lot, expressed more leniency toward the enemy, but made it perfectly clear that he was determined to win. He even told those gathered around the campfire, "War is a waste" but "we must win" and that everyone must be "ready to pay the price" to do so. These comments by Ford were recorded by John Burroughs who wanted all to know that although Ford may have been against the War initially, he was now persuaded that it was a righteous cause. In any event, it was close to midnight before the campers turned in for the night, rolling out their cots with a feeling of comfort "that only a day in the open can give."

The following morning breakfast was called at 8 AM, followed by a visit from the Greensburg mayor and local newspapers. Apparently, the mayor arrived just in time to watch Ford leap over the fire one last time, while daring others to try it. Minutes before, Edison and Ford had both darted around the campfire, with Ford leaping across when the flames were as high as Commissioner Hurley's office desk. Hurley told Ford he had "better look out, you'll burn up your carburetor," but the potential Senator from Michigan showed little concern responding, "I don't care." When the reporters managed to corner Edison for an interview, the inventor used his deafness to convert questions to his liking, converting "Is war man's foolishness" to "man is a fool." However, he made it clear that he believed Germany was no match for Americans, stating, "The reason for American superiority is that the men of this country are of mixed blood. The mixture of various races is good." Edison clearly believed the best dog to be a mutt. An American mutt. Burroughs told the reporters that Uncle Sam was going to give Germany such a licking that "no German will ever want to think of war again." If only he had known as much of war as he did of nature!

The camp was also visited by a Ms. Marion Head, who was described by the senior Firestone as a "young lady friend" of Harvey Jr., and who was apparently, an instant hit with the campers. The morning also included the firing of rifles with target practice though whose idea this was, is not known. However, Harvey Firestone later reflected that some in the party opined that "rifle firing (was) not conductive to restful sleep and that it "takes rank with the rooster or the serenading feline as a capable disturber of sleep." However, nobody seemed to consider it completely out of place. Professor DeLoach, who described the younger Firestone's female friend as a "beautiful young girl," remarked later that she was as accurate with a rifle as any member of the camp. While Firestone and Ford thought they battled for top marksmanship, it was Burroughs who stole the show as he demonstrated his country boy accuracy hitting the bullseye while shooting from a chair. At 11 AM the party broke camp and later bade farewell to Commissioner Hurley, who had been called back to Washington D.C. for a cabinet meeting. Burroughs later described the Commissioner as "keen and competent," and further reflected that the campers all agreed that he was a loyal and patriotic American citizen. Professor DeLoach would later write that Hurley was a "very fine type of public servant," and "could tell a very fine clean story and sit and discuss the problems of his office with perfect clearness." Hurley, for his part, when asked by the press about the trip just a few days after his departure, heaped plenty of praise upon the camping party as well. However, an interesting point of contention did appear between Burroughs and Hurley regarding the starting point of their trip.

While Burroughs later described their initial travel through Western Pennsylvania as "an impressive state, so vast, so diversified, so forest-clad the huge unbroken Allegheny Ranges with their deep valleys cutting across it...; the world of fine farms and rural homesteads ..., and the great manufacturing interests, the source of noble rivers, and the storehouse of many of Nature's most useful gifts to man," he was less enamored with Pittsburgh and her nearby mines. He described Pittsburgh as sitting on the edge of the "devil's laboratory," and further waxed that it seemed fit that "weapons of war and destructiveness should come out of such pits and abysses of hellfire." When he warned the campers that they lived in an age of iron and should do all they could to keep the iron from entering their souls, Hurley pushed back, "it is the fuel being produced here that is providing the steel for the ships which are transporting our soldiers overseas. Without the fuel we could not have the ships and without the ships we could not have the soldiers over there. If we don't have coal and coke, we might just as well not have any soldiers." As for Pittsburgh, Hurley remarked, "there is not a city in the United States that is taking such an active part in this war as Pittsburgh." The United States was indeed leaning heavily on steel mills, coke ovens and coal mines. However, the Commissioner saved his greatest praise for the workers in the nearby mines, reminding all that those who brought coal to the surface, were providing fuel to win the war. Of course, both men were right.

A few words about one of the lesser-known campers on the trip: Professor DeLoach. Robert John Henderson DeLoach was born on December 21, 1873, a few miles west of Statesboro, the county seat of Bulloch County, Georgia. Born and raised on a farm, he was educated in his early years in a one-room schoolhouse, where subjects were far more important than grades. DeLoach would later write that he was acquainted with the traditions and prejudices of the deep South, and by 1892 he "rebelled against ignorance" and made it known to his family that he would get a college education. At the time this was a bold proclamation for a rural farm boy in Bulloch County as very few persons had any formal education. However, the young man would make good on his promise.

In 1893 R.J.H. DeLoach entered the University of Georgia, being initially put on a form of academic probation for the first three months, before receiving classification of a good student. He graduated in 1898 and taught in the Statesboro and Swainsboro local schools for several years and was in the U.S. Indian Service in 1901 and 1902. Thereafter, he returned to teaching in public schools before becoming a member of the staff of the University of Georgia. For sixteen years he directed an educational bureau for the Armour Corporations in Chicago, returning to Georgia on invitation to become connected with the Georgia Teachers College at Statesboro, near his hometown.

In the early 1900s, the Georgian academic became well acquainted with John Burroughs, as a nature writer, and regularly visited him during summers at his New York home. From 1908 to 1921, Burroughs was a regular visitor to DeLoach in the South, and the two also traveled frequently to Chicago for lectures of interest. In the summer of 1916, DeLoach was spending the month of August with Burroughs at his summer home at Woodchuck Lodge in Roxbury, New York, in the Western Catskills, when the nature writer received a letter from Thomas Edison stating that he, Mr. Ford and Mr. Firestone had organized a camping trip through the Adirondacks and wanted Burroughs to join them. DeLoach urged Burroughs to go, telling him he would begin arrangements to return home to the South immediately. However, Burroughs would have none of it, and wrote back to Edison respectfully declining the invitation citing prior obligations and the professor as a house guest. A few days later Edison wrote back and suggested the writer, "Bring the professor along, too. It would be interesting to have a man like him with us."

When DeLoach received word that he had been invited to become a member of an Edison camping party, the professor was elated and felt it a great honor. He later wrote, "My fondest hope has always been to meet, to know, and to cultivate interesting people, and certainly America has not produced any more interesting people than the four members of this camping party...these men have played a very big part, if not a dominating part, in the great changes of human life during the years that they lived." DeLoach also felt a certain kinship with their backgrounds writing, "Of this group, three (Burroughs, Ford and Firestone) were farm boys, and Edison was born in a very small village...." DeLoach believed that Burroughs had changed man's attitude largely from technical studies of nature to a love of nature. As for Edison, he "was the means of replacing the old gooseneck student's lamp with an incandescent light." The Professor further believed that "Ford widened the horizon of man's thought by substituting automobiles for horses and buggies and mules and wagons." Lastly, DeLoach believed Firestone's interest in the development of the pneumatic tire, "enabled man to travel faster from county to county and from state to state." The fortunate professor would be a member of Edison's camping party in 1916 and 1918. We all share in his good fortune as DeLoach provides an "outsider's perspective," and, since very little was written about these trips, his words on the subject help fill in many gaps to these stories.

As for the trip at hand, DeLoach received a telegram from Mr. E.G. Leibold, Henry Ford's general secretary, regarding this camping trip as follows: "Mr. Edison desires that you and Mr. Burroughs be at home on Thursday evening the 15*th*. They expect to leave Friday morning the 16*th*." Burroughs and DeLoach spent the night at Thomas Edison's home in East Orange, New Jersey, and left early the next morning for Pittsburgh, the designated launching site for the 1918 trip.

CHAPTER 5

A Little "High-Kicking"

The caravan motored to Greensburg, Pennsylvania for oil and gas. Burroughs took the opportunity to buy a duster (long coat) to better warm his aging body. Quite pleased with how it looked, he declared that it completed his outfit, and he did not care what else happened next. From there the caravan headed to Connellsville, Pennsylvania. Along the way, one of the bigger cars, driven by the younger Firestone, a Packard, had a cooling fan break, which after running wild, punctured the radiator. Luckily one of the Packard's other occupants was Henry Ford. After a bit of roadside tinkering, they were able to coax the car into Connellsville and found the Wells-Mills garage in the center of town. After much shaking of heads, the initial analysis from the local mechanics was that the radiator was beyond repair and that a new one could be overnighted from Pittsburgh. Several locals, having gotten word of the famous travelers, soon also arrived at the scene and offered their assistance as well. Ford, who undoubtedly knew more about mechanics than anyone else in town, assumed the self-appointed task of deciding what to do. After a few moments of thought, and with a crowd of onlookers, he pulled off his coat, rolled up his sleeves, and began taking off the broken parts. He then carried them into the nearby garage, where the master mechanic spent the next three hours personally repairing them. To everyone's astonishment the car had been fixed and was ready to resume the race. Ford's olive-green suit, spotted with grease, was an unintended casualty.

Road trips in the early part of the twentieth century were quite different than they are today. Fewer roads, often of poor quality, along with constant mechanical challenges, could make for a very uncertain trip. The first "American road trip," might have started over a $50 wager resulting from a bar debate in San Francisco when patrons contemplated the future of the horseless carriage. Some argued it was a passing novelty, while others, including Horatio Nelson Jackson, believed it was here to stay. It is not known if Jackson or the other patron was inebriated. What is known, is that when a patron bet Jackson $50 he could not get from San Francisco to New York City in less than 90 days, he accepted the wager.

On May 23, 1903, in a sea of horse-drawn carriages, Jackson and Sewall Crocker rumbled down San Francisco's Market Street in a cherry-red Winton touring car. Loaded down with sleeping bags, cooking gear and other supplies, these two men and their automobile were embarking on a truly epic cross-country drive that would change travel forever. Jackson was a former medical doctor from Burlington, Vermont who had given up his practice after a bout of tuberculosis. His education served him well as he was smart enough to recruit Crocker, a 22-year-old former bicycle racer, and more importantly, a gasoline engine mechanic, to be his traveling companion. The 20-horsepower Winton touring car, which would be their home for the coming days, was given the name *Vermont* in honor of Jackson's home state. When Jackson and Crocker set out on their journey, there were fewer than 150 miles of paved roads in the United States, with no road signs, road numbers or gas stations.

Problems struck early on their trip. Just 15 miles outside of San Francisco a rear tire blew requiring the travelers to replace it with their only spare. Progress was slow. The racers often slowly motored through standing water, and on occasion were required to stop to remove, by hand, large rocks blocking further passage. When a clutch broke, they had to rely on a stagecoach to bring new parts, and at one point, the car was towed by horses across a desert plain. After 19 days the touring car and its occupants had only reached Idaho. After a gas leak left their gas tank near empty, Crocker set off on a 26-mile bicycle ride only to puncture a tire requiring him to walk most of the way back with fuel and bike in tow. However, somewhere in Idaho -or about 700 hundred miles along their 2,900-hundred-mile drive, luck changed for the better when they picked up a traveling companion. A photogenic bull terrier they named Bud, was placed in the front seat, fitted with his own pair of goggles to protect his eyes from the dusty roads, and officially designated as trip mascot.

In Wyoming, the three companions had to wait five days after a connecting rod to the crankshaft snapped, and the part had to be shipped by rail all the way from the Winton factory in Cleveland, Ohio. By then, word was spreading about their journey. The drivers' spirits were lifted by the tremendous receptions received as curious onlookers gathered in towns hoping to catch a glimpse of an automobile and characters straight out of Jules Verne's *Around the World in 80 Days.* By the time the road warriors arrived on July 12*th* to a cheering throng of people in Omaha, Nebraska, the $50 wager had captivated the nation. They picked up time as travel conditions got better, often averaging 150 miles a day, and on July 20, 1903, a convoy escorted Jackson, Crocker and Bud into Cleveland where the car, named Vermont, had originally been designed and manufactured, and was given a hero's welcome. Six days later, on Sunday 26, 1903 at 4:30 AM, a cherry-finished car, caked in mud, arrived in Manhattan and crawled down a deserted Fifth Avenue. She had traveled 4,500 miles in 63 days, 12 hours and 30 minutes. Although Jackson had won the $50 wager, it had cost him $8,000 to do so. As for Bud, after enjoying his meteoric rise to fame, the lovable pooch retired to a life of peace and quiet and could often be found on the porch of the Jackson family home in Burlington, Vermont. Legend has it, he never lost his love for riding in the front seat of an automobile.

Between Burroughs' search for a coat, and an unplanned visit to the garage following the broken cooling fan, the day was quickly getting away from the campers. The party had also become separated with some vehicles further down the path than others; and one of the trucks with supplies was nowhere to be seen. What was described by the camping party as Truck No. 1 was the commissary, which carried most of the goodies including fried chicken that had been the planned meal for that day's lunch. By mid-afternoon, and without knowledge of where their food had gone, the campers stopped to telephone the Summit Hotel near Uniontown, Pennsylvania, for early dinner reservations. One of the vehicles was sent back to look for the food truck while the rest of the party drove on to Uniontown. After arriving in Uniontown, Pa. the scout car returned with news that Truck No. 1 had a broken driveshaft, that was being repaired and would probably be no more than an hour behind. The campers contemplated setting up camp somewhere outside of Uniontown, Pa. and had looked for sites. However, as time passed, and with no sign of the commissary, it was decided to start for the Summit Hotel and to get rooms for the night.

The register of the Summit Hotel shows that on Monday August 19th, 1918, Thomas Edison stayed in room 18; Henry Ford, Room 20; John Burroughs and Professor DeLouch, room 25; and Harvey Firestone and Harvey Jr., in room 51. It was not what they had planned, but it turned out to be a wonderful evening. It also gave some of the campers an opportunity to get a bathe and shave. Edison, who believed in going all-in on the camping experience, probably frowned upon the chance to get cleaned up, but everyone agreed that dinner was especially good. Opened in 1907 by a group of Uniontown businessmen, who thought a hotel overlooking their town would make a good investment, the Summit Hotel is still in operation today along the old National Road (aka Route 40). With a floor-to-ceiling fireplace and mission style furniture, the hotel lobby remains relatively unchanged from 1918—the outdoor pool was not added until the 1920s. The wrap-around porch is unchanged from 1918 and the late 1800s Steinway grand piano, still sits in the front of the Inn. However, the price has changed. In 1918 the rooms were $4.50 per day, whereas today rooms are in excess of $100. Opened to the public in 1907, the Summit Hotel was a little over a decade old when Thomas Edison and friends made their unexpected stay-over. In the 1950s, the hotel briefly fell into disrepair. However, it was later purchased and beautifully restored by the Shoemaker family who continue its stewardship to this day.

As was often the case, Henry Ford had a hard time sitting still. After dinner, he insisted on climbing a nearby mountain, and was able to convince the elder Firestone to join him on this evening hike with promises of a birds-eye view of Uniontown. At the outset of the walk, Firestone told Ford, "I'll join you in anything." The hike proved to be more strenuous than initially anticipated, and when they arrived at the top, Ford marveled at the view and commented on how beautiful the dark green Pennsylvania valleys looked below. Firestone was apparently not as impressed and wondered "if it were so fine down there, why did we walk up here?"

Past advertisements from the Summit Hotel *include* claims that Ford would have, no doubt, appreciated including: "Above the Clouds in Pennsylvania;" and "Freedom from hay fever and asthma is assured." It is not known what our hikers might have thought about one ad that boldly claimed, "No mosquitoes." After leading his party to the top of the hill, Ford marched his company down the other side, which called forth the quotation from the famous old general of schooldays who had ten thousand men and "Marched them up to the top of the hill, and marched 'em down again."

Later that night Truck No. 1 arrived bringing the entire party together again. At some point during their stay, Burroughs joined Ford and Edison in showing his "pep," as many guests in the hotel lobby lay witness to the three "high kicking" and performing "stair jumping stunts." It appears the great inventor, organized a stair jumping competition, with Ford winning the contest by making ten steps in two hops. Edison made ten steps in three hops, and Burroughs in his attempt to best his adversaries, lost his balance and was rescued from a fall by onlookers. At another point, while lounging in the hotel lobby, Ford placed a cigar on the mantel piece over the fireplace and dared Edison to kick it off. Edison, who responded with a simple, "I'll go you," with little effort kicked the cigar off the mantel three successive times. After initially claiming he was too tired, Burroughs did make one unsuccessful try at the dangling cigar.

The next morning, August 20, 1918, the party made an early start for Keysers Ridge, Maryland for what can best be described as a mail run. When our campers wandered through these southwest parts of Pennsylvania, the Laurel Highlands were the undisputed main attraction. There was no Fallingwater or Kentucky Knob, as they had not been built and the architectural genius of Frank Lloyd Wright was yet to be fully discovered. However, the area was well known for its historical significance and the road they started out on in the early morning hours was well traveled.

The National Road had been the idea of Albert Gallatin, the Secretary of State under President Thomas Jefferson, to "connect the East with the West." Construction began in 1811 on what was the first major improved highway in the United States built by the federal government and was opened to the public in 1818. Starting in Cumberland, Maryland, the road crosses into Pennsylvania, West Virginia, Ohio, and Indiana before ending in Vandalia, Illinois. In the 1830s states began assuming control of maintenance and imposed tolls to cover costs. Tolls varied depending on the mode of transportation so that wagon trains paid the most while those traveling by foot paid the least. During the pike's heyday traffic was quite heavy during the day and into the early evening with the two most common vehicles being the stagecoach and the Conestoga wagon (the covered wagon). Stagecoaches were made for speed and regularly traveled up to 70 miles a day. The Conestoga wagon, the tractor trailer of the 19*th* century, might be lucky to travel

20 miles in a day. Had our group come upon this road a century earlier they would have brought both vehicles with our famous passengers in stagecoaches, while carrying the supplies and help in covered wagons.

The National Road, which is also known as the National Pike or Cumberland Road/Pike, is now Route 40, and in the eastern part largely parallels the military road opened by George Washington and General Braddock in 1754-55. Not long after the road was constructed, towns along the path began to grow and prosper. Uniontown was one such town and was the home to three major stagecoach lines. Taverns and inns began to spring up as well and at one point it was estimated that there was a tavern for every mile of the road. One such tavern is the Mount Washington Tavern—still open to the public today as a museum—which would be considered a stagecoach tavern. A stagecoach tavern was primarily designed with the more affluent traveler in mind. Resembling an inn, the first floor of the Mount Washington Tavern has a dining room for all visitors. However, the bar area sits on one side of a hallway with a parlor on the opposite side. Women would have been prohibited to enter the bar for fear of ruining their reputation. The top floor of the tavern contained rooms for sleeping. However, even the affluent, if traveling alone or without family, might find themselves sharing a room and even a bed with complete strangers presumably only if of the same sex. The other type of tavern for the less affluent traveler was called a wagon stand and would more resemble today's truck stop.

It is not clear if the camping party stopped at the Mount Washington Tavern or visited Fort Necessity which is a relatively short walk away. The site made famous for the events and varying accounts of what unfolded with a young George Washington in the Summer of 1754 is today a National Park and a must-visit for any history enthusiast. Given its importance as the scene of the opening battle of the French and Indian War, it would seem logical to believe the Vagabonds at least took pause, but there is no account or picture from this battlefield site. What does survive is a picture of Harvey Firestone, Jr., Professor DeLoach, and John Burroughs inspecting a Monument to General Braddock.

This is just up the road from Fort Necessity and is a marker memorializing the final resting place of British Major Edward Braddock, leader of the ill-fated expedition to the forks of the Ohio River to try to capture French-held Fort Duquesne. It was near this site on July 9, 1755, that British regulars and American Colonial troops, again with Aide-de-camp George Washington, were routed by Indian warriors who launched a series of lethal attacks under the cover of dense woods. A complete disaster in military history, the long line of red coats suffered heavy casualties including its commander being mortally wounded.

George Washington again found himself at the center of some controversy after his decision to have General Braddock buried under the road in an unmarked grave to keep it from being disturbed by Indians. It was also here that Washington's ability to organize a retreat and to save countless lives, made him a hero in the eyes of many Americans. How they escaped is the stuff of legends. As for the leader of the ill-fated expedition, the exact location of his final resting place remained unknown until 1804 when workers discovered human remains and Officer uniform buttons believed to have been the General's. What has happened since is both sad and bizarre. Some of the remains were kept as souvenirs with hand bones reportedly finding their way to museums in Philadelphia and New York City and a section of vertebrae is even reported to be at the Walter Reed Hospital collection in Bethesda, Maryland. Later, a magistrate ordered the return of the remains and those remains recovered were then re-interred on a small knoll adjacent to the road. On October 15, 1913, just five years before our campers stopped by this site, the monument was erected less than thirty or forty yards off Route 40.

At some point later that morning, the party came upon a sign pointing to Oakland, Maryland which was their next intended stop. Road maps were consulted, and general confusion ensued. While the camping party discussed their next move, Edison took the opportunity to walk to a nearby roadside stand to secure a bottle of pop. It was here that Edison and Harvey, Jr. discovered that the elusive Ridge was just around the corner. Edison, perhaps being proud of his discovery, made the party patiently wait for him to finish his pop before the caravan dared move on.

Pressing on the party stopped for lunch beside a "beautiful stream" and a "handsome grove" of large shade trees causing the campers to comment that Oakland lived up to its name. Mr. Ford wandered to a nearby orchard, while a little girl from a nearby farmhouse followed his every move. After getting the nerve to approach the visitor, the little girl was given a dollar to help the automobile tycoon gather a pail of apples. Pleased with her work, she joyfully skipped home, and soon thereafter her father returned with a pail of apple cider that was happily added as a libation to wash down lunch. For whatever reason, tempers momentarily flared after lunch. After getting gas and oil in Oakland, Harvey, Jr. purchased the elderly Burroughs a box of caramels from a local candy shop. Ford, who was not pleased with such an indulgence, managed to snatch the box and throw it up the street much to the astonishment of many onlookers. It is reported that Ford barked out, "They're no good for you." Burroughs was the oldest member of the party, and at times was treated as a fragile and precious treasure to be guarded every mile along the trip. Apparently, Ford had appointed himself as guardian of the elder writer. The younger Firestone, who was clearly just showing an act of kindness with his gesture, was caught off guard by Ford's knee-jerk reaction. Perhaps typical of men of this age, there is not much else that was said or written about the incident, and we are left to wonder if or how it was resolved between the campers.

Traveling further south towards a lumbering center, Lead Mine, West Virginia, the party enjoyed seven consecutive miles of concrete highway, calming any frayed nerves. Unfortunately, this was followed by an extremely rough and wild stretch causing much shaking and rattling of the vehicles and passengers. At around 5 PM, on Tuesday, August 20th, Firestone and Edison discovered a picturesque area along a small clear river named Horse Shoe Run. Burroughs, who had eyed a smooth field across the road and felt it ideal to pitch a tent, had gotten reluctant consent from the widow who owned it to stay there for the night. Initially hesitant, and equally unimpressed by the names of those in the party, she must have ultimately sensed that the gypsy travelers posed no threat. However, Edison had other ideas. Unimpressed with the open field, he preferred the rough grassy margin of the creek and its proximity to the murmuring, eddying, rocky current. The campers pitched their tents elbowed together in narrow spaces between the boulders, and the mess tent was pitched astride a shallow gulley. Ford later commented that the stream seemed silent, so Harvey Jr. stacked stones along one side creating a waterfall for sound effects. As the campers stretched out around the fire in their sleeping bags, Edison said, "Isn't this great. Nothing but the trees and the air and the fire. This is thc only kind of a vacation."

An interesting object near the camp was an old, unused grist mill, with a huge decaying oaken water wheel. After exploring the mill, the famous campers paused to have their picture taken perched atop the water wheel. The result is an iconic image that not only captures the vagabond adventure, but also reveals the tender, lifelong friendships between these men. Ford, who was visibly annoyed afterwards, lamented the waste of potential water from mountain streams. Thomas Edison quickly chimed in by telling Ford that hydroelectricity could be produced by linking up power from the tiniest brooks. The famous inventor also imagined that homes could be heated, meals cooked, farm drudgery diminished, and whole towns illuminated by all this unused horsepower. In response, Ford stated, "It's a shame, a tragedy, the way this country—every country—is letting this natural resource go to waste." So began an unending search for potential power sources along their journey.

Ford's interest in every stream, caused him to race up and down their banks searching for falls as a potential waterpower. He never tired of talking about how much power might be going to waste everywhere they went. Looking back over the trip, Lester Hopper, commented that it seemed to him that Ford and Edison were obsessed with finding a way to harness the energy of waterfalls. The two believed it would bring employment and contentment to thousands of "mountain-held" people, who they rightly or wrongly believed had been deprived of many of the good things of life.

CHAPTER 6

Wild and Wonderful

Rick Steelhammer writes in *It Happened in West Virginia*, that "In the only state completely encompassed by the Appalachian Mountain range, thunder has frequently echoed across our slopes, but it has not always been the product of lightning." Almost everyone knows the words to John Denver's *Take me Home, Country Roads*

> "Almost heaven, West Virginia
> Blue Ridge Mountains, Shenandoah River
> Life is old there, older than the trees
> Younger than the mountains, blowing in the breeze
> Country Roads, take me home
> To the place I belong
> West Virginia, mountain mama..."

West Virginians know those words as well, and are, likely, also familiar with Debar's Latin inscription, "Montani Semper Liberi," arching across the lower half of the state seal for they have always known "Mountaineers Are Always Free."

The presidential election in 1860 has long been considered one the most consequential elections in American history with Abraham Lincoln being elevated to the highest office in the land and thereby setting in motion a chain of events that would lead to the Civil War. Much has been written about the Republican candidate and Stephen Douglas, the Northern Democrat from Illinois. However, the Democrats ran a second candidate as Vice President John C. Breckenridge ran as a Southerner in the same party. What seems to have also been forgotten is that there was a *third-party* candidate, John Bell, who ran in the Constitutional Union Party. When looking at the area that would become West Virginia, Breckenridge and Bell ran neck and neck, while Virginia proper was carried by Bell. Lincoln finished well behind these two candidates in every region of Virginia.

On December 20, 1860, South Carolina seceded from the Union, followed by Mississippi, Florida, Alabama, Georgia, Louisiana, and later Texas in the winter of 1861. In the spring and early summer Virginia, Arkansas, North Carolina and Tennessee followed. However, each of these states contained large areas with little or no commitment to slavery especially in western Virginia, western North Carolina, eastern Tennessee, and northern Arkansas. The thirty-five counties of Virginia, west of the Shenandoah Valley and north of the Kanawha River, contained a sizable population of whites. The mountains and hollers held no plantations, and for the most part there were very few slaves or slaveowners. Western Virginia looked more to Ohio and Pennsylvania for emulation than to Richmond or Norfolk. For years, the "highlanders" in these western counties had felt neglected and underrepresented in a Virginia legislature dominated by the "tidewater aristocrats." All the state's allocated funds seemed to be spent on roads and railways in the eastern counties. In 1861, a Clarksburg newspaper declared, "Western Virginia has suffered more from her.... eastern brethren than ever the Cotton States all put together have suffered from the North."

On April 12, 1861, Fort Sumter was shelled by confederates, representing, what many scholars consider, the first shots of the Civil War. Shortly thereafter, Abraham Lincoln called for seventy-five thousand volunteers to put down the rebellion, including a telegram sent to Virginia governor, John Lechter. The Virginia governor wasted no time in rebuffing assistance, shooting back his refusal: "The militia of Virginia will not be furnished to the powers of Washington for any such purpose as they have in view." Five days after the Fort Sumter shelling, by a vote of eighty-eight to fifty-five, the Virginia Secession Convention passed an Ordinance of Secession. On April 23, 1861, the Virginia governor offered command of the state's defense forces to former U.S. Army Colonel Robert E. Lee, who accepted. However, the vote for secession was far from unanimous and many questioned the wisdom of appointing a commander for Virginia.

It was not surprising that only five of the thirty-one delegates from western Virginia voted for secession in 1861. In fact, three of four voting citizens in the region initially rejected any form of secession. Although pockets of staunch support of the Confederacy did exist in the Shenandoah Valley, while citizens in the Kanawha River Valley and the southwest portion of the state swore their allegiance to the Commonwealth of Virginia, it is estimated that of the 491,000 slaves in Virginia in 1860, only 18,371 resided in what would become West Virginia. Furthermore, those 18,371 slaves were held by 3,593 owners. Since the population of the region was 376,677, there was only 1 slave owner for every 100 white citizens. While secessionists gathered momentum in many parts of Virginia, mass meetings of unionists simultaneously sprung up all around the northwestern part of the state. The meetings resulted in a convention in Wheeling on June 11, 1861. Realizing that the U.S. Constitution would require the consent of the legislature to form a new state from the territory of an existing one and knowing that the Confederate legislature of Virginia would not consent to such a separate state, the convention instead formed a "restored government" of Virginia. The convention declared the Virginia legislature illegal, thereby rendering all state offices vacant. On June 20, 1861, new state officials were appointed including a new governor, Francis Pierpont, and two U.S. senators from Virginia, and three congressmen from western Virginia, were seated in July of 1861.

In August of 1861, when the Wheeling convention was reconvened, the die was cast for the eventual formation of a new state. Union forces moved into western Virginia and would play a pivotal role in Civil War logistics by protecting the Baltimore and Ohio Railroad and the Ohio River, creating a direct link by rail and water from Washington to the Midwest and ultimately the Mississippi river. It has been said that the Civil War pitted brother against brother, and this is made clear by local troops who volunteered for both the Union and the Confederacy. In fact, scholars believe that 20,000 to 22,000 troops from those counties comprising West Virginia fought equally for both sides. John Snyder Carlisle of Clarksburg, an anti-secessionist, who was elected to the U.S. Senate, was a driving force in drafting a statehood bill. He pushed for the immediate creation of the state of "New Virginia." Carlisle also saw firsthand, brother against brother, as his old law firm split over the secession crisis, with two of his law partners becoming leading advocates to their respective causes.

The battle over slavery came early to West Virginia. On October 16, 1859, a year and half before confederates shelled Fort Sumter in South Carolina, a beloved fanatic attempted an ill-fated raid on a federal arsenal at Harpers Ferry. John Brown, a self-proclaimed abolitionist, believed that by seizing a large stockpile of weapons, that enslaved blacks would become emboldened and would join their fight. John Brown was no stranger to violence, having orchestrated and participated in the 1856 murder of five proslavery men at three different cabins along the banks of the Pottawatomie Creek, near present-day, Lane, Kansas. In August of 1859, Brown had approached Frederick Douglas to see if he could recruit the legendary figure to participate in his Harpers Ferry raid. "When I strike, the bees will begin to swarm, and I shall want you to help hive them," Brown told Douglas. But Douglas would have none of it, believing that Brown was embarking on a suicide mission. He further expressed concern for the abolitionist cause, stating, "an attack on the federal government...would array the whole country against us." Nonetheless, with or without Douglas, Brown was on a mission to start an uprising.

From a nearby training camp on the Maryland side of the Potomac, Brown crossed the river along with a band of followers, cut the telegraph lines entering the town, and captured the armory complex defended by a single watchman. It was just about midnight. Brown sent out a patrol, instructing them to get word out to the countryside as to what was going on and for slaves and other abolitionists to congregate at the arsenal. He also told them to bring hostages, if possible. At around 1:30 AM, an express train from Wheeling arrived at the Harper Ferry station. Heyward Shepherd, a free black baggage handler and substitute clerk for Baltimore & Ohio Railroad, was unaware that the Brown gang was in town and had taken control of the arsenal. Shepherd walked across a trestle looking for the night watchman, was confronted by two of Brown's armed men, turned and ran, and was shot in the back. Shockingly, the first casualty in John Brown's scheme was a freed black man. In the early morning hours, Brown and his followers took hostages, barricaded themselves in the brick building housing the munitions, became surrounded by local militia, and traded gunfire with militiamen and townspeople. Things were clearly not going as planned.

Sixty miles to the east, President Patrick Buchanan was made aware of the situation and by midday dispatched a company of US Marines commanded by Colonel Robert E. Lee and Lieutenant J.E.B Stuart to negotiate a peaceful resolution. Stuart, like Lee, would later become a renowned Confederate General. As for Brown, he was in no mood to surrender and managed to retreat with survivors and prisoners to a thick-walled fire engine house. After the local militias declined the honor of storming Brown's position, Lee sent in the marines. To avoid any casualties of hostages, not a single shot was fired. Instead, they attacked with a battering ram and bayonets. Thirty-six hours after it had started, and after the death of a dozen men, Brown was captured along with what was left of his raiders. Within a matter of weeks, at the Jefferson County Courthouse in Charles Town, Virginia, Brown was indicted, tried, and convicted of treason, murder, and fomenting insurrection. Brown, along with three others, was hanged in Virginia on December 2, 1859. It has been reported that an actor and the future assassin of Abraham Lincoln, John Wilkes Booth, was among the spectators who watched John Brown's execution.

Although Brown was gone, he would have appreciated the tactics used by the warring factions in West Virginia during the early days of the Civil War. Perfected in the early colonial days, especially on the frontier, guerrilla warfare was nothing new for many Americans. Union soldiers were often met with blocked roads, and lurking "bushwhackers" along the rear of their columns ready to take pot shots at anyone worn out or injured. These secessionist guerrillas, when captured, were often given short prison terms and then released only to engage in these same antics again and again, while others never made it out of prison. Some were discovered to have slipped and broken their necks, accidently been shot by the premature discharge of a weapon or found their way to the bottom of a river. Long before William Tecumseh Sherman set a path of terror through the south, Unionists in West Virginia had set forth a "hard war" policy including the torching of property. Such retributive justice did little to win the hearts and minds of citizens on either side, instead widening the banks of the river of division seen throughout the country during this time.

As for Robert E. Lee, he would find himself the commander of Confederate troops in the mountains of what would become West Virginia. On September 12, 1861, he planned and directed the Battle of Cheat Mountain, which ended in defeat in a drenching rain. Itching to make amends, he searched out a suitable spot to defend, hoping Union soldiers would attack and return the favor. As he waited and scouted, he noticed a major in the 3*rd* Virginia Infantry riding past him on a gray gelding with a black mane. Lee took a great fancy in the horse and for good reason. The springy four-year-old, owned by Captain Joseph Broun and raised near Blue Sulphur Springs, was a blue-ribbon winner in 1859 and 1860 at the Greenbrier County Fair. Although the federal troops withdrew from the area ending any hope for another battle, fate would bring Braun and Lee together again in the low country of South Carolina in February of 1862. Braun, who had named the horse Greenbrier, offered to give the horse to Lee as a gift to which Lee declined. However, when Braun offered to sell the horse for $25.00, Lee readily accepted. General Lee renamed his horse Traveller, and without doubt this horse from West Virginia had a front row seat to much of the Civil War.

Forming a state from an existing state would require constitutional contortions never truly anticipated by the framers. Some believed it could not be done, while others could not have possibly anticipated the monumental work required. If a new state could be formed from an existing state, which counties would be included, and what would be the name for the new state? These issues were put to a committee with fifty delegates in favor of an ordinance of dismemberment and twenty-eight opposed, and on October 24, 1861, a dismemberment referendum was put to popular vote and was approved overwhelmingly. Those in western Virginia would have a new state and it would be called Kanawha. Thereafter, on November 26, 1861, in the U.S. Customs House in Wheeling, West Virginia, a convention convened to write a state constitution. After fierce debate, an amendment to the draft constitution included dropping the name Kanawha and replacing it with West Virginia. The other issue to decide was the actual boundaries for West Virginia, with some advocating a "Large-State," while others advocated for a "Small-State." Although the "Small-State" concept initially had favor, the final boundary is closer to the "Large-State" vision. On December 13, 1861, forty-four counties in western Virginia would be included in the new state without conditions while Frederick, Jefferson, Berkeley, Morgan, Hampshire, Hardy and Pendleton to be adjoined if their residents ratified the state constitution. Of those counties, Jefferson,

Berkeley and Morgan had been added beyond the original boundary due to their strategic importance to the Baltimore and Ohio Railroad, and Frederick was included in attempt to protect Unionists living there and to better protect the Union from Confederate invasion. Frederick County would ultimately remain part of Virginia.

The next biggest debate surrounding the new state was the status of slavery. At this point in time, the federal government had taken no stance on the matter, and Abraham Lincoln had not uttered the Emancipation Proclamation. As such, the convention delegates did not know if the state should abolish slavery outright, allow for a gradual emancipation, or just let it continue since it was already not a thriving institution within the new state. In the end, they tried to thread the noxious needle of the time and decided on the prohibition of bringing any new slaves into the state for permanent residence. This all but assured that the U.S. Congress would be forced to decide the fate of slavery in West Virginia.

On the first Thursday of April 1862, 18,862 citizens voted in favor of statehood and the new constitution, while another 541 voted against it. The following month, in a special session, the general assembly of the Restored Government of Virginia passed an act allowing for the creation of West Virginia. On May 29, 1862, less than two weeks later, Senator Waitman Willey, acting as a representative of the Restored Government of Virginia, delivered the request to the U.S. Senate. Fellow Senator, John Carlisle, who had been instrumental in the anti-secessionist movement in western Virginia, fortunately sat on the Committee on Territories and would ultimately draft the statehood bill.

Carlisle's bill set forth the emancipation of children born to slave mothers born after July 4, 1863; the inclusion of fifteen Shenandoah Valley counties in the proposed state; and the election of delegates from all the counties of West Virginia to a constitutional convention. However, the bill was met with stiff resistance when Massachusetts senator, Charles Sumner, balked at admittance unless the new state abolished all slavery as a condition. Senator Willey responded by writing an amendment to the bill that allowed for gradual emancipation, so long as, the delegates to the constitutional convention approve it, along with a majority of the state's voters. Carlisle, on the other hand, maintained that the new state should be admitted without additional conditions. The Statehood Bill with the Willey Amendment passed twenty-three to seventeen. Interestingly, Senator Carlisle did not vote for the bill he had almost singlehandedly drafted, having been thoroughly soured by the demands of the Republicans. Carlisle, sounding much like a new-found confederate, argued that statehood should not be left entirely to the demands of congress especially when it was nothing more than power politics. In any event, on December 10, 1862, the House of Representatives passed the bill along with the amendment and delivered it to President Lincoln five days later.

When the statehood bill arrived on Lincoln's desk, the one-time lawyer, gazed upon it with both curiosity and excitement. Although the 16th President welcomed the idea of a new Union state, he also wondered if carving out a new state from an existing state was constitutional. Furthermore, was the bill sitting on his desk properly before him or had Congress missed some required constitutional step. He asked his cabinet for their opinions, and, not surprisingly, got mixed answers. There was no agreement on either of his questions. In the end, Lincoln signed the bill on December 31, 1862, stating, "It is said that the admission of West Virginia, is secession, and it is tolerated only because it is our secession. Well, if we call it by that name, there is still difference enough between secession against the constitution and secession for the constitution. I believe the admission of West Virginia into the Union is expedient." Clearly the President remained skeptical about the process, but tough times demanded immediate action. Some legal scholars and other constitutional lawyers remain unconvinced to this day. What is undisputed, is that on February 17, 1863, the West Virginia Constitutional Convention voted to adopt the Willey Amendment, and the new constitution was then sent to the citizens for their ultimate approval. Nearly 7,700 Union soldiers voted for their new state, which was ratified by a landslide 28,321 to 522. On April 20, 1863, President Lincoln proclaimed that all the conditions for statehood had been met.

On June 20, 1863, West Virginia became the 35*th* state, becoming the only state created by the Civil War. The new state's constitution freed all slaves born after July 4, 1863, and all others on their twenty-fifth birthday. A year and a half later, in February 1865, the West Virginia legislature finally abolished slavery for all time truly making all mountaineers free.

CHAPTER 7

A Painted Bunting

The campsite at Horse Shoe Run, near the border of West Virginia and Maryland, also proved ideal for Burroughs and Ford as the two managed to spot a painted bunting, a bird rarely seen north of the Potomac. Known by its French name, nonpareil, meaning "without equal," the songbird is vividly colored in hues of blue, red, yellow, and green. Most of the campers might have been considered "birdwatchers," an ambiguous term used for those that enjoy seeing birds in nature, but Ford and Burroughs were accomplished "birders," a term used to describe persons who seriously pursue "birding," a hobby in which individuals' study, list, and otherwise follow bird life. Although detail may vary, birders typically record nest locations, nest types, bird diets, foraging techniques, egg types, breeding habits, and, of course, descriptions and locations of the birds themselves.

The two friends also engaged in "twitching," which is a British term used to describe the pursuit of previously located rare birds. Bird watching as a popular pastime developed almost entirely in the 20*th* century, made possible by the development of optical aids, particularly binoculars, and primarily started in Great Britain, spreading later to the Netherlands, Denmark, Ireland, Finland, Sweden, and the United States. Birders, like many homeowners, set up feeding stations to attract birds, but they might also join local bird watching societies, and maintain a life list of all the species of birds eyed during their lifetime.

Birding also involves a significant auditory component, as many bird species are more easily detected and identified by ear rather than by eye, and it can probably be said that almost every person has at one point, or another tried to whistle like a bird. Henry Ford showed a profound, if not, sometimes unusual, fondness for the auditory life of birds, so much so that he was known to let out bird calls in public, among friends, and to his wife Clara to announce he had returned home to their residence at Fair Lane. Like many hobbies birding can turn competitive, and, in fact, competitions can include teams or individuals that have 24 hours to identify as many species as possible, called a "Big Day," or over the course of a year, called a "Big Year." The latter was made into a movie in 2011 starring Steve Martin, Jack Black and Owen Wilson, that followed these three birders as they crisscrossed the globe trying to spy as many birds as possible in 365 days.

In retrospect, it may very well have been a love of birds and the gift of an automobile that ultimately brought these famous campers together. When Henry Ford rolled out his Model T in 1908, it was appreciated by most, but not John Burroughs. The nature writer denounced it with outright hostility describing it as a "demon on wheels" that would "seek out even the most secluded nook or corner of forest and befoul it with noise and smoke." Burroughs had also made it clear that he was no fan of industry, the noise of factories and railways, and the corrupting power of money which he believed created vulgar people to despoil the lovely countryside.

As an avid birder, Ford was a big fan of John Burroughs, and, in fact, had been given a complete set of his writings as a gift from his wife Clara. The blistering review hurt Ford especially since he believed his affordable family vehicle would create greater access to America's great outdoors. He adamantly believed Burroughs had let his emotions get the better of him which had sent him down the wrong path. As such, Ford penned a letter to Burroughs explaining that the car was not a way to destroy nature, but to enjoy it. He also sent the disgruntled writer a brand-new model T. Even though the nature writer managed to accidently drive that same automobile through the side of a barn, the peace offering worked as Burroughs was persuaded by Ford's vision. Ford later wrote that with a car the whole countryside outside was made open, and that John Burroughs made nearly all his bird hunting expeditions behind a steering wheel. The two would go on exchange letters, ultimately meet, and form a strong friendship. Ford would also introduce his nature-writing friend to two other titans of American industry: inventor, Thomas Edison and tire manufacturer, Harvey Firestone.

Burroughs quickly learned that Henry Ford was devoted to birds, buying land and creating bird sanctuaries, almost from the first day he began to make money. At one point, Mr. and Mrs. Ford had five hundred bird houses on their farm lovingly referred to as bird hotels. One of them, the Hotel Pontchartrain, a martin house, had seventy-six apartments. Ford did not confine himself to local birds either. In *My Life and Work*, Ford mentions, "About ten years ago we imported a great number of birds from abroad: yellow-hammers, chaffinches, green finches, red pales, bull finches, jays, linnets, larks, some five hundred of them. They stayed around for a while, but where they are now, I do not know. I shall not import any more. Birds are entitled to live where they want to live." During winters food was hung on trees from wire baskets and a big basin for water was kept from freezing by an electric heater, while in the summers the birds feasted on cherries from trees and strawberries in the beds. Henry was most proud when he wrote that John Burroughs said he believed Ford had more bird callers than anywhere else in the northern states, and that one day, when he was staying at Ford's place, he had come across a bird that he had never seen before.

In 1909 a bill was brought before Congress for the protection pf migrating birds, in the form of creating sanctuaries, and was known as the Weekes-McClean Bird Bill. However, by 1911, the bill was in danger of dying a natural death as the bill's sponsors could not drum up enough support. When Burroughs drew Ford's attention to the plight of the Weekes-McClean Bird Bill, the automobile manufacturer swung into action by getting all six thousand car dealers in his network to lobby congress on behalf of the birds. The bill was ultimately passed in 1913, near the time that John Burroughs personally guided Henry Ford through Concord, Massachusetts with stops at two of the author's favorite spots: the home of Ralph Waldo Emerson and Walden Pond made famous by Henry David Thoreau.

As dusk neared on the banks of Horse Shoe Run in West Virginia, dinner was prepared for the campers, but soon they were joined by a hoard of visitors including lumberjacks and mountaineers from nearby mines. The crowd, being large in number and rough in appearance, mixed with the famous campers, made for quite a spectacle. Some of the crew sensed potential trouble as the initial conversation was loud and unscripted. At one point, R.V. Kline, Ford's appointed chauffer, even managed to reveal his holstered Smith and Wesson to anyone who might have thought the party traveled unarmed. Ford, who was always inclined to seek peace, diffused any awkwardness between the parties by offering cigars and handshakes to all of those gathered. In no time the parties sat intermingled around the campfire like old friends talking shop and swapping stories. In fact, so friendly had things turned, that the campers, mainly Edison, were offered the opportunity to see a nearby logging engine. The lumbermen pointed out that the campsite was near a railroad used as a logging route that traversed the mountains for miles around and this interested Edison tremendously. By the end of the evening, promises were made to bring the engine down the next morning so that the great inventor could climb into the cab for a closer look. Still, some of the crew remained unconvinced and offered to remain up and to guard the camp throughout the night.

The following morning much of the crew remained unconvinced of the promises made the night before. In fact, a member of the trip, who had been assigned driving duties along with chronicling parts of the trip, later recalled that he had made a bet to himself that the wood cutters would not bring down the old locomotive and if ever seen again would most likely claim to not have had enough time to do so. But he lost the bet with himself and wryly commented that he slipped a five-dollar bill from his left pocket to the right as the next morning the entire lumber camp, including wives and children, escorted "the little old one-lung engine" down near their breakfast table.

The entire camping party thoroughly enjoyed playing in and around the engine with Edison at one point assuming the role of engineer much to the delight of a motion picture photographer who filmed the brief event. Another photograph shows Ford at the helm, while Firestone serves as fireman and Edison fearlessly rides the cowcatcher afront the steam engine. Many photographs were taken much to the delight of the families gathered, perhaps memorializing the fun and games enjoyed for generations to come. What had started out the night before as a tense initiation for all practical purposes ended in a gala the following day.

Taking to the highway again, the six motor vehicles ventured further south on their way to Elkins, West Virginia. There being no road signs, and with mountain turns often obstructing their views, the party often would get off route and several times after driving down a mountain road, they found it necessary to drive back up that same mountain road. In Parsons, West Virginia, gasoline and supplies were purchased, and many of the townspeople came to the neighborhood drugstore to shake hands with the visiting celebrities. Edison, as he often did, located sweets to soothe his constant craving and laid into a supply of milk chocolate. Ford offered advice to those with car trouble, and even helped fix a leaky water jacket on a small white truck.

At lunch that day, by the side of a spring, a twelve-year-old girl appeared on the road above with a pail of fruit for sale and was invited to sit down with the party. She made quite an impression as John Burroughs later recalled her "shining eyes" and remarked about her being a "very firm, level-headed little maiden." Burroughs, who had a soft spot for children and the world as they see it, also remembered another girl perhaps thirteen years old, who hitched a ride with the campers for a few miles on her way. He recalled her telling him that she had "been on a train five times, and once had been forty miles from her home." She told the author that her mother was dead and that her father lived in Pennsylvania. She was apparently living with her grandfather, and when asked how far it was to Elkins she said, "Ever and ever so many miles."

When reflecting on this trip, Burroughs described in detail the conspicuous roadside flowers for hundreds of miles, from Pennsylvania all the way to North Carolina including "Purple eupatorium or Joe Pye weed, and ironweed-tall, stately hardy flowers and very pleasing to look upon; the ironweed a vivid purple, the eupatorium a massive head of soft pinkish purple." However, it was the people that he remembered most, stating, "Birds and flowers and trees and springs and mills were something, but human flowers and rills of human life were better." The great writer also described his feelings about traveling to the South for a Northern man, by describing it as a plunge into the past. "As soon as you get into (the Virginias) there is a change. Things and people in the South are more local and provincial than in the North."

The roads, for the most part, were inconsistent with some roads being nicely paved in one county, while others remained rough and dirty in the next. In one place one would pay a toll at a rate of two cents a mile for their cars, and five cents a mile for their trucks. The caravan passed grist mills, busy at work, driven by an overshot wheel. Burroughs described seeing a man or a boy on horseback with a bag grain or meal behind him going to or returning from the mill as a frequent sight. His attention was also drawn to a woman on horseback on a side-saddle with a baby in her arms. Another "old-fashioned feature," much to be commended by the famous campers, was the larger families in the South. In a farmhouse near which they made one of their camps one night there were thirteen children, the eldest of whom was on the front lines in France. The senior Firestone further described the local schools as already in session in late August, with school rooms well filled with children.

By the time they reached Elkins, West Virginia, it seemed that almost everyone in town had learned about their trip as they were met by throngs of well-wishers. The spontaneous welcome included the mayor and prominent business owners, along with autograph seekers and anyone with a camera. Edison and Burroughs seemed more than happy to brave the crowds, pose for photographs, and to sign their name to whatever was stuck in front of them. Firestone and Professor DeLoach were told by some local businessmen that they should stop for the night at the Cheat Mountain Country Club as it was some twenty-five miles down the road, just beyond Beverly, West Virginia near Durbin. On the way out of town, another vehicle had some trouble described by Firestone as involving a "spring shackle bolt" that had been "sheared off." It looked like mechanical difficulties had struck again and the party feared the vehicle would be laid up along the road for at least another hour for a part to be located back in Elkins.

Edison, along with the other vehicles, moved ahead with instructions to find a suitable camping place for the night. Henry Ford took his self-assumed mechanical duties to study the situation for a few minutes. Looking for a certain size bolt, none could immediately be found anywhere in the car. Ford, then stood up and looked around as a distant hum came to the ear of those that had stayed behind with him. There, a quarter of a mile away, across the field, was a threshing machine. Taking Firestone with him across the field, Ford located a suitable bolt on the thrasher, and after some negotiations with several farmhands, a bolt was obtained and within minutes was "doing regular duty on the disabled touring car."

CHAPTER 8

"Knock-me-down-fever"

Just Southwest of Manhattan, Kansas at the confluence of the Smoky Hill and Republican Rivers, was a U.S. Army training camp established at the outbreak of World War I. Nearly 50,000 recruits would train at the camp, including the 89*th* Division, deployed to France in the Spring of 1918. Camp Funston, which was one of sixteen camps set up nationally, was located on the Fort Riley Military Institution on the Kansas River and resembled more of a city than training camp with stores, libraries, schools, and workshops. The camp even included a coffee roasting house. Social centers and theatres provided entertainment including an orchestra from St. Louis and the singing voice of Madam Schumann-Heinke. However, the Camp's main purpose was to train soldiers drafted in Midwestern states to fight overseas, and the recruits spent many more hours drilling with officers from France and Britain than they did enjoying the opera. Although nothing would compare to the actual horrors of war, for many it was their first introduction into a concept or fighting style that would become known as trench warfare.

Private Albert Gitchell, by all accounts was a cook and was about to be shipped out to join the fighting overseas. It had been an unusually cold winter in Kansas, and Gitchell, like many others, had struggled to stay warm in the overcrowded barracks and tents. Just before breakfast on the morning of March 11*th* he reported to the hospital at Fort Riley complaining of cold-like symptoms. He had a sore throat, a fever, and a headache. By noon, another one hundred or so of his fellow soldiers were reporting similar complaints and given the numbers and fever as a symptom, it was believed to fit grippe, or what was considered the old English name for flu, "knock-me-down-fever." For those unfortunates who have experienced the flu, it meant two or three days of pure misery followed by a rapid recovery and in the case of these young soldiers, back to duty, training, and being hurled into the misery that awaited overseas.

Across this long state and catacorner to Camp Funston, some fifty miles west of Dodge City and what was once upon a time the wild west, sits Haskell County, Kansas. Flat and mostly treeless, this sparsely populated corner of the state is home to spectacular prairie sunsets. In 1918 it was also home to Dr. Loring Miner. Miner, who was a graduate of Ohio University, had come to the region in 1885 along with farmers and ranchers hoping to claim land promised by the Homestead Act. The big burly man, with a handlebar mustache, had set up shop as a medical doctor, and when not treating patients, he attended to the drugstore and grocery that his family owned. Being in an isolated part of the state, Miner's practice extended over several hundred square miles, and as a classic country doctor, Loring Miner was known to travel many miles making house calls at all hours of the night. Although isolated, Miner took great pride in keeping up to date in the advances in his profession and even built a laboratory in his office. When not working he enjoyed reading the classics in Greek, especially while drinking a spirit or two. The good doctor also enjoyed watching thousands of migratory birds, including sandhill cranes, geese and ducks as they migrated north across the plains.

In early February Miner became concerned after several patients, one followed by another, experienced violent headaches, body aches, high fever and a nonproductive cough. Over the years, Dr. Miner had seen his share of influenza, but this seemed different, so he reached out to the U.S. Public Health service to report an "influenza of a severe type." Just when he seemed completely overwhelmed, the disease began to disappear. By then it was mid-March. Given the isolated part of the state, perhaps the virus might have died there. However, with a World War raging on across the Atlantic that would not be the case. To keep the fires of war burning, soldiers, much like kindling, had to be continually added to the embers. On February 21, 1918, in nearby Copeland the local Kansas paper had reported, "Most everybody...is having lagrippe or pneumonia." A week later the paper reported that John Bottom just left Copeland for Camp Funston, printing: "We predict John will make an ideal soldier."

Viruses are tricky, and potentially destructive, little things. They exist on the fringes of life as we understand it. Their origins remain a mystery, though one hypothesis asserts they may have predated primitive forms of life and may have played some role in the emergence of cellular life itself. Other virologists believe viruses began as more complex living cells and have literally devolved into more simple organisms. Regardless of where they come from, viruses have hitched a ride through millennia doing one, and only one, thing: replicating themselves. They do not do this alone, but by invading cells. John M. Barry, in *The Great Influenza*, gives an accurate, yet disturbing description of this process, writing: "It invades cells that have energy and then, like some alien puppet master, it subverts them, takes them over, forces them to make thousands, and in some cases hundreds of thousands, of new viruses." In other words, a virus literally invades a cell and inserts its own genes into the cell's genome essentially seizing control of the cell's own genes. The result is new viral particles burst through the cell's surface to invade other cells usually destroying the host cell in the process.

Influenza constitutes one of these creepy viruses. There are three types, including A, B and C, although the last of these rarely causes disease in humans. Type B does cause disease, but not epidemics (a national outbreak) or pandemics (a worldwide outbreak). In 1918, the world would feel firsthand the blistering assault of a type A influenza.

Historically the influenza virus did not originate in humans, but in wild aquatic birds. The Spanish flu may very well have found a home in one of the migratory birds that Dr. Loring Miner gazed upon in Haskell County, Kansas. Then again, perhaps not. Although there is strong evidence that Haskell represents the site of origin, no one will ever know for certain. What is known, is that a new variant of influenza virus adopted itself to humans and spread like wildfire across the globe.

In the spring of 1918, influenza was also being ominously trailed by pneumonia in many cases but was only given a modicum of attention. Today with our 24 hours news cycle this would most likely have caused "Breaking Reports" or "This Just In" but in 1918 there was no such access to the news and much of the country would have been considered "unconnected." Besides there were other attention grabbers in the first part of 1918, most notably the Great War. On April 21st, the world learned that Manfred von Richthofen had been shot down and that the 25-year-old German pilot had died. How could the flu compete with the death of the Red Baron?

Another reason the spring (and later the fall) wave of influenza went largely unnoticed is a bit more ominous, as it may very well have been by design. When the United States finally entered World War I in 1917, many Americans, including Henry Ford, were quite disheartened. Pacifists, together with isolationists, wanted the United States to remain neutral and were quite vocal in their dissent. Fearing anti-war speech might undermine the war effort, President Wilson pushed the Espionage Act through an all too willing Congress. The Act criminalized the publication or distribution of any "information" that could harm or hinder US armed forces as well as of "false reports or false statements" intended to promote America's enemies. This essentially enabled the Postmaster General the right to refuse to deliver any paper or periodical deemed unpatriotic or critical of the administration. In 1918, since almost all the news flowed from publications or word of mouth, President Wilson would now essentially control any narrative as to the health and well-being of America and her war efforts.

The Sedition Act, adopted on May 16, 1918, essentially extended the Espionage Act of 1917 and took a battle axe to an already bloodied First Amendment. This truly intolerable act made it punishable by twenty years in jail to "utter, print, write or publish any disloyal, profane, scurrilous, or abusive language about the government of the United States." Although intolerable, such action had been taken before. In 1798, after John Adams had faced criticism for an undeclared war with France, the first Sedition Act made it unlawful to "print, utter, or publish...any false, scandalous writing" concerning the government. When America is at war, or when issues of national security are at stake, Presidents Adams and Wilson cannot alone be singled out for such harsh and questionable actions as Abraham Lincoln suspended the writ of habeas corpus during the Civil War. As a result, hundreds of people were wrongly imprisoned.

On April 13, 1917, President Wilson had also unleashed a propaganda machine when he issued an Executive Order creating the Committee on Public Information or CPI. George Creel was put in charge of CPI and set out to galvanize every American behind the War by flooding the press with tens of thousands of press releases. Such articles, often completely unedited, found a welcome spot in most newspapers. As a result, patriotism swelled, and Americans rallied behind a single cause: to win the War at any cost. Bad news was forced aside to make room for stories of bravery, commitment and service. Nobody had time to be sick, let alone dwell upon it. Furthermore, editors dared not print anything they believed might hurt morale. News of an entire army base falling ill surely would be helpful information for an enemy. Wouldn't it? Who would want to risk going to jail for printing such a story anyway?

In the end, it was a perfect opportunity for a destructive little virus to fly below the radar. In an ironic twist, news of the virus did flow more freely in countries not involved in the War. One such country was Spain. Spain was neutral during the War, and unlike other European countries, Spanish papers did not shy away from stories of influenza or other stories that might hurt morale. Since Spanish newspapers regularly published accounts of the spread of the disease in the Spring of 1918, while other countries did not, the virus came to be called the "Spanish Flu." The truth might set you free, but forever link your name to a virus. So unnoticed was the Spring wave of influenza in the United States that it is not even mentioned in the index of the 1918 Volume of *The Journal of the Amercian Medical Association.* To further complicate things, influenza was not a reportable disease and most death certificates from the time listed the cause of death as pneumonia, a perfectly natural cause of death in the early 1900s.

Those involved in the planning of war, knew the greatest killer in war was not combat but disease. For instance, during the American Civil War two men died from disease for every soldier killed on the battlefield. If a soldier was well enough to fight, they might survive the battlefield only to succumb later to the wounds inflicted in combat. The Spanish-American War had even more appalling numbers, as approximately six soldiers died of typhoid for every combatant killed in battle or from their wounds. What they feared most was about to happen. Within several months the U.S. Army would balloon from tens of thousands of soldiers to several million. Tight quarters, together with many soldiers being from rural areas where immunities were far less acquired than those born and raised in urban centers, was a recipe for trouble. Whooping cough, chickenpox, and mumps were all potential dangers, as was a potential epidemic of measles. What nobody knew was that by late April the essential characteristics of a new strain of influenza virus had already been established, mutated, and continued into France where it most likely nuzzled up with exhausted soldiers stuck in crowded damp trenches near rotting corpses and scurrying rats.

Although no longer an active military base, Camp Devens still sits along the Nashua River about thirty-five miles Northwest of Boston and a little over 1,500 miles Northeast of Kansas. It rests upon 5,000

acres of rolling hills leased and later bought from the towns of Ayer, Harvard, Lancaster and Shirley, Massachusetts. Established in 1917, this base, much like Camp Funston, was built to be more like a city than a fort. By 1918 tens of thousands of soldiers had already trained at Devens, with many already in France. On August 20*th*, Major General Henry P. McCain, who was training the newly created Twelfth Infantry Division, made it clear that he wanted them in France within fourteen weeks which meant round the clock drilling. Camp Devens was built to encamp approximately 35,000 men, but as most Generals or war historians are quick to point out, war, or in this case war training, never goes as planned. By the Autumn of 1918, there were 45,000 men with 5,000 of them under canvas. Overcrowding coupled with sheer exhaustion made it a prime candidate for an epidemic.

On August 27, 1918, some 30 miles from Devens, two Navy Seamen, stationed on Commonwealth pier in Boston, entered a sickbay with flu like symptoms. The next day there were eight, the following day there were 58. The first Devens victim, a soldier of Company B, 42*nd* Infantry, went on sick call. However, it was believed he had meningitis as his symptoms seemed far too extreme to be influenza. Up to then the flu was that unfortunate family ritual, and although completely unpleasant, was not the kind of thing to strike terror. The following day additional soldiers from Company B reported similar symptoms and this began a pause in the meningitis diagnosis. By September 12*th* medical officers believed it was indeed influenza, and just four days later 36 members of Company B had been hospitalized. Even more alarming was it had spread to other companies and regiments and by September 18*th*, 1,176 men had been hospitalized at Camp Devens with a total of 6,674 cases of flu. Unlike the Spring outbreak that had started with Private Gitchell in Kansas, and which had largely gone unnoticed, this second wave of grippe was about to catch everyone's attention.

On September 23, 1918, William Henry Welch, one of the most distinguished early 20*th* century physicians in the United States, arrived at Camp Devens to assess the situation. As past president of the American

Medical Association, he was also a distinguished pathologist and scientist having also been president of the National Academy of Science. Dr. Welch, who had more recently done a stint at Johns Hopkins, had joined the Army and was given an assignment to assist the Army Surgeon General in inspecting the conditions at military camps across the country. If the United States was going to win the "war to end all wars," it needed a healthy fighting force. The Surgeon General's office had dispatched Colonel Welch to Devens to find out what exactly was going on and to otherwise verify distressing telegrams coming from the camp. By the time he and a team of other doctors arrived at Devens, what would become known as Spanish Flu was being reported by civilians as well all along the eastern coast. Influenza can spread exponentially but the 1918 flu had an ominous twist. This strain showed a great propensity for pneumonic complications and history had taught mankind that pneumonia is often lethal.

When Welch and his colleagues arrived on September 23rd in a cold and drizzling rain, there were at least 12,600 cases of Spanish flu with a rapid spread of pneumonia. Initially it was believed to have been 750 cases, but so overwhelmed was the hospital that it was determined a few days later that the number of those with pneumonia was just shy of 2,000. The scene was downright pathetic. Men stumbling, covered in blankets when available, often with a blue or purple coloring especially in the face. Nose bleeds, a common symptom with this wave of flu, just added to the horrific scene as bloody linens lay about everywhere. The Devens hospital had been built to accommodate roughly 3,000 patients, so now with nearly 8,000 patients, there was nowhere to put them. Empty barracks and nearby buildings were used as a waiting area for this overflow until a nurse or doctor could break away just long enough to check in. The medical staff was completely overwhelmed and since there is no cure for influenza or pneumonia, most care was directed towards comforting the soldiers with cooked meals, warm blankets, fresh air or just a hand to hold or an ear to listen. It was equally tough on the medical staff physically and soon nearly one-third of the nurses were ill as well.

William Henry Welch had enjoyed a completely different scene just the week before. Having finished his tour of southern army bases with his last stop at Camp Macon in Georgia, the doctor had taken in a few days of rest and relaxation at the Grove Park Inn in Asheville, North Carolina. Taking in a concert with several colleagues who would ultimately join him at Camp Devens, discussions turned to issues of pneumonia, immunity and, of course, the best cigars. They may very well have learned from staff that they had just missed Ford, Edison, Firestone and Burroughs who were there just several weeks before. Nobody had any idea what awaited them upon their return, nor the battle that would need to be waged in the months ahead.

By 1918, modern science had begun to finally coalesce with medicine. Physicians and scientists had already developed vaccines, antitoxins and procedures that are still in use today. Much was understood about genetics, blood circulation and bacteria. Much of the world enjoyed access to hospitals where surgeries might be performed with anesthesia. Physicians carried stethoscopes, took blood pressures and recommended medications to their patients for a variety of illness. Furthermore, the X-ray machine, a foundation for modern diagnostic testing, had been around for over twenty years. Medicine, which had remained largely unchanged since the time of Hippocrates, had lunged forward during the nineteenth century when a microscope equipped with achromatic lenses literally revealed another world which had remained largely unseen to physicians and scientists alike. Germ theory, which held that minute living organisms invaded the body and caused disease, had largely replaced competing theories of disease including miasma theory. This theory speculated disease came from some type of putrefaction in the atmosphere. After Louis Pasteur, a French chemist and microbiologist, seemingly proved germ theory, surgeons raced to institute antiseptic conditions in the operating room. By 1918, infections following surgery had been greatly reduced.

In 1882, Robert Koch, a German physician and microbiologist, discovered the tubercle bacillus as the cause of tuberculosis. This disease, often referred to as "consumption" as it literally consumed people, had been identified as the thief who stole life. By shining the spotlight on this killer, science had finally triumphed over disease. In 1880, Pasteur successfully inoculated chickens with the cholera bacteria creating another win. The smallpox vaccine developed nearly one hundred years before by a British doctor, Edward Jenner, would finally be joined by a plethora of new vaccines for typhoid, rabies and anthrax. Finally, over the Christmas Holiday in 1891, in Germany the first attempt to cure a person with diphtheria was made and succeeded. Science and medicine had not only learned to prevent infectious disease but now had notched a new type of victory by curing someone who was dying of a disease. By the outset of World War I, humanity had remedies for, vaccines against, or at least methods for limiting the spread of smallpox, typhoid, malaria, yellow fever, cholera and diphtheria. With those big boys covered, corona or influenza hardly seemed a threat.

On the eve of America's entry into World War I, she had at her disposal a new arsenal of healthcare research and treatment centers. Johns Hopkins, an American entrepreneur and philanthropist from Baltimore who died in 1873, had left behind a trust worth $3.5 million dollars to create a university and hospital. Three years later a research laboratory was established, followed by a medical hospital which opened in 1889 and a medical school in 1893. Johns Hopkins had set out to not only change education but to change the world of medicine. When William Henry Welch, known to later be called "Popsy" by younger scientists and students, had taken the helm of Hopkins he set out to do just that. By the turn of the century, he would become one of the most prominent faces of American medicine and Johns Hopkins would become synonymous with medicine itself.

In the early days of the 20*th* century another behemoth in medical and biological sciences was the Rockefeller Institute for Medical Research. On January 2, 1901, John Rockefeller's grandson, John Rockefeller McCormick died of scarlet fever. In 1903, the Institute opened its own laboratory followed by a hospital in 1910. The mission, which remains the same today, was to support intensive scientific research in medicine, especially infectious disease. When Welch joined the war effort, he essentially brought with him the Rockefeller Institute as it had become an auxiliary laboratory for the army during the war. The country also brought forth the beginnings of reformed medical education. Starting in 1901, Harvard joined Hopkins in requiring medical students to have a college degree, and in 1904 the American Medical Association formed a council to review medical schools—many of which were ultimately found wanting. However, the examination had been fruitful as many schools raised standards, updated curriculum, and instituted other reforms. Lastly, on the eve of war, America had seen the birth of public health as a scientific matter. The CDC (Centers for Disease Control and Prevention) would not be created until several decades later, along with the WHO (World Health Organization). In the meantime, Welch and others understood the importance of public health and in the fall of 1918 the Johns Hopkins School of Hygiene and Public Health was scheduled to open with Welch as the first dean.

Clearly the government was worried about Devens as included in the group who joined Welch was Colonel Victor C. Vaughan, another ex-president of the American Medical Association; Rufus Cole of the Rockefeller Institute; and Simeon Walbach of the Harvard Medical School. The Grove Park Inn must have seemed more like a distant dream than a recent trip. After observing the pitiful scene in the hospital, the esteemed group asked to be taken to the morgue. Answers, if any, might come from the autopsy room. Bodies the color of slate were "stacked like cordwood," while others remained lying about the morgue floor. Chaos reigned here as well, with the doctors having to navigate around and over bodies to get to the autopsy room. On the table was the corpse of a young man, who had been alive and relatively healthy just a few days before. When his body was moved in the slightest degree fluid poured out of his nostrils. Welch and company had seen their share of autopsies. They had also seen the damage caused to the lungs when a person has succumbed to pneumonia. However, they had never seen anything quite like this. The lungs of those who had died looked completely abnormal and contained an enormous quantity of thin, bloody fluid. Suddenly a sniff of fear filled the room. The other doctors naturally looked to Welch for reassurance, but found they gazed upon a man much like themselves. Several decades later, Doctor Cole remembered, "It was not surprising that the rest of us were disturbed, but it shocked me to find that the situation, momentarily at least was too much even for Dr. Welch."

When Welch finally spoke, he said, "this must be some new kind of infection or plague." Everyone within earshot surmised it must be pneumonic plague, or Black Death from medieval times. Perhaps the European cesspool of filth and death, with rotting corpses left to be eaten by rats, had spawned some new disease. Or perhaps the earth had become so saturated with mustard gas that it was causing irreversible damage to mankind's lungs. Would anyone ever really have a chance to breathe again? After his initial shock, Welch managed to make a series of phone calls to laboratories and hospitals. Any chance to find a treatment or cure would require methodical scientific research. Like Thomas Edison, he also knew such investigation takes time. Time perhaps they did not have. In the meantime, the assembled doctors recommended no more troops should be ordered to Devens or dispatched to other camps from Devens. They also recommended that, when practical, the camp should be reduced by 10,000 soldiers, quarters should be enlarged to allow more space for troops, and additional medical personnel and supplies should be obtained.

A few weeks later, on October 1*st*, the Johns Hopkins School of Hygiene and Public Health was officially christened. The ceremonies were not attended by the new dean. He had fallen ill.

II.

GENTLE STAR

CHAPTER 9

Watching Clouds

From a Treasury Window, one might be able to peer down an alleyway and catch the sight of a tall stovepipe top hat and a "best-natured looking man" with a "kindly, almost homely, face." However awkward he might be, one could not help but look at him. Abraham Lincoln, who was fond of taking shortcuts on foot down back streets and alleyways throughout the capital city, was occasionally spotted by a young John Burroughs as he worked at his desk at the Treasury building. It was an exciting, if not alarming, time to be working in Washington D.C. as the Civil War raged on. The population of Washington was only 60,000, and most streets were unpaved with dirt and mud everywhere. The Dome of the Capital was not yet completed, and skirmishes between the Union and Confederate sometimes came so close that residents could hear gunfire.

John Burroughs was twenty-seven years old when he went to find work in the capital city. Initially leaving his wife behind in New York to maintain their family home, the country born youngster made his first headquarters in the rubber store of Allen, Clapp & Co. Sleeping in the store on a camp cot, Burroughs would wash his clothes in a sink in the store, drying them at the stove. Years later, when he was an honored guest at the White House, the famous writer was driven along Pennsylvania Avenue with President Theodore Roosevelt on their way to Yellowstone Park and would find himself reminiscing about those days of poverty and early struggles finding it almost too incredible to believe. How he had changed. How the country had changed.

One night as he was sitting in the back part of Allen's Store, there had come in at the door a tall figure in grey, wearing a broad-brimmed felt hat. "There he is, there's Walt!" cried Allen. E.M. Allen was "Allen," and he had convinced Burroughs to come to Washington D.C. to look for work and in his correspondence had mentioned that he had seen Walt Whitman saunter into the store on occasion. Allen went forward to meet the famous poet, followed by his quiet companion, who, though outwardly calm, was in a state of seething emotion. "Walt, here is the young man from the country I told you about." Burroughs later said, "I shall never forget Walt's kindly glance, his big soft hands, and his friendly grasp when we first met." The young aspiring writer might have been a Lincoln man but was also a huge Whitman fan.

After weeks of searching, Burroughs secured work in the Quartermaster General's Department and his first job was to supervise the burial of African American soldiers. He later looked after supplies for the calvary. However, things were slow. He often found himself with a great deal of free time to wander about the city, walk to the Capital Building, and listen to Senators and Representatives. The fortunes of the Union seemed to be getting better, but the future of the young Burroughs was still in the balance. Becoming somewhat despondent with his lack of work, being away from his wife, and regretting his not enlisting when the war first started, Burroughs felt like he was at a crossroad in his life. He had missed being a soldier in the armies of the Union during the Civil War, later saying it was "the greatest miss of my life...." One day the young man walked over to a nearby battlefield to catch a firsthand look at the war. As he approached the frontline, shocked by the level of blood and carnage, bullets whistled by his head leaving him scared and shaken. Perhaps he was not made to be a soldier. Then again, who really is?

On January 4, 1864, John Burroughs was installed as a first-class clerk in the new Currency Bureau of the Treasury Department. His wife having finally joined him in Washington, the couple rented a brick house where the Senate Office Building sits today. Remarkably the house included an acre of land, and the young couple grew small crops, kept chickens, and tethered a milk cow that would often graze freely on Capitol Hill. Working at his desk at the Treasury Department, he penned essays for the *Atlantic Monthly* and now regularly discussed his ideas with his newest friend and hero, Walt Whitman. The famous poet, who was in his forties, began to have a positive influence on the younger writer encouraging him to write about the things Burroughs knew and loved best: country life and the outdoors.

After the chance meeting at Allen's store, the two had met again on a Sunday afternoon along a footpath under a patch of shaded trees. The elder poet, who carried an especially large sack, was on his way to visit an army hospital and asked "Jack" to come along with him. If the battlefield had frightened Burroughs, the crowded wards full of wounded soldiers left him completely numb. Whitman had come prepared. From his sack, the poet pulled out an assortment of goodies including tobacco, pipes, newspapers, magazines and foods. Whitman's empathy, moving from cot to cot with gifts and letters, expressing soft words of encouragement, clasping every hand, and even stopping to peel an orange for one young lad, left Burroughs inspired. From that point on, he was always eager to accompany his friend when the chance presented itself.

Some days they would take baskets of fruit, and Whitman was fond of taking flowers, including daisies, clovers and dandelions, to scatter on cots. They often were given notes for certain needs, would run errands for the boys, were asked to write and read letters, and were just there to talk about all aspects of life. Later, after Mrs. Burroughs had moved to Washington D.C. to join her husband, she would make pies, cookies, doughnuts, and the like for the two writers to distribute as they made their hospital rounds. Burroughs came to believe America owed Whitman a debt to his devotion to the boys of the North and South stating, "He helped them to bear their pain, braced them for their operations; and sat by the dying until the end. He was home, father, mother, sister, and sweetheart to those sick and homesick boys." America no doubt owes a debt to Mr. and Mrs. Burroughs for their actions as well.

Although John Burroughs was a great admirer of Abraham Lincoln, he was not among those gathered at the Capital when the President took his second oath of office on March 4, 1865. His journal reveals that he "went to the woods instead," but that Mrs. Burroughs went to see the President. It was a dark day in the city, but just as Lincoln was taking the oath of office, Mrs. Burroughs told her husband that "a burst of sunshine came out, illuminating his face and almost making a halo above his head." The nature writer went to see Spring inaugurated instead, describing the afternoon in the countryside as "deliciously clear and warm" though "the wind roared like a lion over the woods." A month later Richmond fell, followed shortly thereafter by Lee's surrender on April 9th at Appomattox bringing the collapse of the Confederacy. Washington was a wild scene, filled with celebration and relief. A spirit of reconciliation filled the streets.

The feelings of euphoria did not last long. On the morning of April 15*th*, Washington was blanketed in a fog of gloom. Shouting and singing was replaced with tears and whispers. President Lincoln, who had attended the theatre the night before, was shot and killed by John Wilkes Booth, an actor and leader of a band of fanatic plotters. What had originally been planned as a kidnapping of the President as an exchange for Confederate prisoners-of-war, was changed hours before into a plot to murder the President, Vice President, Secretary of State and General Grant. Mr. and Mrs. Burroughs had been waiting impatiently for a milk delivery for their breakfast, after which a frazzled elderly Irish woman arrived with the milk proclaiming "The President is shot! They do say he is dead!" She detailed the crowds of people she encountered often blocking her route thereby causing her delay. Although they initially thought she must be mad, the horrible news was confirmed after Mr. Burroughs rushed out for a morning paper. Breakfast went untouched. Soon much of the country was in a deep state of sorrow, with flags at half-mast and much of the land draped in black. Andrew Johnson took the oath of office of the Presidency while the tolling of bells could be heard throughout the landscape. Work was suspended that day for Burroughs and all other government workers. Finding himself with nothing to do he ventured out hoping to go beyond Fourteenth Street to a nurseryman in search of strawberry plants only to be held up by a sentry. No one could pass, martial law had been established, and every exit from the city was now guarded in hopes of apprehending any conspirators to the grizzly crimes.

When work resumed, Burroughs would tend to his garden every morning and then walk a mile or so to the Treasury where he would sit at a desk outside the door of a great iron vault. The young man's work was simple enough. Burroughs was fond of saying, "Uncle Sam was a very easy master (and) he paid us well and didn't insist on our working very hard." To help pass the time, Burroughs continued to write his essays and at four o'clock every afternoon he would begin his walk home. To be keeper of a vault where fifty or sixty million dollars in bank notes were stored was a big responsibility even if the young writer suggested otherwise. After Grant was elected President, he came into the Treasury Vault and was shown around by Mr. Burroughs who, though somewhat abashed at being in close quarters with the silent man, explained things as best he could. Burroughs described Grant as walking about the vault with hands behind him, asking a few questions but "saying little else."

Often accompanied by his Devonshire cow named Chloe, Burroughs would discuss life and literature on the Capital steps with Walt Whitman. By the time Burroughs had met Whitman, *Leaves of Grass* was already in its third edition with mixed reviews. Although Ralph Waldo Emerson had declared the work a masterpiece, most critics of the era felt otherwise. Burroughs agreed with Emerson, and along with Henry Thoreau's *Walden*, believed the work to be pure literary genius. The young writer never did meet Henry Thoreau, but in 1863 he had met Emerson, as the New England poet and philosopher had come to West Point to give a lecture during the June examinations of the cadets. Burroughs got the chance to walk and chat with Emerson, who he initially described as "a man in a silk hat with sharp-peering eyes," and even managed to carry his valise to a boat landing. The two would see each other several more times in the coming years. As for Whitman, he often took breakfasts on weekend mornings in the Burroughs household. He was very fond of the good coffee and pancakes that Mrs. Burroughs made. However, he was rarely on time, which was a sore trial to the most punctual of women.

Before John Burroughs ever came to Washington D.C. and mingled with famous writers and Presidents, he made his home a few hundred miles north of Manhattan in New York State's Catskill Mountains—his beloved Catskills. West of the Hudson River and south of the capital city, Albany, the Catskills got their name from Dutch settlers who named them "Kaatskills" for their populations of mountain lions and bobcats and maze of valleys and streams or "kills." In actuality, the Catskills are not technically mountains at all, nor were they when John Burroughs was born there on April 3, 1837, on a Catskill peak nicknamed "Old Clump" by local farmers. The Catskills do boast impressive peaks including Slide (4,204 ft.) and Hunter (4,040 ft.). This much is certain. However, it is not the size of the peaks, but how they were made that has scientists casting doubt on their mountain status. Mountains are typically made by force and lift when the earth's tectonic plates collide, or when the earth spits out its innards with volcanic activity. The Catskills were not made by such fireworks, but instead are the remnants of an ancient plateau formed millions of years before at the bottom of a prehistoric sea, sporting flat tops and regular contours resembling western mesas.

The descendants of John Burroughs, who came to America from the West Indies in 1690 and settled in Connecticut and Massachusetts, most likely had little concern for the Catskill's Mountain status. One such descendant was Ephraim Burroughs. Born in 1740, the great-grandfather of John, came to New York from Connecticut as a small boy just after the Revolutionary War. The Yankee farmer ultimately had a large family with six sons and several daughters. Having passed away in 1818, Ephraim is believed to be buried in a field somewhere between the New York villages of Hobart and Stamford. His son, Eden, born sometime around 1770, later married Rachael Avery and moved with his bride to the town of Roxbury sometime in 1795. Hauling what they owned on a sled by a yoke of oxen, the couple cut a road through the woods and constructed a rude shelter consisting of four poles driven into the ground and horizontal plates covered with elm bark. This same bark was also used for the floor. Here, atop this highly wooded summit in Delaware County, New York, the couple, along with the help of neighbors, later built a more permanent log house in a small clearing nearby.

In this humble log house, the father of John Burroughs was born. His name was Chauncey. He married Amy Kelly, son of Edmund Kelly, who had fought in the Revolutionary War and had endured the hardships at Valley Forge during the terrible winter in 1777-1778. Years later Kelly was fond of saying, "Zuckers! but it was monstrous cold." John Burroughs later told others that his grandfather had personally seen George Washington and the Marquis de Lafayette, and that on one occasion Washington had given the orders to the soldiers to dress-parade for inspection. Some had good clothes while others had scarcely any and no shoes. The General apparently made all the well-dressed men go and cut wood for the rest, while excusing those dressed in rags. Burroughs recalled his grandfather Kelly ("Granther") as being a small man with pronounced Irish features, usually wearing a military coat with brass buttons. He also described his grandfather as liking the life of a soldier far better than the humdrum of being a farmer. In fact, when the War of 1812 broke out, and one of John's uncles was drafted, he went in his stead. Brave as Granther was on a battlefield, he adamantly believed in spooks, witches and hobgoblins. When he told scary stories to the children, everyone, including his grandfather as storyteller, would shudder with "hair standing on end." His grandfather was also an expert trout fisherman, and Burroughs enjoyed rising early to steal along the streams with him. When it came to fish, that was one area for which Edmund Kelly could provide a bounty. Burroughs would later say that he believed he got his dreamy, lazy, shirking ways from Granther.

As for his maternal grandmother, Lavinia Minot, Burroughs described her as a big, practical woman, who did more to raise his mother's family than anyone. Lacking in education, she was a prolific housewife, who showed her displeasure of any war stories or other human hardships described at the dinner table. On more than one occasion, Burroughs was convinced Granny might pick up Granther and take him across her knee. Apparently, she made everyone toe the mark. In their last years, Burroughs recalled his grandparents living in a small house on the east end of the family farm. One morning, after having breakfast with his grandparents and a black man, who had stayed at the house overnight, Burroughs recalled the heart felt prayers offered to all who were present. It was only later in life that he realized he had dined and prayed with a fugitive slave.

His paternal grandfather, Eden Burroughs, was described by his grandson as a sparse man, serious-minded, and a hardworking farmer. Besides being an old school Baptist, who read his Bible daily, he was also described as being an exemplary man with a love for peace and solitude. Grandmother Burroughs (Rachael), who was of Celtic origin with red hair, a sandy complexion and a freckled face, was recalled by her grandson as being warm hearted and with a cheery disposition. Both Burroughs paternal grandparents died in their seventies, leaving just these small snapshot memories for the famous writer.

As for his father, Burroughs described Chauncey as a sturdy man, with red hair and a ruddy, freckled face. Easily moved to emotion, Burroughs recalled his father as being as transparent as a child. Not generally considered sophisticated, he had a harsh and strident voice. However, his bark was worse than his bite. Burroughs found his father to be tender-hearted, who although would initially establish strict rules, was often willing to go along with breaking them. His father refused to hunt, never picked up a fishing pole, and seldom read anything beyond his bible or the local newspaper. Like many others in the Burroughs clan, John's father was a farmer through and through. Born on December 20, 1803, his father had received a fair amount of schooling for the time. However, he was known as a saucy lad with a mean streak, who was fond of horse racing and playing cards. In early adulthood this all changed after he "experienced religion" and joined the Old-School Baptist Church. He stopped swearing, quit going to the track, and became an exemplary member of the community.

Chauncey met his wife in a schoolroom, while he was working as a schoolmaster, and she was his pupil. Later they courted, married, and moved to the nearby Burroughs homestead. Amy Kelly, John's mother, was described as a plain and unlettered woman. She was just seventeen when she married Chauncey, and although she would never read any of her son's books, she would treat the writer with marked tenderness. Looking for ways to grant her son's desires, she would often take John's side over his father, even if she did not fully understand him. With ten children, Amy Kelly probably exhibited more of the characteristics of her hardworking mother than the shirking ways of her father. However, the one area where she was like her father was her attraction to wild places. When not laboring on the farm, Amy enjoyed venturing the slopes of Old Clump to collect harvests of blueberries, huckleberries and chestnuts. She considered John, who was her seventh child, as her best berry picker and would often take him with her to roam over the hill meadows in search of berries and adventure. In time her love of venturing off the farm was shared by her son, who also said, "I owe to Mother my temperament, my love of nature, my brooding, introspective habit of mind—all those things which in a literary man give atmosphere to his work... My idealism, my romantic tendencies, are largely her gift."

When John was born in a house not far from where his father had been born, he entered the world with three brothers: Hiram, Wilson, and Curtis. His two sisters were Olly Ann and Jane. Another brother, Edmund, had died as an infant. Martin Van Buren was President of the United States, all twenty-six of them including Michigan which had been given statehood just a few months before. Six months later, another occurrence took place, far more important to him than Michigan's recent statehood and involving a person far more impactful to the newborn writer than the Democrat that occupied the White House. On October 22, 1837, a young Harvard man named Henry David Thoreau began keeping a journal. In time, these captured thoughts would become the flesh for a work called *Walden*. Three other siblings later joined John-Eden born in 1839; Abigail; and Eveline, who unfortunately passed away at the age of five. However, his oldest brother, Hiram, who was a beekeeper, would always hold the author's greatest affections.

The Burroughs farm was an expansive enterprise, sitting on some three hundred acres, with a herd of dairy cows and a smattering of sheep and hogs. Although field crops included hay, oats, buckwheat, potatoes and yellow corn, the sale of butter was the primary source of income. All in all, the family was well off for the time. Nonetheless, farm life was not always easy. The wooden house, being uninsulated, was usually cold and drafty in the winter, making the sleeping arrangements of two to three children per bed a little more agreeable. The kitchen's open fireplace not only created additional warmth during the cold New York winter, but also served as a gathering spot for the family. By all accounts, the farm was self-sustaining with cattle providing beef, butter and milk, and the family sheep providing wool for clothes and other household items. Every crop and farm animal served a purpose. Farm life began early in the morning, usually before the sun had risen. When he was old enough, John, along with his siblings, would begin the day with a trip to the barn to turn the cows out to pasture, before returning to the house for breakfast by candlelight. After breakfast, the Burroughs brood walked down the road, up a hill, down a smooth rolling meadow, and across a creek in the valley, about a mile and half in total, to a one-room schoolhouse nicknamed the "Old Stone Jug." The walk was manageable, if not whimsical, in the Spring and Summer, but trudging through the snow and wind in Winter could be downright miserable.

When Spring came to New York, and the last of the snow had melted, Chauncey and the boys would drive sheep into nearby streams and wash them. On a spinning wheel, John's mother would then twirl the wool into yarn that was then woven into cloth to make carpets, socks and mittens. During the Summer months household chores were plentiful, including work in the fields and the time intensive task of butter making. Life on a farm meant the family made their own soap, sugar, cheese, candles, dried apples, pumpkins, berries, preserves and pickles. In the fall, John and his brothers were given the not so pleasant assignment of walking through the fields with long sticks to knock apart and scatter cow droppings. The Burroughs boys made this task into sport finding ways to launch the excrement much like a golfer might swing at a golf ball. It is not clear how, or if, they kept score.

From an early age, the young lad took an interest in nature and those creatures around him. One Sunday in May, when John was seven years old, he and his brothers were in the woods and as he lay on the ground idly gazing into the branches above him, he spied a small bluish bird with a white spot on each wing, flitting amid the branches. When he asked his brothers as to what type of bird it was, they had no idea and hardly seemed to care. As for Burroughs, it fired his imagination. He was quite excited about his discovery, viewing it as a great event. The little boy wondered whether he would see this bird again and where could he learn what they were?

Twenty years later, Burroughs learned that what he had seen was a black-throated warbler. The next year, when he was eight years old, John grew very curious as to what was making a shrill cheery sound in a nearby swamp area. One evening, while it was still light, he settled at the water's edge in the brush, scrooched down along the ground, and stayed there as still as a mouse. The lad was rewarded for his patience when a tiny, yellowish brown, mottled frog, less than an inch long, climbed a nearby bulrush. As the little boy held his breath, hoping his pounding heart would not be heard by the tiny frog, scaring it and causing it to jump away, the creature burst forth with his nightly song: *Phee, phee!* Cautiously he stretched forth his hand and grasped the little piper, and after a few moments, sensing no danger from the pure heart that provided his perch, the frog continued to pipe from the boy's hand.

The young boy would also come to find refuge near a big rock in a hillside pasture over the east end of the Burroughs farm, in an area called "the Rundle place." Later the area would become his home and would be named Woodchuck Lodge. Here John would climb atop the huge drift boulder of red sandstone dropped by a glacier, tens of thousands of years before, to gaze upon a great panorama of valley and mountains. It was here that the lad would go to sit and dream. Perched upon "(his) boyhood rock," he would often spend the afternoons watching the shadow of Old Clump as it was slowly thrown on the broad mountain slope across the valley. In the spring he would go there to listen to the call of the highhole or flicker, and in the summer to hear the bobolinks as they soared and sang above the meadows. Early mornings, sitting upon his rocky throne, Burroughs could look out over a great lake of fog that had settled in the valley. Sometimes he would spend hours, loafing on the rock, watching the clouds drifting across the New York sky. As an adult, Burroughs often returned to this spot to ponder, write and reminisce. This everlasting rock, near a perennial spring, just a few yards away and along a wooded hill with its sheltering ironwood trees still provides a quiet spot for those who wander the nearby hillside. It also keeps guard over the final resting spot of John Burroughs, who is buried among the grass, stone and wildflowers just below.

The young John Burroughs not only found himself with a burning desire to learn more about nature, but also to learn about almost anything. Since there were perhaps only a few dozen books in the school library, John would take them out regularly, reading them over and over. The printed word, moved him differently than his friends or siblings, causing him to carry a book in his hand, stopping to read aloud a certain passage which caught his fancy. Soon literature created an exalted emotional state, and the young man was known to tramp about the woods, often drunk with a wild joy of living, shouting his favorite passages to any critter within earshot.

When in school, Burroughs sat in front of several students, including Jay Gould. Gould, who later became an American Railroad magnate and financial speculator, would amass a fortune throughout his life. As youngsters, the two played, wrestled, traded knives and marbles, and helped each other in a scrape. Once in class, before John had taken the literary plunge, he had copied a required composition straight out of an almanac, passing it off as an original. The teacher, not too pleased by this blatant theft, had told him that he would be required to stay after class to write a new composition. Apparently, Gould slipped him another composition under the desk, saving his friend from missing out on the after-school activities with friends. Interestingly, Burroughs still had no shame as he passed it off as his own. Several years later, after Gould had left the school and was living over his father's store and tinshop, Burroughs bought two books from him for eighty cents. Gould was in a tight spot, and Burroughs bought the books as a good faith gesture. Whether the eighty cents came to be included in the eighty million dollars, left by Gould when he passed away, is not known. It is also unknown if the financier's pen played a role in the writer wanting to produce his own, original works. What is known is that John Burroughs apparently never saw Jay Gould again after those early years as schoolboys in the Catskills of New York. However, the nature writer, throughout his life, would have no problem attracting other tycoons into his inner circle.

During the summer of his fifteenth birthday, Burroughs took an interest in broadening his education while following the progress of a close by village Academy as it neared completion. The young man had no trouble envisioning himself entering the walls of the new establishment as one of the first pupils, and after some initial discussions with his parents, things looked bright. His father promised that if John stayed and worked on the farm through the fall, that he might go to the Academy for the winter term. Although the young man kept his end of the bargain, his father did not. John was crushed. The following summer he took up the notion that he should go away to school, and that the school should be even further away at a school called Harpersfield. Again, he pleaded, this time along with his mother, and again his father promised a winter term if he would work through the fall. But, alas, it was never meant to be as the winter came and went leaving the young dreamer mired in farm chores and a sizable level of discontent.

Recalling this disappointment many years later, an elder Burroughs seems to have forgiven his father, stating, "he didn't mean to break his word, but there was very little money." In fact, John Burroughs further reflected that although it was a bitter disappointment at the time, he was made better by the experience. He also readily acknowledged that none of his siblings, although noticeably less interested in going away to school, were given such an opportunity either. Although he may have sulked in silence, the young man continued his required chores on the farm, all while keeping an eye on future opportunities to learn more about the world. Every March, he would help his father and brothers tap 250 or so big maple trees. To earn extra money, Burroughs would tap four or five smaller trees, and would then carry the sap to the kitchen where it was boiled on a cookstove over a wood fire and the resulting sugar was then poured into cake molds. The maple sugar cakes were sold in the nearby villages for two cents apiece, and these profits were immediately applied to the purchase of any book the entrepreneur could get his hands on.

Late in March of 1854, near the end of another sugar season, John Burroughs set out for Olive in Ulster County in search of work as a schoolteacher. It was just a few days before his seventeenth birthday. Walking many miles through a heavy snow squall, with his black oilcloth satchel in hand, and a few dollars in his pocket, he crossed Batavia Mountain into Red Kill and right into manhood. Just a few weeks later Burroughs found work in nearby Tongore, an obscure hamlet, at the foot of Olive Mountain. Here in a little red one-room schoolhouse, John began his career as a teacher. His wages, being quite meagre, were supplemented by invitations to eat and sleep in the houses of students and their families. The students, twenty or thirty in total and ranging from six to thirteen in age, left quite an impression on him as throughout his life he could recall their names and faces, including a chubby freckle-faced girl and a thin talkative girl with a bulging forehead. Three of his boys became soldiers and fell in the battle of Gettysburg.

Burroughs furthered his education by enrolling in a three-month course of study at the Hedding Literary Institute, a small private school in the Catskill village of Ashland. Here he learned algebra, geometry, chemistry, logic and French. John was also required to write compositions, which usually received favorable comment. One outdoor essay, read in part, "The last sun of 1854 was gilding the tops of the western hills." Around this same time, Burroughs began to keep a writing journal of sorts in a pocket-sized writing tablet, jotting down thoughts, expenses and often misspelled prose. By his own admission, spelling would never be his strong suit. As a young single man, Burroughs strived to keep his expenses low, spending his earnings on Saint Pierre's *Studies of Nature,* Locke's *Essay on the Human Understanding,* Spurzheim's *Phrenology*, and the works of Thomas Dick, a Scottish philosopher. John later recalled spending most of his time then with an empty pocket and an empty stomach, but with a bagful of books.

A few years later, during a second stint of teaching, an attractive dark-eyed niece of one of the trustees, caught the young man's eye. Ursula North was not only intelligent and high-spirited, but she was also available. In his trusty notebook he practiced writing her name, paying close attention to the letter "U" writing it out again and again. This, of course, he kept to himself. As for formal writing, the first appearance of John Burroughs in print was in May of 1856, in a small rural newspaper called the Bloomville Mirror. Adopting the pen name, Philomath, or lover of learning, the article about spiritualism was primarily a reply to a credulous writer in a previous issue. A month before this first published writing, Burroughs had resumed his formal education by enrolling in Cooperstown Seminary, a small private school in a neighboring county. Here he continued his studies in math and French, while taking up Latin and English literature. The young man, who although remained clean-shaven, let his hair grow long, joined the Websterian Society, often debated in a grove along the shore of the nearby lake, and dabbled in the homegrown sport of baseball. It was during this time, that the young man got his first dose of Emerson, and to Burroughs it was like tasting a green apple. The writer later recalled not initially being ready for Emerson, but a year later he found his understanding had ripened and Emerson had proven an acquired taste. Soon he devoured all that he could find.

In September of 1857, after being given an ultimatum from his future bride to cut his hair, John Burroughs convinced Ursula North to marry him. He also took a teaching job at High Falls. The newlyweds, being strapped for cash, lived apart with John living at High Falls while Ursula remained with her family. Every Friday, after dismissing his students early, Burroughs would set out on the sixteen mile walk to visit his wife. After spending the weekend with Ursula, he would make the journey back to High Falls, often leaving in the early morning hours on Monday, and on more than once occasion, he made it just in time for the start of school.

During these walks, nature and literature continued to slowly shape his life. In February of 1859, after John took a new teaching job in East Orange, the two settled in a little three-room apartment in the suburbs of Newark. The walk was only a few miles and did not require any late-night departures. However, Burroughs also began to realize that work as a teacher, although it paid the bills, carried many of the same pitfalls as work as a farmer. It was hard work, paid little, and was nearly as monotonous as work on the farm. At night and on the weekends, he turned his attention to his notebook and began to write in earnest. Soon his works, published under the pseudonym "All Souls" appeared in *The Saturday Press*, a literary periodical.

While living in East Orange, Burroughs also developed an important friendship that would ultimately lead him to the nation's capital. E.M. Allen was a member of a Newark debating club, while the slightly younger Burroughs was a member of the East Orange debate club. When the Newark team challenged the boys from East Orange, Burroughs was one of the speakers that night and spoke with such force and eloquence, that all the glory belonged to East Orange. Even though the Newark team was soundly beaten, John had won the admiration of a magnanimous Allen. The fellow debater was later described by Burroughs as being of a winsome nature, cheery, witty versatile and companionable. He also wrote poetry and stories, made clever caricatures, was a born mimic, and was at home on the lecture platform. In short, he was the first real comrade in the life of John Burroughs. This dear friend to Burroughs not only introduced the young writer to the works of Walt Whitman, but also to the man himself. He also encouraged John Burroughs to continue writing.

"A Thought on Culture" was the first published work to bear the signature of J. Burroughs. While John Burroughs might have a writer's heart, his wife remained unconvinced that teaching offered any real future for him or his family. She believed he should try his hand in business. Answering advertisements, Burroughs found work as a draughtsman in a carriage factory, but soon discovered he did not know what he was doing. Feeling discouraged, John Burroughs returned to work on the family farm.

In November 1860, the *Atlantic Monthly* published an essay by John Burroughs entitled "Expression." James Russell Lowell, the editor of the *Atlantic*, read the essay submitted and at first thought it might be some pilfering of an Emerson work, but having found no such title, realized he might well have discovered a new and powerful writer. Its prose, both strong and polished, was coupled with the wisdom found in more established writers. In part, Burroughs wrote, "As men grow earnest and impassioned... and speak from their inmost heart, and without any secondary ends, their language rises to the dignity of poetry."

Publication in this journal may very well have given John Burroughs a sense of accomplishment, but it did not pay the bills and he began to feel that his writing was looked upon by those around him as a kind of "lazy self-indulgence." As for his initial writings, although he received favorable reviews, Burroughs correctly surmised that he must not copy Emerson and his philosophical themes. Rather, he would be better served writing about country themes for which he was more familiar. Here he could "bury his literary garments in the earth and let it extract the Emersonian musk."

Still not quite finding his footing in business, John Burroughs returned to teaching and for the next few years alternated such posts with stints on the family farm. Starting in 1861 he also began a series of newspaper columns for the *New York Leader,* titled "From the Back Country," which explored the many facets of farm life. Although he received no money for these essays, Burroughs was sent by the editors a three-year pass on the Ulster and Delaware Railway and received his first fan mail from a fellow farmer and poet, Myron B. Benton. Benton, who praised the country sketches for their charm and fidelity, in time would become a dear friend.

In the spring of 1862, Burroughs received word from his neighbor, who having jumped his horse over several fences in the remaining April snow of New York, that General Grant had inflicted great losses to the Confederates and their cause at the Battle of Shiloh. The neighbor further relayed the news that the gallant Confederate General Albert Sydney Johnston had been killed, perhaps setting the war on a more favorable path for the Union. These bits of news from the war, together with letters from his pen pal, E.M. Allen, made it harder and harder for Burroughs to remain working in New York. Allen regularly urged Burroughs to come to Washington to make his mark or, at least, his fortune. He also tried to lure his friend with reports of Walt Whitman sightings.

In 1863 John Burroughs began teaching at a school at Buttermilk Falls, near West Point. He also began reading anatomy in the office of an old friend, Dr. Hull, and although he remained interested in writing, medicine had also caught his attention. The twenty-six-year-old also had taken up the study of plants, and after discovering a copy of one of John James Audubon's books with its spirited coloured illustrations, at the library at the U.S. Military Academy, he rediscovered his interest in birds. With an inflamed enthusiasm, Burroughs quickly discovered that a walk in the woods, while carrying an arsenal of knowledge, was only made more delightful as a storehouse of possible treasures. It also helped that he regularly invited Professor Eddy, a local scholar and botanist, to join him for these meanders. One gloomy November night, while sitting in a dingy little office with a copy of *Gray's Anatomy*, John Burroughs pushed aside the book and scribbled in his notebook, "...What matter if I stand Alone? I wait with joy the coming years; My heart shall reap where it hath sown, and garner up its fruit of tears...." The poem, "Waiting," which would be published two years later in *Knickerbocker's Magazine*, struck a chord with many readers and probably brought the writer more friends than anything else that ever came from his pen.

Sometime in June of 1863, when John was walking around West Point, he spotted a tall striking looking person with a "much too large silk hat pushed back on his head, and an air of eager curiosity." Pondering it further as he continued his sauntering, he wondered who this alert and eager countryman might be? Later that evening, John's pal Myron Benton, the fellow farmer and poet, who had come to town unannounced, raced into the Burroughs home and in a scattered and excited demeanor, announced that Ralph Waldo Emerson was over at West Point. Burroughs had his countryman, and meeting this hero the next day, was like water to a thirsty heart. Early in August of that same year, shortly after the country had endured the significant war battles at Vicksburg and Gettysburg, Burroughs sojourned in the Adirondack wilds with his two good friends Benton and Allen, along with another fellow named Jasper from New Jersey. Allen, who had traveled from Washington, managed to miss his stage at Poughkeepsie, and had to walk twenty-eight miles to Benton's home in Leedsville.

Despite the unending chatter about the war, whether it was too late to join the ranks as soldiers, and what might come next for the Union and the Confederacy, the trip was a welcome break for all. However, it also proved to a breaking point for John Burroughs. After returning to his classroom, Burroughs contemplated joining the army, and tried to convince his "buddy" Benton to join him. Benton, whose two younger brothers had already gone to the war, declined as he was the only remaining sibling left to manage the family farm, and in the end, Burroughs could not seem to muster the courage to enlist by himself. Later, when the draft came to his village, John's wife had taken ill making it impossible for the young man to leave her unattended as he had no housemaid in his vicinity. Although his wife would soon make a full recovery, John Burroughs realized something had to change for his wellbeing.

One evening in late October, after giving his students their lessons for the next day, John Burroughs locked the schoolroom door, put the key in his pocket, and walked away. He never went back. His complete unrest, in farming and teaching, and his confusion and hesitation as to how to assist the Union cause, culminated with his abandonment of the school. No doubt this snap decision would end his career as a teacher, but as he walked away from the schoolhouse, he rationalized his decision. If he was so unhappy, with his heart so conflicted, what kind of teacher was he to his students anyway? They deserved better. As did their parents. With the schoolhouse slowly disappearing behind him into the night, he also pondered his many failed business ventures and his brief and unfinished study of medicine. He told himself, "John Burroughs is not a businessman and never will be." Furthermore, it was unrealistic to believe he would ever find himself becoming a doctor. His heart was in the woods and meadows, with the birds and plants. It was then, on a crisp Fall night in late October as he walked alone, that John Burroughs decided he would become a full-time writer. However, before he could begin his new career, he realized that he would need to turn his back on the Highlands of the Hudson and migrate South to Washington D.C. to lend a hand in ending the war.

CHAPTER 10

Founding Campers

Ford and Harvey senior hurriedly drove over and around the mountains looking for their fellow campers. Dusk was setting in, and they did not want to lose them to the dark West Virginia night. The potential of a heavy rain only made the prospect of searching unknown roads more ominous. Coming to a bridge, they spotted the younger Firestone waiting nearby the Packard to guide them about a mile down the road to the campsite and on to the Cheat Mountain Country Club. It was just before 9 PM, August 21st1918. The Cheat River in West Virginia, was, and still is, a large, clear mountain trout brook. Crossed multiple times by our travelers and flowing in a devious course Northwest toward the Ohio, the river made for another ideal camping site. The Cheat Mountain Club being next door, made it all the better. The site came as a bit of a surprise to Ford and Firestone, as Edison usually refused to go to any club. Perhaps an even bigger surprise to the stragglers, was the announcement that dinner at the club would be served within the hour at 9:30 PM.

In 1918, the walls in the main room of the clubhouse were adorned with paper outlines of big brook trout and told the story of the rare spot the club members enjoyed. The Club was built in 1887 by the Cheat Mountain Sportsman's Association as a private hunting and fishing preserve. Just prior to the association's 50-year lease running out, the lodge was purchased by the Western Maryland Railroad. In the mid-1960s it was purchased by Mower Lumber Company to be used again as a hunting lodge and private executive retreat, and in 1987 the Club was purchased by a group of families and was at last opened to the public. Today the Great Room, with its large stone fireplace, provides a rustic, restful atmosphere. The lodge, which sleeps twenty-three people, is available for rent and guests are served three meals daily. Specialties include homemade breads and cookies, along with hearty soups and dinners from the grill. Outdoor recreational opportunities include fly fishing on the Shaver Fork, mountain biking, cross country skiing, snowshoeing, hiking, horseback riding, skeet shooting, and yard games including horseshoes and badminton. There are also miles of trails on the property and in nearby national parks.

Our travelers, feeling welcomed and warmed by the big open fireplace, also made note of the hospitable welcome from the staff. By all accounts it was a splendid dinner and Edison was heartily praised by all for his acquiescing, and even suggesting, a little indoor eating. Following dinner, a peek into the cozy, inviting rooms proved too much for "the tenderfoots" of the party and many of the crew, along with Harvey, Jr., chose a hot bath and a warm dry bed over the cold drizzly tents pitched aside the trout brook. While the senior Firestone snuck in a hot bath and a shave, he ultimately joined Edison, Burroughs, Ford and Professor DeLoach by the river. Together the old-timers stuck to their gypsy ideals and party traditions and slept outside. Later that night the clubhouse bedrooms must have seemed a world away, as Burroughs recorded that the "mercury dropped to thirty."

Sleeping outside, or roughing it, has gained a certain appeal in modern times. This was not always so. Although camping is by no means new, it did not become a widespread phenomenon, and was certainly not viewed as a meaningful form of recreation, until after the Civil War.

The earliest "American campers," be they explorers, pioneers, hunters, or indigenous peoples would never have thought about camping as a vacation or a form of leisure. Camping, or roughing it, was done out of necessity. The wilderness was a scary, dangerous place, and these early campers often faced great hardships. Through strenuous labor, survival might be achieved if nature was tamed by clearing, cutting, and building something more permanent than a pup tent. When settlement was not the intended goal, the wilderness was not a place to linger but a place to be traversed as quickly as possible. Of course, with time, the modern world would change all that.

In April 1869 a groundbreaking book, *Adventures in the Wilderness*, was published by an unlikely author, William H.H. Murray, the new pastor of the Park Street Church in Boston, Massachusetts. Also known as *Camp Life in the Adirondacks*, the work was part memoir, part guidebook, and part advertisement for the beauty of upstate New York. Murray, who was then hired as a reporter by the *New York Daily Tribune,* returned to the Adirondack's the following Summer to report that the area remained "Enchanted Ground."

In a series of newspaper articles the young pastor wrote about the sporting life, appealing to those feeling trapped in the city, aspiring to be in a more peaceful place. Murray, knowing what his audience wanted to hear and having a natural gift of persuasion like any good preacher, also made it clear that it was possible for anyone to escape to the woods. Camping seemed easy. It was simple, anyone might try it. He also made promises. A week in the woods was sure to cure any physical or mental ailment a person might have. Plentiful fish, game, and tasty breakfasts were all but guaranteed. As for the unpleasantries of camping, he easily downplayed being cold, wet, or sore. Lastly, Murray assured any camper that the bugs were manageable and even took specific aim at the dreaded black fly, describing the ruthless biting pest as "the most harmless and the least vexatious of the insect family" and "a monster existing only in men's feverish imaginations."

Between Murray's book and his series of newspaper articles, American camping was born. Tens of thousands of his books were sold, making it a best seller of the time, and making the Adirondack region a prime tourist location. A stampede of visitors from Boston, New York and other northeast cities arrived daily, usually following the routes outlined and otherwise recommended by Murray, filling any hotel or cabin within miles, overrunning any tourist infrastructure, and thereby causing many to have no choice but to camp in the forests. In the end, this created an unintended consequence. Lured into a promise of a blissful escape, many were just not prepared for rain, mud, wild animals, unidentified insects, crowds of people, drunken locals and the typical assortment of rip off artists. However, the blackflies would not be outdone in creating mayhem. They came, wave after wave, circling campers, flying into everything and everybody, biting their helpless victims with no mercy or discrimination. The blood and welts proved the monster was real and not simply a figment of any wild imagination. American camping may have been born, but it was on life support. Murray, who had made a great deal of money and notoriety the year before, now faced ridicule and scorn for inviting the novice camper into the wilderness with all her dangers.

Maybe camping was not for everyone. Maybe camping was only for those who sought a strenuous adventure, or for those who wished to make themselves stronger. If so, American camping was about to get the poster child for such a person. As a child "Teedie" suffered from severe bronchial asthma, which would often leave him gasping for air, feeling as if drowning. Opening his mouth, searching for air, the young boy's chest would contract causing horrible gasping and wheezing. His parents, in turn, would be struck with terror watching their child struggle to breathe. Soon they sought out a variety of remedies which included, among other things, a search for fresh air with trips to the countryside, mountains, and seaside. The young lad hit his books hard, was an avid reader, and loved learning about everything. However, he continued to suffer from asthma attacks and bouts of stomach ailments. Following a visit to a doctor for a thorough checkup, "Teedie's" father took his son aside and told him, "You have the mind but not the body, and without the help of the body the mind cannot go as it should. You must make your body." Teddy Roosevelt looked up at his father, accepting the challenge, and said, "I'll make my body!" He wasted no time, creating a gym with his parents help, lifting weights, and getting outside at every opportunity. His health so improved that by August 1871 he was permitted to go on a camping trip to the same Adirondacks glorified by Murray just the Summer before. He loved it, slept on the ground, shot rapids, and climbed mountains. Many Adirondack adventures followed. However, on a later camping trip to Maine, Roosevelt, who was fourteen, suffered an asthma attack and was made fun of by two boys his age. Upon his return home, he took up boxing to further strengthen his body and to be better able to defend himself.

Mountain climbing and wilderness exploring, along with stints as a Dakota rancher, Rough Rider, and Police Commissioner of New York City, were proof that the young lad had made his body. Years later, as Governor of New York, Roosevelt set aside nearly seventy thousand acres of land in the Adirondacks and the Catskills as forest reserves. He would never forget America's original campground. Roosevelt's life story would be further intertwined with outdoor adventuring in his ascent to the White House.

After President McKinley's assassination, the nation had no president for twelve anxious hours, as Vice President Roosevelt, totally unare of the crisis, was climbing Mount Marcy, the highest peak in the Adirondacks. It was an exhausting climb filled with clouds and mist so thick the climbers could not see more than ten feet in front of them, made worse by slippery rocks from all the recent rains. After climbing the summit, the mist had cleared for a short time, briefly bathing the climbers in sunshine. On the way down, the party had stopped to eat. Sitting on a ledge with friends near a lake named *Tear-of-the-Clouds*, Roosevelt was about to bite into a sandwich when a runner approached carrying a telegram outlining the dire situation. Teddy Roosevelt, who was about to become the 26*th* President of the United States, would also become America's most beloved camper. He would go on to establish one hundred fifty national forests, eighteen national monuments, and five new national parks. By setting aside these beautiful places, Roosevelt hoped others might also build their character and lift their spirits. He knew outdoor living had done more than just make his body.

Coming after Murray's writings, camping got more sophisticated when John B. Bachelder offered alternatives to traveling throughout the Adirondacks by canoe in his 1875 book, *Popular Resorts and How to Reach Them*. Bachelder essentially identified three modes of camping: on foot (now called backpacking); on horseback; or by horse and wagon. While a horse allowed for more supplies than a single backpack, the wagon allowed for even more gear and supplies, but could alternatively be more limiting by poor roads and the need for additional funds. Most writings on camping and travel had mimicked Murray's focus on the Adirondacks. Bachelder's work greatly expanded the geographies to be explored with sections on Kentucky, Illinois, Wisconsin, Minnesota, and the western states.

What followed can best be described as the development of camping rituals. Having introduced the public to the ideas of camping, followed by potential areas to explore while suggesting the best routes and means to get there, the last piece was to educate campers on what to do once they reached their destination. Horace Sowers Kephart was perhaps the most influential provider of how-to-camp manuals, and his book, *Camping and Woodcraft*, gave any would be camper every detail they could ever imagine. Written in 1906, *Camping and Woodcraft*, addressed proper camping attire, tents, equipment, campsite selection and design, hunting, fishing, cooking, pests, fire building, and forest travel. The book would go through multiple revisions during and after Kephart's lifetime, all while his reputation continued to grow. Before he died in an automobile accident on a mountain road in North Carolina in the spring of 1931, Kephart had become known as the "Dean of American Campers" and was unanimously elected to the National Council of the Boy Scouts of America two years before his death.

Over the following decades, camping slowly modernized, while creating a paradox of sorts. Born out of a need to return to nature and escape modernization, camping has simultaneously embraced sophisticated technologies seeking ways to improve comfort and convenience. In short, "roughing it" has long been distinguished from suffering—at least by some. From the beginning, there has been tension between campers and what it means to camp. Although all agree that camping requires leaving town or an urban setting to temporarily stay in nature, and that some form of restoration is the desired goal for such a journey, that is where the agreement ends. Most conflict exists in the level of challenge required in camping, and as camping has modernized, it has become safer, less demanding, and generally more comfortable. This has been applauded by many, while others frown upon every improvement as further infringement of a noble antimodern practice.

Tensions between the modern world and wanting to return to nature, would quite literally be laid bare for all to see in the summer of 1913. On August 3, 1913, at 10:40 AM, Joseph Knowles, a middle-aged painter from Boston, took off his brown suit exposing his pale unconditioned body, and wandered into the woods of Maine wearing nothing more than a white cotton jockstrap. In the weeks leading up to this morning, Knowles had promised to enter the Dead River wilderness of Maine without any clothing where he would dwell alone for two months. After being examined by a doctor and taking a few puffs on a cigarette, Knowles smiled and said, "See you later, boys!"

Shortly after entering the woods, he supposedly lost the jockstrap. Cutting notches in a tree with a makeshift axe made from the forest, he would mark the days before his return to civilization. The Boston painter would also dispatch stories of his exploits to the *Boston Post*. Knowles, who has been described as America's first outdoor "realty star," initially had a few rough days, finding his feet in agony and being unable to build a proper fire to drive away the giant herds of mosquitoes that followed him around every tree. However, he would later write, that it was the feelings of isolation that caused his greatest suffering. Dressed head to toe in natural materials, Knowles emerged from the woods on October 4, 1913. The superstar had lost thirty pounds, now donned a matted beard, and was considerably darker than when he had entered the woods two months before. Knowles had delivered as promised, and in the process, managed to help double the daily circulation of the *Boston Post*. Wearing a bearskin robe, he was given a hero's welcome by thousands of adoring fans as he sauntered down the streets of Boston.

For the next month, Knowles gave lectures and camping demonstrations, shook many hands, and filled his pockets with money. However, in late November, the *Boston Sunday American* ran an expose entitled "The Truth about Knowles: Real Story of His 'Primitive Man' Adventures in the Maine Woods" alleging the camping superstar and his two-month jaunt in the woods was nothing more than a fraud. The story told of how Knowles was never naked as clothes had been stashed in the woods; that he had stayed at a cabin with an accomplice for most of the time; and had frequent visitors including a certain lady friend. To top it off, the paper quoted an eyewitness as alleging the bearskin robe had been purchased for $20, and that a close examination of the skin would reveal four bullet holes proving its owner had fibbed about how it was obtained. Much like William Murray several decades before, Knowles originally sold a ton of books only to later become a target of ridicule and shame. However, Murray was only accused of leading novices into the woods, whereas Knowles was accused of staging an actual fraud on the public. Embittered, and wanting some form of vindication, Knowles filed a $50,000 dollar lawsuit against the *Boston Sunday American*, and went on a tour of sorts to prove his survival skills, including an exhibition where he jumped into a river and pulled fish out with his barehand.

After the turn of the century, the pace of camping's modernization accelerated by growing salaries and, in part, car sales. Although the first modern tent, which used canvas instead of buffalo hides was designed by a U.S. Army officer in 1855, it was only after 1900 that tent sales proliferated. For instance, the Boy Scouts established a camp in New York in 1910 and the 1st Boy Scout handbook published in 1911 contained

10 different types of tents. The Girl Scouts followed shortly thereafter, with a camp built in Georgia. A few years before, W.C. Coleman had developed a liquid fuel lantern with a small base tank pressurized using a hand pump. In 1908, Thomas Hiram Holding, long considered another founding father to modern camping, wrote his first edition of *The Campers Handbook*. The British traveling tailor had developed a love of travel and the great outdoors as a child when in 1853 his family had crossed the American prairies in a wagon train in route to the Oregon territory. Later, as a 33-year-old, he would canoe through the Scottish Highlands.

On August 21, 1915, almost exactly three years before our campers gathered in Pittsburgh to start their journey, the Conklin family departed Huntington, New York for a cross country camping trip in a 25 ft, 8-ton custom-built vehicle. The family trip took nearly two months in part because of the poor roads encountered along their journey. The vehicle, nicknamed the "Gypsy Van," was built by Roland Conklin's Gas-Electric Motor Bus Company, and included many innovations, including: an electrical generator and incandescent lights; a full kitchen; pullman-style sleeping berths; a folding table and desk; a concealed bookcase; a phonograph; convertible sofas with throw pillows; a variety of small appliances; and a "roof garden." The Smithsonian has described the van, which featured room for 17 passengers, as a "marvel of technology and chutzpah." The first recreational vehicle, or RV, was hand-built onto an automobile in 1904, and this proto-motorhome slept four and included an icebox and radio. Camping trailers, usually consisting of a plain device made to hold tents, sleeping bags and other equipment also entered the market around this time. However, it was Conklin's vehicle that caught the fancy of America. According to American Heritage magazine, the Conklin van "gave the upper class a play home that combined some of the appeal of a yacht or a private railroad car with the flexibility of the automobile." This, in turn, poured over into the middle class and inspired a cultural phenomenon. The Ford, Edison, Firestone and Burroughs camping trips simply offered a glossy sales brochure of sorts to help convince many Americans to take the plunge and try their luck at hitting the road. Today, nearly ten percent of all U.S. homes own an RV, with 400,000 Americans making it their permanent residence

CHAPTER 11

"Apalachen"

John Burroughs observed that the mountains and valleys of the Virginias presented a stark contrast to those of New York and eastern Pennsylvania as they had not been rubbed down and scooped out by glaciers. The valleys were markedly V-shaped rather than U-shaped, making for steeper valley sides that could rarely be cultivated. As for the farmland, it was atop the broad, open river valley that held mile after mile of beautiful farms producing hay and oats. Burroughs further described seeing large fields of buckwheat, "white with bloom" and "humming with bees" and that "here and there" he saw by the rocks and boulders strewn over the landscape, evidence of a large local glacier that had hatched these mountains during the great ice age.

Burroughs wrote in his journal that on August 16, 1918, the campers set out for a two-week automobile trip into the land of Dixie. However, a more accurate description of the trip would be a romp into the heart of Appalachia. This region, long being considered the essence of America, is also home to what has been described as a "strange land and a peculiar people." Some have argued that Appalachia is a state of mind, while others doubt the mere existence of such a place at all.

Many historians maintain that Appalachia is really nothing more than an invention of northern writers. In John Alexander Williams comprehensive and compelling, *Appalachia, A History*, he reminds us that Appalachia is both a real place and a territory of imagination, and that social reality there lends credence to both aspects. In fact, most scholars agree that Appalachia is home to a distinctive and important regional variant in American culture. Today, major tourist attractions, including the Blue Ridge Parkway and the Great Smoky Mountain National Park, are considered to represent Appalachia in pictures more than words. These pictures capture two important elements that define Appalachia: a rural society with a strong and enduring presence of wilderness.

In 1861, during the early days of the Civil War, a Minnesota newspaper first attempted to define the area in a series of articles identifying the region as "Alleghenia." Included in this region were 161 counties in the mountains of Virginia, Kentucky, Tennessee, Alabama, Georgia and the Carolinas. The articles dubbed the area as more a "land of corn and cattle," distinguished from the deeper south which was more a "land of cotton." Most importantly, in this attempt to define the area, Alleghenia represented a land with little slavery, stronger Union sentiment, and ripe for its own independent internal revolutions. These highlands and her mountaineers, which may have been apt to take issue with any overbearing influence of the east coast, would also not be bullied by the low country culture of the deep south. Some, but not all, had been cast out from colonial society. Those who chose to call these mountain ranges home would not bend.

The biggest problem with attempting to define this region, especially in a world of maps, is there are no agreed boundaries or borders. John Burroughs was correct that the trip would take the campers south of the Mason-Dixon line, the 233-mile-long line mainly between the Pennsylvania and Maryland border and marked by large blocks of limestone. However, unlike the Mason-Dixon line, Appalachia has not been measured out by an astronomer (Mason) or a surveyor (Dixon), and there are no borders between states representing an obvious demarcation in topography, politics or culture. In the twentieth century and today, the Mason-Dixon line has been and is used to assist in understanding Appalachia, but it is only a tool and in no way represents a border to the area. In fact, in the postmodern approach to regionalism, which looks to the interaction of global and local human and environmental forces, boundaries can and do shift with time and environmental landmarks lose their significance. Nonetheless, geologists have marked off distinctive provinces within Appalachia, including the Piedmont, the Blue Ridge, the Great Valley, the Allegheny, and the Appalachian Plateau. These provinces represent a huge territory extending from New York to Mississippi, and further includes parts of Alabama, Georgia, South Carolina, North Carolina, Tennessee, Virginia, Kentucky, West Virginia, Ohio, Maryland, and Pennsylvania. However, regardless of definitions, the core remains in six states: Georgia, North Carolina, Tennessee, Kentucky, West Virginia, and Virginia. The 1918 trip never left the broader definition of Appalachia, remaining in the core almost the entire time.

Appalachia owes its name to the Spanish empire's unquenchable search for gold. Explorers converged upon the Apalachee Indians in northwest Florida, and the tribes having no gold to offer, pointed the potential plunderers to the north and the distant mountain ranges. Later, French explorers who arrived in Florida, continued to fuel speculation, spreading stories of gold deposits in the internal mountain range where lakes and waterfalls were also in great abundance. In all fairness to the Apalachees and the French, there have been some gold discoveries made in the eastern mountain ranges even if nothing like the finds in the western United States.

The name, "Apalachen," appeared on European maps as early as 1562, and the eastern mountain ranges would come to be called the Appalachians after the American Revolution. In 1839 Washington Irving even went so far as to propose changing the name of the United States from America to Appalachia. Perhaps Irving was on to something as to this day there is some confusion when one calls themselves

American as in reality this includes several continents. Peruvians and Canadians might be surprised to learn they are so alike.

Regardless of its name, John Burroughs would have no doubt known he was not the first naturalist to venture into the region as that honor belongs to William Bartram. Bartram, generally considered America's first native-born naturalist, was a friendly chap with the heart of an artist. The Quaker from Philadelphia could often be found exploring the back country with a smile on his face and a sketchbook in his hand. His father, John Bartram, had been appointed a royal botanist to King George III, and had earlier explored Iroquois territory. He also had managed to make his son an assistant. Starting in 1773 the younger Bartram, looking to make his own path, rambled through Georgia's barrier islands, not to conquer or search for gold, but to catalogue.

In May of 1776 the naturalist, with a few English pounds in his pocket, found himself traveling from the safety of Keowee in South Carolina into the upcountry over the Blue Ridge towards the lands of the Cherokee. As a white man, he cautiously followed a ridgetop trail across South Carolina into Georgia ultimately meandering his way through the western tip pf North Carolina. The young man was enchanted by what he saw, describing in his journal a "magnificent landscape, infinitely varied and without bound." He was especially enthralled by the large array of trees, plants, and shrubs, paying particular attention to the blossoming azaleas and rhododendrons. Stunned by the height of many trees and delighted by the discovery of a multitude of waterfalls, Bartram filled his packs with small rocks, leaves and flowers all while sketching pictures captured in his eye and feverishly scribbling descriptions in his journal. Relatively untouched by the hand of man, Burroughs would have been properly jealous knowing what Bartram had witnessed. Learning that George Washington, Thomas Jefferson and James Madison came to call on Bartram for his expertise in nature, would also make most anyone jealous.

The eighteenth century, along with Pennsylvania and Virginia, hold the keys to a better understanding of what started Appalachia. Being reminded that the European and native peoples, who collided in this frontier in the later part of that century, were by no means monolithic but rather multiethnic and multilingual societies is equally important for any true enlightenment of the history of this region. The eighteenth century presented an age of frontier and settlement in Appalachia, and Pennsylvania provided the easiest and safest gateway to this new frontier. With no mountain ranges blocking a western migration, Europeans, especially Quakers, were able to travel between the Piedmont and the Great Valley. Generally considered less scenic, these routes avoided deep gorges and cliffs. It also helped that these regions of Pennsylvania were more sparsely populated with Indians creating less displacement and potential for conflict. William Penn, for whom the state is named, was an aristocratic Quaker and investor in lands just west of the Delaware River. Although he passed away in 1718, Pennsylvania would soon become a haven for religious minorities and refugees looking for a fresh start. In contrast, Virginia, where the Great Valley is located much further inland from the coast, initially saw more hunters and soldiers venture into the mountainous backcountry. When they did, they often encountered Indians resulting in conflict and displacement.

This western push from the center part of the United States, much like flowing water in a stream, initially went where it could with the least resistance. At the time, important boundaries, political, and otherwise, directed any potential migration of peoples. To the north were French territories, along with the Iroquois, while the southern parts of North America had been previously carved out by Spanish explorers. The French and the English claimed lands further to the west, along with multiple Indian tribes, including the Cherokee. The "sweet spots" in Pennsylvania were soon settled by German immigrants, who in time came to be referred to as "Pennsylvania Dutch" by their English-speaking neighbors who confused *Deutsch* for *Dutch*. Virginia's "sweet spots" also saw a migration of "Dutch" settlers from Germany and Switzerland. Irish Protestants also began migrating to America in droves during the middle part of the eighteenth century, but unlike their German counterparts, they were much more willing to mix it up with Indians. They also were known to challenge local authority. This, in part, was because German settlements had driven up the price of property causing the newer Irish immigrants further into the western frontier in search of affordable land.

In time, this Irish migration came to be one the greatest influences in the history of Appalachia, and many of the characteristically Appalachian speech patterns heard to this day are remnants of this original Scotch-Irish base. Irish migration included Protestant and Catholic alike, although there were many more of the former. "Scotch-Irish" generally refers to those persons who primarily immigrated from Ulster in Northern Ireland, whose ancestors before them had originally migrated from the Scottish Lowlands and Northern England. Regardless of these distinctions, the Irish soon outnumbered Germans and would leave their mark on this region for generations to come.

Although rare, free African Americans also found their way into this migrant stream, sometimes only to find themselves captured and enslaved by Indians. However, the Indians made no distinction based on race, often capturing whites or Indians from other tribes as well. While often comprised of different nationalities, migrants shared much in common as they, for the most part, were made up of a principal class: folk looking for small, independent land ownership. They were also often dirt poor, with many having arrived in America as indentured servants. Those not looking for land, were drawn to the forests of Appalachia by the fur trade.

Appalachia was for all practical purposes largely forged in war, as long before the arrival of Dutch, French, German and English settlers, the mountainous areas of eastern North America were fought over by numerous Indian nations. With a dizzying variety of wildlife, and an abundance of water and rainfall, the mountains provided an optimum location for hunters. When European migrants arrived, they initially went to areas of least resistance, but as the river of migration increased, it soon became a flood, going around and over nearly everything and everybody in its path. At the same time, many Indians, being enticed by European trade, actively and purposely engaged traders and settlers alike. Rather than retreat, many came forward. Much has been made of the tragic addiction to alcohol, but many tribes became addicted to guns, powder, tobacco, blankets and food as well. Skirmishes from New York to the Carolinas were commonplace. Treaties were regularly ignored or broken. Confusion and misunderstanding brought on in part by different languages and cultures, hung over Appalachia like a morning fog in a wooded valley.

Beyond the hinterlands, along the western front, Protestant England and Catholic France boxed these peoples in. As these two countries vied for sole world superpower status, their struggle would spill over into Appalachia. Following this heavyweight battle, and just when it looked like peace might gain a foothold in the region, the colonies began to quarrel with London. The result was another war: The American Revolution. When the colonies pulled off one of the greatest upsets in military history, control of the mountain regions passed from the Kings of Europe to a newly formed government of the United States. Betting heavily on the British empire, many tribes had picked the wrong side to cozy up with which ultimately spelled the beginning of the end for Indian strongholds in Appalachia. The outcome, at least initially, ensured continued bloodshed in the region. Following the Revolutionary War, migration into Appalachia was greatly accelerated as veterans were provided large tracts of land as severance pay for their military service. Veterans joined "sunshine patriots," Loyalists, Negroes (runaway slaves or freed), Indian "hold outs," and a smattering of European immigrants in this new frontier.

Castoffs and other wanderers had long made homes in the mountain regions of Appalachia—with or without Indian consent. However, for years, by grant or purchase, the Revolutionary royalty had gobbled up millions of acres in the region as well. Many had a hunch the wilderness might one day be valuable. The result was many settlers wrote and recorded deeds, surveying by metes and bounds, land belonging to another. Others, knowing full well they were essentially squatters with no clear title, settled in the more remote regions of Appalachia hoping their presence would go undetected. For many this is exactly what happened. Land speculation is as old as time, and many owners, living along the eastern coast, filed their deeds and forgot about them. In fact, many never personally viewed their property and remained completely unaware of the frontier life that unfolded on their land. This was especially true as much of the land belonged to just a handful of people. However, some owners sold their land to others, or decided to travel west to gaze upon their acreage. Lawsuits and evictions ensued. What followed has haunted the region to this day.

Outside investors have long had an interest in Appalachia's valuable commodities: first, timber, then coal and natural gas. By 1810 it is estimated that as much as 93 percent of the land that is present day West Virginia was held by absentee owners. Furthermore, by the 1880s outside interests began purchasing extensive timber and underground mineral rights on land whose residents retained only the surface rights. As the value of property became known, landowners and local government began to secure land titles through legislation, court actions, and taxes. Following the Civil War, another phenomenon developed as the eastern elites, no longer needing the assistance of the backcountry folk to assist with defending the Union, began to look upon the region with a sort of fascination. For some this fascination morphed into outright disdain. The initial admiration for frontiersmen was replaced with a certain condemnation of the lifestyle.

With the American Indian having been pushed further West, or outright eliminated, these elites invented a new race of people considered isolated, poor and otherwise backward. In 1900, a journalist for the *New York Journal* described a person he had never seen before. "A Hill-Billie is a free and untrammeled white citizen of Alabama, who lives in the hills, has no means to speak of, dresses as he can, talks as he pleases, drinks whiskey when he gets it, and fires off his revolver as the fancy takes him." While hillbillies evoked hostility in some writers, they were most always viewed with pity by social reformists. Why won't they assimilate? How can we end their isolation? What can be done to alleviate their plight?

Hints of this lifestyle conflict started many years before when Alexander Hamilton essentially invaded the mountains of the region to bring economic control to an area deemed out of step with the necessary progress of a newly formed federalist/capitalist society. Hamilton surmised a tax on whiskey was reasonable—after all the backwoods should pay its fair share. He also believed it would tie them to the central government, thereby making them citizens of the newly formed country. Daniel Shays, having returned to Pennsylvania after his service in the Continental Army, saw things a little differently. For his service in the cause, he found himself wounded, never paid, and in arrears. He was not alone. A tax on whiskey was viewed by many as an afront to their livelihood, and on August 29, 1786, an army of 600 led by Shay stormed a Court of Common Pleas setting in motion the Whiskey Rebellion. Believing the people of the frontier would be better served by making things for money, and that a tax is an important step in this process, Hamilton was caught completely off guard by the mountain man's angry response. In time, he would not be alone in miscalculating the will of her people.

If Hamilton could not extract value from Appalachia in the form of taxation, the industrialists that came in the following century surely would. During the Civil War, both armies had found much of the region impenetrable, or otherwise undesirable for arranged battles. As such, raids and small skirmishes were the norm. Appalachia's unique geography created roadblocks for development, as it is, for the most part, a landlocked and mountain-bound location. With the bulk of Appalachia sitting south and southwest of the Ohio River, there is no similar waterway creating an avenue for travel. George Washington understood this problem and envisioned roads and canals linking western commerce and expansion, not knowing that the railroad (originally called a "steam wagon") would provide the key to unlocking the door to Appalachia.

The Baltimore and Ohio Railroad was the first to be chartered in 1827, followed soon by others including: The Chesapeake and Ohio Railroad; The Norfolk and Western Railroad; The West Virginia Central Railroad; The Western Maryland Railroad; The Virginian Railway; The Shenandoah Valley Railroad; and the Clinchfield Railroad (also known as The Charleston, Cincinnati and Southern). As these trains began crisscrossing the region, their steam engines were fed on a diet entirely made of coal. Geologists had determined that the area, especially near West Virginia and Kentucky, had an abundance of coal, with reports describing it as "incredible" and that "there is nothing equal to it anywhere." With railroads in place, and land that was for the most part unoccupied except for a smattering of small, seemingly inefficient, farms, the area seemed a capitalist dream. Land not rich in coal deposits, or otherwise suitable for easy mining, was equally valuable to industrialists as large trees created a canopy as far as the eye could see. Commercial logging, along with mining, would drastically change the landscape and the lives of many who called Appalachia home.

By the turn of the twentieth century timber barons had turned their sites to the Southern Appalachian Forest, driving farther and farther into the mountains, with vast cuttings leaving entire mountainsides bare. Farming, as difficult as it already was, became more difficult as in these mountains cattle often lived in the woods. While farm productivity in the region had diminished steadily between 1840 and 1880, largely replaced by the flatlands of Ohio, Indiana, Illinois and Michigan, industry had simultaneously gained strength. Farm life was replaced by cutting down trees and digging for coal.

Following the Civil War, the South's cheap labor and easy access to cotton had resulted in a seismic shift in the cotton mill workforce from New England to the New South. At the same time, coal company towns and timber camps emerged throughout southern Appalachia all while local land ownership continued to dwindle. By the time Henry Ford and company motored through Appalachia, a unique coal town/timber camp culture had developed. While timbering peaked in 1909, the region continued mining at a frenetic pace well into the 21st century. Companies, providing work in remote areas, created villages where workers lived, shopped, socialized and worshipped. Some towns were literally owned entirely by one company, and Appalachia had a much higher concentration of company towns than any other area in the nation. Intentions aside, this industrial paternalism, sometimes referred to as "corporate feudalism," usually turned out badly for the workers. Thrown into wage work, and having abandoned their land and farms, workers leased land or rented houses from the company. Furthermore, a trip to the company owned store, or any other nearby establishment, resulted in a tab ultimately deducted from pay checks. To add insult to injury, company stores sold food and other necessities at exorbitant prices. Lastly, coal towns often operated like small police states, where company rules were the law. As a result, it instigated a sort of class warfare, putting everyone on edge.

Thomas Edison and Henry Ford were famous men by the time of their 1918 road trip. However, they were also well known for being wealthy businessmen. When the campers encountered the hoard of visitors deep in the heart of West Virginia, including lumberjacks and mountaineers from nearby mines, it was recorded that the initial conversations were "loud and unscripted," but that Henry Ford diffused the situation by offering cigars and handshakes. Although we are left to wonder what was said and what made the situation feel potentially hostile, one cannot help but think this encounter reflected the growing resentment of local laborers towards the wealthy businessmen they had encountered in their camps and company towns. One can also sense a certain naivety from Harvey Firestone and company as they gazed upon the area through the lens of business aristocracy. Ford and Edison believed better living conditions might be obtained through harnessing local energy sources from nearby rivers and streams, while Firestone searched for better local business practices to improve living conditions. Although true, none seemed to sense the role that business itself had played in the harsh conditions for Appalachian workers. What is known is that a sort of peace was made that night, and that the same group arrived again the next day with their wives and children to give Thomas Edison a ride on a nearby steam engine. The image is stark, if not ironic, given the role of the iron horse in removing lumber and coal from the mountains and her folk.

Any peace achieved was tenuous and would soon be shattered, as after World War I, West Virginia would be ground zero for some of the worse mine violence in U.S. history. Between 1890 and 1917 more than 26,000 miners were killed on the job, with another 12,000 or so maimed each year. Simply put, conditions were deplorable. Stuck deep below the earth's surface, often in close quarters, labor had easy contact with each other. Further, it was often outside managements control. The United Mine Workers, which had begun in Pennsylvania in 1890, not surprisingly, had taken root in the "El Dorado" regions of Appalachia, including West Virginia and Kentucky. In 1912-1913, thousands of West Virginia miners, acting on their own, staged a walk-out at Paint Creek-Cabin Creek. This was followed by thousands of walkouts throughout 1919—with both sides on edge, things were about to get much, much worse.

On a dreary morning in May 1920, a dozen or so men from the Baldwin-Felts detective agency boarded Norfolk and Western trains bound for the small mining town of Matewan, in Mingo County, West Virginia. These detectives carried badges, and bags packed with Winchesters and pistols. Tom Felts had personally selected these men and would rendezvous with his brother Albert who was already posted at the Urias Hotel in Matewan. Acting as a private police force, the detectives later piled into three cars and drove to Stone Mountain property, where they began clearing miners' cabins. As the miners and their families stood by, furniture was hauled out of the dwellings and piled along the street. At some point, the crew was interrupted by the mayor, Cabell Testerman, and the police chief, Sid Hatfield, who demanded to know under what authority the detectives had for the evictions. Albert Felts assured them a circuit judge had given approval, and ordered his men to continue with the evictions, at which point the mayor and police chief walked away.

After getting back to town, Testerman and Hatfield phoned the nearby sheriff's office in Williamson and ultimately spoke with the county prosecutor, who told them the evictions were illegal and warrants for arrest should be issued against the detectives. The mayor sent Charlie Kelly, one of the evicted miners, to Williamson to swear out the warrants. Unbeknownst to the mayor, a phone operator loyal to the coal company, relayed the conversations to Anse Hatfield-owner of the Urias Hotel and a close friend of Tom and Albert Felts. By mid-afternoon, regardless of allegiance, the whole town was acutely aware that Charlie Kelly was due to arrive with the warrants on the 5:15 train from Williamson which just happened to be the same train the Baldwin-Felts gang planned to take back to Bluefield on their way out of town. Sensing trouble, Sid Testerman told Hugh Combs, a miner loyalist, to select a dozen "sober minded men" to back up the police chief as special officers. At around 4 PM, after being sworn in by Testerman, the new officers, began gathering at the rail station. Nearly all brought their own guns.

Felts had also sensed trouble, especially after getting the tip from Anse Hatfield. Returning to the hotel, his men broke down their Winchesters and hid them in their bags. Lee Felts, and a few others, decided it might be best to keep their pistols on their belts. As the detectives approached the station, they were confronted by Sid Hatfield who advised them they were under arrest. Albert Felts laughed him off and told Hatfield that he had a warrant for his arrest as well. The mayor, who had also happened upon the scene, asked to see Felt's warrant. Felts handed over a warrant, which in vague language, charged Hatfield with taking a prisoner from a local constable a few days before. After examining the warrant, the mayor declared, "It's bogus." What happened next is disputed to this day. Although most versions begin with Albert Felts reaching for his gun, they diverge thereafter. What is agreed upon is that all hell broke loose as a string of gun fire rang out from nearly every direction. The detectives, having packed up their Winchesters, were heavily out armed, while the newly appointed officers were lousy shots. However, they were relentless in their attack. In the end, detective Troy Higgins, a former Virginia police chief, was shot dead. A. J. Boohrer, another detective and former Virginia police chief was also killed in the gun fight. Detective C.B. Cunningham, who had also arrived in town earlier that day, was so riddled with bullets his body was nearly unrecognizable. E.O. Powell, another Felts detective, was also gunned down that afternoon. J.W. Ferguson, hit in the first rounds of gun fire, was helped by a bystander to a chair on a nearby porch, only to be later discovered dead in a nearby alley. A bullet hole was later discovered in the back of the chair. Albert and Lee Felts, along with two miners, were also killed before the 5:15 train rolled into the station. Mayor Teterman, also shot in the melee, died later that night. The remaining detectives somehow managed to escape with their lives on foot, by train, or swimming across the nearby river.

Three months later, Anse Hatfield, the hotel owner and tipster, was shot dead on the porch of his hotel. The bullet, which ripped through his chest, came out his backside and struck a local dentist in the jaw as the two were chatting. Sid Hatfield, who had escaped death in the massacre, but who remained under heavy suspicion and scrutiny for the series of events that had transpired in the small mining town, met his own demise when he was allegedly gunned down by a group of Baldwin-Felts agents outside a courthouse in 1921. Hostilities, between miners and coal companies, far from over, would boil over a month later at the Battle of Blair Mountain when America would see her largest labor uprising yet.

CHAPTER 12

A Time to Play

The party broke camp from the Cheat Country Club starting the fifth day of their journey south. It was August 22, 1918. According to one of the drivers, he looked down at his wristwatch and saw that it was exactly 10 AM on the dot when Edison gave the "all clear" signal to move out. The cars rumbled through the West Virginia countryside only for a short time before Henry Ford shouted "Look, there's a cradle." In the Allegheny Mountains, somewhere near Bartow, West Virginia, Ford and Firestone, who knew a thing or two about farm work, ordered the procession to stop. The two farm boys could not help themselves. Hopping a fence, they asked to borrow a scythe from a local farmer and began a contest of "cradling" and "sheaving." Cradling, which is cutting grain with a scythe, is not an easy task. A smiling Harvey Firestone went first, much to the delight of Henry Ford and the local farmer. Soon he was entangled in oats and weeds. Henry Ford was up next. He seemed to have not forgotten his days on the farm in Michigan as he proved to be quite proficient at it. Not to be outdone in proving his country credentials, John Burroughs stunned everyone with his perfect form and surprising endurance. Years of raking and bundling oats in Roxbury, New York made him a natural at cradling. Edison, who was the self-appointed official score keeper, all but crowned Mr. Burroughs the winner. Burroughs later presumed that Professor DeLoach would have been a clear winner had the contest involved cotton picking given the professor's early days passed as a youth in Georgia. Having worked up an appetite from the unexpected stop and resulting exercise, it was decided to have lunch on the side of the road before hitting the road again.

Following the roadside meal outside of Bartow, West Virginia, maps were again consulted under the watchful eye of Edison, and it was decided that the party would pass through Warm Springs, Virginia with a scheduled stop in Hot Springs, Virginia. Somewhere along the way, the caravan crossed the wrong bridge, journeyed up the wrong mountain, and ended up in the wrong town: Bolar Springs. Learning of their mistake and running out of daylight on the 22*nd* day of August, they made camp in a fine grove with warm springs and a concrete bathing pool. Tents were pitched among the sugar maples, and some, if not all, of the party availed themselves of the public bathhouse that spanned the overflow of the great spring. The charge for a bath was fifteen cents and based on some accounts not everyone had remembered to pack a swimsuit. Dinner included a Virginia ham purchased at a village store. Once in camp, Mr. Ford again showed his skills, this time as a woodcutter. He cut all the wood that was used in the camp, revealing what the others regarded as "great training in this art." Professor DeLoach later recalled Mr. Ford remarking that he would give $50,000 for the springs in Bolar if he could move them to the State of Michigan and everyone agreed that the fifteen-cent bath "felt like a million dollars."

Hot Springs are located throughout the United States including Alaska, Arizona, Arkansas, California, Colorado, Hawaii, Idaho, Illinois, Indiana, Massachusetts, Montana, Nevada, New Mexico, New Mexico, New York, North Carolina, Oregon, South Dakota, Texas, Utah, Virginia, Washington, West Virginia, and Wyoming. The term "hot spring," also known as a thermal spring or geothermal spring, specifically refers to a spring of naturally hot water produced by the emergence of geothermally heated groundwater that rises from the Earth's crust. While some springs are perfect for bathing, others, mostly found in the Western states, are so hot they might result in injury or death. In fact, many are literally boiling. The term "hot spring" is often used loosely to describe any natural spring or spa, and bathing waters are not always made naturally hot. However, along the border of Virginia and West Virginia is a stretch of natural thermal springs, providing "warm" waters between 68 and 122 deg. Fahrenheit. Bath County, the county in which are travelers made camp, was established in 1745 and is named for the English resort town of Bath.

Bath County should not be confused with the town of Bath, West Virginia, near Berkeley Springs. Although both are named for their English counterpart, the town of Bath sits further North near the Maryland border and is in Morgan County, West Virginia. It was in the town of Bath, that George Washington escaped the calls for his removal as Commander of the Continental Army in October of 1777, searching for warm pools of water with healing powers. British victories at the Battle of Brandywine and at Germantown had resulted in the evacuation of the capital, Philadelphia. Shaded by giant hardwood trees, Washington had first visited the springs in 1748 at the age of sixteen when working as a professional surveyor. Like many, he was drawn to the crystal-clear water pouring from the mountainside at a comfortable seventy-four degrees. He had revisited the springs many times over the years, even bringing his ailing brother, Lawrence, who was afflicted with tuberculosis in hopes that he might find some relief from his misery. While soaking in these rock-lined pools he was able to put the harsh realities of the war behind him, clear his mind, and formulate plans for future victory.

Native Americans were the first to experience the healing power in these heated waters in what would become Bath County. In the 1700s Europeans traveling west discovered these same pools and by the 1740s small guest lodges were built nearby. The first gentleman's bathhouse was built in 1761 in nearby Warm Springs, Virginia, and the structure still stands today making it one of the oldest spa structures in the United States. Thomas Jefferson, suffering from what he called "rheumatism" visited Bath County for three weeks in 1818 seeking aid from the healing waters. Eighteen years later, in 1836, a separate women's bathhouse was built allowing for greater privacy between the sexes as swimsuits were, and in many cases remain, optional. It is not known if our party of famous travelers forgot to pack swimsuits, or simply decided to follow local practices. However, what is known is that one of the helpers, brought along as a driver for the journey, later recalled a "famine of swimsuits."

The history of vacations in the United States begins with a handful of these springs, a few seaside locations, and a small number of eighteenth-century colonial elites. South Carolina planters, hoping to escape stifling heat on plantations during the summer months, would sail their families north to Newport, Rhode Island. Only a few, usually less than 100 to be exact, elite Americans could afford such a long and expensive voyage, and the four or five-month stay on the Rhode Island coast. By the late eighteenth century and into the early part of the nineteenth century, additional resorts had sprung up throughout the United States catering to wealthy Americans searching for ways to protect or improve their health. With outbreaks of cholera and yellow fever in the cities often during summer months, families with the means to do so would quite literally flee their homes to escape disease.

In the early 1800s, medicine began to change moving away from such practices as bleeding, leeches, and the use of powerful chemical compounds, to alternative treatments. These treatments looked for less dangerous and painful options for patients and spawned a variety of new physicians including homeopaths, hydropathists, and "electromagnetists" to name a few. Although traditional medicine took issue with many of these new treatment practices, in time most doctors agreed that good hygiene, when combined with exercise and disciplined eating habits, was beneficial for overall health. Most doctors also agreed that nature, in the way of fresh air and water, might also play a role in good health and in recovery from some ailments. Finding a more moderate climate, might be just what the doctor ordered. With a seal of approval from the medical community, the 1820s and 1830s saw the openings of more springs and seaside resorts. Saratoga, New York began to develop as a resort during this time and was joined by multiple springs scattered throughout the western part of Virginia. Seaside resorts, such as Cape May, New Jersey, with a multitude of visitors from the Philadelphia area, boasted two hotels by the early 1820s.

At some point along the way, travel itself began to be prescribed by doctors as a cure for illness. For instance, in 1847, a young lawyer in Ohio, Rutherford B. Hayes, found himself with a nagging sore throat that doctors believed had been brought on by his confinement to his office. The future president was advised to take a year off from practice, but instead settled on a two- month trip to New England where he visited with friends and family, fished and even climbed Mt. Washington. He returned to his law practice invigorated and the rest, well, is history.

In *Working at Play: A History of Vacations in the United States*, Cindy S. Aron describes the three "r's" of early nineteenth century travel in America, including "recuperation," "restoration" and ultimately "recreation." Her review of letters, diaries and journals of those who visited springs and seaside resorts during this time, reveals that a primary motivation for visiting was not health, but rather pleasure and fashion. In Saratoga, with activities including rifling, concerts, games, parties, balls, and cotillions, this is not surprising. In fact, one guest traveling to Saratoga in 1839, commented that for every person who was sick, there were forty others in perfect health. However, it should be noted that any infirmed person would most likely not be traveling alone and that many of these activities may have been initially designed or intended for those who traveled with them. Although billiards and card games became a male staple, many other activities were gender neutral. In fact, those visiting resorts and spas, for the most part, enjoyed more integration in activities than in any other area in society, and women were able to engage in amusements that may have been forbidden back at home. One primary exception involved bathing, with men and women being given different times and facilities. However, evening activities involved both men and women and were popular opportunities for socializing and potential courtship. Balls and dances were common, as were singles looking for romance.

Regardless of gender, and varying degrees of illness, these early travelers shared one thing in common: they were all, for the most part, extremely wealthy. Only the elite had the time and resources to travel to such locations and to indulge in such activities. This excluded many modern-day professionals such as lawyers, teachers, businessman and farmers. Abon points out that diaries from these professionals from the first half of the nineteenth century, seldom mention anything resembling a vacation. However, there is one major exception and that is what can best be described as camp meetings. The middle and lower class, looking for a reason to get away from home, could partake in a search for salvation with fellow Christians or those looking for answers about life. Primarily a Methodist undertaking, the church encouraged these meetings to reinforce teachings while simultaneously growing the flock. However, like all well-intentioned undertakings, these meetings also attracted throngs of rowdies and other troublemakers who often set up adjoining camps just outside the perimeter of the Methodist camps.

For those that came in search of spiritual restoration, they lived in conditions far different from the Seaside hotels and natural spring spas enjoyed by the wealthy. Most campers stayed in tents, while others lived in wagons or small cottages. Thousands of Americans flocked to these encampments every year, usually staying anywhere from four to eight days. In time, these campgrounds became more permanent with cabins, and other smaller homes, with the locations for these camps becoming middle-class vacation resorts after the mid-nineteenth century.

As for the term “vacation,” it did not appear with any regularity in travel writings until the early 1850s. Magazines and newspapers, including the *New York Times*, slowly began referring to “breaks” and “excursions” as “vacations.” Between the church camps and high-end resorts, Americans were beginning to see that a vacation might be beneficial not only for a person's physical well-being, but also from a psychological and spiritual standpoint. Still a friction existed between recreation and amusement or leisure, with many persons hearing sermons on Sunday at their local church exalting the virtues of hard work and warning of the dangers lurking in idle time. Americans, long entrenched in the Protestant work ethic, grappled with determining what might be considered acceptable leisure activities. Surely time spent replenishing the body and mind, might be beneficial in offering a certain level of reinvigoration that could be re-applied to work activities when returning from a break or excursion. This is commonly referred to as "sharpening the saw" and goes hand in hand with the idea of not working on the sabbath. However, what activities were worthy endeavors or would truly sharpen a saw, remained tricky. Some religious leaders argued that getting out and seeing all of God's wonderful creation, was a blessing in and of itself and could not possibly be considered as wasting time. Others, such as Minister Horace Bushnell, took a much more brazen approach, claiming that work was done so that a person might take time to play. This is much more in line with how many people view work and vacations today. Lastly, Henry Ward Beecher, a prominent nineteenth century minister who was fond of searching for breathtaking views in nature and quoting noble passages from great books and poetry, openly preached that leisure and relaxation could be a route to God.

By the late 1800s vacations had taken hold in the United States. As the economy grew, especially after the Civil War, more Americans found themselves in less labor-intensive jobs. As a result, white collar jobs were being created all while a middle class began to take form. Workers found themselves with more free time, with some even being encouraged to take time off from work all while being paid to do so. Marketing vacations also took hold around this time as well. Aimed primarily at city folk, advertisements and travel columns began appearing in major newspapers. Soon resorts were popping up just about everywhere, and although most catered to a Northeast crowd, all the states could boost a multitude of potential vacation spots.

As the economy expanded, so did the railroads. Rail travel simultaneously contributed to the growth of vacations by providing an easier, quicker, and more comfortable means of travel. Gone were the long bumpy carriage rides and the slow-moving steamships with a few stops along a handful of rivers. Although the automobile and the airplane would be the final pieces in making travel the twenty first century colossus it is today, the railroad was the first block in this expansion. As demand grew for new vacation spots, the railroads were happy to oblige by adding new routes and additional stops along the way. Small towns, hardly known before, became destination points. In fact, some railroads developed land they owned into resorts as a means of increasing ridership and increasing the value of their land holdings. For instance, the Camden and Atlantic Railroad owned the land company that was instrumental in building what would become Atlantic City. By reducing the time needed to travel, railroads further made vacations more obtainable to the middle and lower class. The costs of long journeys, often taking weeks, if not months, were largely eliminated. The costs could now also be spent on the destination and not just getting there.

Families were not the only ones to catch the traveling bug. By the end of the nineteenth century, the convention circuit also began to take hold in earnest. A variety of organizations, professional and otherwise, began picking vacation hot spots to hold their meetings. Martha's Vineyard, along with the other previously mentioned destinations, welcomed a multitude of meetings during this time, and in 1886, the Michigan Central Railroad and the Grand Rapids and Indiana Railroad, along with the Detroit and Cleveland Steamship Navigation Company, formed the Mackinac Island Hotel Company. After the Grand Hotel on Mackinac Island opened its doors in 1887, the hotel soon hosted conventions for insurance agents, teachers, and newspaper editors.

Following the increase in salaries, and the greater ease and lower costs to journey to vacation spots, an important shift began to set in in the American psyche. Now, for the first time, many believed vacationing was an integral part of a meaningful life. However, others remained concerned about whether vacations offered a sufficiently productive use of their time. The protestant work ethic would not go quietly. Could a person really turn a work ethic back on after being idle for a considerable amount of time? These concerns were only exacerbated by the fact that many vacation spots and fancy resorts featured gambling as a recreational activity, further calling into question the morality of a vacation lifestyle. In the end, the American vacation could not be stopped, even for those with concerns. Many simply chose to vacation in more out of the way locations, choosing a simpler path and avoiding high end resorts and other potential vice that might await. The church, along with other organizations, stepped in to help anyone who might be waffling. Much like the early Methodist church camps, resorts sprung up offering formal instruction and training, religious or otherwise. These resorts gave birth to the self-improvement vacation.

One such resort was near Lake Chautauqua in New York. Founded in 1874 by John Vincent, a Methodist minister, and Lewis Miller, an inventor and manufacturer, the spot chosen had previously been the location for a Methodist camp meeting. However, the resort set out to avoid a revival, instead focusing strictly on education and self-improvement. The resort was a smashing success, and in time drew hundreds of thousands of students from across the country to the shores of her lake. Thereafter, Chautauqua's success spilled over onto other sites in other states, with many even using the lake's name regardless of how many miles separated the two. While many were no doubt drawn by the affordable price tag, most sought out a resort vacation to gain additional skills and knowledge. As it turns out, self-help has always sold in America. This is especially true given the nature of education at the time. Although many Americans attended schools, including high schools, this is usually when formal education ended. Higher learning, or University study, was a privilege enjoyed primarily by wealthy white men. As such, a place like Chautauqua offered opportunities to the middle and lower class to continue education even if it was only for a few days or weeks. Here a middle-aged woman might have the opportunity to study philosophy or to read classic literary works, while her male cousin, usually engaged in farming, received basic instruction in a second language such as French or Japanese. "Black Chautauquas" also took hold during this time, focusing on self-improvement and racial uplift, often focusing on community issues and searching for political solutions. Regardless of the location of a resort, or whether it catered to Black or white Americans, entertainment was a vital part of the programming. Not surprisingly, these activities often mirrored what might be enjoyed at the high-end resorts including swimming, boating, concerts, fireworks, and other more relaxing evening get togethers. One major deviant from the higher end resorts, and clearly a remnant of the Methodist camps, was a strict prohibition on alcohol.

Another type of trip also evolved in America during the nineteenth century. A vacation might not only be spent at a resort or natural spring, but might include visiting sites such as historic places, natural wonders, and places of cultural or artistic significance. In all actuality, such touring dates back as far as persons traveled for work or out of necessity as curiosity inevitably led persons to explore spots of interest. Furthermore, Europeans, especially of great wealth, had made touring an art form in the preceding centuries. What made this new type of touring different, was that Americans, wealthy or otherwise, were purposely leaving home to visit spots all with the intention of returning home. The expansion of railroads and other infrastructure greatly aided in the development of tourism, as did the birth of travel agents. Unlike the resort, where the trip involved one single destination, touring might involve visiting multiple sites perhaps with great distance between them. If not carefully planned, the trip might create more stress than not traveling at all.

Travel agents found a valuable niche, coordinating rail and coach schedules, while arranging for food and lodging. One such agent, was Thomas Cook. Originally catering to British tourists, he came to America in 1865 looking to learn more about the United States and to plot out trips for clients wishing to visit the States. British tourists were especially fascinated with visiting Civil War battlefields and related sites. However, Cook soon discovered that Americans also needed assistance with travel, so in 1872 he opened an office in New York City. Within no time, offices were also opened along the Northeastern corridor including Boston, Philadelphia, and Washington D.C. Business, although brisk, was never great. Soon Cook faced homegrown competition from Lamm's Tourist Offices and Raymond and Whitcomb Travel Agency. Tourism, along with vacationing, became an industry unto itself.

Not surprisingly, the crown jewel for American travel was the western part of the country with its vast natural sites and parks. However, more surprisingly, Americans were also drawn to touring places where other people were working. This phenomenon, both fascinating and curious, has led scholars to ponder why there was, and still is, such an attraction to see work while not working. Such a discussion naturally wanders into issues involving sociology and psychology. However, it is interesting to note just how much of the Vagabonds journey through Appalachia actively sought out what might be considered simple or mundane sites, and how often they were drawn to work sites or related work activities.

Another popular form of vacation that took hold in America in the latter part of the nineteenth century and the early part of the twentieth century was a visit to a world's fair. Before amusement parks, a trip to the World's Fair might offer a family a relatively inexpensive vacation. Visitors were welcomed into a variety of grand structures housing art, science, technology, history, and agriculture. There was an exposition for just about anyone. Providing the host city with great pride, millions of travelers would arrive by train, stay at local hotels, and attend the fair for a few days or longer. In fact, it is estimated that nearly one fifth of the U.S. population attended the Philadelphia Centennial Exposition in 1876.

Today, replaced in part by theme parks and alternative travel destinations, the world's fairs are largely forgotten. However, not entirely. Here are a few structures that remain: The Palace of Fine Arts, having been part of the Louisiana Purchase Exposition at the 1904 fair, is now the St. Louis Art Museum; The Palace of Fine Arts from the 1893 fair, is now the Museum of Science and Technology in Chicago; the Space Needle in Seattle is from the 1962 fair; and the Unisphere in Corona

Park in Flushing Meadows, which sits just outside the U.S. Open facilities in Queens, was from the 1964 fair. However, the most famous landmark is not to be found in the United States, as the Eiffel Tower was built for the 1889 world's fair in Paris, France.

As previously mentioned, camping has long faced tensions between those that find primitive camping to be a lost art, and those who welcome every new advancement with open arms or at least their debit cards. Almost everyone can sense that the backpacking crowd will not be joining the RV folk for dinner anytime soon. Not surprisingly, this same friction has spilled over into travel itself. Rolf Potts describes the battle between *traveler* and *tourist*, in his brilliant modern travel companion *Vagabonding*. As early as the 1920s the divide was described by G.K. Chesterton, writing in essence: "The traveler sees what he sees, whereas the tourist sees what he has come to see." Potts correctly and succinctly points out how the distinction between traveler and tourist has largely degenerated into a "cliquish sort of fashion dichotomy." He further points out that any attempt to distinguish the two only creates a "flimsy façade" of presumed insiders and outsiders. Just as there are no "real campers" to be distinguished from "fake campers," circumstances dictate the moment anyone might be considered a tourist instead of traveler.

Americans, forever vain, have become obsessed with worrying about whether they will be viewed as a tourist and not a traveler. The ugly tourist is as much a creation of our own imagination as it is a reality. The rest of the world is no better, willingly playing along with this false narrative. The problem is only compounded when viewing travel through the eyes of politics and what it means to be openminded. To define what it means to be truly openminded, we are inadvertently perpetrating a closeminded outlook. Although most of our society now views everything through a political lens, the beauty of travel and vagabonding comes from leaving that, along with everything else, at home. Potts beautifully concludes the foray into such follies by offering the following:

After all, as Thomas Merton retorted when asked if he'd seen "the real Asia" during his trip to India, "It's *all* real as far as I can see."

CHAPTER 13

Katherine

As the sun set on August 22, 1918, Sato announced to the party that there was an unexpected shortage of bread. Mr. Firestone described this as "an oversight in the Commissary Department," but it was more a result of ending up in the wrong town as supplies were intended to be purchased in Warm Springs. A call to the general store found no bread to be had, but it was suggested that perhaps a hotel on a nearby hill might have bread for purchase. Firestone took a small group with him to inquire with the hotel owner, Mrs. Eagle (Eahles), but she insisted that she had no bread to spare. When asked if she might bake a loaf or two, she indicated that she was out of flour. At last, the group found a solution as the campers *did* have flour, so she relented and agreed to bake some bread if they would bring her flour and split the loaves with her. Harvey Jr. and Mr. Kline took a sack of flour back to Mrs. Eagle, and in talking with them she learned that Mr. Edison was fond of apple pies and decided to bake a couple pies with the excess flour.

Later that night, she brought the apple pies down to the campsite. Edison, who had just finished dinner and was reading *A Life of Thoreau*, insisted that he would have the pie for breakfast, and although great care was taken to secure the pies, neighborhood dogs got into the commissary truck during the night and ate his highly anticipated breakfast. The following morning, Mrs. Eagle did return with loafs of bread, but is not known if she was told about the dogs. It is also not known, if the campers would have told her that her flat bread had an odd taste. Although some in the party immediately suspected it, no one said a word, and it was only later confirmed that gasoline must have leaked into the sack of flour. Nonetheless, the camping party ate the bread—gas and all. At one point during the raucous breakfast someone asked Edison if he wanted some prunes. "No" he replied, "I was once a telegraph operator and lived in a boardinghouse!"

The baking tragedy, along with the prune quip, was followed by additional unexpected levity. Mr. Edison gave several children nickels for candy, and when asked if they knew his name, a little girl answered, "Yes, Mr. Graphophone." And, alas, an incident involving Mr. Ford resulted in plenty of friendly ribbing. A traveling salesman, on his way to his next town on his route, experienced a breakdown near the campsite. Ford, with his screwdriver and pliers, lent his hand, fixing the car in question. When he was done, the man said, "How much do I owe you, stranger?" Ford replied, "Not a cent, friend; I really don't need the money." The man looked at Mr. Ford, then at the car that Ford was driving. Not convinced, he then said, "My good man, I insist on paying you for this work...I don't agree...(as) no man would be driving a little Ford car if he had all the money he needed." This exchange brought a hardy laugh to all, especially Mr. Edison.

The next stop was Hot Springs, Virginia which they reached before noon. It was August 23, 1918. Being in Virginia, the party wasted no time in finding a village store and buying another ham. While making a quick stop at the Homestead, a well-appointed resort and hot spring spa, the party received word that Mr. Hurley would not be able to rejoin the trip. Motoring another seventeen miles, the outfit stopped and lunched beside a fine stream of water along the roadside. A large concrete pool was discovered nearby, and one of the members of the party inadvertently shut off a water gate. As the party ate their lunch, a gentleman, in a rather foul mood, approached the diners to inform them that they had shut off his power. Apologies were made for this mistake, and readily accepted. It was learned that the pool was part of a waterpower system used by the O.C. Barber phosphate plant, known for being a very modern plant in the south. Harvey Firestone took his son, and along with Henry Ford, ventured to the plant for a full inspection and to better understand the workings of the hydropower.

The drive to White Sulphur Springs, West Virginia was described by Harvey, Jr. as long and tedious, while the senior Firestone described the road as one of the dustiest yet encountered on their trip. The dust covered caravan rolled up to the Greenbrier, commissary truck, baggage cars, and all. The party was met with hesitation by the resort staff, not knowing what to make of the spectacle that had just arrived at their doorstep. Did they gaze upon royalty traveling incognito or just touring tramps in the wrong place? Arriving in this fashionable resort town at 5 PM, the senior Firestone, feeling a bit scruffy, found a convenient bathhouse for a bath and a local barber for a shave. Ford and Professor DeLoach waited for Firestone, while Edison led the others to a camping place on the Tuckahoe River about three miles outside of White Sulphur Springs. The party named their location Camp Tuckahoe, not only for the nearby river, but in honor of "Indian names being plentiful in this vicinity." The river-side location would make it easy to wash up in the morning. Harvey Jr., along with a male friend, went back to the Greenbrier to pick up his father, Mr. Ford, and Professor DeLoach and returned them to Camp Tuckahoe. The younger men then returned to the resort for dinner, and dancing in the White Ball Room, followed by games of bridge with other younger folk.

Joshua Coleman may very well have been one of the Greenbrier staff who gazed upon the dust-covered campers with a bit of hesitation. Besides working several side jobs, including cleaning and driving rich people around with his show horses and buggy, he also worked as a bellman for the resort. Wearing his uniform, he carried steamer trunks up to guest rooms and assisted with any general requests made by guests. As a "person of color," Coleman was permitted to work at the Greenbrier but would not have been permitted to stay there as a guest. The wealthy guests of the Greenbrier ensured a source of income for everyone in White Sulphur Springs, regardless of race. Coleman, like many others, moved into the town that developed around the Greenbrier to take advantage of plentiful work and to make it easier for his kids to go to school. He built himself a house called the Big House, better known as Dutch Run, which was the first house on the block to have indoor plumbing. His wife Joylette, who found work as a teacher, was pregnant with their fourth child on the night the campers came a calling. Just three days later, on August 26, 1918, while the camping crew passed over Virginia into Tennessee, the Colemans' welcomed their little girl, Katherine, into the world.

Katherine, along with her two brothers and sister, would grow up in White Sulphur Springs in the shadow of the Greenbrier, their lives forever entangled with the resort. Although the resort was open to whites only, some of the amenities were made available to the town folk including movies in the private theatre. The youngest Coleman clearly loved her "daddy" and her "mama," but she also loved numbers. She would later say, "I loved numbers and numbers loved me." She would count everything from trains, floorboards, trees, and even cracks in the sidewalk. She excelled in all her studies, graduating in the spring of 1932 during the depression when she was just 13 years old. The following fall, when she was fourteen, she started college at the West Virginia Colored Institute.

After finishing her freshman year, she took a summer job in the small antiques shop at the Greenbrier, when one day she heard a guest speaking to her husband in French. Katherine, who had practiced the language, was met by the gaze of the woman who asked her, "You understood every word I was saying, didn't you?" The young worker looked the heavily perfumed woman in the eye, just as she had been taught by her family to do when speaking to someone, and said, "Yes, ma'am, I did." The woman was not only stunned, but curious. Katherine Coleman introduced herself, told the woman that she had learned French in college, and explained that she was working to help pay for school. She never saw the woman again. However, later that week, she was approached by a manager who asked her if she was Katherine Coleman. When she told him she was, he told her "The chef would like to see you." When she approached the chef, a larger-than-life figure, he asked her, "You're Katherine Coleman?" When she responded affirmatively, he asked, "Parlez-vous francais?" Oui, monsieur. Un peu" (I speak French a little bit), she responded. At that point, the Greenbrier chef asked her if she would like to learn French from him. So, every Monday morning at 7 AM, the teenager practiced her French with the seasoned Frenchman. She was also introduced to the many exciting flavors and sauces that are staples in French cuisine, and, not surprisingly, developed a taste for more than just the language.

Still, it was her mastery of math, that caught the attention of her professors. She later described her love of math, with its simplicity and elegance, as being apart from life's uncertainties and racisms. What Katherine held onto, was that the answer was either right or wrong, and that the answer today would be the same tomorrow. Setting out with the goal of becoming a research mathematician, although the young woman was not entirely sure what that would entail, Ms. Coleman soon found herself tutoring other college students in math. In 1937, she graduated summa cum laude with degrees in mathematics and French, having the highest-grade point average of any student in the school's forty-six years of existence. After graduating she took a job at Carnegie Elementary School in Marion, Virginia, teaching mathematics and music in a little two-story red building. Named after, and perhaps funded by, Andrew Carnegie, the school was for colored children in the segregated south. It was here, when putting on a play for a school fundraiser, that she met her first husband, Jimmie Goble. Although she would play the piano, and could also sing a variety of soprano parts, she needed a man with a decent singing voice. Jimmie sang bass, and after the play had concluded its run, the two began a courtship resulting in their marriage on November 9, 1939.

In time, Katherine Goble packed her belongings and traveled to Morgantown, West Virginia to begin graduate school at West Virginia University. The school, which had been an all-White college, and wanting to avoid forced integration, had reached out to several highly recommended students to extend offers for higher education. Mrs. Goble, along with a handful of others, would be among the first Colored students to integrate a university.

After a house fire, the couple moved their family to the Hampton Roads region of Virginia, near the largest ice-free harbor in the United States and home to a multitude of military bases. It was also home of Hampton Institute, a college for colored students. Looking for leisurely activities following Sunday church service, the family would sometimes stroll through the tree-lined campus, peaking in classrooms and admiring the school chapel. It was here, below the sprawling hundred-year-old limbs of the famous Emancipation Oak, that Katherine would, in a hushed voice, tell her daughters, "This is where the first reading of the Emancipation Proclamation took place in the South." Imagine, she would say, how it must have felt for a person, who had lived their entire life as a slave, to learn that they were now free.

Determined to find work, Katherine became aware of the National Advisory Committee for Aeronautics (NACA) located at the Langley Field in Hampton. She also learned that there was "some sort of secret government project" going on there and that they are "looking for Colored women who are mathematicians." One morning, after dropping her daughters off at school, Katherine drove her car to the NACA base, and after finding the Administration Building, walked in and filled out an application for a job as a mathematician. She was thirty-four years old. A year later, Katherine touched up her navy-blue tweed pleated skirt and jacket, checked her stockings for runs, and reported to work for her first day as a mathematician for NACA. She would report to Dorothy Vaughan, an honors' graduate of Wilberforce University, also with a degree in math. Originally recruited in 1943 on a temporary basis, Dorothy Vaughan had become a NACA section head in 1951. She was also the base's only black manager. Vaughan's first assignment for Katherine involved working with engineers focused on airplane aeronautics, and although much of the work focused on designing missile warheads during the height of the cold war, there were also discussions about flying humans in outer space.

A decade later, after Katherine had lost her first husband following a heartbreaking illness and had remarried another *gentle man*; and while collaborating on America's first manned orbit of the earth, her love of math would become legendary. At the last moment concerns arose over computer data, and Katherine was called upon by NASA to verify the trajectory calculations of the entire voyage to ensure a safe reentry into the earth's atmosphere. Astonishingly this would all need to be done by hand. At first, the prospect seemed overwhelming. However, Katherine Johnson realized she had been preparing for this moment her entire life. Math—her trusted childhood friend—knew nothing of segregation or soviet threats. Rather the answers were there to be had in the countless stacks of computer data sheets. After a day and a half, she had taken her calculations two decimal places beyond the hulking computers of the time, further factoring answers for eleven different variables.

Compared to the star quality given to many early astronauts, scant attention has been given to the many engineers, mathematicians, physicists, and scientists involved with the early days of NASA and space travel. More recently, in part by the enormous success of the movie *Hidden Figures*, the enormity of what goes into a space launch is better known or understood. Thankfully, the little girl born in August 1918 in White Sulphur Springs, West Virginia, in the shadow of the Greenbrier and the twilight of The Vagabonds visit, has finally been noticed as well.

CHAPTER 14

Shakespeare Reproduced

By all accounts, Camp Tuckahoe provided a good night's sleep for the entire party. The following morning, after washing their faces in the river, the travelers set out for Narrows, Virginia. Harvey Firestone, Sr. later recalled passing many summer hotels located on mountain tops and in the valleys. Their first stop was Sweet Springs, a sleepy little town, with quaint brick buildings. Although many of the well-preserved buildings appeared empty, and occupancy in the nearby summer hotels was said to be less than 25%, the water from the springs was described by one of the campers as "unusually sweet and pleasant." However, not all agreed, as others found it "not very tasty." The town also had a bathing pool where there were a few people bathing, but the campers declined to take a dip as the pool looked as if "the frogs had been bathing more than the people." The party later lunched by an old mill stream at a little place called Gap Mills, the location being chosen only after a local doctor had tried to bully the campers into dining on his front yard. Nonetheless, residents still gathered to pay homage to the famous campers, and one bold citizen went back to his home and returned with a can of maple syrup for Edison as a token of his regard for the inventor.

Apparently, news of his sweet tooth had traveled far and wide. Meanwhile the nearby mill captured Ford's attention for nearly half an hour, with its ancient mechanism in stark contrast with more modern machinery.

After leaving Gap Mills, the countryside became rough and wild as they ventured southward. Narrows, which was primarily a railroad center, also proved to be a bit rough for the campers liking. However, somewhere along the way, they managed to convince one of the citizens, who was well acquainted with the nearby countryside, to help them find a place to camp. The result was one of the best sites on the entire trip. On the evening of August 24*th*, the party set up camp on Wolf Creek, and for the first time were completely alone. Set on a narrow, grassy margin of a broad, limpid creek in which the fish were jumping, the spot made for a beautiful location. Firestone remarked to Edison, "This is the only place we have struck where they don't know any of us." "Good," said Edison, "we shall have a good time here." The only interruption came from a nearby dusty highway, when an automobile drove by and a woman's voice could be heard shrieking, "What the hell is that?" Otherwise, the rest of the evening was completely quiet.

Burroughs later described that, after settling on a camping site, "Mr. Edison settles down in his car and reads and meditates; Mr. Ford seizes an axe and swings it vigorously till there is enough wood for the campfire." Since provisions were again in short supply, and there being no nearby town, Harvey Junior and Kline drove through the countryside, later returning with chickens, fresh milk and eggs. Perhaps the fresh food, along with the surroundings, helped create such great memories for the evening and the site. Naming it Wolf Creek Camp, the Vagabonds marveled at the smooth unruffled stream that flowed by, reflecting their images and the outline of their tents in its mirror-like surface. During the evening, as the party gathered around the campfire, the conversation turned to their trip and West Virginia. Edison remarked that West Virginia had always been a "rather hazy proposition to him" and he was "glad to get a clear impression of it." The other travelers full-heartedly agreed, happy to have seen firsthand the backbone of the Allegheny Mountains. The following morning, Edison, who was known to bestow the virtue of early rising, slept late and came out of his tent with a hand hiding his face in small-boy shame. After breakfast, he went out and collected flowers, while Burroughs and Ford ran off on another bird hunt. Along the way Burroughs told Ford that he had not recalled seeing a single woodchuck on the entire trip.

John Burroughs, who was the only camper to have his sleep disturbed by some grazing horses, reflected that the party was nearly a week in West Virginia and Virginia, crossing many times the border between the two states. He would later write, "Now in one, then, in the other, all the time among the mountains, with a succession of glorious views from mountain tops and along broad, fertile valleys." He further offered the following humorous reflection, "Now we were at Warm Springs, now at Hot Springs, then at White Sulphur Springs, or Sweet Water Springs, soft water and hard water, cold springs and warm springs, and trout brook springs, alternate with each other in these mountains."

Camping life is a primitive affair no matter how many conveniences one has, drawing all to the center usually around a table or fire. Occasionally around the campfire the campers drew Edison out on chemical problems and according to Burroughs "heard formula after formula come from his tongue as if reading them from a book." All agreed that when it came to practical chemistry, he had few equals in the United States. Burroughs also recalled it being easy to draw Mr. Ford out on mechanical problems and that, "there is always a pleasure and profit in hearing a master discuss his own art." As for Professor DeLoach, being a lifelong student of physics and agriculture, the campers found him a storehouse of knowledge when it came to such matters. Burroughs, being the only writer of the lot, was proclaimed by all as the only true literary man in the party and often served as referee in such matters. Lastly, Harvey, Jr., was described as "being all ears."

Although Burroughs was often worn out after a day of driving and described his wits as "being shaken like a bag of corn," he could not help but jump in on a conversation when he overheard Edison proclaim the two greatest works of poetry and fiction in his time as being *Evangeline* and *Les Miserables*. Burroughs told the inventor that *Evangeline* was certainly a sweet and tender poem, but with no elements of greatness, and lacking creative power. As for Hugo's novel, Burroughs believed it had power but could not yet, from an artistic point of view, be considered the greatest work of fiction. Far from it. The eldest member of the outfit told Edison to read any of Balzac's stories and then get back with him. If Edison had been able to invent a crystal ball, he might have hummed a bar or two from *Les Miserables*, the Broadway Musical, as it clearly ranks as one of the greatest pieces of modern theatre.

One morning, as the party ate breakfast, Edison asked Burroughs if Shakespeare could be reproduced, without loss, in common, everyday speech. Edison further commented on how he believed it had lost an audience for the common, more modern man. Burroughs told the inventor that it was hard to put any piece of pure literature into another language without some loss; that Wordsworth wrote poetry in the simple, everyday speech of the people, as did Burns and others, but you cannot substitute other words for those they selected without a loss of poetic value. The elder writer further elaborated by stating that to put Shakespeare's highly artificial, stage-begotten verse into simple language would, in most cases, kill its poetic value entirely. Burroughs believed Shakespeare's style reflected the style of courts and royal personages; that it reflected the feudal ages and all the pomp and circumstances that went with life in those times. Therefore, it is the language of kings and queens and knights and courtiers, and is, as it were, rich in drapery and ornament. Burroughs then offered to those around him with the following example:

> *"Full many a morning have I seen*
> *Flatter the mountain tops with sovran eye"; or*
> *"The jocund day stand tiptoe on the mountain tops."*

Burroughs explained that if you put these wonderful Shakespearean passages into common speech, as used in the early 20*th* century, one would simply say, "*The Sun is shining on the tops of the mountains.*" He made it clear that no person in an ordinary democratic, industrial life would speak as Shakespeare's characters spoke—it would seem preposterous. Shakespeare's writings were deliberately formal and ornate as were the manners and dress of the aristocratic circles of the day, creating an exalted, highly artificial language, and thereby attaining great poetic power.

Burroughs had brought literature with him for his travels including Channing's book on Thoreau. Edison asked if he could borrow it and delved into it a great deal. Edison later asked Burroughs if he thought Thoreau had "not overdone the matter," and whether he thought Channing was a good writer. Burroughs replied that he considered Channing a "clumsy, ineffectual writer," but that Thoreau himself was an "extreme, uncompromising idealist," and although he has "stroked the world the wrong way of the fur," the value of his contribution to American literature "ranked next to that of Emerson's."

Later, while in a dining tent, and perhaps as retaliation for the literary dust-up, Edison accused Burroughs of overeating. Often contenting himself with toast and milk, Edison had many special theories concerning diet. Burroughs in self-defense declared he ate mostly bulky foods, such as cereals, vegetables, and fruit, and very little concentrated food. Burroughs further stated, "If I'm underfed, my capacity for intellectual work falls off." and "We're not all made on the same plan, and it's not safe to generalize in such matters from one's own experience. I come of a lean, hungry tribe-flat-bellied and raw boned, but active and industrious." Edison, who was not impressed, continued to air his ideas about sugar forming crystals in the blood and in the inadvisability of heating food under 212 Fahrenheit. All those present momentarily wondered how he could make such comments, knowing his love of apple pies, sweets, black coffee and cigars. At last, Burroughs offered the following response, "Cane sugar is bad for me, is it Edison? I notice you take two spoonfuls of it three times a day in your coffee. O consistency, thy name is not Edison." Edison, called out for his hypocrisy, quipped, "I know coffee and smoking are bad for me, but I'm usually so good about my eating that I allow myself these little indulgences." The original exchange, or literally dust-up, is quite revealing, especially about Thomas Alva Edison. Henry Ford later told the story of signing a guest book at a hotel after Edison had signed in before him. Besides listing name and address, the guest book had a final column entitled "Interested in." Edison had completed this section by writing, "Everything." For all those who knew Thomas Edison, he literally was interested in everything, including the arts and literature.

The next morning, on August 25th, Ford took his soap and towel to the creek, while Burroughs, Firestone and Edison washed in cold water at a folding camp table. As breakfast was being prepared, many in the group took to target shooting. Edison refrained, but Burroughs again was on the mark. Breakfast consisted of eggs, toast, cereal, bananas, oranges, coffee, and hot water for the elder writer. While eating breakfast under an open-ended dining tent, Sato and others prepared lunch in advance consisting of sandwiches, chicken, and an assortment of other goodies.

Loaded with provisions, the group got a late start from Wolf Creek Camp. Almost from the outset, the passenger cars, followed by the trucks, encountered bad roads on the way to Bluefield, West Virginia. John Burroughs grew very tired, and with Professor DeLoach, boarded a train at Oakvale heading for Bluefield. About 1 PM, Edison was convinced to stop for lunch a short distance from Princeton, West Virginia. Somewhere along the way, the car carrying lunch got a punctured tire, and the others, thinking that lunch was in one of the trucks, drove right by the car letting them fix their own tire not knowing that they were inadvertently delaying their meal by not offering additional assistance. Lunch delayed, was nonetheless enjoyed by all. During lunch Henry Ford chatted with a local farmer, learning much about the surrounding farm country and discussing the absence of bridges over the small streams as a novel southern feature. Edison called these fording places "Irish bridges." The caravan also stopped in Princeton for gasoline.

After leaving Princeton the party started out over what they described as "the first macadam road encountered in many a day." Dirt roads were replaced by broken stone of even size in successive compacted layers, making for a much smoother drive. This type of road construction was pioneered by a Scottish engineer, John Loudon McAdam around 1820. After amassing a considerable amount of wealth in New York, McAdam returned to his native Scotland in 1783 and set about to remedy the terrible conditions of local Scottish roads. The resulting method had roads composed of a compacted subgrade of crushed stone or granite designed to support a load, covered by a surface of light stone. In modern macadam construction crushed stone or gravel is placed on the compacted base course and bound together with asphalt, cement or hot tar. A third layer to fill the interstices is then added and rolled. Today, the engineer is indirectly honored with this revolutionary improvement as his name is generally used when describing types of finished roads.

From there it was on to Bluefield, West Virginia. The smoother roads proved to be a blessing as not only did they make better time in trying to catch up with John Burroughs and Professor DeLoach, but they had also run out of tubes for the 38+7 pneumatic tires on one of the trucks. Harvey Firestone was on top of this potential issue and had ordered a tube to be shipped by parcel post, but when they arrived it was Sunday, and the post office was closed. An appeal to the hotel proprietor prompted him to telephone a friend, who accommodated the senior Firestone by answering a knock on a side door and providing him with the necessary package. With the tube in hand, and reunited with Burroughs and DeLoach, the caravan set out for Tazewell, Virginia with great speed

Camping trip, August 21, 1918, Lead Mine, West Virginia. *Left to right:* Thomas A. Edison, Harvey S. Firestone, Jr., John Burroughs, Henry Ford, Harvey S. Firestone; *seated below:* R.J.H. DeLoach

Resting after lunch, 1918

The Vagabonds, posing with an unknown logger, near Camp Horse Shoe Run, Lead Mine, West Virginia, 1918

Thomas Edison, Harvey Firestone, Henry Ford and John Burroughs enjoying breakfast in camp at Bolar Springs, Virginia

Camping, 1918

View of Camp Robert E. Lee, 1918

Harold Sato, carries one of the cameras for the expedition, 1918

Henry Ford dangling his feet in a stream with Harvey Firestone, 1918

Tents at Camp Tazewell, 1918

Henry Ford presumably drinking a cup of cool spring water, 1918

III.

A NEW HORSE

CHAPTER 15

"You have it, keep at it."

Having no other helper, the young man brought his engine into the kitchen, hooked a wire at the cylinder end into the kitchen's electric power cord, clamped it to the kitchen sink after grounding it to a water pipe, and then asked his wife to trickle gasoline into the intake while he turned the flywheel. It was Christmas Eve 1893 and Clara Ford had also been without a helper while she was preparing a Christmas dinner for extended family visiting Dearborn the next day. Built from mostly salvaged scrap parts, the contraption had steam pipes, steel tubing, a handwheel from an old lathe, and looked much like a small toy cannon attached to a board. The little engine had a hole drilled in it with an inserted piece of wire, and as he turned the flywheel and she dribbled gasoline, Henry Ford waited for a spark that would ignite the mix of air and gas.

Ford had been frantically tinkering on his contraption before the holidays, and at last thought it just might work. Earlier that year he must have sensed that he was embarking on what would become his life's work when he pedaled around Detroit on a bicycle, contemplating future mechanical modes of transportation. A visit to the 1893

Columbian Exposition in Chicago brought him face to face with a Daimler engine from Germany and would further convince the mechanic that he could build his own internal combustion engine. Up to this point his ideas and contraptions had been a hobby pursued in his spare time, while his regular work was still at the Edison Illuminating Company. Yet, again, he had initially gone to work there to gain greater knowledge of electricity while working as an engineer and mechanic hoping to apply this knowledge to his obsession with engines.

At the time Edison Illuminating Company was focused on the residential market and was delivering electricity to nearly all the homes in Detroit. Ford, who was initially given the night shift and a five-month salary, quickly impressed his supervisor with his almost unnatural mechanical skills and knowledge of steam engines. Co-workers marveled at his ability to make engines run better, faster, and more efficient. Soon he was given a raise, moved to the day shift, and was transferred to the company's main station on the southeast corner of Washington Blvd. and State Street. What he did not know or understand he set out to learn, always with his tools and hands.

At first nothing happened. After a quick adjustment, Henry resumed spinning the flywheel and again asked his wife to pour a few more drops of gasoline into the intake. This time the engine roared to life causing the sink to shake violently. Flames shot out of the exhaust, and the kitchen was suddenly filled with black smoke. The engine ran for thirty seconds before sputtering out. The horrible, wonderful, racket was over, but Ford's manic tinkering had just begun. It is not known what, if anything, became of the Christmas meal Mrs. Ford had been preparing just moments before.

Henry Ford was born on a farm in Springwell Township, Michigan. Today it is essentially a suburb of the Motor City, but in 1863 it was a rural forested area with just a scattering of farms. He was born in an upstairs bedroom in his parent's house on July 30, 1863, just several weeks after the Civil War had been forever altered at the Battle of Gettysburg. He was the second child. The couple's first child, a boy born in 1862, died in infancy. Henry would ultimately have five younger siblings: John, Margaret, Jane, William Jr. and Robert.

Henry's father, William Ford, left Ireland in 1847 after his family was essentially evicted from their small stone cottage near the town of Clonakilty in County Cork. Ford's father was just 21 years old when he crossed the Atlantic in steerage class on a packed ship with his parents, John and Thomasina. During the crossing the Ford's suffered a terrible loss, as Thomasina fell ill and died en route to America. She was presumably buried at sea. Recovering from this cruel twist of fate in time the family managed to make it to Michigan and built a log cabin in Springwell Township. Not as much is known about Ford's mother, Mary Litogot, as she, along with her three siblings, was an orphan. She was born in 1839 and grew up in Wyandotte, Michigan. Her father, William Litoget, a carpenter, died when Mary was just three. One account has the carpenter falling from a roof, while another through the ice of the Rouge River. What is known is that she was informally adopted by Patrick and Margaret O'Hern and became the pride and joy of her foster parents and that her siblings all found loving homes.

Ford's parents would meet in 1850 when William Ford signed on as a laborer at Mary's parents ninety-one-acre property in Dearborn. She was ten or maybe eleven years old. A decade later, on April 25, 1861, the two were married. William Ford, who was treated like a son by the O'Herns, continued to work on his wife's family farm and with the help of his father-in-law built the wood framed, two-story, white painted house that would become the home of Henry Ford.

Life on a farm introduced a young Henry Ford to wide open spaces and hard, often tedious, chores, and with time, sparked the boy's imagination. Like many children, the youngster was not enamored with work, but unlike many children, Ford set about how to make his chores easier or how to avoid them entirely. His clever mind also set out on ways to cross the great expanse of this sweeping landscape. Although clever, he was not a particularly good student and it has been said that he never learned to spell, to write with any precision, or to read freely. On the other hand, it has also been said that he was a "master of mechanical logic" knowingly or unknowingly ditching pen and paper for hammer and steel. Ford's lifelong friend, Thomas Edison, was cut from the same cloth and as a boy cared little for his formal school lessons, wanting instead to fiddle with gadgets and chemicals. Perhaps the two youngsters were always bound to be friends.

It seems Ford never entirely warmed to his father or to a life as a farmer, instead clinging to his mother and dreaming of another life somewhere else. While his father did manage to pass along a love for nature and the great outdoors to his oldest son, Henry found life on a farm to be slow and dull. His little sister, Margaret Ford Ruddiman recalled her older brother's dislike of cows and horses, but also recalled her brother taking apart just about everything including Christmas toys. By all accounts his parents provided the children with ample books, toys, and time to allow them to pursue their interests outside of their farm chores. Although Henry was not a fan of books, there was one exception that he held close to his heart throughout his life. The McGuffey Eclectic Reader series was used in Dearborn's one-room, eight-grade schoolhouse and taught fundamentals such as spelling and grammar. More importantly, for Ford, the series were filled with life lessons and stories reflecting what has been described as "American values." It has been speculated that Ford's fondness for rural life, can be attributed more to these lessons than his actual experiences as a young boy living on a rural farm.

Henry's mother took great pride in keeping an orderly house, but also made it a fun place to be a kid. Her love for her children meant allowing them to do the things they enjoyed, and in the case of Henry, allowing him to set up a workbench in the kitchen to help fix his siblings toys and to help with other household repairs. He was crushed when his mom died. She was just 37 years old, and he was not quite 13. Two years later he quit school abandoning any formal path for higher learning or college. However, his mother's influence would go with Ford wherever he ventured and in whatever he did. In fact, after Ford had been one of the world's richest men for quite a while, he told an interviewer, who had asked him for the secret of his success, that "(he) had tried to live life as (his) mother would have wished."

On December 1, 1879, Ford headed to Detroit in search of work and adventure and took up residence with his father's older sister. He quickly found a position at the Michigan Car Company Works, which built streetcars. Six days later he was fired. His father, upon learning of this false start, bailed him out by securing an apprenticeship for him at the James Flowers & Brothers Machine Shop, which designed and manufactured machine parts. The job only paid $2.50 a week, and since his room and board cost a dollar more, he took a night job repairing clocks and watches for a local jeweler. During this time, his friend, Fred Strauss, had taken a job at a nearby factory and the two spent their free time discussing and planning to build a steam engine. The engine never went very far, but Strauss recalled that Henry was always pursuing different ideas and that, "Every Sunday we started something and never finished it."

When Ford returned to the farm in Dearborn in 1882, his father had hoped that his son had gotten any big city wanderlust out of his system and would decide at last to stay put and run the family farm. Ford was nearly twenty so it seemed logical that he might consider settling down. The elder Ford's hopes were quickly dashed when Henry announced that although he would live on the farm, he had accepted a job as a regional representative for Westinghouse servicing steam engines throughout Michigan and Ohio. For the next few seasons Ford worked elsewhere and when he was home, he spent much of his free time in a tool shop he had set up to help with his inventions including a farm locomotive (tractor). During the winter months, Ford also entered a Detroit business school called Goldsmith, Bryant & Stratton Business University. Here he studied mechanical drawings, bookkeeping and general business practices.

In 1886, Ford's father saw another opportunity to make a farmer of his son. Henry, who had developed a regular work routine and had become well acquainted with farm equipment, was offered eighty acres of land known as Moir place. Purchased by his father sometime in the 1860s, the land, named after the previous owner, also included a small house and plenty of forest growth ideal for timber. Ford later recalled that his father's proposition came with a catch as he was to "give up being a machinist." The younger Ford accepted the offer, not because of any newfound love of farming, but because he saw an opportunity to put his mechanical knowledge into practice by setting up a lumber business. Another, and probably much more important reason he accepted the offer, was that Henry suddenly wished to do anything he could to stay in the Dearborn area. On New Year's Eve, 1885, while at a dance at the Martindale House in nearby Greenfield, Ford had been introduced to Clara Jane Bryant. The pretty local girl had left Ford enthralled and certain that he was not leaving town any time soon. In fact, Henry told his sister Margaret that it was love at first sight.

The petite eighteen-year-old with chestnut hair, was not only pretty but popular and smart. She also came from a prosperous local farm family and lived just a short distance from the Ford homestead. Clara was the eldest of her sisters and was generally responsible in assisting her parents for the care of her nine siblings. As a result, she had little time for social activities, boyfriends, or any of the other rituals that are typical in teenage life. However, there was something different about Henry Ford. Clara Jane Bryant was quickly drawn to his intensity and enthusiasm. Ford carried himself well, enjoyed music, and was a good dancer. He also had a secret weapon: a cutter. Back in the day, people traveled by horse and buggy during the summer months and would switch to cutters and sleighs for the Winter months. Unlike a sleigh, which are made for families are larger groups, cutters are meant to be snug requiring a couple to sit close together. Ford's cutter, like most cutters sat low to the ground, but unlike other cutters it was not built for slow straight rides. His cutter was also made for speed, limited only by the stamina of the horse that pulled it. Long before Steve McQueen in the movie *Bullitt* had made a green Mustang the burning desire of every young man, Ford could be seen in his green cutter in the wintry streets of Dearborn with a pretty, young woman by his side.

Ford purchased a large circular saw, got engaged to his sweetheart on April 19, 1886, and set about getting married and running a lumber business. In no time, he built a successful business supplying lumber to not only locals, but also to shipyards and factories in nearby Detroit. Two years later, on April 11, 1888, he married Clara at a ceremony at the Bryant's house with the bride wearing a wedding gown she had designed and sewn herself. The newlyweds moved into an old farmhouse on Moir place, and together planned and built a charming story-and-a-half cottage with a wraparound porch. Made entirely from lumber harvested from the Ford farm, the couple moved into their new home in June of 1889 and settled into what looked like a path the elder Ford would heartily approve. However, it would not last long.

Ford was soon restless. More importantly, he was quickly becoming obsessed with a new idea and continually spoke about building a "horseless carriage." A few years before, while working for Westinghouse, he had been called to repair an Otto engine from England. Nobody knew much about the "silent Otto" combustion engine, but it was thought Ford might be able to figure it out and indeed he did. The young man also came away with a keen sense that a gasoline engine had enormous potential as a viable alternative to the comparably clunky steam engine. Ford, who could be quite headstrong, had a solid partner in Clara as she believed in her husband and his ideas. Ford came to call her "The Believer," and one night the groom excitedly drew a sketch for his bride of his idea for an engine on the back of an old piece of sheet music. In a 1938 issue of the *New York Times Magazine*, Ford went one step further when he stated, "The greatest day of my life was the day (he) married Mrs. Ford" and credited her for supporting him even when others thought he had taken risks not befitting a family man.

Drawing a picture on the back of a piece of sheet music was one thing—building a working model was quite another. The combustion engine and it's firing cycle was a revelation to Henry, and he knew what he didn't know and soon set out to find a way to get a hands-on education with electricity. When he applied for the job at the Edison Illuminating Company, he might have believed it would help him conquer the combustion engine, but he could not possibly have known it would also lead to one of the greatest friendships of his entire life.

In September of 1891, Henry and Clara left their farm life for Detroit and the Edison Illuminating Company. They would never return. By 1893 Ford had become an invaluable asset for Edison's company serving as a trouble shooter and largely working his own hours. Ford was never known as being a hard worker in the traditional sense preferring to work efficiently as opposed to putting in long hours. He was seldom the first one to work, was considered by co-workers to be good natured, relaxed, and was known to be a bit of a prankster. Working as a chief engineer, he doubled his salary to $90 a week and had plenty of down time to tinker. That same year the Ford's moved to 58 Bagley Avenue where Ford built a small workshop in a shed behind the home, and on November 6*th* their first and only child, Edsel, was born.

With a newborn child, and a supportive wife, Ford plowed ahead with his engine culminating with the Christmas Eve breakthrough for which he had been waiting. Typical of Ford, he immediately set upon making another engine, this time a two-cylinder engine that he believed would be powerful enough to run his "horseless carriage." When he was not tinkering at home, or at work, Ford would wander across town picking up any ideas or clues about how to improve his engine. At one point, he even took a teaching job at night at the YMCA so that he could gain access to the school's metal shop.

As Ford continued his exploration, he was often joined by fellow engineers, mechanics, and curious neighbors. Besides the workshop behind his home, Ford also set up another informal workshop across the street behind the Edison facilities. Here he was often joined by two fellow Edison mechanics, Jim Bishop and George Cato, who helped him with physically creating a carriage body. Charles King, another co-worker who had been working on his own engine designs, helped Ford with electrical issues, and Oliver Barthel, a former student of Ford's from the YMCA, helped with just about everything. Ford also went looking for outside help and again recruited Frederick Strauss, the fellow mechanic and longtime friend from his first venture to Detroit over a decade before. Strauss brought with him a wealth of knowledge he had built up since their first foray with steam engines. However, it was his former student, Barthel, who turned Ford onto an important invention from an article in *American Machinist* that described a gasoline engine design and how a machinist might build one on their own.

In the late 1890s, bicycles were all the rage and so it makes sense that Ford would refer to his horseless carriage as a quadricycle. This contraption had a small box carriage frame with a seat in the front of the engine; a steering bar connected to the front wheels; and four bicycle wheels with rubber tires. The engine was a four-cylinder motor with two cylinders that generated about four horsepower. The ignition system was a spark breaker fitted into a hole of the cylinder, and the transmission system featured a clutch and two speeds, low and high, and a neutral gear. A flywheel was spun to start the engine and a gasoline tank held roughly three gallons. To brake, the vehicle would have to be in neutral, and there was no reverse gear. All said it weighed about 500 lbs. and was a far cry from what we consider a car today.

For six months the quadricycle sat in the workshop usually mounted atop sawhorses. Although it had taken shape, there was no moment of immediate completion, but rather daily tedious work that often went late into the night. Ford, who was often hit with setbacks and unanticipated problems, for all practical purposes took up residence in his workshop emerging only occasionally for a meal or nap. After two straight days without rest, at 4 AM on June 4, 1896, a sleep deprived Ford finished his creation. Henry unveiled his quadricycle not to the world or an adoring press, but to his long-time partner and biggest fan, his wife, Clara. That morning he was also with Jim Bishop, who had become his primary assistant in the last stages of building the horseless carriage. This seminal moment in American history was later idealized by

Norman Rockwell in 1953 for the 50th anniversary of the Ford Motor Company. It was still dark outside, and the shed was dimly lit. Detroit, still sleeping, was damp as a drizzle fell across her streets. And then, as if in a moment of comedy (or terror), Ford and Bishop realized that their car would not fit through the door of the workshop. This embarrassing oversight was quickly resolved, although probably not to the liking of any sleeping neighbors, as Ford and Bishop took an axe to the structure and widened the size of the door by knocking out bricks.

After rolling the quadricycle onto a cobblestone alley, Ford reached into the engine compartment and jerked the fly wheel to start it spinning, and with the motor running, he jumped into the driver's seat. With Clara watching under an umbrella, her husband pulled back the lever and was lurched forward into history. Bishop had to hurry ahead on a bicycle to warn unsuspecting pedestrians of the approaching vehicle. At one point, the vehicle came to a complete stop and would not start, but after a bit of tinkering Ford had it running again. Henry was able to successfully drive back to the shop just in time for a quick nap, and a breakfast prepared by Mrs. Ford, before heading back to work at Edison.

The Summer of 1896 was one that Henry Ford would never forget. Just two months after his inaugural voyage, he met his hero, Thomas Alva Edison. In August, one of the company's acting managers, Alexander Dow, invited Ford to accompany him to a professional convention in New York City at the Oriental Hotel. Henry was so excited that he packed a camera so that he could prove to friends and family that he had come face to face with greatness.

On the evening of August 12th, after several days of attending lectures, Ford was invited to a dinner at the hotel's private banquet room and managed to be seated at the same table as Edison. When the conversation turned to electric car batteries, Dow helped the young engineer again when he said, "There's a young fellow here who has made a gas car." While still pointing directly at Ford, he added "I've seen him with his wife and child in his horseless carriage," at which point the young man was bombarded with questions from those around the table. Edison, who was hard of hearing, could not quite make out the conversation and moved closer and ultimately summoned Henry to sit next to him. The always inquisitive Edison was completely fascinated with what the young man described and after peppering him with more questions about how the engine worked, Ford took out a pencil and sketched his engine on the back of a menu. Ford would later acknowledge that he "could convey an idea quicker by sketching it." It helped that the Electric King, was also fond of sketching out his ideas. Edison was clearly impressed and explained to Ford and those gathered at the table that electric cars would not work as they need to be kept near power stations, and that the batteries are simply too heavy. Edison further offered to his listeners that steam cars would not do either as they carry a boiler and fire. Edison continued to encourage the young Ford by indicating that, "Your carriage is self-contained...carries its own power plant, with no fire, no boiler, no smoke." According to Ford, Edison then said: "Young man, that's the thing, you have it, keep at it," and banged his hands upon the table as if to settle the matter once and for all.

These words of encouragement would never be forgotten by Ford. Not only had he met his idol, but the master inventor had validated the direction of his work. Ford would later recall, "The Edison who came into my life (that evening) had been my ideal since boyhood...." Henry Ford was not only infatuated with Edison as an inventor, but also Edison as a worker—someone he considered to exhibit a combination of mental habits that were inspiring. Edison's work ethic, Ford found to be worth emulating, and his concern for improving the lives of common folk was downright heroic. To fully understand the full admiration Ford felt toward Edison consider that the car maker would later co-author a book entitled *Edison as I Know Him*, in which he penned, "Edison has done more toward abolishing poverty than have all the reformers and statesmen since the beginning of the world." So much for the notion that you never want to meet your heroes.

The Oriental Hotel at Manhattan Beach, just a few miles from Coney Island, where the encounter between these two men occurred, also serves as the official location where their famous friendship began. Beginning that August evening at an oval dinner table, with a spirited conversation and a drawing on a menu, the friendship would endure for the rest of their lives. Equally remarkable, is that this conversation between these two heavyweight titans is still going on today over 120 years later. Astonishing in retrospect is that the father of electricity encouraged Ford to not bother with an electric car as the gas engine made more sense. In many ways, the problems outlined by Edison at the banquet table have plagued the electric car and engineers for years. As for Ford, he had just been told by the world's greatest inventor, and his idol, to plow ahead with his ideas. Despite any local naysayers, Ford had always felt in his heart he was on to something big. Now he knew that he was right. When he returned home from New York, Ford told his wife, "You won't be seeing much of me for the next year."

With one car behind him, Ford set out to build a second. He sold his first car for $200 to help raise funds to assist in this endeavor. He also assembled much of the same crew to help him do so. By late 1897, a larger, more elongated carriage had replaced the original boxlike design, and Henry Ford began to look for a vehicle he could manufacture for the masses. He soon realized he would need capital and resources he did not have. Like Edison before him, Ford would need to dip his toes into the pool of finance required in manufacturing operations. To do this, the mechanic would need to be a businessman. At the time, Detroit was home to a multitude of entrepreneurs, many of whom had joined the horseless carriage craze. What Detroit also had was money. By the turn of the century the city boasted forty-four millionaires, many of which were looking for a way to bet a little on the future of the automobile.

Following completion of his third car in the summer of 1899, which was his biggest and heaviest yet, Ford snagged several local financial backers and formed the city's first car manufacturer: The Detroit Automobile Company. Ten days later, on August 15, 1899, Henry Ford resigned from the Edison Illuminating Company and walked away from his title as general superintendent and his $1,900 a year salary. Within a year, the move looked like a gigantic mistake as the new company floundered. The car itself, a rather clunky design, was not a very good automobile, and despite solid capitalization, Ford was found equally wanting with his endless equivocating on a final prototype for production. When he was not wandering about in the woods, he found other ways to hide from the investors, even telling his crew to tell them "(he) had to go out of town." Henry Ford admired Thomas Edison for his work ethic, but he also managed to emulate his hero as neither one worked well for others. Ford had no interest in the car that had been previously designed, and in November of 1900 the Detroit Automobile Company ceased doing business. His first attempt in car manufacturing had crashed and burned. Ford realized the lousy design of his third vehicle, and turned his attention to a smaller, lightweight automobile. He also turned his attention to what he believed was lacking in manufactured vehicles: speed.

The following year articles of incorporation were filed for the Henry Ford Company. Not only had he landed on his feet, with many of the same investors, but Ford also had managed to increase capitalization to $60,000 and he kept his team of mechanics largely intact. However, once again, Henry Ford failed to produce a commercial vehicle for manufacture. The investors knew Ford was interested in building a race car of some sort but did not realize that he was spending nearly all his time on it. Finally, after the primary investors had become frustrated by the lack of progress and brought in an outside expert to review the situation, Ford left the Henry Ford Company. It is unclear if he quit or was fired. While his first go around had ended after a year, this second venture lasted only five months. Things appeared to be accelerating in the wrong direction for Henry Ford. Following his departure, the investors reorganized as the Cadillac Automobile Company and in 1909 were purchased by General Motors Corporation.

Despite these enormous setbacks, Ford hardly seemed to notice, taking on a rather unconcerned, even lackadaisical attitude. Perhaps he simply had a case of racing fever. To be certain, Henry Ford had no interest in allowing wealthy capitalists to dictate his future, instead he would choose his own path and follow his own instincts. Steven Watts, in *The People's Tycoon: Henry Ford and the American Century*, beautifully captures the young automaker, writing, "Ford, made clear that somehow he intended to hold on to a populist ethic of old-fashioned individualism as he strained to create a modern corporate bureaucracy." Around this time, Ford shared with crew members that, "From here in, my shop is always going to be my shop and that's the way it is going to be. I'm not going to have a bunch of rich people tell me what to do." The same year he appeared to be washed up, having burned up all the goodwill and capital he had previously garnered, Henry Ford emerged with his race car. The slender framed, two-cylinder, 2,200-pound, low lying machine would ultimately show that Henry Ford was not finished after all. In fact, it was about to make him a celebrity.

On October 10, 1901, on a dirt track in Grove Pointe Township, a star was born. Coming into the race, the most famous automobilist in the country was Alexander Winton, a Scotsman with a car company in Cleveland, Ohio that bore his name. What his car might have lacked on the roadway, Winton compensated for with an assured belief, bordering on arrogance, about the quality of his automobiles and his prowess as a driver. His confidence was well founded, as he had set the world record for the fastest mile in 1897, and then had done so again earlier in 1901 clocking in at one minute and fourteen seconds. At the turn of the century, automobile racing was new, but had immediately caught the fancy of a new emerging mass culture. Engineers and mechanics throughout the developed world scrambled to build an automobile that might become the first to eclipse one mile in one minute (60 mpg). As for racing, it was, and still is, extremely dangerous, requiring physical endurance and unflappable courage. In 1901, it also required two occupants: one to steer and one to provide balance.

Organizers had agreed the first official automobile race in Michigan would include a program of preliminary events featuring an assortment of electric, gas and steam vehicles, followed by the main event. Henry

Ford and Alexander Winton would be joined by Henri Fournier, a French racer and undisputed European speed champion, W.N. Murray, another record holder from nearby Pittsburgh, and William K. Vanderbilt, Jr., who raced a $15,000 French-built car nicknamed the "Red Devil." These speed demons would vie for a $1,000 cash prize, as well as, a crystal punch bowl, for which Winton had reportedly already found a spot to showcase in his living room. However, Fournier never made it to Michigan and Vanderbilt and Murray were scratched from the race after discovering mechanical difficulties. This left only two entries: Ford and Winton. To be expected the eight thousand or so fans who had packed the grandstand were initially disappointed in learning that only two vehicles would compete in the main event. In retrospect this only magnified the drama that was about to unfold. With Winton as a well-established racer in his appropriately named "Bullet" automobile, up against the local newcomer in an odd-looking vehicle that looked more like a train, the stage was set for a classic David and Goliath moment.

Prior to the ten-mile race, Henry Ford made two slow, overly cautious, practice laps on the unfamiliar track. In fact, as it turned out, he had never even been on a racetrack before. Any attendee, who might have placed a wager on his fellow Detroiter, would have been anything but reassured especially as Winton's Bullet roared around the track with ease. The local engineer and novice racer, who had spent countless hours building the car, had hardly ever driven it. He was joined by his fellow crewmate, Edward "Spider" Huff, who would ride shotgun and act as a human ballast. As race time approached the atmosphere turned electric. Not surprisingly, Winton shot ahead for an early lead, literally leaving his challenger in a cloud of dust around the first corner. For the first few laps, things looked bleak as Ford swung high and wide around the curves all while Huff hung far out of the car to ballast her. At one point, Ford even cut the power to better manage the curves.

Meanwhile, Winton, with his vast racing experience, neatly hugged the inside fence and opened a sizable lead. However, like all good come-from-behind-scenes, about halfway through the race, Ford began to get a better handle on the monster he drove. Slowly he began to cut into Winton's lead. On the sixth lap, thousands of fans roared with approval as Ford, hunched behind the steering wheel with Huff tucked down low, shot up the straight away to tighten the gap. Now the race was on, and the underdog had all the momentum. On the seventh lap, a thin line of blue smoke could be seen streaming from Winton's car, brought on by the relentless and unexpected strain of the challenger. What happened next is best described by the *Detroit Free Press*, who wrote, "Mr. Ford shot by them as though they were standing still...." Ford may not have been a better race car driver, but he clearly had a better car. Engineering had won the day, and Henry Ford's string of inexcusable business failings were erased on that oval track with thousands watching.

With the thrilling victory, Ford was the talk of the town. More importantly, for purposes of being a car maker, he had given himself another chance to get himself back in the game. Following the race Henry Ford agreed to build two identical new race cars, one for himself and the other for Tom Cooper. Cooper, a successful young bicycle racer with a bunch of cash to burn, had caught the racing bug and figured he would try his luck on four wheels as well. As for Ford, he painted his car red and named it "999" after the New York Central monster train. Despite winning his first and only race, Ford was notably unnerved by the four great big cylinder-80 horsepower, one seat, window rattler he had built and designed. So much so, that he and the boys hauled it by horse through the city, and when behind the wheel, Ford quipped, "going over Niagara Falls would have been but a pastime after a ride (in the "999" or her sister car Arrow)." If Ford wouldn't race the "999," Tom Cooper knew someone who would.

In the summer of 1902, Cooper arranged for Berna "Barney" Eli Oldfield, to make the trek from Ohio to test drive the "999." A former bicycle racer with Cooper, Oldfield was also a former boxer who had fought earlier in life as "The Toledo Terror." Half daredevil, but all showman, Oldfield, with his trademark goggles across his face and handkerchief knotted around his neck, would become synonymous with American racing. After meeting Oldfield, Ford immediately acknowledged that he had found a natural racer, commenting that, "the man did not know what fear was." In his first race for Ford, on October 25, 1902, Oldfield powered the "999" to a victory over Winton and a circle of others, winning the five-mile race by a full lap and setting an American speed record. Between 1902 and 1918 he would string together countless victories, making the blue-eyed, square jawed Ohioan, the face of early racing. Years later, when the two were reunited, Henry Ford told Oldfield, "We started together at the bottom, and we owe each other a lot. After all, it could be said that you made me, and I made you." Oldfield, still lightning quick even when not behind the wheel of a car, replied, "but I did a damn sight better job of it than you did."

While Oldfield raced the demon on the track, Ford returned to his original plan of building a car for the people. This time, the third time, would prove to be the charm. A week after the Oldfield victory, Henry Ford set out to mass produce a successful commercial vehicle. His newest backer, Alexander Malcomson, who owned Detroit's biggest coal company, would inevitably clash with Ford much like those financiers who came before him. However, the coal man brought along more than money. He also brought along a young Canadian born coal yard cashier named James Couzens. In time, his contributions to Ford would be immeasurable.

By 1903, an actual assembly plant had been established on Mack Avenue, and a prototype for a new car had been completed by Ford and his team. They would call it the Model A. Unable to build parts on site, Ford and Malcomson struck a deal with the Dodge Brothers to provide engines, transmissions, and axles for the new automobile. John and Horace Dodge, two rough and tumble brothers from western Michigan, had received offers from other companies including Oldsmobile but picked Ford. Meanwhile Malcomson sent Couzens to watch over the automobile venture, while he tended to his coal empire. More importantly,

Couzens would do what he could to keep Ford on task. On June 16, 1903, or thereabouts, the Ford Motor Company was born, and by that same summer Model As were being assembled, driven out of the plant, and given a rudimentary test run around the nearby blocks. The car was a solid vehicle, and fit Ford's vision of a simple, reliable car. Harold Wills, a visionary toolmaker and draftsman, who had been with Ford through the initial business misfires, set the letters F-o-r-d in cursive script. The logo, purposely set with the now famous *F*, was meant to look old-fashioned representing a symbol of timeless quality.

As the cars were assembled, the company's balance sheet shrunk to a paltry $223.65. When the menacing Dodge brothers came a knocking and demanded payment, they were paid in shares of stock as there was simply not enough cash on hand. Finally, on July 15, 1903, the company sold its first car for $850.00 to Dr. E. Pfennig, a dentist from Chicago. Within a month the balance sheet would swell to over $23,000. As sales climbed, Ford emerged as a dominant force on the shop floor, offering words of encouragement, lending a hand, and otherwise providing leadership to his team. By the end of the year the company had built over 1,500 vehicles, and employed well over 100 assemblers, designers, and mechanics. In many ways, this new Henry Ford was aided by James Couzens. Although the young clerk knew nearly nothing about cars, he was sharp as a tack in matters involving finances, billings, and sales. What Henry Ford did not want to do, he simply let the young Canadian tackle. This trade would prove sublime for nearly everyone involved except Couzens' other boss: Alex Malcomson.

With business on the upswing, Ford and company did not rest on their newfound success. Not only did they continue to make improvements to the model A, but they also set about creating a radically different car. This car, was bigger and faster, and would be called the Model B. To help sell the public on the engine for the Model B, Henry Ford would climb back behind the wheel for his second and final time. Ford had reacquired the Arrow racer from Tom Cooper after Cooper had wrecked the beast in a 1903 race. Cashing in on his new fame, and craving even more publicity, Henry Ford announced he would outfit Arrow with his Model B engine. A publicity stunt to be sure, Ford then proclaimed that he would set the world record for the mile driving the modified car across the ice-covered surface of Lake St. Clair. Harold Wills and Spider Huff, helped Ford make the necessary modifications to the race car installing a V-shaped fuel tank, replacing the old tiller with a steering wheel, and adding a "blast breaker" windshield.

On January 12, 1904, on a bitterly cold day on a lakeshore north of Detroit-bordering the United State and Canada, the dynamic duo of Ford and Huff battled the weather and ice in their second and final race. Prior to the race, local farmers had cleared a path through the snow and spread hot cinders from a nearby powerplant along the course. The hope was that this might cause enough melting of the ice to create traction along the surface. In preparations for the race, Ford had noticed he was having trouble keeping his foot on the accelerator as the car slid across the ice, so it was decided that Huff would crouch on the floor of the car and hold the gas pedal down with his hand. This would allow Ford to concentrate entirely on steering the glorified sled across the frozen lake. A poster, serving as an advertisement for the race, predicted that Ford "...would clock a mile in 36 seconds. Come and see the fun." Braving the cold, a crowd consisting of locals, family and friends, watched as Ford and Huff were hurled down the ice. Their reward was witnessing a new land speed record of 91.37 miles per hour. Years later Ford would ponder this massively dangerous undertaking recalling, "I shall never forget that race...When I wasn't in the air, I was skidding, but somehow, I stayed top side up and, on the course, making a record that went all over the world."

In performing under such terrible conditions, Henry Ford had created the best advertisement money can buy. If you bought a Ford, you were purchasing a reliable car. Oh, and it was fast too. In the early part of 1905, Ford Motor Company moved from the Mack Avenue factory to a much larger facility on Detroit's Piquette Avenue. By then a workforce of nearly 300 was cranking out 25 cars a day. The Model B was joined by the Model C, as annual profits soared to $200,000. This enormous upswing in sales and production, was not based on good publicity alone as the assembled team was loaded with talent, and the vehicles were well- built, solid little things. Equally important was the alliance forged between Henry Ford and James Couzens.

Originally, when Malcomson had entered the automotive world, he feared that the venture would be viewed unfavorably by bankers and other business partners in the coal business as his credit was already stretched thin. This, in part, was another reason he had transferred Couzens to the automobile business. Working side by side, Ford and Couzens developed an understanding of how to make things work efficiently. They also began to share a vision for the future of the Ford Motor Company. As Couzens got closer to Ford, he drifted further from Malcomson. Things slowly reached a breaking point. Malcomson, who at times had seemingly drifted away from the venture entirely, reemerged with the idea that the car company should focus on building an expensive, luxury automobile aimed at prosperous customers. The coal man was looking for large profit margins. Ford, on the other hand, envisioned inexpensive cars, built through a standardized manufacturing process, and aimed squarely at the masses. These differing visions created an impasse. Ultimately, in the summer of 1905, Malcomson decided to make his move by submitting a formal proposal to have Couzens removed, and the management responsibilities given to him. When Couzens refused, he called for a vote to have him fired, and with the directors deadlocked, Henry Ford cast the decisive vote to keep Couzens. Alex Malcomson, frustrated by his inability to wrestle control from Ford and Couzens, decided to wage war by announcing that he would start his own car company to compete directly with the Ford Motor Company, even as he remained the treasurer. Furthermore, he would use the Ford Motor dividends that had been pouring into his bank account to do it—but plans made largely in spite often backfire.

In November 1905, Henry Ford and James Couzens set up the Ford Manufacturing Company, the function of which was to provide parts used at Ford Motor Company. With business booming, the Dodge brothers already could not keep up with demand anyway. Every member of Ford Motor Company was given stock in the new enterprise, every member but one: Alexander Malcomson. The next move was to cut off dividends in the Ford Motor Company, while simultaneously starting them with the Ford Manufacturing Company. This essentially cut out Malcomson, while not angering any other stockholder. If he was going to create his own car company, he would not do it with profits from Ford Motor Company. The Board of Directors also demanded his removal as treasurer citing his obvious conflict of interest. Finally, in 1906, Malcomson realized his situation was dire so cut his losses and sold his stock in the company. The result left Henry Ford with 58.5% of the company and James Couzens with 11%.

Out of deference to Malcomson, the Ford Motor Company had developed the Model K. This six-cylinder automobile, weighing in at eighteen hundred pounds, was priced at $2,800. With the coal tycoon out of the picture, the company came untethered and was free to focus on lighter, less expensive cars. Henry Ford was firmly entrenched as the man in charge, while James Couzens, his staunchest ally, was second-in-command. The vision they shared, was simple, yet revolutionary. Some have called it one of the world's greatest "paradigm shifts." Rich folk were more than welcome to buy a Ford, but the focus would be on the common man. Farmers and mechanics would not only want to drive a Ford but would be able to afford to buy one. This market was immense, and Ford told anyone who would listen, that "there are a lot more poor people than wealthy people. We'll build (a) car for the poor people."

The Model N, which premiered in the 1905-1906 season, weighed in at just over 1,000 pounds and sold for $600. The culmination of many months of hard work, this vehicle was an instant sensation. The vehicle had a streamlined body, offered reliable engine performance, and at a time when the average car cost over $2,000, it was a bargain. As a result, sales skyrocketed. In 1906, after selling more than 8,500 cars, Ford Motor Company emerged as the top sales leader in the industry. Harvey Firestone, the tire maker from Akron and good friend to Henry Ford, scrambled to keep up with orders from the Piquette Avenue factory.

Still, the Model N was not without fault. The car was rather small and offered a rather unimpressive ride. Henry Ford and his engineers soon gathered again in the same room where the Model N had been conceived. Just outside of Ford's office on the second floor of the plant, this unimpressive space had been nicknamed the "experimental room." It was also where Henry Ford spent most of his time. Looking to improve his car, Ford, along with a cadre of engineers, developed a list of components that could be improved. The room contained a blackboard, several drafting desks, a kitchen table and a few chairs. At any given time, it was also filled with plenty of parts, new and old. People, plenty of people, also crammed the room, with Henry Ford usually in his favorite rocker or stretched out on a low-lying couch. Like the furniture, and the people, the room was also filled with ideas, all vying for a spot on the blackboard. As they gathered day after day, Ford came to imagine a bigger, yet lighter car. Initially considered incompatible, Henry Ford searched for a design that would wed these opposites. First, it was agreed a simpler design could reduce the weight. Secondly, using different, or better, materials, could also unlock the key to a lighter automobile. Ultimately, Ford, along with his chief designer Harold Wills, and John Wandersee, whom Ford had originally hired as a sweeper only to make him into a self-taught metallurgist, discovered vanadium steel. By adding this element, steel is made a stronger and lighter alloy. It was in this room, with these men and these breakthrough ideas, that the Model T was first conceived. In just a few short years, the world would witness a miracle

CHAPTER 16

Birthplace

The campers had become anxious. With unexpected stops, poor road conditions, and countless mechanical issues, it seemed they had not made good time when traveling through Pennsylvania and West Virginia. Driving fast towards Tazewell, Virginia, with open roads and no mountains for a change, the party put the pedal to the medal. Somewhere along the first hard-surfaced highway, part of the caravan got off the road, perhaps so used to being in the mountains where there were scarcely any roads at all, that when they came to two roads they got lost. Otherwise, the Blue Grass Country was on its best behavior and the rolling hills and patches of woodland lightly shrouded in a purple haze soothed any jolted nerves and ironed-out wrinkles that the rutty roads had left in their memories.

When the party finally reached Tazewell, Virginia, Edison drove on to find a camping site while Firestone remained behind near a hotel to direct the other vehicles as they approached. With some vehicles getting on the wrong road earlier in the day, Firestone remained behind for several hours and took the opportunity to talk with local citizens, including a circuit Judge of West Virginia. Finally, Sato and another crew member named Wilmott came along in one of the Ford cars and picked up Firestone. After driving a bit further, Firestone, Wilmott and Sato came upon a party of young people from Bluefield, who invited them to stop and eat with them. Firestone would later state that he believed they were intrigued with Sato, finding his Japanese heritage to be a novelty. After eating they drove on under the direction of the Bluefield youngsters, and finally met Harvey Jr. and Mr. Ford who had returned to find them.

Driving back to Camp Tazewell, the party was reunited as dusk neared. After dinner, which was later than usual, Firestone and his son took a walk through the countryside and heard some people off in the distance singing and playing accordions. Struck by the evening music and laughter, father and son spoke about the great pleasures and joys found in the simple parts of life. The elder Firestone, playing his role as dad, took the opportunity to teach his son another life lesson: Happiness is found in simple pleasures, with family and friends, and regardless of the Firestone wealth, a simple life would result in an abundance of enjoyment.

The following morning, around 10 AM, with the camping equipment packed and the travelers ready to roll, the caravan broke camp and made a short run through Lebanon, Virginia, on their way to the immediate objective of Hansonville, Virginia. It was August 26, 1918. After reaching these destinations in fair time, the road to Abingdon, Virginia, stretching some six miles, was quite rough. One of the campers described this patch of road as putting his Christian training and patience to a test. Burroughs further remarked, "These roads are the most damnable and despicable in the United States, probably built by the Germans as being one of their most cruel acts." He even went so far as to stop people along the road to inquire as to the cause of its current condition making it clear to anyone who would listen that he found it unacceptable. Edison, who had picked the route, and was bounced around like everyone else, remained rather tight lipped during the other campers' complaints.

An hour later, the group reached Abingdon, Virginia. Just north of the Tennessee border and tucked into the southwestern side of the Commonwealth at the foot of what is now known as the Virginia Creeper trail, sits this gem of a town. Founded in 1778, the city, located in Washington County, boosts a population of roughly 10,000 as of this writing. Blessed with a natural beauty found in so many Virginia towns, it features many fine arts and crafts, along with a smattering of great restaurants and pubs, including the *Tavern* located in the oldest historical building in Abingdon. Originally built as a tavern and overnight inn for stagecoach travelers, the *Tavern* lists famous guests including Henry Clay, Andrew Jackson, and the famous designer of Washington D.C., Charles L'Enfant. Nearby, also in the heart of town, sits *The Martha Washington Inn & Spa.* Originally built in 1832 as a private residence for General Francis Preston (of the War of 1812 fame) and his wife Sarah, the living room now serves as the main lobby of the hotel.

But any talk of Abingdon must include its crown jewel, the world-famous *Barter Theatre*. Opening fifteen years after our travelers rumbled through this Virginia town, the *Barter Theatre* has been in operation since 1933. A young aspiring actor, Robert Porterfield, had an idea that would bring this theatre to his native southwest Virginia by allowing local farmers to barter products from their farms and gardens to gain admission to a play. Money was always appreciated, but so were vegetables, dairy products and livestock. Afterall, it opened during the great depression. According to the theatre, the idea of trading "ham for hamlet" caught on quickly and by the end of the first season, the theatre had "cleared $4.35 in cash, two barrels of jelly, and a collective weight of gain of over 300 pounds." Besides dogs and barn animals, actors performing for this quirky theatre company also had to contend with the town jail which sat directly below the stage.

When Harvey Firestone and friends visited Abingdon, they most likely would have seen some of the buildings that house the current theatre as the earliest theatrical event is believed to have occurred there in 1876. The main building, which was made the town hall in 1890, is one of those buildings that quickly catches your attention. In fact, along with the other buildings that now make up the theatre, you can hardly keep your eyes off any of it. Built of solid brick in a multi-floor A-frame design, it is not surprising that this main building was also used as a fire-hall up until the 1990s complete with a large fire alarm mounted to the roof. Apparently, the actors learned to simply stop their performance when the alarm sounded, remaining frozen in position, and resuming when they got the "all clear."

Today a visitor is greeted with a large marquee proudly proclaiming "The State Theatre of Virginia" along with a multitude of flags mounted across the roof's edge. Inside the theatre is equally charming. The main stage, named Gilliam stage, has 505 seats with 216 of those in the balcony, and the Barter stage II located in a nearby building, was once a Methodist church and holds an additional 167 seats. Many of the interior furnishings were salvaged from the *Empire Theatre* in New York City when Robert Porterfield learned that the Empire, originally built in 1875, was to be demolished. Given just one weekend to remove furnishings and equipment, Porterfield and a crew of helpers, came away with seats, light fixtures, carpeting, paintings and tapestries. Portfield even managed to take the lighting system which was originally designed and installed by Thomas Edison himself. The theatre crew's ingenuity and resourcefulness would have surely pleased the Wizard of Menlo Park.

Famous alumni of *Barter Theatre* include Gregory Peck, Patricia Neal, Ernest Borgnine, Hume Cronyn, Ned Beatty, Gary Collins, Wayne Knight and Larry Linville. Today, despite the most recent pandemic, the theatre is going strong, playing year-round to sold out audiences and although there are no more animals running about or fire alarms regularly going off, when one visits this majestic theatre, you're sort of glad they one time did.

Beyond Abingdon, Virginia, and much to the delight of the travelers, the roads turned better again with pavement all the way to Bristol, Virginia-Tennessee. However, again the caravan had become divided into three parts, described as "without much semblance of good marching order" and "something like Caesar's description of Gaul." After arriving in Bristol, a fair-sized town even in 1918, the disjointed party faced an immediate problem. Unlike many of the smaller towns they had passed through, Bristol had many streets or possible meeting locations, and they had no idea where to rendezvous. The car carrying the younger Firestone was the first in town and the occupants decided to camp outside the Hotel Bristol with the hope that the others would find them near such a landmark especially since it was approaching lunch, and all were hungry. Their hunch soon paid off.

The hotel was the setting of a rather active lunchtime, and seating for the entire camping party was found to be difficult. A request for seating together was dismissed out of hand by the head waiter, who responded by stating, "the tables are not large enough for such an arrangement." The waiter, who may not have initially recognized the famous campers, made it clear he did not care much for making any effort to seat them together. After they had been seated in various locations, but before they had ordered, word spread that Thomas Edison was part of the lunch party. Apparently, the head waiter did an about face, quickly had the tables rearranged to seat the entire party together, and even went to the kitchen to personally supervise the food preparation. By all accounts, the service they received was "wonderful" with the Senior Firestone even commenting about how the party had been doted upon.

Bristol is a unique, if not remarkable, location. The main street divides Virginia and Tennessee, and with a single step one might stroll from Bristol, Virginia to Bristol, Tennessee. Being downtown is literally like being in two places at once. Anyone who says you can't be at two places at the same time has never been to Bristol. Or maybe they forgot. On July 10, 1852, Joseph R. Anderson, having a hunch that railroads might meet near the border of Virginia and Tennessee, purchased 100 acres from his father-in-law's plantation. The King plantation property he acquired included forty-eight acres in Tennessee and fifty-two acres in Virginia. Two days later he chose the name "Bristol" for his planned city. The following year he built a combined residence and business house on what is now the southwest corner of State Street, generally considered the Birthplace of Bristol. In 1856, the conjoined cities were separated, and Virginia's Bristol became incorporated into Goodson, Virginia. The train station, which sits on the Virginia side, continued to be called the Bristol Station, so in 1890, Goodson once again took the name Bristol.

Today, the twin-cities share a water system, library, emergency medical services and a historic downtown where main street is the state line. These siblings even take turns paying the electric bill on the city's giant 1,330 bulb electric welcome sign, declaring Bristol (Va. & Tenn.) "A GOOD PLACE TO LIVE." Made famous throughout the years, the Bristol sign was donated to the city by the Bristol Gas and Electric Company in 1910. Now an icon on State Street, the sign was originally erected on top of the Interstate Hardware Company building near the railroad tracks off State Street and contained a more peculiar slogan: "PUSH! THAT'S BRISTOL." Within a few years the hardware company became concerned that the weight of the sign would cause long term damage to the building, so it was moved in 1915 to its current location where it rises 25 feet over the line dividing Tennessee and Virginia. When Ford and company visited Bristol, the slogan remained the same which at times provided locals and visitors with a good laugh especially when lights burned out resulting in the sign to proclaim "PU __! THAT'S BRISTOL." In 1921, the Bristol Advertising Club offered a contest for the best new slogan for the sign, with the winning slogan being, "A GOOD PLACE TO LIVE."

Word of the whereabouts of the famous lunch guests quickly travelled throughout the town, and before lunch was finished, a mayor and others holding political office organized an impromptu reception party as a welcome to Bristol. When the meal was finished many came to greet the camping crew, including local newspaper men. Henry Ford, recently turned politician with his Michigan senate run, was asked, "What will you do if you're nominated by both Democrats and Republicans?" The automaker, described as bright eyed and brown skinned from his life in the open, laughed like a boy, and vigorously responded, "Why, I will pitch a penny to settle it, or leave it to my secretary to decide." He also made certain the nearby reporters understood he had no desire to be in politics, further saying, "I would give a million dollars to be out of the matter and I wouldn't have been in it except for the request of President Wilson."

The famous guests were also greeted at the impromptu reception by the local Edison phonograph agent, the local Ford agent, and the local Firestone agent, Charles J. Harkrader. Whether these agents were thrilled, or perhaps more filled with trepidation, we are left to ponder. What we do know is that Firestone and Ford later went to the Firestone branch store to pose for pictures and to pick up more truck tires. What we also know, is Burroughs, who had no local agents, was said to have sat back and enjoyed the festivities. The writer later said that "when a man of letters like himself goes a-junketing with...such well-known men as Edison and Ford, he shines mainly by reflected light." He noted that the public is often eager to press the hand and hear the voice of such giants, but a writer of books excites interest only now and then. However, while the crowds gravitated towards Edison and Ford, Burroughs did have his share of schoolteachers, editors, lawyers, and nature lovers who took notice in him.

Some in the group, made a quick stop to the telegraph office to send a message to F.L. Seely at the Grove Park Inn, in Asheville, North Carolina, with notification that the travelers would arrive in his backyard either Tuesday evening or Wednesday morning and asking him for assistance with arrangements for a camp on Sunset Mountain. After returning to the hotel, many other locals had joined the festivities including a Mr. W.H. Cox, a leading merchant, who insisted that the party stop by his farm (Maplehurst) on their way out of town. The senior Firestone accepted his invitation on behalf of the travelers, at which point Cox phoned his wife, and was heard to say, "Sarah dear, I am going to have some very distinguished guests, Mr. Edison, Mr. Ford and Mr. Burroughs. They will be out in a few minutes and have everything all primped up. They want some milk, apples, etc..." He seems to have not mentioned Firestone, who had accepted the invitation. He then asked if it would be permissible for him to take the leading newspaper editor with him, and after being told it was totally agreeable to the party, Cox rode in one of the cars while the editor rode in another. When the party arrived at the farm, which was about ten miles outside of Bristol and described as "a very fine place," Mrs. Cox would not come outside. Mr. Cox managed to get his daughters outside to meet the entourage, but his wife would not venture out. Firestone and Ford asked if they could go inside, and after getting permission to do so, found the local merchant's wife baking in the kitchen. Sarah believed her husband had not given her enough notice to be properly dressed for such an introduction. When Ford and Firestone insisted that she must come out to meet Thomas Edison, she was only persuaded to do so, if they would wait five minutes for her to change her clothes. After running upstairs, Mrs. Cox eventually emerged outside wearing her finest Sunday dress perfect for the pictures taken outside of the family farm.

Nine years after the party visited Bristol, the city that straddles two states would be ground zero for what has been described as the "Big Bang" of country music. In July of 1927, Ralph Peer, a producer for Victor Talking Machine Company, came to the Tennessee region with a new technology. What he brought with him was the new Western Electric electronic microphone. Before this time, making field recordings was difficult and required bulky equipment with the resulting music often of poor quality and of limited use for the public. Most musicians in the early 1900s had to travel to New York City to record their music. When Peer showed up in Bristol, it was as if he brought the New York studio with him, making it possible to record music to be released to the public of a much higher quality.

At the turn of the twentieth century, Thomas Edison's company, along with Alexander Graham Bell and Charles Sumner Tainter's company, American Graphophone (better known by their distribution company name Columbia), was well immersed in the phonograph industry. The third major player in this industry was the Victor Talking Machine Company. Victor, formed by machinist Eldridge Johnson, was originally named the Consolidated Talking Machine Company. Johnson had originally worked for Emile Berliner, inventor of a hand-cranked device he called a gramophone. After Johnson developed a better process for recording and duplicating records, he was sued by Berliner for patent infringement in 1900. Ultimately Berliner lost the lawsuit. The following year, Johnson renamed his company Victor Talking Machine to commemorate his court victory. As for Edison, it is reported that he along with Henry Ford and Harvey Firestone, somewhere along their 1918 trip, stopped at a local music company to listen to phonographs and to personally inspect a stock of his New Diamond Disc. Phonographic.

Most recordings of this time featured band music, comedians or opera. Records used raw sound energy without the assistance of electricity making the use of string instruments almost impossible as they did not produce the required volume to be fully recorded. In the early days of recording there were no amplifiers or microphones. Instead, artists sang or played in front of a horn (cone), with the sound waves traveling down the horn, creating a vibration pattern into a metal diaphragm. The pattern was then transmitted to the recording stylus, cutting a groove in a soft wax blank. Recording sessions of the time were often described as frustrating, or even comical ordeals, with artists being required to be positioned in different locations or literally on top of each other. An opera singer might be required to sing from the corner of the room while another musician stood directly over the horn. The goal was to direct as much sound as possible into the recording horn with the hope of making a recording that picked up all sounds or instruments equally or otherwise appropriately. Much of this was done through trial and error and could take a great deal of time and patience.

In 1918 a new type of recording also emerged. Looking to increase listening audiences, and facing competition from radio broadcasts, recording companies created a new category of "ethnic recordings." Previously unrecorded music was welcomed by those who had not heard their local sounds recorded, while also holding a novel appeal to mainstream audiences. Artists with accents became all the rage, with Irish, Jewish, and Negro musicians recording and performing for live music broadcasts. Soon this ethnic category was expanded to include "hillbilly" music from Texas and Oklahoma and from Appalachia.

Following 1919, the Western Electric Company's J.P. Maxfield and H.C. Harrison began work on an electronic recording system that would improve sound volume and allow for acoustic instruments to join the recording bonanza. Their system was introduced in 1924 and employed an electronic amplifier and a newly designed microphone. These breakthroughs captured softer sounds, including acoustic instruments, and allowed musicians more freedom in positioning themselves behind a microphone. Now, each singer might be heard equally behind a separate microphone. No longer would the opera singer be refined to the corner of the room. Another great advancement was that the equipment was portable, making it possible to record in remote locations outside the company studio.

The Victor Talking Company had begun issuing electronically produced recordings to the public in 1925 and made phonographs available later that same year. By this time, Maxfield and Harrison had designed an affordable acoustic phonograph with a six-foot-long folded horn allowing an acoustic phonograph to have the frequency response necessary to adequately reproduce electronically recorded music. The Victor Orthophonic Victrola was the first consumer phonograph designed specifically to play electrically recorded phonograph records. Victor advertisements from the time, with the trademark Smooth Fox Terrier "Nipper" listening with puzzlement to a phonograph, use the phrase

"Electronically Recorded" to show their state-of-the-art recording technology. An interesting sidenote is that the dog, Nipper, was born in Bristol, England in 1884. In 1898, three years after the dog's death, the owner, having happily recalled the Terrier listening intently to a wind-up Edison-Bell cylinder phonograph, painted what would become the advertising icon. The painting was entitled "His Master's Voice," and Nipper's image has been used by Victor, HMV, RCA, EMI, and JVC, making the dog an advertising legend.

By 1927 Victor Talking Machine Company, later named RCA Victor, had successfully released "hillbilly" records, and was in search of broadening this new market. Ralph Peer, who had been hired as a producer for Victor in 1926, had conducted location recording sessions throughout the South in the 1920s. These early recordings, unique but flawed, caught the attention of Victor Talking Machine. Victor, lagging behind their competitors in capitalizing on the country music boom, hired Peer to build its catalog. "I had what they wanted," Peer later recalled. "They couldn't get into the hillbilly business, and I knew how to do it."

Ralph Peer identified Bristol, the small city near several Appalachian areas known for distinctive music traditions, as an ideal center for making recordings. Bristol was also part of an urban area with 32,000 people called the Tri-Cities, with Johnson City to the south and the new "planned" city of Kingsport to the west. If Appalachia had any urban centers, this area might be considered one. For this trip, Peer would also implement a new business model, signing artists to three separate contracts: a recording contract with Victor that paid $50 per side up front, as well as a modest royalty on each record sold; a song publishing contract with Peer's newly formed Southern Music Publishing Company; and a personal management contract with Peer himself. He also brought with him $60,000 that Victor had appropriated for his southern trip.

On Friday, July 22, 1927, Peer and two recording engineers, Edward Eckhardt and Fred Lynch, set up a portable recording studio in the Taylor-Christian Hat Company building on the Tennessee side of State Street, and set about the business of finding talent and repertoire. Compared to Atlanta, Savannah, and Memphis, Bristol had a relatively small population and would need to draw upon the region. Peer initially turned to local broadcasting stations, music stores, and record dealers to help in the search for talent. At first, few candidates appeared. Not discouraged, Peer then turned to the editor of a local newspaper, who after realizing the great benefit to be derived to the community, decided to run a half-column story/advertisement on the front page. This worked like a charm, with a deluge of calls from the surrounding mountain regions pouring in the next day. Singers, many who had never visited Bristol during their entire lifetime, arrived by train, bus, horse and buggy, and on foot.

Ralph Peer later recalled that, "The best things in life seem to occur by pure accident. We strive to accomplish something worthwhile; success finally comes to us, but usually from an unexpected source." One of the first calls received by Peer, was from Jimmie Rodgers who telephoned from nearby Asheville. He told Peer he was a singer with a string band, had read the newspaper article, and was quite sure Peer would find his group to be satisfactory. Peer assured Rodgers he would be given a try-out and to make the visit to Bristol. Peer was delighted to be alone in the studio with Jimmie, quickly realizing the personal and peculiar style along with his yodel, just might spell success. However, Peer could not possibly have known that Rodgers would become "The Father of Country Music." The Carter Family, known affably now as the "The First Family of Country Music," travelled to Bristol from nearby Maces Springs, Virginia. Their talent was immediately obvious to Peer and to any others blessed to have been present during the legendary recording sessions.

Ernest V. "Pop" Stoneman was the original reason, in part, that Peer had picked Bristol as a recording site. Stoneman was already a recording veteran when he showed up in Bristol, having recorded some two dozen sides for Victor Talking Machines and countless other sides for different labels, including Edison. He would be the first artist to record at the Bristol sessions. Red Snodgrass, who along with his small dance band worked at a local Bristol hotel, recorded just one song on the second to last day. It has been speculated that Peer was staying at the same hotel and allowed Snodgrass and his band to record as a favor. As for the hotel, it is not known if it was the Bristol Hotel where the Vagabonds had vied for adjoining tables less than a decade before. Perhaps the most remarkable performer, was a blind fiddler, singer and composer from nearby Princeton (Pipestem), West Virginia, named Alfred Reed.

Over the course of two weeks, seventy-six performances by nineteen different acts were recorded on the 2nd and 3rd floors of the building used by the Taylor-Christian Hat Company located at 408 State Street. On Monday, July 25th the recording sessions began at 8:30 AM and ultimately ended on Friday August 5th at 3:30 PM. What happened in between was legendary. The schedule was as follows: Monday, July 25, (1927), Ernest Stoneman ; Tuesday, July 26, Ernest Phipps and His Holiness Quartet; Wednesday, July 27, Uncle Eck Dunford and various artists, and The Blue Ridge Corn Shuckers; Thursday, July 28, The Johnson Brothers, Blind Alfred Reed, and El Watson; Friday, July 29, B.F. Shelton, and Alfred Karnes; Saturday, July 30, & Sunday, July 31; Peer auditions new acts and takes a driving tour into the mountains; Monday, August 1, J.P. Nester and Norman Edmonds, the Bull Mountain Moonshiners, and the Carter family; Tuesday, August 2, The Carter Family, the Alcoa Quartet, and Henry Whitter; Wednesday, August 3, The Shelor Family, Mr. and Mrs. J.W. Baker; Thursday, August 4, The Tenneva Ramblers, Red Snodgrass and His Alabamians, and Jimmy Rodgers; Friday, August 5, The West Virginia Coon Hunters and the Tennessee Mountaineers.

The term "country music," is really the result of record executives advertising music and musicians based on what they assumed different audiences would like. "Hillbilly music" and "race records" are two examples of such early marketing, with the first catering to whites and the latter to black audiences. On the other hand, a genre is generally defined as a category of artistic, musical, or literary composition characterized by a particular style, form, or content. Through time, genres can blur or splinter, as musical styles borrow from each other. As such, country music is now both a genre and the marketing term used to describe hill or non-city music. It was forged from a variety of American music, including Southern gospel, bluegrass, Western, Cajan, blues, and Tin Pan Alley. Today, country music is a national, and international, behemoth.

At the turn of the century, there were no standard band lineups or instruments. Voice was the primary instrument on the Bristol Sessions, mixing traditional Scots Irish ballads with African American folk traditions. In fact, of the 76 recordings made in Bristol, only 7 could be considered instrumentals. The Bristol Sessions are considered by many music historians, to be the first major field recording sessions to emphasize voice. Peer reportedly did not hesitate to offer alterations to the performers style or delivery, knowing the artist would sell more than any given instrument. All in all, he understood the voice must be heard above the band, and he had the equipment to make it happen.

The acoustic instruments brought to early country music were often created by rural musicians or purchased through mail order catalogs, borrowing upon instruments from the British Isles (fiddle), the European continent (guitar and mandolin) and from Africa (banjo). In total, 35 of the 76 performances would be considered traditional pieces. These early musicians also brought their church and faith. The people of southern Appalachia considered faith a central component to everyday life, with the church being an essential part of creating a strong community. Music was an important way to share and express faith. As a result, many religious songs were recorded at the Bristol Sessions, with 31 of the 76 performances being gospel songs.

In 2003 the Bristol sessions were placed in the Library of Congress on its inaugural list of the fifty most significant historical recordings as compiled for the National Recording program. Today, Bristol is home to the Birthplace of Country Music Museum—a must see for any music fan or history buff.

CHAPTER 17

Schlieffen's Plan

Shortly before two o' clock on the afternoon of May 7, 1915, a German submarine under the command of Lieutenant Walter Schweiger, spotted a large steamer off the southern coast of Ireland. With general orders to sink any British vessel, the German sub shot and hit the starboard side of the ship, right behind the bridge. At first nothing happened, then a moment later an "unusually heavy detonation followed by a strong explosion cloud...she has the appearance of being about to capsize. Great confusion ensues on board...In the bow appears the name *Lusitania*." A little more than twenty minutes later the ship sank below the sea taking with her 1,195 men, women and children including 128 Americans.

One week before this tragedy, on May 1, 1915, New Yorkers turning the pages of their newspapers, probably wondered about an unusual notice that had been placed next to a Cunard Line advertisement announcing the sailing of the Lusitania that day. The notice had been placed by the German embassy in Washington and warned passengers that the waters around Britain were considered a war zone and might be subject to an attack. In retrospect the warning is haunting and downright odd. Odder still is how or why it was placed in the newspapers, and what consideration, if any, the U.S. government might have taken to such a "notice." Americans were clearly outraged and confused by the attack of the *Lusitania*, yet many were still not ready for war.

That same Spring, as the weather began to finally warm from a brutal and cold winter, clusters of poppies sprung up on and around the battlefields of Belgium and France. Seeds may lie dormant, but if the soil is disturbed it causes the seeds to germinate and grow. The ground, which was disturbed by fighting and washed in blood and sacrifice, would return red poppies again in the Spring and Summer of 1916, 1917 and 1918. The sight of these flowers caught the eye of a Canadian solider and physician by the name of John McCrae who noticed how the flowers had sprung up near the burials around the artillery position he was in. Believed to have been written following the death of a friend, he wrote these words:

> "In Flanders field the poppies blow
> Between the crosses, row on row,
> That mark our place, and in the sky
> The larks, still bravely singing, fly
> Scarce heard amid the guns below."

Long before this European tragedy and the sinking of the *Lusitania*, there were plans for peace and plans for war. At the turn of the 20*th* century, diplomacy was an art, a convoluted European art, built on centuries of conflict, alliances, royalty, and embassy intrigue. Much, of course, has been written about the diplomatic breakdown, tangled alliances, and the bizarre happenstance of the assassination of Archduke Franz Ferdinand of Austria in an alley in Sarajevo ultimately ushering in a world war. What is surprising is that very few people are familiar with the *Schlieffen Plan.* Perhaps even more surprising, is how few people in Germany had any knowledge of this plan especially since it is considered as one of the most important documents written in any country in the first decade of the 20th century and some historians have even argued that it is one of the most important documents of the last hundred years.

Field Marshall Alfred Van Schlieffen was appointed Chief of the German Great Staff in 1891 and set about almost immediately devising ideas on how to assure his country's security. What the Field Marshall realized, and what most German military strategists have also realized, is that Germany sits in what could best be described as a lousy location when it comes to potential hostilities or war. Just to the West, sits France, historically hostile and made even more so following the defeat in 1870, while Russia, having forgiven France and Napoleon long ago, sits just to the East. As such, Germany faced the real possibility of a two-front war, and with history giving us 20/20 vision in a rearview mirror, that is exactly what happened in both world wars.

As Schlieffen surveyed Europe in the early part of the 20th century, this is what he observed: France had a series of forts built to rebuff a German attack yet they had very little else in the way of a military; Russia was no doubt weaker than Germany as well, but was protected by vast amounts of land and a treaty of neutrality with Germany so long as Germany did not attack France; Austria was an ally, but a weak ally at best; and Britain was separated from the mainland of Europe and could be ignored at least for a time. Given the landscape, and the Field Marshall's belief that Germany was stronger militarily than any other country, he believed that should there be a war, an overwhelming offensive against France was the surest way to victory. By committing most of Germany's strength, it amounted to an "all-in" strategy that could risk everything, but Schlieffen was convinced that attacking France would work. Beginning in 1894 he had begun to craft plans for eliminating French fortresses along the France-German border.

With time he began to realize that Germany's artillery alone would not sufficiently damage the French forts and that the best approach was to find a way to outflank them. However, this would require German troops to cross Belgium and Luxembourg, both neutral countries. Although multiple war games staged between 1899 and 1904 placed German troops in these neutral countries, it was the final plan, commonly referred to as the "Great Memorandum," that was beyond shocking. Not only would neutrality be infringed, but it would also be purposely shattered. Under the final plan, almost the entire German army would line up on the Swiss frontier and in a huge sweeping movement, march straight across Belgium passing just North of Brussels, then across the plains of Flanders and into the French frontier. The plan called for this to be done within 22 days. On the 31st day the German line would then turn south to envelop Paris from the West, with the goal of driving the French towards the left wing. The plan was to essentially encircle the French army, pinning them in, and hopefully within 42 days crushing their army once and for all. The victorious German army would then be free to take railway cars back across Germany to the eastern front where they could take their time in defeating Russia or convincing them to seek peace.

Schlieffen retired in 1905, continuing to refine this plan up until his death in 1913. With a passion for military history, and a driving work ethic, he often worked past midnight molding his creation, envisioning a recreation of Hannibal's crushing victory when Roman legions were successfully encircled in 216 BC. Such a massive and decisive victory could surely be recreated with the power of the German army, and unlike Hitler, who would devastate the West with his infamous Blitzkrieg campaign only to fail by trying to do it again in the East, Schlieffen was rightly afraid of the massive space that is Russia. Schlieffen was also concerned about the size of his country's army. It was not that he believed the army should be bigger, but that it should be an optimum size to move quickly and effectively through the Belgian and French road networks. His focus was also the infrastructure of France and Belgium, and how many soldiers it could accommodate without creating what might be best described as a bottleneck or traffic jam. For Paris to be taken in six weeks, it would require enough troops, pushing through given sectors, and at a speed that allowed for a continuous flowing column. The retired military man knew the margin of error was razor thin, and that any deviation or delay might leave Berlin vulnerable to encroaching Russians or other massing armies to the East. His final writings on the matter contain a hint of desperation regarding troop size, troop speed, and the exact specifications of the right wing of the great wheel turning through Belgium and northern France. The plan required an understanding of mathematics, together with a dose of reality. Like all war plans, it also needed a little luck.

In the Spring of 1918, the German army launched a series of attacks commonly referred to as the Spring Offensive. In a war that had otherwise become a legendary stalemate, this was more than a calculated risk. It was more an act of desperation, brought on by years of utter fatigue. With Russia finally out of the war, Germany poured an additional half million troops from the Eastern front into France, hoping to punch a hole through the lines of the Western front, finally capturing Paris. This would defeat France, hopefully deflate the British, and perhaps allow the Germans to claim victory before millions of fresh American doughboys could properly enter the fight. The stakes were high, but victory close. Paris, the coveted prize, was just barely out of reach. In fact, the Germans were encamped in what would be considered "commuter distance," just 40 miles out, when they started their "final" push in July of 1918. Panic gripped the capital city in anticipation of the city falling to a bitter enemy. On July 14, 1918, the German army set about to end the war, and just as Robert E. Lee had crossed into Pennsylvania on a date with destiny in Gettysburg, the German commanders must surely have felt that this was not part of any prior war plans.

Four years earlier, in August of 1914, declarations of war were greeted with enormous enthusiasm throughout European capitals. Crowds gathered on streets and in town squares to cheer and sing patriotic songs. In Berlin, the Kaiser appeared high atop a balcony to address throngs of Germans and told them about their fateful hour, commanding them to go to church, kneel before God, and to pray for their gallant army. In Paris cries of *Viva La France! Viva L'Armée* rang through the streets and train stations from crowds waving handkerchiefs and hats. Similar scenes played out in England, providing the French great relief, while going largely unnoticed, or at least not fully understood, in Germany. The British, who under the Schlieffen plan, it was assumed, would stay out of the war initially, were carrying on at the outset like the other combatants.

The German army mobilized 715,000 men while the Austrians mobilized an additional 600,000. Along with men, thousands of horses were also readied for battle as armies at the turn of the 20*th* century remained Napoleonic in their dependence of the horse. Thousands of young German soldiers boarded trains awaiting to whisk them to the French border. Departure was nearly as festive as the declaration of war, as German soldiers marched to war with flowers in the muzzle of their rifles, and French soldiers dusted off their heavy wool uniforms in the sweltering August heat to much fanfare. In Russia soldiers paraded in their new uniforms and sang the Russian national anthem to the Tsar, signaling another ominous sign for Schlieffen's plan.

The German soldiers had the furthest distance to travel and were expected to traverse 20 miles a day while pulling their supplies and weapons to keep on their strict timetable. Before it was over, the right wing of the army was expected to march some 200 miles to the French capital. The French, on the other hand, only had to take up arms and prepare to defend their border, making for much shorter movements. On August 14, 1914, a small British Expeditionary Force disembarked near Boulogne, France near the Northern Belgian border, marking another unexpected response as by all accounts they should have been sitting on the sideline deciding what to do. However, the biggest military turning point, occurred several weeks before. On August 2, 1914, the Germans delivered a 24-hour ultimatum to Belgium demanding the use of its territory and threatening to consider her an enemy if she did not comply. Not only did Belgium not agree to such demands, but the British cabinet stepped in finding this to be a cause for war and thereby made their own demand on August 4th to cease and desist by midnight. When they failed to do so, Britain, France, Russia were at war with Germany. Austria would declare war on Russia on August 5th and against Britain and France on August 12th after those two countries declared war against them.

Comprised of roughly 320,000 men, the German 2nd army crossed into Belgium on August 4, 1914, with the goal of attacking France and ultimately sacking Paris. Starting on August 5th, and lasting twelve days, the Battle of Liege is generally considered the first battle of W.W. I. and resulted in a moral victory for the allies. General Emich, with the force of 30,000 men, met very stiff resistance and sustained heavy losses attempting to capture several forts along the Meuse River. The Belgian Forts were stouter than anticipated, and the Belgian King, Albert I, was unexpectedly solid as well. Upon receiving word of the approaching German army, he did not retreat or surrender, but instead ordered the destruction of river bridges, railway bridges, and tunnels. He also gave orders to hold the forts at all costs. The German army, overly confident in their size and strength, expected nothing more than a "show of defense" from the Belgians. They also did not expect the world to be engaged in every move they made. When Belgian citizens were seen valiantly defending their homeland, being killed for no reason, the Germans immediately faced a publicity crisis throughout the world including in the United States. The stiff defense also slowed their movement towards France.

The French Commander-In-Chief, Joseph Joffre, decided that France could not wait to be attacked and launched several offensives at the same time as the German Chief of Staff Helmuth Von Moltke. These battles, known as the Battle of the Frontiers, also took place in August, inflicting equal damage on both armies, and further slowing the German plan for a quick victory. One of the battles, the Battle of Mons, was the first encounter between British and German forces on the Western Front. The British Expeditionary Force (B.E.F) made up of four infantry divisions and one calvary division had arrived on the French coast on August 16*th*, and although they ultimately had to retreat under superior rifle fire and much larger German forces, the British had made a good first showing.

By the end of August, the Germans had made many hard-fought gains in Belgium, and, in fact, had even managed to penetrate the French border. What followed has been referred to as the 'Great Retreat," and which would carry the French armies and the B.E.F. back near the outskirts of Paris over a two-week period. However, in retreat a funny thing happened. The French positions were made stronger, while the German positions were made more tenuous as they became stretched in their chase, fighting further and further from their home. No doubt the French and British forces were dejected while the German forces were refreshed in the belief that the plan was working after all. As the fighting continued, with the stakes seemingly getting higher, the German lines began to get off-track. The army which was intended to stay north and west of Paris under the Schlieffen Plan began to slide south and east as it pursued the French armies. By September, the German First army was essentially lined up directly against the B.E.F and French troops in a position approximately 40 miles east of Paris, when it should have been well West of the city. All the while, French troops began pouring in from the French railway system. Any attack of Paris would not be from the north as planned, and any hope of encircling the city was out of the question. As the French forces continued to strengthen, it was the German army that had a seriously exposed right flank.

On September 4, 1914, the Germans launched an attack east of Paris, making some progress, only to see the allies carry out counter offensives from September 5*th* through September 8*th*. These dates are significant to the original war plan, as they essentially represent the halfway mark of the 40*th* day since the outbreak of hostilities, the day believed by Schlieffen to be the day that Russia would finally be able to assemble sufficient strength to launch an offensive against Germany in the East. The clock was ticking for Germany.

The French Commander, Joseph Joffre, authorized General Maunoury's Sixth Army, comprising of 150,000 men, to commence an attack to the right flank of the German First Army. Starting on September 6th, when the Germans turned to meet the French attack, a 30-mile gap appeared, and although French and British troops poured into this gap, they were unable to encircle the German army. Exhausted the French troops received aid from 6,000 French reserve infantry troops ferried in from Paris by some 600 taxi cabs. The next evening, the French launched a surprise attack against the German's second army, resulting in a further widening gap between Germany's armies. This left open a full-scale Allied advance to the Marne, and eastern tributary of the Seine River. Sensing the risk to the right wing, and perhaps impending catastrophe, the Germans ordered a stop to the offensive against Paris and to fall back to safer more defensive positions beyond the Marne.

The Battle of the Marne, as it would come to be known, was a strategic victory for the allied forces as they had succeeded in halting the German offensive, even managing to recapture small amounts of lost ground in the process. However, the battle came at a staggering cost for all with the French incurring an estimated 250,000 casualties, the Germans roughly the same amount, and the British nearing 13,000. If the Battle of the Marne did not effectively kill the Schlieffen plan, the next few weeks surely did. After falling back, the German army encamped on the high ground of Chemin des Dames ridge on the North bank of the river Aisne. Determined to not lose all the land taken in their early gains, the Germans began digging defensive trenches to secure positions and to avoid further withdrawals.

Starting on September 12, 1914, and lasting three days, allied forces consisting of the French Sixth Army, the British Expeditionary Forces, and the French Fifth Army, tried unsuccessfully to dislodge the Germans in what came to be called the First Battle of the Aisne. In what would be a preview of things to come, the Germans showed the superiority of using defensive warfare by deploying machine gun fire and heavy artillery. Soon both sides grew weary of the futility of frontal assaults. This was followed by what has been referred to as the "Race to the Sea." From late September through early November, the allied forces and the Germans attempted to outflank one another by trying to capture unoccupied territory on each other's northern flank resulting in a continuous movement towards the French-Belgian coast.

By the second week of October, as British reinforcements arrived daily to shore up allied defenses, any potential gap in the western front through which a decisive advance might be made, was narrowed to an area of Belgian Flanders. In what has been described as one of the dreariest locations in Western Europe, a battle raged until late November with both sides hopelessly trying to punch a hole through this last narrow corridor of Flanders wet open fields. With Winter quickly approaching, and both sides completely exhausted, the fighting, which had been at a fever pitch, began to slow and then completely stopped. All the moving and marching also came to a sudden halt. Everything seemed to stop. Everything, except for the digging. After five solid weeks of fighting, neither side was willing to give another inch. The allied forces had successfully rebuffed the sacking of Paris, even managing to push back the enemy line. The Germans, after making such large gains in the early days of the war, dared not take another step backward. Front lines were consolidated with trenches, wire fences, mined dugouts, bunkers, and reinforced concrete emplacements. The result was one continuous defensive line, 475 miles long, stretching from the North Sea to the Mountains of Switzerland. And, when the first lines were sufficiently fortified, second and third defense lines were created, and likewise fortified. Two weary armies, exhausted and no doubt in shock, stared across a narrow and empty zone of no-mans land. All was quiet on the western front. To the east, the shadow of Russia loomed large in the minds of the Germans. As for the Schlieffen plan, for all practical purposes, it had been laid to rest.

CHAPTER 18

Before World War II

In the United States, Teddy Roosevelt arrived in New York to little fanfare in May of 1914. His exploration of the River of Doubt (Rio da Du'vida), a black colored, previously uncharted tributary of the Amazon, that snakes through treacherous jungles filled with Indians armed with poison tipped arrows and stocked with man eating piranhas, had nearly killed America's most famous camper. The robust former President had become delirious with infection and fever, enduring emergency surgery on his leg, and at one point, had demanded the party leave him behind in the jungle to die alone as he was convinced, he was so slowing the expedition that he was putting everyone at risk for survival. His twenty-three-year-old-son, Kermit, who was one of the members on the expedition, would have none of it and managed to bring his father out of the jungle alive. The *New York Times* reported that he was "thinner and older looking," and many wondered if he may have lost his interest in politics.

Although he would never be the same, the Bull Moose wasted little time in talking politics. On June 30, just two days before the Serbian nationalist assassinated the Archduke Franz Ferdinand, Roosevelt launched a full throttle attack on Democrats and Republicans believing they were underestimating potential aggression from Germany. However, most Americans were paying little attention to the events unfolding in Europe. On August 4th, President Wilson officially proclaimed the neutrality of the United States and urged the American people to keep an open mind and not rush to judgement. The following day, Roosevelt, knowing that the country had no stomach for a major war, did an about face, and came out in favor of Wilson's policy of neutrality.

To better understand the reluctance for war, it is important to remember that it had only been forty-nine years since Grant and Lee had met in Appomattox to negotiate the surrender of the Confederate army, thereby ending the Civil War. Bruised and battered the county had weathered the great storm and slowly rebuilt itself from within. The Spanish American war, fought between 1898 and 1901, was a much smaller conflict, and although it had made the United States a world power, the country was not about to squander any newfound prominence on the world stage. After the sinking of the *Lusitania*, Americans were clearly outraged and confused, yet many remained wary of war. President Wilson responded by declaring, "There is such a thing as a man being too proud to fight. There is such a thing as a nation being so right that it does not need to convince others by force that it is right." Starting on May 15, 1915, Wilson sent Berlin a series of protest notes until at last an apology of sorts was returned by the Germans with an agreement to pay indemnity and a promise to not target any other passenger liners.

Although the United States was not formally at war in 1915, this did not stop many young American's from joining the fight. Some sailed to England, while others made their way up to Canada to get around America's initial declaration of neutrality. These early soldiers provided Americans with their real-life stories of what was going on in Europe's great war. One such fellow, by the name of Arthur Guy Empey, gave his firsthand account of a Yank who went off to fight the Kaiser in an autobiography of sorts entitled, *Over the Top*. The book, which was quite popular, gave his readers a gripping tale and told of the terror faced by soldiers when they were required to come out of the trenches and literally go "over the top" into no-man's land and enemy fire. He also gave Americans a phrase that a dozen years later Erich Maria Remarque would use as the title for one of the most famous war novels ever written: *All Quiet on the Western Front.*

While there were others like Empey who joined the battle early on, most young men did not. Furthermore, many Americans sought to find ways to end the war immediately. One such person was Henry Ford. Initially distracted in the early days of the war by the Dodge brother's declaration to produce their own automobile after having worked for Ford as auto suppliers for many years, Ford made it known he was against America's involvement in the war. Ford initially used his publication, the Ford Times, to convey pacifist views and later to question the wisdom of intervention in this massive conflict. In 1915 he reprinted George Washington's Farewell Address, with its warnings of the dangers to getting involved in foreign entanglements. Ford, believing he represented the interest of the common man, insisted that ordinary folks wanted peace and that it was politicians and the ruling class that sold the public on war.

Quickly, Ford developed a national reputation as an anti-war activist, warning that the United States was confronted "by the danger of militarism," pledging at one point to burn his factory to the ground before he would turn it over to the war production. Ford would later claim that he inherited his dislike of war from his mother. His dislike of war was also rooted in his vision of creating a new and better world through engineering and industry, and his dislike for old and archaic concerns. To Ford, European rulers represented a by gone world set on interfering with America's glorious future, and although many business owners saw profit in war, he had dedicated himself to improving human life, not destroying it.

In late 1915 Ford began to look for ways to put his beliefs into action and found a most unusual partner in a radical Jewish Hungarian pacifist named Rosika Schwimmer. Ms. Schwimmer, who was a journalist, had been trying to find ways to end World War I through some form of neutral mediation, regularly traveling and speaking at anti-war gatherings. The American press, often aligned with Schwimmer and her ilk, made her a favorite spokesperson. Upon learning of Ford's views of war, she used her connections and managed to schedule a personal meeting with Henry Ford. In early November, Schwimmer, along with another American pacifist by the name of Louis Lochner, visited Ford's Dearborn home for a luncheon where she laid out plans for convening a commission of representatives from neutral nations who would work to negotiate a peace acceptable to the warring countries. Often described as bespectacled, portly and squat, perhaps to suggest that Ford was not simply taken with the beauty of a European woman, Schwimmer won him over before lunch was even finished. Ford not only rifled off a series of telegrams to President Wilson, but later signed on to what would be one of the most questionable and downright embarrassing chapters of his life.

The Peace Ship, as it came to be known, was a Scandinavian American ocean liner named the Oscar II, leased to Ford for his ill-fated journey. After great fanfare, the Peace Ship set sail for Europe on December 4, 1915, with high hopes for brokering a peace before Christmas, providing the ultimate gift for a world in need. Henry Ford initially enjoyed favorable press as a peacemaker with noble intentions, but he would quickly learn that peacemakers can be turned into naïve buffoons by the same ink and paper. There were early signs that the voyage would not go as planned when many prominent individuals, including Thomas Edison and John Burroughs, offered their moral support, but politely declined their invitations to join Ford who found himself largely alone, without any close friends, on a mission for which he really knew little about and for he which he was the designated pitchman and chief financier. As a result, he also found himself, the primary target of ridicule and scorn. Alton Parker, the former Democratic candidate for President in 1904, offered the following scathing view: "If we could only be sure that all the other nations would estimate him as we do, as a clown, strutting on the stage for a little time, no harm could come of it, but we need have no such assurance. The chances are that his antics will be taken seriously, and they will tend to bring us into contempt, if not hated."

On the ship was Dr. Charles Griffen Pease, head of the Anti-Smoking League; editor S.S. McClue; Judge John B. Lindsey of Denver; Governor L.R. Hanna of North Dakota; and what can only be described as an oddball mix of counter conformists advocating everything from temperance to sexual liberation. Halfway across the Atlantic the carnival became a full-blown circus. Arguments broke out between different factions on the ship, and the journalists assigned to covering the voyage, who were not drunk or passed out at the bar, wired back stories of the complete and utter dysfunction of the Peace ship with one headline back home decrying, "Ford Ship is Scene of War." Henry Ford quickly realized his massive miscalculation, keeping to himself when possible, and only venturing out of his quarters at mealtime. Ford also found himself at odds with nearly everyone on board the ship, finding many to be "intellectual snobs" with views so impractical as to be taken seriously. The millionaire entrepreneur turned industrialist was completely amused that while he ate his meals in the third-class dining room, many of the other self-proclaimed delegates for the people, vied for the best tables in first class. His amusement was probably tinged with agitation knowing that he was footing the bill.

Stuck at sea, Henry Ford wasted no time in plotting his escape. At the first stop in Oslo, Norway, Ford checked himself into a hotel, went into hiding, and after finding a doctor to announce he had fallen ill, he booked his own passage home. While the Peace Ship was never met by cheering crowds, and the war grinded on for many more years, Ford managed to earn the respect of the reporters assigned to cover the ill-fated voyage, being described as honest, genuine, and otherwise as a good man. A *New York Times* article stated the reporters on the ship, "have learned an immense respect and liking for the charm and abilities of Henry Ford." As for Ford he summed up the odyssey by stating, "I didn't get much peace, but I learned that Russia is going to be a great market for tractors." Ford's initial misgivings about World War I as being wasteful, economically destructive, and a hindrance to long term growth, would in time be proven correct especially in hindsight of a second World War which would shortly follow the first. In the meantime, Ford, and the country, began to explore a position of war preparedness if, and when, the time might come.

By early 1917 Germany was beginning to feel the full impact of an Allied blockade and concluded that if American merchant ships were going to continue supplying the Allies with food and arms, that it had no choice but to start sinking those ships. This, of course, would probably bring the United States into the war as would a recent intercept shared by the British intelligence with Washington. A cable intended for Germany's ambassador in Mexico had contained a proposal for Mexico to enter the war on Germany's side in exchange for the return of Texas, New Mexico and Arizona to Mexico once victory was secured. For once, Germany had not miscalculated.

On April 6, 1917, congress voted to declare war on Germany after President Wilson had asked congress for a "war to end all wars," and on June 26 the first 14,000 U.S. Infantry troops landed in France to begin training for combat. The Commander of the American Expeditionary Force (AEF) was General J. Pershing, who arrived in France, parading with his armies on the 4*th* of July to commemorate American Independence Day. The symbolism was by design and lost on no one. Just as the Marquis De Lafayette had made certain the American's received French assistance during the American Revolution, the United States would now return the favor to the French people.

Americans were well received in Paris. After three years of war, the Doughboys efficacious attitude lifted the spirits of the French citizens who had seen their boys killed by the thousands and their homes and villages destroyed. Almost the entire war had been fought in their backyards. Everywhere American soldiers went, they assured the French that the war was going to be settled soon, leaving little wonder as to why they were often the guests at French homes for dinner, drinks, and sometimes more.

While the people were impressed, the Allied Commanders were not. The Americans were viewed as completely deficient in military skills and training. It is now hard to imagine, but at the time, the American Army, made up of approximately 107,000 men, was only the seventeenth largest army in the world. They were also poorly equipped. The United States Marine Corp., although numbering in excess of 15,000 and considered to be battle ready, was scattered across the globe, primarily in Central America fulfilling commitments as remnants of the Spanish American War. The French and British top brass initially saw the American forces as capable for replacement or subordinate units, further wishing to put them under Allied command and not under American command. General Pershing, who would win great praise both during and after the conflict, insisted that there should be a United American Army under American command. This greatly lifted the morale of the soldiers, giving them a sense of purpose and pride. Just as importantly for the home-front, this helped avoid any appearances that American soldiers were being improperly used or sacrificed by other Allied Commanders. If Americans were going to die in battle, it was going to fall squarely on American Commanders and General Pershing.

On November 20, 1917, three regiments of the Army Engineers were attached to support the British 3rd Army's attack at Cambrai, thereby commencing the United States military engagement with the enemy. The battle, which raged for three weeks and marked the first large scale use of tanks in any military engagement, resulted in 77 American casualties. A little over three years after the outset of World War I, American blood had been shed in France. Later the Americans would notch their first victory at a place called Cantigny located North of Paris in the Somme region. On May 28, 1918, some 4,000 troops from the American 1st Division under Major General Robert Lee Bullard, aided by French air cover and heavy artillery, captured the village held by the German Eighteenth Army commanded by Von Hutier. However, it was a battle several days later, that would forever change how American soldiers were viewed by Allied Command and would make the U.S. Marine Corp. legendary.

Several months before, on March 3, 1918, Germany and Russia signed the treaty of Brest-Litovsk essentially terminating hostilities against each other, thereby allowing the Bolsheviks to put down any anti-Bolshevik uprisings in what was for all practical purposes a civil war, and which allowed Germany to move nearly all its forces from the Eastern front to the Western front. This amounted to thirty-seven divisions or roughly 500,000 troops, giving the Germans numerical superiority over the Allied forces. However, Germany knew that with American forces pouring into Europe daily, any numerical advantage would not last long. So, just as it had been at the outset of the War, Germany went on the offensive seeking the elusive crown jewel as outlined in the original Schlieffen plan. As always, they had to take Paris to end the war.

Hearing the desperate pleas from the Allies, General Pershing committed the 2nd and 3rd Regular Army divisions, consisting of 50,000 soldiers to assist in defending the French Capital. The 2nd Division was comprised of two Army regiments, the 9th and the 23rd, and two regiments of Marines, the 5th and the 6th. Starting on the last week of May, the Allied forces battled the Germans, with the American contingency beating back the enemy at Chateau-Thierry, just 50 miles Northeast of Paris. The Germans fell back into the nearest fortified position just a few miles away in an area called Belleau Wood.

Before the Marines landed on the Island of Iwo Jima in 1945 and so famously hoisted the Stars and Stripes atop of Mount Suribachi, in 1918 they entered a "quiet sanctuary of graceful old growth trees teeming with birds and game (and Germans)." Just outside of Paris, these woods were the private hunting grounds of wealthy Frenchmen remaining largely undisturbed for centuries, and until then, untouched by the war. The retreating German soldiers all but disappeared into this densely wooded forest and all but dared the French and Americans to follow. The French exhausted from the chase, began to pull back and suggested the Americans do likewise, but Americans would not retreat from the gains made over the prior few days. Instead, they dug in, even managing to withstand German attempts to break out. When the French soldiers again urged them to retreat, the response was famously summed up by Captain Lloyd Williams of the 5*th* Marines, who said, "Retreat? Hell, we just got here." Before World War I, the Marine Corps. was a relatively small force that specialized in protecting U.S. interests abroad, largely performing security duties on military bases. Although known for being impeccably trained, Pershing and others remained skeptical of the Marine Corps. ability to serve as a major ground force especially against the battle tested German army.

Separating the Marines from the enemy was a large open wheat field, and after the Americans, dug in, they discovered that any attempt to move across the field towards the forest, would be met by machine-gun fire from well protected German positions just inside the woods. James Harbord, who had originally been Pershing's Chief of Staff and who was an old friend of the General, had been promoted to Brigadier General and put in charge of the 5*th* and 6*th* Marine regiments. What happened next is truly remarkable, if not in retrospect, inexplicable.

On June 6, 1918, under the command of Harbord, the Americans launched a daring attack against the entrenched German defenses without the aid of any prolonged artillery barrage. Getting to the edge of the woods, across the open field, was difficult, yet wave after wave of Marines did just that. By chance, a dashing, if not flamboyant, reporter named Floyd Gibbons from the Chicago Tribune, was with the Marines and recorded a bit of what happened and what was said. Early on, Sergeant Dan Daly, is said to have rallied his squad while crossing the vast openness between the Americans and the and the edge of the woods by yelling out, "Come on you sons of bitches! Do you want to live forever?" Gibbons, who was completely unarmed, crawled across the field only to be shot three times including in his left bicep, his left shoulder, and his left leg. The reporter was not alone in sustaining injuries, as the Americans suffered nearly 1,100 casualties on the that first day alone.

Three weeks later, on June 26, 1918, Major Maurice Shearer sent a message to top command that simply said, "Woods are now entirely U.S. Marine Corp." What happened in the forest is haunting, as well as, legendary. Countless Americans and Germans never left those woods, and those that did rarely, if ever, spoke about it. What we do know is that the fighting was fierce, almost barbaric, and often involved hand to hand combat. The Americans were initially successful in pushing the Germans back through the forest, followed by a German counterattack, and then wave after wave of counterattacks by both sides. Those that ventured into the woods after the battle described trees literally being decimated and such carnage that there was little left of any soul who perished. In total the Americans sustained 9,777 casualties including 1,811 killed in action. Although German casualties were not recorded it is believed they were quite high, with another 1,600 captured. The battle would become an essential part of Marine Corp. history and forever established the Marines as a major force capable of sustained ground operations. In short, many acknowledge it was the birth of the modern Marine Corps., and immediately following the battle the French renamed it the Bois de la Brigade de Marine.

As the Summer of 1918 unfolded, American importance and strength began to grow exponentially, and although every inch of land was purchased with blood and sweat, the tide was beginning to turn. Many Americans would spill their blood on French soil, including some well-known names. One such person was Quinten Roosevelt, the former Presidents' youngest son, whose plane was shot down on Bastille Day, July 14, 1918. Taking several German machine gun bullets to his head, Quinten was dead before his plane hit the ground. Teddy

Roosevelt, who had warned America about Germany's growing power and ultimately urged U.S. involvement in the war, was made to suffer a father's loss of a son all while feeling he had somehow played a role in his death. Broken hearted, he would be laid to rest himself just six months after his son.

The battles of 1918 were also pivotal for Americans, who though not yet famous, would one day become household names. Consider that in Meuse-Argonne, beginning in the latter days of September 1918 and considered one of the greatest U.S. battles of the War, Americans who served included: Captain Harry Truman of the 129th Field Artillery's Battery D; Colonel George S. Patton of the 1st Provisional Tank Brigade; Brigadier General Douglas MacArthur of the 42nd Infantry Division; and Colonel George C. Marshall, who played a key role in planning the offensive. It is also fascinating to consider that a young twenty-two-year-old Second Lieutenant by the name of Erwin Rommel sat on the other side during this same battle.

IV.

ROLL ON

CHAPTER 19

Harvey

Jim McElreath's car caught on fire on lap 24, bringing out the first yellow of the day, and on lap 87, Arnie Knepper crashed on turn four, prompting the second caution in the race. A.J. Foyt had led for 66 laps, while another twelve racers had watched their days end early with mechanical issues. On lap 99, Mario Andretti caught a break when Foyt pitted with engine problems. The gritty Texan would not get back on the track for another twenty minutes, but by then he was many laps down and out of contention. Andretti caught another break on lap 105 when his primary challenger, Lloyd Ruby, who had led for 11 laps of the race, misunderstood a signal from his crew and accelerated out of the pit area with the fuel hose still attached instantly rupturing his fuel tank.

Leading up to the race in May of 1969, Andretti was considered a favorite to win at the Brickyard, as he was a two-time United States Auto Club (USAC) champion and was the Rookie of the Year in 1965, along with a podium finish that same year. He had qualified on the pole in both 1966 and 1967. Besides Andretti, Andy Granatelli, owner of the Granatelli STP team, had a strong team of racers in 1969 that also included Art Pollard and Carl Williams. Earlier that Spring it had been decided that Andretti would drive an all-new Lotus design, the Type 64, powered by a turbocharged 2.65-liter Ford V-8 and featuring Ferguson Four-Wheel drive. Modifications to the car included reversing the Ford engine and Lotus/Hewland transmission. To reduce the grip advantage of Four-Wheel Drive, the Type 64 was required to run on tires not exceeding 10 inches in width while the Two-Wheel drive cars were permitted to run on tires up to 14 inches in width. A delay in delivery meant that Andretti had just a single test session prior to Indianapolis qualifying, made more ominous as the turbo charged Ford engine was difficult to master. Crew chief, Clint Brawner, was also concerned with the car's construction expressing doubts about the car surviving a 500-mile race. Any concerns were initially alleviated when Andretti clocked laps in excess of 171 mph.

On May 21*st*, during practice laps, a rear hub of the Lotus failed at speed, putting Andretti forcefully into a wall. The car was destroyed, and Andretti sustained facial burns. Remarkably he suffered no other serious injuries. With just three days before qualifying, the Granatelli crew worked tirelessly to prepare the backup car, a turbo charged Ford powered Brawner Hawk III. Andretti was more comfortable in this car, as it had driven him to victory in April at the California 200. However, with that race being less than half of the 500 miles at Indy, much about the car remained unknown. On May 25*th*, after a week of rain and a revised Pole Day, Andretti lapped the Speedway at 169.851, just behind Foyt's 170.568 putting him in the middle of the first row and next to Bobby Unser. Embarrassed by his facial burns, Andretti asked his twin brother Aldo to stand in for him in the traditional front row qualifying pictures.

On May 30, 1969, just after the Purdue Marching Band had finished the National Anthem, and at the green flag, Andretti passed Foyt for the race lead heading into turn one. He held that position for the first five laps but sensing that he was already riding the car too hard and remembering the old racer's adage—to finish first, first you must finish—he backed off the throttle enough to cool his car and his nerves. Later in the race, when it appeared Andretti had it in the bag, the unthinkable almost happened when the leader was passing a slower car and went wide finding himself wide of the race line. Andretti avoided a spin out, got himself back on the track, and moved closer to victory. In the closing laps overheating remained a constant worry and the race leader was dealing with a severe driveline vibration with the gears nearly falling out of the transmission as he reached two hundred laps and the checkered flags. Mario Andretti won the Indy 500 in three hours, eleven minutes, and fourteen seconds, breaking the existing record by nearly 5 minutes.

Firestone Tires had their man, Mario Gabriele Andretti, the Italian born American race car driver. Although he would not officially win the Indy 500 again, he would become one of the most successful drivers in the history of the sport, winning in Formula One, IndyCar, World Sports Car, and NASCAR. His name would become synonymous with racing, and the relationship between Andretti and Firestone Racing would last beyond 50 years. As for the Indianapolis 500, considered one of the greatest spectacles in sport, Firestone was there from the beginning. In 1911, the first 200 lap race around the 2.5-mile oval, was won by driver Ray Harroun who crossed the finish line on Firestone Tires. In 1964, A.J. Foyt set a new speed record of 145.35 mph on Firestone's and became the first driver to complete the race at the brickyard on just one set of rubber. When French driver Simon Pagenaud won the 2019 Indianapolis 500, it marked the 70*th* time the winner drove on Firestone's. In fact, Firestone tires account for over two-thirds of all wins including 1911, 1913, 1920-1941, 1946-1966, 1969-1971, 1996-1997, and from 2000-2019. Goodyear is second with 29 race wins, followed by BF Goodrich with 2, Michelin with 1 and Palm Cord Tires with 1. Firestone provides about 5,000 tires to the Indy 500, with each entry getting 36 sets of tires for practice, qualifying and the race.

A decade after Andretti's historic win at Indy, Firestone rolled out a series of commercials featuring another American icon. James Maitland Stewart, born on May 20, 1908, was ten years old when the Vagabonds made their trip to North Carolina, and was in his early 70s when he appeared as himself alongside another actor playing the role of Harvey Firestone. James Stewart, better known as "Jimmy," had served his country in WWII in the United States Army Air Corps. fighting in the European theatre and attaining the rank of Colonel. Returning home, a hero, he was doubly blessed with a voice for radio and a face for the big screen. His roles in *It's a Wonderful Life, The Spirit of St. Louis, and Mr. Smith Goes to Washington*, not only made him a movie star, but also made him a person who the public considered kind, trustworthy and believable.

The commercials are, for the most part, mini period pieces, except for Jimmy Stewart who appears in a modern suit and tie. With his trademark delivery, Stewart, remarks, "You know Harvey sold a lot of tires, because Henry sold a lot of cars," and "Harvey always said give people a good product, and they will buy it." These Jimmy Stewart quips were used best at the end of the commercials when he concludes Harvey wanted his "Products to be the best today, and still better tomorrow," and the 721 tire was a "product he (Firestone) would have been proud of, of course, he still wouldn't have been satisfied."

Harvey Firestone never saw Mario Andretti win the Indy 500, and never got the chance to see Jimmy Stewart's biggest movie roles or to see him starring alongside his likeness in his company's commercials. But he was alive in 1930 when Shojiro Ishibashi, using the capital accumulated from Jika-tabi and the rubber shoe business, decided to make tires, which was an industry that did not exist in Japan at that time. However, he did not live to see Bridgestone acquire Firestone for $2.6 billion dollars in May of 1988, thereby setting up a new global competition with Goodyear and Michelin.

As a shrewd and practical businessman, he would have understood the need for this merger, and would have appreciated watching Firestones' stock price go from $35.75 before the initial offer to $80.00 a share when the deal was finally inked. Harvey would also have enjoyed watching new and inventive marketing techniques take hold within his company and elsewhere. Harvey Firestone was a visionary when it came to marketing and its ability to sell products. In many ways, this is not surprising as Firestone, who set up shop in Akron in 1900, had to sell tires in a town dubbed the "rubber capital of the world." His local competition included B.F. Goodrich, started by Benjamin Franklin Goodrich moving to Akron from Jamestown, New York in 1870; Goodyear Tire & Rubber Company established by F.A. Seiberling and C.W. Seiberling in 1898; and General Tire & Rubber incorporated by William F. O'Neil in Akron in 1915. These companies, literally on top of each other, engaged in tire wars for decades making marketing and finding product niche critical for survival.

Firestone was considered the "general manager" and commissary officer for the camping trips, and was described by Burroughs as "belonging to an entirely different type: the clean, clear-headed, conscientious business type, always on his job, always ready for whatever comes, always at the service of those around him, a man devoted to his family and his friends, sound in his ideas, and generous of the wealth that has come to him as a manufacturer who has faithfully and honestly served his countrymen." What Burroughs might have also noticed, is that Firestone enjoyed the comradery of the camping trips, but also saw an opportunity to market Harvey Firestone, the Firestone family, Henry Ford, the Ford Motor Company, and the Firestone Tire & Rubber Company.

Nearly a century before the creation of social media and reality TV, Firestone glimpsed the future and saw that business tycoons would do better out and among the people as opposed to hiding behind large stone walls. In retrospect, it was truly visionary. This is not to say that the camping trips were simply a publicity stunt. Clearly, they were not. However, in tipping off the press to their routes and destinations, he allowed the public to share in their adventures and in doing so made them average, and even approachable, people. While Edison made his laboratory a theatrical stage, and Ford made his manufacturing plant a highly coveted destination spot, Firestone took their show on the road for a cross-country tour.

The Vagabonds were born along with another arm in modern marketing. Harvey Firestone and his sons (Harvey, Jr. and on later trips, Russell), kept diaries and notes and following the trips would write up an overall account. Firestone also always provided for photographers, either professional or a member of the crew, to create a visual record of the trips, and it appears that Firestone came to believe the trips made for good reading, privately publishing two books and distributing them to his fellow campers and close associates.

The first of these, *In Nature's Laboratory*, published in 1917, chronicled the 1916 trip; and the second, *Our Vacation Days of 1918*, published in 1926, is largely a collection of thoughts and writings in collaboration with fellow camper, John Burroughs. A project to complete the preservation of the trips in book form, or a series of books, also appears to have been contemplated but never realized. When reviewing Firestone's notations following the trips, much of it is written as scenes, like the outline of a screenplay, probably formatted for a book with room for pictures, but leaving open the possibility that he may very well have also envisioned a motion picture at some point.

Harvey S. Firestone arrived in Akron, Ohio with his wife and infant son during a January snowstorm. With Harvey Jr. snug in his arm, the couple walked from the train depot to the Windsor Hotel about four blocks away. The hotel would serve as their shelter until they could find a suitable home. Firestone was 31 years old, Akron was a bustling city of 43,000 people, and the year was 1900. Previously known for the manufacturing of harvesting machinery which had begun to move west towards Illinois and Wisconsin to be closer to the newer grain sources, Akron had caught the bicycle craze just like the rest of the country in the 1890s. It was well positioned, along with New England, in the rubber goods industry, and the production of bicycle tires had become the newest major industry in the area. This was followed by a demand for solid rubber tires on carriages, spurred by salesmanship and promises of a more comfortable cushioned ride without the constant jarring to both vehicle and occupant. It was the turn of a new century, and the city was considered a land of opportunity.

Firestone had returned to Ohio from Chicago to join Whitman & Barnes, a firm that manufactured twist drills and produced a line of carriage tires and rubber horseshoe pads. Harvey had appreciated the cushioned ride from rubber sporting the first rubber-tired carriage in Detroit in 1893 while serving as manager for the Columbus Buggy Company. The depression of the 1890s had caused a collapse of many businesses including the buggy works. The young businessman dusted himself off, moving to Chicago to open his own shop where he would transverse cobblestone streets to pick up wheels at livery stables. His business was a retail service business, and he bought his tires from a manufacturer.

By 1898, the Firestone Rubber Tire Company on Wabash Avenue, bought out rival Imperial Rubber Tire Company, making for the largest carriage-tire business in the city. Soon thereafter he was approached to sell the business at an attractive price to the Rubber Tire Wheel Company in Springfield, Ohio, which in turn became part of Consolidated Rubber Tire Company. Not only did he receive a handsome payoff, but he was also initially retained to work as the manager of its Chicago wholesale-retail business placing large contracts with Akron tire factories. After a few months, Firestone realized that he was at odds with the home office in Springfield over policy and direction, and with $42,000 from the sale of his company, he offered his resignation and left with his wife and child for Akron, Ohio.

Harvey Firestone came to Akron with more than just a large wad of cash in his pocket. He also brought with him a patent he owned on a device for applying tires to carriage wheel channels, proposing to take command of the Whitman & Barnes tire department. A common problem of the day was how to keep tires from slipping off any standard channel, and most solutions involved springing the tire into place after joining the ends. Firestone's patent fit standard channels applying even tension to the retaining wires, prior to the joining, thereby holding the tire firmly and evenly in the channeled rim. While Whitman & Barnes pushed for sales of shoe pads for firetrucks and ambulance horses in New York and other major cities, Firestone worked with little support as manager of tire sales, being paid a royalty on tires made and sold with his patent at a Buchtel Avenue factory down by the railroad tracks. Not seeing any future in tires, the firm offered him an option on the tire department.

Later that summer Firestone was invited to the home of James Christy, who was involved in the leather business, to discuss an invention that was believed would further improve carriage tires. Also present at this meeting was Dr. Louis E. Sisler, the county auditor and a retired physician; James A. Swinehart, the originator of the invention; and W.D. Buckman, one of Sisler's deputies. Together these men shared a patent for a sidewire device that they believed would reduce the danger of wire cutting at a tire, and in the case of a heavier commercial vehicle, prevent creeping on a rim. On this steamy July night, Firestone examined the new tire and quickly realized that if the tire worked as promised, it would open a large market for tire sales. As for the others present, they hoped that Harvey Firestone, who they had invited for his experience and dependability, might also have brought his checkbook.

Harvey Samuel Firestone was born in Columbiana, Ohio on December 20, 1868. His father, Benjamin, who was a childless widower at thirty-two, married Catherine Flickinger whose family had settled from Hanover, Pennsylvania and lived along the road going into Columbiana. The couple had two other sons, Elmer Sylvanus, born in 1864, and Robert James, born in 1873. Not long before this little family came to be, many land seeking Americans had poured across the Alleghenies, from eastern Pennsylvania and western Virginia, looking to farm or establish a cottage industry. Many arrived before the region had been properly surveyed, while others arrived buying sections of land for $2 an acre from the Government Land office down river in Steubenville. In 1803 Ohio was carved out of the territory northwest of the Ohio river becoming the 17th state. The General Assembly at Chillicothe carved out Columbiana County from a northerly corner along the Pennsylvania border. While log cabins were being built, many families lived in covered wagons including Harvey Firestone's great grandfather. He carried with him a deed bearing the signature of President Thomas Jefferson, outlining a square-mile section of gently rolling countryside good for cultivating grass and grain.

The Firestone story more properly begins in a German Lutheran church in Alsace, France with the birth of Nicholas Firestone in 1712. The area had numerous Firestones, and Nicholas grew up to become a farmer, living in a stone house, married, and with nine children. One night in 1752, without any farewell, he slipped his family out of the Village of Berg, abandoning his farm and setting sail for America. Nicholas was not yearning for a new life in a new world, but did so to protect his eldest son, who was turning eighteen, from military service to the bourbon king, Louis XV. This left Nicolas without passage money, and like thousands of others during this time, he came to America as an indentured servant.

Nicholas worked on a farm in eastern Pennsylvania until fulfilling his contract, and then moved his family to Conococheague Creek. His firstborn son, who was also named Nicholas, married a "Dutch" girl and managed his own farm nearby. They in turn had another son, also named Nicholas, who was barely fourteen when he signed onto the Cumberland militia along with his father during the Revolutionary War. The third Nicholas, who was the first American born, married a local girl, and joined a caravan out of Frederick, Maryland setting out with his new family for the western frontier. Ohio only had a few straggling Delaware and Iroquois, when Nicholas built a two-bedroom log cabin in what would become Columbiana County. He soon acquired several more tracts of land including an area heavily timbered with oak, elm and hickory, where he enjoyed visiting a bubbling limestone spring along with friends including a few Indians. At sixty he put up a cabin on this track of land for the use of his children, and the following year, in 1828, he helped his son, Peter, build a large brick house on land inherited by Peter's wife. The house was built to be a country showplace, making Peter the "big man in the neighborhood (who) had the biggest house."

After losing his wife, Peter remarried Sally Ann Allen, who bore him seven children. He expanded the farm to include sheep farming, which by all accounts was a success. In 1853 Peter died leaving his farming business to be divided among his sons, and the brickhouse was willed to his widow with her being given authority to choose a child to help her maintain it and occupy it with her. Living in just two rooms upstairs, she chose her eldest son, Benjamin, who was twenty-two at the time. He shared a love of horses with his father, bringing with him a wealth of knowledge of how to manage sheep and sell wool. In time he came to possess 148 acres in Fairfield township and avoided hiring more than a single hand by using labor saving devices including a mechanical cornhusker.

Benjamin approached farming with a businesslike approach, favoring care and efficiency over sweat and debt. He was a nimble man, who enjoyed planning and thinking over working long hours. In *Men and Rubber, The Story of Business*, written by Harvey Firestone in collaboration with Samuel Crowther (who was also a co-author with Henry Ford on *My Life and Work*), he describes his father as "by and large, the best businessman I have ever known." He further heaped the following praise when describing his father's farming prowess, "he seemed always to be able to balance his affairs," and "he always had some money on the side and was therefore able to use his best judgement under the circumstances, instead of being forced into a decision by financial pressure." Firestone, and Ford for that matter, solidly believed that a man with a surplus could control circumstances, and that the first task in business ought to be to set out to gain that surplus. Firestone was fond of saying that his father had the rare foresight to know that a fine crop one year, was a fortunate accident and could not be guaranteed the following years. Lastly, Harvey observed that his father in every farm operation used just a little more care than did the others and, consequently, his crops were always just a little bit better.

Young Harvey, along with his brothers, had plenty to do on the Firestone farm. When the boys were not sweeping stables on Saturdays, they were busy plowing, hoeing potatoes, weeding the gardens, and greasing harnesses. Firestone recalled his father with chin whiskers, as affable in nature, hesitant in speech, and fond of muted chuckling, preferring it to laughing aloud. His mother, Catherine Flickinger, Firestone described as lovable, kind and intelligent, and as a diplomat, who kept the family running smoothly. Later, after his tire company was up and running as a viable and profitable operation, Firestone's mother, acting as an unofficial executive, would host superintendents, foremen, department heads, and others at the family farm. She also regularly traveled to Akron to meet with these same people and did so up until she died in 1916. Firestone sincerely believed that she had a splendid mind for the human side of business as she understood people and how to get on with them.

In 1876, when Firestone was nearly eight years old, he traipsed off to school about a mile and a quarter from Columbiana in nearby Pleasant Valley. The school was a brand new, one-room clapboard building with huge windows and a bell tower. His mother's sister, Aunt Nannie, grabbed him by the hand, opened the schoolroom door which led to a long room with rows of desks and two round coal stoves in the middle, and introduced him to his frock-coated teacher. Lessons for the younger pupils went from September to mid-November, thereafter the class size swelled considerably with older students finally relieved from family required farm chores. The desks were graduated in height, with the smallest of children placed in the front of the class. Being young and undersized, Firestone found himself up front. The lad carried a slate pencil, bordered with twisted colored yarn, and sometimes before or after school, he would stop off at Grandma Flickinger's for cookies, cheese, or apple butter on bread. On Sundays, the boys attended Sabbath school at the Grace Reformed Church in Columbiana, where their father was an elder of the church. Riding in a spring wagon, their mother would give them each a penny for the offering.

From an early age, Harvey was viewed by his instructors as an industrious young man, who stayed out of trouble. He was generally well liked by his classmates, even if he was a bit modest about going bare while bathing at "the arch," a pool formed by a nearby brook and stone bridge. Young Firestone, with his knee pants and rubber boots, enjoyed hunting squirrels, fishing any day but Sunday, puffing on burning bits of hollow grapevines as a form of adolescent smoking, and swinging by a rope in a familiar barn from one haymow to another. "Harve," as he was known by his friends, also had a deep appreciation for horses, and at an early age he had learned to ride and to break in colts. Firestone would later recall that since childhood, no matter how hard up he might be, he was seldom without at least one good horse.

He would also accompany his father to nearby village fairs, and although he was regularly seduced by the sweet cider and gingerbread offerings and the excitement and dust from harness racing, he also got the opportunity to see his father engage in horse and cattle trading. Lessons from his father included, "never rush a deal, let it come to you," and "be satisfied with getting a good price when the market was high and don't be sorry if it was not the peak." What Harvey may have initially kept to himself was an immediate understanding that buying and selling appeared to be easier and more profitable than farming. When Firestone turned fifteen, he convinced his father to let him run the family horse business. Benjamin, who would focus on the cattle trading and other aspects of the farm, would defer to his son's judgment when it came to horses. He would also defer to his son's judgment when it came to separating trading opportunities from farming. This decision, while proving to be more profitable, also created good will between Harvey and his parents and helped to avoid a classic tragedy in farm life where children feel forced to stay on the farm just to get the work done.

The Columbiana High School Class of '87 met for commencement exercises on a rainy night in May at the Methodist Episcopal Church across Pittsburgh Street, where all fourteen graduates were obliged to give an oration. Open to the public, but with a ten-cent admission to avoid overcrowding, the church was filled with mounds of presents and flowers and a cheerful buzz saturating nearly everything. The girls were dressed in white dresses, while the boys were dressed in their finest dark suits. Harvey Firestone was sweating profusely through his. Nervous with public speaking, the graduate had practiced his speech, "Agitation," over and over, and now five minutes stood between him and the freedom of graduation. With his heart thumping, he stood before his peers and began his well-rehearsed lines, "Nature is never at rest...Encourage opinions, discussions, investigations...Encourage agitation. Yes, give the widest scope to opinions and discussions in the mental and moral world, and from their discordance will come truth and wisdom." And, just like that, it was finished. The last unpleasantry of High School was over. Returning to the haven of his seat, he glanced at his classmate, Ella, knowing he had successfully passed the baton of public speaking to her. It was now her turn to get through five minutes of terror. Ella was determined to teach, as was Loma and the valedictory, Ida. Bill Strickler was going to stay on as a clerk selling groceries at his father's store, and Charlie was off to Heidelberg College with a calling for the ministry. One lad had lined up a job at Shilling's bank, while another planned to move to Pittsburgh to work at a drug store. Hattie remained undecided. As for Harvey, he had made up his mind. Harvey S. Firestone would become a businessman.

On a June morning, a little after 10 AM, Harvey boarded a train for Cleveland. He was eighteen, and had enrolled in the Spencerian Business College, where he would pursue a three- month course to learn the fundamentals of bookkeeping and to learn more about the art of penmanship. Cleveland was a city of roughly a quarter million people, making it a little over half the size in 1887 as it is today. The school, before it became known as the Spencerian, was also the path taken by Cleveland's petroleum behemoth, John D. Rockefeller. Besides school and life in a large metropolis, Firestone had arrived with the hope that he might make himself valuable and thereby worthy of a job at his cousin Clinton's Columbus Buggy Company. Clinton made a fine-looking, expensive buggy and was one of the best-known buggy makers in the entire United States. Clinton Firestone was the principal owner and although he had previously hired Harvey's older brother Elmer, he had written Harvey to tell him that he had currently had no work for the youngster, but that the situation could change.

Living with a childhood friend, Firestone found quarters in a dingy downtown boarding house, and set about starting his career as a businessman. Or at least as a student. Soon, Harvey discovered the college proved no great chore, leaving him with plenty of time to explore the city, visit with friends, and work on his penmanship with frequent inquiries to his cousin Clinton. After finishing his three-month course, Firestone still had not got his foot in the door at his cousin's buggy shop, but Clinton did help him find a job as a bookkeeper in the coal business of John W. Taft in Columbus. Harvey was paid thirty dollars a month by the Royal Coal & Mining Company, which sold coal at wholesale, and was owned by a distant relative of the future President, William Howard Taft.

Moving to the capital city at the beginning of 1888, further from home and the Firestone family, Harvey found himself perched on a high stool in the basement of a coal company that was not doing well. Nor was its owner or its bookkeeper. Firestone earned a dollar a day, barely squeaking out a living. To supplement his income, he also took on work as a bookkeeper for O.D. Jackson, a middle-aged man, who as a tenant of sorts, occupied an office in the same building. By the fall, Mr. Taft fell ill and shut down the business leaving Firestone without his primary job. Upon learning the news, his cousin Clinton swooped in to play the role of savoir to Harvey by finally offering him a job. However, the younger Firestone turned down the job, having been offered a sales job working with Jackson to pedal bottled patent medicines, lotions and flavoring extracts. Clinton, who was clearly caught off guard by his younger cousin's perceived ungratefulness, lashed out, stating, "All right, young man do as you like. I'll give you three months to be around here again begging me for a job."

With his pride hurt, Harvey set out as a traveling salesman, not knowing, that in time, his cousin would ultimately be proven right. Harvey Firestone, along with another dozen or so "crack salesmen," went from one small town to another selling tonics, cough syrup, a liniment, and an "Arabian Oil," which was a horse liniment. Finding resistance from smaller stores, Firestone learned to focus on the biggest store in town, and in the process discovered that even though he did not possess the gift of gab and would never be one of those persons who could "sell anything," he did have a basic talent for salesmanship. He also learned that the easiest way to sell something was to believe in the product you were selling, causing the young man to ditch the tonics and focus on the extracts and the other products offering some tangible benefit and which might result in a repeat customer down the road.

What Firestone would also learn is that being a good salesperson, does not always result in success especially when the profits made by the young man were being consumed by the salaries and expenses incurred by the other men. When his salary and expense check did not arrive on a Monday in Crestline, Ohio, Firestone was not surprised as the checks seldom arrived on time. However, when Tuesday came and went with neither check, Harvey began to worry as he was out of money. Afraid to telegraph Jackson for fear that word might get around the small town situated about a hundred miles from Columbus, Firestone decided to wait. He was also afraid the hotel might wonder what he was doing just sitting around, so he pretended to work, walking the streets past supper. His hope was to receive his check and then escape. The following Saturday, the check came, but it was Jackson's last money.

When Harvey Firestone returned to take a job at the Columbus Buggy Company it was in the shipping room, and although his cousin Clinton might have had the opportunity to rub salt in the wound, he apparently allowed the younger man to dine alone on his humble pie. For nine months he worked in shipping, until he was promoted to salesman in the Columbus showroom where he learned to sell buggies. After the Des Moines branch of the company ran into considerable trouble, Firestone was transferred there to assist with the bookkeeping. He worked there for several months before being shifted to Detroit. There he would continue to work as a bookkeeper, but soon managed to edge himself into the showroom during any spare moment to assist with sales. Working alongside his brother, Harvey proved himself a natural at selling buggies, and by 1892, when Elmer was transferred to Des Moines, Harvey was put in charge of the Michigan sales district. His earnings of $150 a month was used to purchase a horse, and then another. Soon he managed to acquire and maintain a stable. He also began to look the part of a well-to-do Detroiter. Firestone, who parted his hair down the middle with a full-blown mustache with twirled points, might be spotted along the Grand Boulevard on a late afternoon or Saturday in a fine horse and buggy, wearing his fine clothes, gloves and lap robe. Harvey also developed a reputation for training horses, including those considered big, wild sorts, converting them to racing horses which might be entered in gentlemen's race on a private mile track near Detroit, and on more than one occasion he drove such horses to victory himself.

While enjoying his newfound prosperity, Harvey Firestone met Idabelle Smith of Jackson, Michigan at a dancing party given in her honor in the home of a seminary classmate. Her father, George, was the inventor of the process that turns out "patent" and "half-patent" flour. The daughter of Mr. and Mrs. Smith was fair haired and classic, with aristocratic features, and a very engaging personality. The handsome Firestone made an equally favorable impression, and when Idabelle was invited for a carriage ride in the only buggy in Detroit with rubber-tired wheels (a show model from the store), she readily accepted. By all accounts it proved to be a "smooth ride," as the couple married on a cold icy day in November of 1895 in the same house where they had first danced together. She was just twenty-one, while he was not quite twenty-seven.

Returning to Detroit following their honeymoon, the newlyweds found Detroit still suffering from a hangover left from the nationwide depression of 1893-1894. Although the unemployment, bank failures, and labor unrest had slowly started to stabilize, Harvey found it more and more difficult to sell farmers expensive buggies. The Columbus buggy might run for $110 a carriage, whereas a competing Durant or Nash model was only $35. A farmer, who initially might purchase the more expensive buggy as a matter of pride, eventually realized a cheaper model made more sense as a new buggy could be purchased every few years instead of holding on to an old expensive one. Just a few months after he was married, the Columbus Buggy Company failed leaving Harvey without a job again. However, this time he had the responsibility of a wife and a home.

One afternoon, while driving around town in his rubber-tired show model, Firestone was suddenly struck with the realization that his future was literally right below him. Although his rubber tires were unique to Detroit, it was not the only such buggy in the United States. Furthermore, he recalled learning that a London cab company had already fitted all its buggies with rubber tires. Although farmers wanted a cheaper buggy, in time all buggy customers would also come to expect a smoother ride. Instinctively he knew this. His own buggy had reminded him daily, that steel rimmed wheels were no match for rubber. The problem was that the tires were expensive, usually a $40 markup on the buggy price, and such tires were generally hard to buy in the United States. "Why not make them easy to buy," Firestone wondered. Calculating the number of buggies, he further realized that if he only convinced half the drivers to switch, he might also be sitting on a goldmine. Firestone went to work on selling his closest friends on the idea, by literally driving them around town in his rubber-tired buggy. Firestone believed his demonstration was better than any proposition, and after an evening with a business acquaintance, he found a willing investor.

Setting up shop in an old, rundown rubber factory in Chicago on Wabash Avenue near Harrison Street, Firestone went to work on putting buggy owners on tires. Purchased for $1,500, the building was filled with an allotment of largely unusable machinery, but Firestone was not looking for much in the way of machinery anyway. He would buy tires in strips that looked a good deal like a garden hose, cut them to size on the buggy, and cement it on the wheel over the steel rim. He continued the practice of selling a set of tires for forty dollars, and with the cost incurred to the Firestone-Victor Rubber company at about fourteen dollars for a set, he was easily able to pay his monthly rent of twenty-five dollars for a little house and a weekly grocery bill of five dollars.

Equally important for the future of Harvey Firestone was a visitor to the Columbus Buggy Works in Detroit in 1895. Although Firestone did not recall the exact details of the meeting, Henry Ford clearly did. Ford later recalled, "At the time I was building my first automobile. It was about complete, and I was using bicycle tires. The car weighed 500 pounds, which was too much for the light tires. I went to the buggy works to see about obtaining some solid rubber tires as a substitute. Firestone told me he had just received new tires, that were a great deal softer on a buggy being unpacked in the rear. They were pneumatic tires and I had him order me a set." This casual meeting between Firestone and Ford set in motion a series of events that would alter the 20*th* century as it not only helped put Firestone in the tire business, but it also accelerated the development of the automobile. In time, it would also blossom into a strong business relationship and an even stronger personal friendship between these two men. Five years after this chance meeting, at the dawn of the automobile age, and as the horse and carriage began an inescapable descent, Harvey Firestone moved to Akron, Ohio to be part of the "Rubber Capital of the World." In the decades that followed, Ford would buy tires by the millions from Firestone.

CHAPTER 20

Campfires and Story Telling

It was raining heavily as the party drove into Elizabethton, Tennessee, requiring the drivers to seek refuge in a nearby garage. News of their arrival from Bristol had reached the town located in the Tri-Cities area of northeast Tennessee (encompassed by Bristol Johnson City and Kingsport) and crowds of people were lining the streets.

Moving on to Johnson City, Tennessee, the Vagabonds were again met by a large crowd of five-hundred or so well-wishers. It had stopped raining and Burroughs, Professor DeLoach and Mr. Kline, who were the first to arrive in Johnson City, got out of their car to greet the locals. Burroughs and DeLoach decided to grab a cold drink, and when wandering through town, DeLoach heard a young fellow say, "There goes Rip van Winkle!" Another youth was heard to say, "I wonder if that's Mr. Edison?" His companion immediately replied, "No, that ain't Edison, cause if it was, he would have invented a razor to shave hisself with!" While in town a young boy named Abe jumped up on one of the cars, and at the urging of his father who was an editor for a local newspaper, sold Mr. Edison a copy of the daily news. He quickly became the envy of his barefoot friends who had tagged along for a sight of the great inventor.

Although many of the local citizens offered accommodations in town, the party would set up camp in a field a few miles outside of nearby Jonesborough. Those in Jonesborough had gotten late word of the visiting caravan and hastily tried to organize a band to play music as the campers approached the town. Unable to pull it off in time, they were left with a scattering of persons who waved as the caravan rumbled through. Camp Robert Lee, which appears to have been named for the owner of the land and not the Confederate General, was nestled in a field with the only entrance being through a barn making it quite difficult to enter. The passenger cars passed through with relative ease, but the supply trucks required more care and a little digging to allow the tops to squeeze through without any scraping of structure or vehicle. There is some indication that one of the trucks may not have been so lucky.

Once a site was chosen to pitch the tents, Edison hired some boys, including the owner's son, to gather firewood and run some errands. Ford, who was sawing wood, asked a young lad to help him. As they worked, Ford asked, "Do you know with whom you are sawing wood?" The boy responded that he did not, and Ford said, "Well, my lad, you are sawing wood with Henry Ford." The boy brightened up and said, "And I, Herbert Lee, am at the other end of the saw." Another young lad named George, who was no more than nine years old, shouted to Thomas Edison, "I've read about you." "You have," asked a smiling Edison "And what was it you read?" Young George responded, "Why I read about you sitting on those eggs to hatch 'em." As everyone enjoyed a good laugh, Edison responded, "Don't ever try it, son. It won't work."

With one newspaper in hand, Edison sent some of the boys in search of others. One privation suffered most by Burroughs and Edison, was the scanty or delayed war news. Local papers, picked up here and there, gave brief summaries of the war. Bigger papers from Cincinnati, Philadelphia, or New York could be found in the larger railroad towns but were often a day or two old. Burrough readily admitted that "persons who have hung on the breath of the great dailies for four years miss something when they are cut off from them." When it came to his tent,

Burroughs, who was beginning to show his age on the trip, insisted on having his tent placed back in the field next to the woods. He insisted that he was not seeking space from the others, but that such a location gave him a greater degree of protection from uncertain elements. However, he did later claim that the crew and the boys made too much noise, that they never went to bed and always woke him in the morning. The wisdom of such a decision was proven in the early morning hours, not by inclement weather, but by the presence of barnyard animals including cattle, hogs and dogs who gathered near the other tents to voice their protest at the land poachers.

Dinner was served at dusk and by all accounts was quite tasty, being described as "proving again the goodness of things that grow in Southern soil." Following dinner, the campers gathered around a large campfire for their nightly discussions, but soon headlights appeared on a distant road signaling they had company approaching. As the members of the party had learned along the trip, a night around the campfire often evolved into a local reception of sorts. Men and women from nearby Jonesborough brought with them treats and stories, joining the famous campers around the fire. Edison took the ladies up and showed them each one of the tents, how they were equipped, how the electric lights were installed in each tent, and how the current had been bottled in battery form and brought all the way from Orange, New Jersey to be let loose each night in any spot desired.

The locals, not to be outdone, impressed the visitors with stories about Jonesborough being the oldest town in the state of Tennessee. It was also once the capital for the State of Franklin. Founded in 1779, or 17 years before Tennessee became a state, Jonesborough was originally under the jurisdiction of North Carolina and was named after Willie Jones, a North Carolina legislator who supported westward expansion. The travelers might have been surprised to learn that this town, sitting in the heart of the southern Appalachian Mountains, was a hotbed for the abolitionist movement. In 1819-1820 *The Manumission Intelligencer* and *The Emancipator* were edited and published by Elihu Embree and printed by Jacob Howard. Monumental in their importance, these were the first periodicals in the United States devoted exclusively to the abolition of human slavery. The original weekly publication, forcefully outlining the evils of slavery, was well received and, at one point, even after becoming a monthly journal with some 2,000 paying subscribers, was one of the most widely circulated papers in Tennessee and Kentucky.

Unfortunately, Embree succumbed to "bilious fever" in December of 1820, thus silencing an early voice of compassion and reason. Although the stain of slavery remained, and even with Tennessee later joining the confederacy, East Tennessee consistently maintained a strong anti-slavery sentiment. The locals might also have shown their pride in mentioning that nearby Elizabethton, where the caravan drove through a heavy rain earlier that day, was the site of the first independent American government West of the original thirteen colonies. Today, while wandering about downtown, one might stumble upon a plaque near the Doe River that reads: "In 1772 the first court West of the Alleghanies was held under this tree."

Stories of Tennessee that evening surely included discussions of her favorite adopted son, Andrew Jackson. A few miles from where the campers settled for the evening, sits a log house built in 1777 by Christopher Taylor, who was a veteran of the French and Indian War and a major in the American Revolutionary War. That same house was later the home for Andrew Jackson while he was practicing law in Jonesborough. The seventh President of The United States, and founder of the Democratic Party, was most likely born in South Carolina but is forever linked to Tennessee. His father died three months before he was born, leaving his mother to raise three boys on her own. Andrew Jackson would come to be known for sudden flashes of rage and for guarding a grudge like a Spanish war chest. His hatred for the British crown, began in earnest when his older brother Hugh died from war injuries in 1779, and carried forward when his other brother, Robert, died of smallpox, which he and Jackson contracted while British prisoners of war in Camden, South Carolina. He and his brother, considered too young to fight, were caught delivering messages for the Continentals. While being held as a prisoner, Andrew was ordered to clean a British Officer's boots, and when the young Jackson replied that he was a prisoner and not a servant, he was struck across the face with a Sabre.

However, it was only after his mother had helped negotiate his release that his hatred became unhinged. Having successfully gotten her two sons out of British hands, she turned north towards Charleston to offer care for her nephews who had been held captive on a British prison ship. Andrew's mother succumbed to "ship fever," most likely cholera, and along with countless others, was buried by the British in an unmarked grave on Charles Town Neck. At fourteen, pitted with smallpox and what would become a permanent scar across his forehead, Andrew Jackson was an orphan without a living sibling. His revenge against the monarchy, would make him a national hero and ultimately propel him to the White House.

After having great success in dealing with the Creeks during the Creek War, Jackson was made a Major General in the U.S. Army over the 7th Military District which included Tennessee, Louisiana and the Mississippi Territory. When the young general learned of a rumored British invasion of the South, he entered New Orleans on December 11, 1814, with the hope of strengthening its defenses. Along with regular U.S. troops, Jackson gathered a ragtag group of soldiers including volunteer militia from Tennessee, Kentucky, Louisiana, and the Mississippi Territory, Native Americans, free blacks, Creoles, and even a few of the local pirates. With not much time, and greatly outnumbered, this inexperienced lot stared down the mighty British throughout the month of December. Finally, on January 8, 1815, the British launched a full-scale attack on New Orleans, but to the amazement of the world Jackson's ragtag army handed the British yet another crushing defeat. Literally, overnight, Jackson was America's next George Washington.

Andrew Jackson is by all accounts a complicated, if not colorful, character in American history. Today, he is both loved and despised. The man who defeated the Creeks and who gave us the "Trail of Tears," also adopted and reared Indian orphans. He lived in a mansion (the Hermitage, near Nashville), and he owned slaves, all while seeking to act as a direct representative for the common man. A notorious gambler, he was also a strong leader, who was tough as nails. His willingness to suffer alongside his men ultimately resulted in his being given the nickname "Old Hickory." Unbeknownst to Jackson, he married his wife before she was legally divorced from her first husband, and he was the target of the first attempted Presidential assassination. When a deranged house painter's pistol misfired twice at close range, the lanky 6'1, 130-pound President subdued the man by charging with his cane.

Throughout his life, Andrew Jackson also had a propensity for duels. By some accounts, he was in over 100 of them during his lifetime. However, his first occurred in Jonesborough and it involved a well-known attorney in town named Waightstill Avery. Avery, who was a graduate of the College of New Jersey (later Princeton) and a Revolutionary War Veteran, found himself matched against Jackson in a civil suit. At one point in the trial, seemingly having a better case, Avery openly ridiculed a legal position taken by Jackson. The future President, and future habitual dueler, took offense, grabbed a pen, and wrote a peremptory challenge to his legal adversary. At first, Avery believed it to be a lark, but the next day Jackson reiterated the challenge by stating, "My character you have injured, and further you have insulted me in the presence of a court and a large audience. I therefore call upon you as a gentleman to give me satisfaction." To avoid any further misunderstanding, Jackson continued by stating, "This evening after court adjourned." After the trial concluded, the parties met in a low-lying area north of town. It was just after sunset, and apparently Jackson's anger had sufficiently cooled, as both parties, after stepping off the agreed-upon distance, fired and deliberately missed. The two lawyers then shook hands, and maintained a friendly, if not professional, relationship from that point on.

A few steps from where Jackson practiced law, the Chester Inn was built in 1797 by Dr. William P. Chester, originally hailing from

Lancaster, Pennsylvania. It has been continuously occupied as an Inn, a hotel, and an apartment house. Among the guests there have been three United States Presidents including Andrew Jackson, James K. Polk and Andrew Johnson. In the summer of 1832, just a few years before Andrew Jackson became the only President to pay off the national debt, the local hero held a reception for his friends on the porch of the Inn. Avery, his former colleague and dueling partner, was not present having passed away in 1821.

Any discussion surrounding travel through Tennessee and Appalachia would have no doubt caused the locals to mention two other American icons who have a solid claim in the region: Daniel Boone and Davy Crockett. Kentucky may well consider Boone a first-born son, but Tennessee, along with other states, also has a valid claim on kinship. Daniel Boone, who was born in a log cabin near Reading, Pennsylvania, had little formal education, having learned to read and write from his mother. His father taught him wilderness skills, which came naturally to the lad. He was given his first rifle when he was 12 years old, and by the time his father had moved the family to Rowan County, North Carolina, Daniel had started his own hunting business. The young entrepreneur was just 15. The year following Braddock's defeat, and his harrowing escape from the ensuing slaughter, Boone and his young bride, Rebecca Bryan, set up their home in the Yadkin Valley in what is now Davie County, North Carolina. The couple would ultimately have ten children, and at first Boone seemed content to live a simple and happy life, describing the perfect ingredients for same as "a good gun, a good horse and a good wife." During this time, he continued to hunt and explore the region, sometimes alone and sometimes with other long hunters. In 1767, Boone led his own expedition for the first time and somewhere along the way became infatuated with exploring the American frontier.

By 1769 Boone had formed a relationship with Richard Henderson, a North Carolina promoter, who planned to purchase large tracks of land from Indian tribes with the hope of establishing a fourteenth colony. Boone, along with six other explorers including his brother, set out that same year to explore Kentucky in connection with the proposed purchase. Although some of his companions abandoned the expedition, Boone carried on and ultimately passed through the Cumberland Gap and along the Warrior's Trace into Kentucky. The trail would become the main avenue for settlers to access the frontier. Daniel Boone continued to explore the region until spring 1771, and about this time he also moved his family to the Watauga settlements in upper East Tennessee. When Henderson delayed purchasing lands, Boone formulated his own plans for starting a settlement in Kentucky. In September of 1773 he led a group of settlers, including many of his in-laws, through Cumberland Gap. The expedition unfortunately ended following an Indian attack in Powell's Valley Tennessee, in which Boone's son, James, was killed.

Two years later, after Richard Henderson had completed preliminary negotiations with the Cherokee to purchase a large chunk of land consisting of what is now Kentucky and Middle Tennessee, Boone's knowledge of the West and reputation as an American explorer would be used to boost interest and sales in these newly acquired tracts of land. Daniel Boone was also put in charge with clearing a road to the new settlements and assisting settlers as they migrated west. Along with the purchased lands, the Cherokee had also agreed to an access corridor known as the "Path Deed" which would essentially run through the Cumberland Gap and on to the settlements in Kentucky. With a crew of thirty axmen, Boone created the "Wilderness Road," and by April of 1775 he directed colonists to an area in Kentucky he named Boonesborough.

That same year he brought his family to live in this settlement he had created and for which he would lead. Local Indian tribes, including Shawnee and Cherokee, were not pleased with Boone's settlement in Kentucky, and began a resistance movement that culminated with the kidnapping of his daughter, Jemima in July of 1776. Boone was able to obtain the release of his daughter, only to be captured himself by the

Shawnee in 1778.The frontiersman would manage to escape his captors but was never able to escape furious settlers after he was robbed of their money on his way to buy land permits. Many of his own land titles had come to him as pay for his services to Henderson's land company and were made questionable after the Virginia legislature invalidated Henderson's land purchase. His other land claims were improperly filed, leaving Boone virtually propertyless.

In 1788 Boone left the Kentucky settlement that bore his name and moved to Point Pleasant in what is now West Virginia. He would serve as a lieutenant colonel and legislative delegate, before venturing west one last time. Daniel Boone would spend the remainder of his life as an outdoorsman in Missouri.

A thirteen-day siege, followed by an early morning attack lasting roughly 90 minutes in 1836, will forever make Davy Crockett an honorary Texan. His death at the Alamo, along with others including William B. Travis and Jim Bowie, would also make him a bonified American hero. David Crockett, the frontiersman, Tennessee legislator and U.S. Congressman, had spent the last few months of his life in Texas, after uttering his famous quote, "You may all go to hell, and I will go to Texas." However, before these pivotal moments in American folklore, the 49-year-old icon had spent almost his entire life in Tennessee. Born on August 17, 1786, in Green County on the banks of the Nolichucky River in East Tennessee, Crockett was never a big fan of school, preferring to play hooky. When he was twelve, he ran away from home for nearly three years to avoid attending school in what Davy described as his "strategic escape." Not surprisingly, upon his return home in 1802 his family barely recognized him.

With little formal education, Crockett used the frontier as teacher where he became an efficient woodsman, scout and hunter. In 1813, Davy Crockett joined the Tennessee militia as a scout and fought against the Creek Indians in Alabama, and later fought in the War of 1812 as a Third Sergeant where he helped Andrew Jackson clear British forces, including British-trained Indians, from Spanish Florida. Following his discharge, his first wife Polly died, and a year later Crockett remarried moving his family to Lawrence County. In 1817, after starting several businesses, Crockett entered political life when he became public commissioner of Lawrence County and was elected justice of the peace. He also became a lieutenant colonel in the Tennessee militia but resigned these posts when he won a seat in the Tennessee General Assembly. As an assemblyman he fought for the tax and land rights of poor settlers, while refining his public speaking skills, especially his gift for storytelling.

Crockett's foray into national politics took a jagged path, initially losing his first bid for Congress in 1825, followed by victories in 1827 and 1829. He lost in 1830, won again in 1833, but lost his final bid in 1834. His political fortunes became intertwined with those of his fellow Tennessean-Andrew Jackson. Initially elected as a Jacksonian candidate to the Twentieth Congress in 1827, he later became an Anti-Jacksonian candidate in his reelection to the Twenty-first Congress. Crockett, who had fought directly under Jackson at Talladega and marched with him back to Ten Islands in search of sorely needed provisions for survival, came to have a political falling out with "Old Hickory."

When Andrew Jackson advocated for the power to forcibly remove all Indian tribes living east of the Mississippi River, Crockett became a fierce critic of the President and the Indian Removal Act of 1830. Crockett, who would be proven right to criticize Jackson for what later led to the Trail of Tears, also disagreed with the seventh President about a return to the gold standard and what Davy saw as a total withdraw of government funds from the Bank of the United States. Jackson came to see Crockett as an opportunist, seeking to turn his days of Indian fighting and bear hunting into a possible run for the White House.

Davy Crockett was indeed becoming a national celebrity, being the model for Nimrod Wildfire, the hero of James Kirke Paulding's play, *The*

Lion of the West, which opened in New York City on April 25, 1831. When *Life and Adventures of Colonel David Crockett of West Tennessee* was published in 1833, resulting in an eastern tour, Crockett had emerged as living proof that Andrew Jackson did not speak for all the common men in the country, let alone Tennessee. In the end, Jackson did speak for enough of the people in Crockett's congressional district as the frontiersman was defeated at the ballot box. After telling off his constituents, Davy Crockett rode off to Texas and his date with destiny.

The townsfolk might have asked the campers, especially John Burroughs, to imagine thousands of buffalo (bison) roaming through the Tennessee backcountry, for their massive herds trampled a deep, open trail through the forest over time. Some estimates put the total count of Bison in North America at sixty million near the arrival of the first Europeans to the continent, but by 1918 the majestic creature was nearly extinct, having been driven west and ruthlessly butchered. Their mighty comeback was still many years away, but their paths had evolved into trails for stagecoaches, tracks for rail lines, and paved roads for automobiles. The Great Buffalo Trail, or Trace, cut a path followed by Native Americans and explorers alike. The first Englishmen to visit the area, James Needham and Gabriel Arthur, were sent from Fort Henry to explore the Great Valley of Tennessee in 1673. They were also charged with creating a trading path with the Cherokee which would come to follow Buffalo creek, ultimately bending around Buffalo Mountain, just south of Johnson City past the land and spring on what would become Tipton-Haynes farm. When Colonel John Tipton purchased the site in 1784, after having moved from Shenandoah County, Virginia, little did he know that his peaceful home would become a battleground of sorts.

After the American Revolution, North Carolina claimed all the land between the mountains and the Mississippi River causing more settlers to venture West. However, being at the western tip of the state, and much outside the areas reasonably under her control, these settlers soon learned that they were essentially on their own. Warfare with Native Americans was a part of daily life and North Carolina was simply not able to protect them. When North Carolina decided to give back their land west of the Appalachians to the federal government, the settlers saw an opportunity to make their own state—the State of Franklin. However, the federal government had no plans for new states, and ignored the fact that the state had a constitution, a legislature, and a governor named John Sevier. Instead, it just gave the lands back to North Carolina.

For four years, between 1785-1788, Franklin languished in obscurity, becoming the only state to never become a state. Meanwhile, on the national stage, delegates had met in Philadelphia to correct the glaring weakness of the Articles of Confederation. The result was a new proposed constitution. Colonel Tipton was one of five delegates representing Washington County who met in the Summer of 1788 to consider ratification of the Constitution. Along with one-hundred and eighty-one other delegates representing North Carolina's western territory, he voted against ratification of the Constitution until a list of rights were added to it. Earlier that same year, in February, tensions between the Franklinites and the North Carolina loyalists (sometimes called Tiptonites), boiled over when the North Carolina sheriff of Washington county, Jonathan Pugh, was ordered by the county court under Tipton to seize the property of Sevier for taxes owed to the state. Sevier's property, including several slaves, were brought to Tipton's cabin for safe keeping by sheriff Pugh.

Sevier, who had been absent from his home during the seizure, was furious when he learned the news. He also felt the actions taken by Tipton were in direct violation of the Franklin Act, which stated, in part, that any party attempting to perform an official duty on behalf of North Carolina was subject to punishment. On February 27, 1788, Governor Sevier, along with 100 men, arrived at Tipton's cabin and positioned themselves a few hundred yards from the house. Tipton, along with his family and a handful of supporters, were surrounded. However, earlier, when he had learned of the march towards his homestead, Tipton had sent a dispatch with his subordinate, Major Robert Love, requesting assistance from any nearby militia. When Sevier sent Tipton a flag of truce, it included a thirty-minute deadline to surrender to the people of Franklin. This was met with no response. The first outside force to arrive was a company from Washington County under the command of Captain Peter Parkinson, but as they approached Tipton's cabin they were fired upon by the Franklinites. Several horses were shot and five of Parkinson's men were taken as prisoners. No further movement was made by any party until the following day, when Sevier again asked Tipton to surrender. This was met with a response from Tipton that he was more than happy to accept the surrender of Sevier.

By the evening of February 28, 1788, Major Love, with a small party of reinforcements, finally reached the outskirts of Tipton's property. The weather was bitterly cold, and some of Sevier's men had left their posts seeking the warmth of several nearby campfires. This left an easy path back to the cabin for Love and his reinforcements. Later that night, spilling into the following morning, the cold turned to heavy snow making it nearly impossible for Sevier and his men to detect the arrival of Colonel George Maxwell and his North Carolina loyalists from Sullivan County. It is not known, who fired first. What is known, is that after both sides fired a volley at each other, Colonel Tipton decided to attack Governor Sevier. The battle that ensued can be described as more like a duel. Both sides wishing to save their honor could not back down, but neither side was keen on shedding blood. As a result, most men shot in the air or directly at the top of the cabin. Nonetheless, three men were killed in the battle, including Sheriff Pugh. The battle itself lasted no more than ten minutes and resulted in a route of the Franklinites, who fled back towards Jonesborough. Sevier may have lived to fight another day, but the State of Franklin was now on an accelerated slide towards extinction. The days of Jonesborough being a capital city were also numbered.

The Constitution of the United States went into effect in March of 1789 without the approval of North Carolina and Rhode Island. Later, in the fall of 1789, delegates at a second convention for North Carolina, including John Sevier, ratified the Constitution after the addition of the Bill of Rights. In December of 1789 the North Carolina legislature essentially ceded the state's western territory back to the newly formed federal government. These came to be known as "The Territory South of the River Ohio" or "Southwest Territory," but unlike the first go around the federal government now had a roadmap as to how to form a new state. George Washington put William Blount in charge of this new territory, and after a census revealed enough people to form a legislature and a new constitution, Tennessee was well on its way to statehood. On June 1, 1796, Tennessee became the 16*th* State to join the Union, joining Vermont and Kentucky as the first states added to the original 13 colonies. The capital would be Knoxville. Franklin's former governor, John Sevier, would also serve as the first governor of Tennessee perhaps making him the only man to serve as first governor for two newly formed states. As for Tipton, he was a delegate from Washington County to the state constitutional convention, which crafted Tennessee's first state constitution. He also served as a state senator, aligning himself with the political powerhouse Andrew Jackson. He and Sevier never did manage to bury the hatchet and remained political adversaries throughout their lives.

Storytelling comes easy to many southerners, including Tennesseans. However, Jonesborough, and her folk, have taken it to a whole new level. Not only does this town stage a National Storytelling Festival, but it also is the home of the International Storytelling Center. In fact, the *Los Angeles Times* has proclaimed, "What New Orleans is to Jazz...Jonesborough is to storytelling." In 1973, after a small group, numbering sixty or so, had gathered around an old farm wagon in the Courthouse square to hear a few Appalachian tales, a festival was born. That small group has now grown to tens of thousands of persons who descend upon this town to be part of the festival hosted by the story telling center. The wagon has been replaced by large, circus like tents, attracting world-renowned tellers to spin their tales. The International Storytelling Center, located on three acres in downtown Jonesborough, opened its doors to the general public in 2002 and is the only facility anywhere in the world devoted solely to the tradition of storytelling. The importance of storytelling cannot be overstated. Consider the greatest and most important story ever told: the human story. Our story. C.K. Chesterton, C.S. Lewis and J.R.R. Tolkien remind us that the human story remains a story and the fact that we continue to tell stories is significant because it flows from the fact that we are a story. Donald T. Williams in his book *Mere Humanity* points out that this is the narrative argument for Theism: as a contingent universe needs a Creator, a dynamic universe needs an unmoved Mover, an intelligent and orderly universe needs a Designer, and a moral universe needs a Lawgiver. So, a universe containing a creature whose life is utterly inexplicable except as a story demands a Storyteller.

No wonder the travelers described their evening with the locals as "one of the happiest and most interesting evenings of storytelling on the entire journey." It also explains why the campers stayed up past midnight.

CHAPTER 21

Unexpectedly Detained

Earlier that same evening, while the Vagabonds swapped stories with local Tennesseans, John Burroughs had expressed his concern that cattle would come up in the woods and bother him. But in the morning, they failed to make an appearance near his tent. Rather cows and pigs did appear around the main camp especially near the makeshift kitchen, upsetting utensils and other paraphernalia. Nonetheless, breakfast was served on time. It was August 27, 1918, and just as the campers were finishing their meal, a group of the visitors from the night before, returned bringing gifts for the journey that lay ahead including eight large watermelons. Apparently, only a few of these "fine fruits" survived the breaking of camp as they made for a great breakfast dessert.

The Jonesborough delegation informed the travelers that Asheville, North Carolina was due South, some eighty miles away. Before breaking camp, a route was made for each car with instructions to meet at the Grove Park Inn in Asheville, where they would hopefully set up camp near the inn. Harvey junior's car contained Henry Ford, John Burroughs and Professor DeLoach, while Thomas Edison, Kline, and

Harvey Firestone rode together in another car. Unfortunately, the caravan was short on gasoline, and some of the vehicles were running near empty, when they pulled up to a store pump in a remote village about ten miles from Greeneville, Tennessee. The storekeeper was short on gasoline, but did part with three precious gallons, just enough to make their run to Greeneville.

When arriving at Greeneville, the caravan made a pit stop for gasoline at the first garage they set eyes on. This garage was also low on gasoline, managing to part with only six gallons. After a few minutes, a crowd of people again began to gather. The senior Firestone strolled up to a nearby store to buy a pair of glasses and discovered that the store also had a gasoline tank. While getting gas at these various locations, the mayor and the chief of police, along with many other fine citizens, made multiple invitations to the travelers to visit local sites. Firestone, acting as the party diplomat and sensing Edison's growing frustration at the progress being made towards their camping destination for the night, respectfully declined citing a strict schedule including previous obligations in North Carolina. Escorted out of town by the mayor, who was described as "a very fine man," the party assured those present that it was a great honor and was greatly appreciated.

The weather had grown exceedingly hot and humid, and after traveling twenty-six miles, the party stopped for lunch in Newport, Tennessee. Eating at two long tables, the travelers had another "fine meal." Apparently, the manager of the hotel, described as being "a very nice woman," was quite taken with John Burroughs. So much so, that Henry Ford agreed to send her a set of Burroughs' books. As for Edison, who had initially gone unnoticed, he slipped into a nearby room, sat down and read his paper. However, after devouring the news, he put down the paper only to realize that a crowd of citizens had gathered around to meet him and get his autograph. He obliged, while Ford, as usual, mingled with the crowd. As for Harvey Firestone, he waited under the hot sun while receiving a battery of questions from the town-folk, as one of the vehicles got gasoline and received some other small adjustments.

On the way out of Tennessee, Firestone persuaded Edison, who was still worried about the caravan getting too far behind schedule, to make a side excursion to Hot Springs, North Carolina, with a visit to a nearby German prisoner-of-war camp. With the aid of an army colonel, the travelers were guided through the camp housing approximately twenty-two hundred men, mostly sailors from interned German ships, who had been there since the outbreak of the war. What they saw and learned, quite frankly, stunned them.

The Mountain Park Hotel in Hot Springs was built in 1886 and served the wealthy as a luxury resort and spa that featured hot springs, with desired healing properties. The hotel had enjoyed a thriving business until the outbreak of World War I, when travel to the hotel slowed considerably. Sometime after the start of the war, the owner of the hotel, Col. Rumbough, approached the War Department with a proposal to convert the hotel to house prisoners-of-war. After Great Britain declared war on Germany in 1914, many German citizens and crew members of German commercial ships, took cover in American ports. Included in this group were members of a German orchestra, as well as, the crew of the world's largest ship, the "Vaterland" (Fatherland). Because these persons were citizens, and not soldiers, they were not technically prisoners-of-war, and instead were designated as "enemy aliens" by the Department of Immigration.

Brought by train to Hot Springs, these passengers, officers, and crew members would spend the remaining years of the war living in and around the Mountain Park Hotel. Immigrants who had been held at Ellis Island since the beginning of the war, were also brought to Hot Springs. Officers were housed in the hotel, while crew members and others were placed in barracks built on the lawns of the hotel. As for women, they were placed in rooms throughout the nearby town, and children went to the local public schools. In time, the Germans built a small village on the lawn of the hotel using scrap lumber and driftwood, including a chapel made almost entirely of flattened Prince Albert Tobacco tins. With no paint to be had, the crafty builders improvised with mixed berry juices and colored clays bringing much needed splashes of color to the makeshift village. Thankfully, one of the detainees, Adolph Thierbach, was a photographer and chronicled his time while in Hot Springs so these black and white images survive to this day.

In time, many friendships developed between the German detainees and the local townspeople. The atrocities of the war on a distant continent, were nowhere to be found in Western North Carolina. Far from what might be found in a traditional prisoner-of-war camp, relatives of detainees were granted permission to visit detainees and many Germans were often guests in the homes of the townspeople. Guards would dine with detainees at their homes for dinner, while Germans passed along their crafts to townspeople including informal classes in dressmaking. With so many talented musicians on board the ship, rehearsals were held daily, culminating in concerts for the town every Sunday afternoon.

Not all experiences in Hot Springs were pleasant for the detainees as much of the village was washed away in the 1916 floods that ravished the area, even causing extensive damage to the Mountain Park Hotel itself. During that time, most detainees were forced to take refuge in higher ground. Things were equally bad in 1918, with many German detainees succumbing to the Spanish flu and a wave of typhoid. However, when the armistice was announced in November of that same year, the German band could be heard playing for the entire town all night long. After the war had ended, the Germans were transported to Oglethorpe, Georgia with some returning from there to Germany. However, many decided to stay in America, and many returned to North Carolina with their families to visit or to live. When the Vagabonds visited Hot Springs in 1918, they observed homemade bowling allies, and were shown local crafts including homemade pocketbooks and other "small trinkets." The campers also commented that everyone appeared "well fed" and that many appeared to be "having a nice vacation."

The roads in and around Hot Springs were rough and mountainous country. After spending time at the German camp, the party drove towards Asheville, encountering another tortuous twenty-five miles of steep inclines and harrowing cliffs along the way. The caravan came close to the edge of precipice several times, and although nobody seriously believed they would survive driving over one of these overhangs, some occupants nonetheless vied for those seats towards the inside of the automobiles. Perhaps, if nothing else, it allowed them to not see what was going on or just how close they were to the bluff. The senior Firestone, who knew a thing or two about tires and issues of road grip, was not ashamed to express his concerns later saying that he "took no chances and...changed seats with my companion every time the side of the mountain changed." Edison, on the other hand, was not such a person, preferring to stay in an outside seat to enjoy the birds eye view.

The next stop was Mars Hill, North Carolina, a small college town deriving its name from the local University, nestled aside the Blue Ridge Mountains. The party was well received, as the pilots, Harvey, Jr., Burroughs, Ford and DeLoach, were greeted with flowers and fruit from school children and female college students. Prominently displayed, hanging in the street, was a service flag with one hundred-and twenty-eight-stars representing enlistments from the local college.

Mars Hill University, founded in 1856, is the oldest college or university in Western North Carolina, changing its name from Mars Hill College to Mars Hill University in 2013. Originally named French Broad Baptist Institute, sharing this name from the nearby French Broad River, the private university changed its name in 1859 in honor of the hill in ancient Athens on which the Apostle Paul debated Christianity with the city's leading philosophers. Acts 17:22 says, "Then Paul stood in the midst of Mars' hill and said 'Ye men of Athens, I perceive that in all things ye are too superstitious." The college was founded by local families who wanted their children instructed in the Baptist faith. The school, like much of the mountain regions of North Carolina, was hit hard by the civil war and the divided loyalties between the Union and Confederate Armies, even shutting its doors for several years. However, by the turn of the century the school became more stable, and three years following the campers visit, it became an accredited junior college. In 1962 Mars Hill became an accredited four-year college. Founders Hall, the first campus building, is still in use today, and the university is home to the Rural Heritage Museum which at one point exhibited, among other things, included crafts made in 1916 by the interned Germans in Hot Springs. Today the campus is on the U.S. National Register of Historic Places and is listed as a U.S. Historic District.

When asked by the assembled crowd if someone might make a few comments, Edison placated the crowd by rising in his usual gallant way and bowing to each side of the auto. The eldest writer, who was never called upon to say a few words, had nonetheless prepared a few words to say in his mind. Ready on his tongue Burroughs would say, "Ladies of the college, I write books, and Mr. Ford makes cars; I hope you will read my books and ride in nothing but Ford cars." Brief enough, and to the point, the ladies of the college never got the chance to hear those words. After the latest in a string of impromptu receptions, the caravan headed south albeit in pieces toward Weaverville, North Carolina.

The first to get on the road was Henry Ford and the occupants in his car, followed by the trucks. Firestone and Edison brought up the rear and found themselves several minutes behind the others. During the ten mile stretch between towns, Firestone began to formulate a way to carry out a plan that was hatched by the other campers to convince Edison to camp on the grounds of the Grove Park Inn in Asheville or preferably stay at the Inn itself. Somewhere along what is now route 26 south, Firestone told Edison that given the time and Burroughs growing exhaustion, that staying at the Inn could not be ruled out and might be their best option. Edison was not receptive to such propositions, and for the time being held out for a camping site somewhere further south near Asheville. What he did not know is that everyone in the caravan had already decided that they would be bunking at the Grove Park Inn.

In Weaverville, Edison and Firestone were again met by local citizens, including several ladies who were operating a Red Cross booth set up on one of the streets. These ladies invited the two to join them for tea, but the weary duo graciously declined the invitation. As he had done earlier in the day, when asked to speak, Edison instead bowed to the assembled audience and received great applause. However, this time he did briefly speak by offering Firestone as his replacement. Initially Firestone also refused to speak, but the crowd insisted that he must do so as Ford had spoken to them earlier. Firestone relented and spoke to the crowd, thanking the citizens of Weaverville and Western North Carolina for their great hospitality. Harvey had taken one for the team earlier, when he was chosen to bring up the subject of camping arrangements for the evening. Now, he had taken one for Edison in speaking for the two of them. Maybe, just maybe, he could find a way to convince Edison to sleep at the Inn.

CHAPTER 22

Land of the Sky

Asheville, North Carolina is no longer a remote mountain village, trading in mountain craft, for a chic and modern city usually making travel magazines "must see" travel spots. Home of the legendary Biltmore Estate, the region has long attracted rich and famous guests, with even former president, Barack Obama, at one point mentioning Asheville as a potential retirement site. Long before Asheville was filled with hipsters, art galleries, alt-bluegrass, and countless micro-breweries, it was home to quiet mountain peaks, rushing rivers, and spectacular waterfalls. Most geologists agree the Appalachians are the oldest mountains in the world, making this city a new tenant on ancient property. Although Western North Carolina still boasts some of the highest peaks in the Eastern United States, years of wind and water have worn on these tall and rugged peaks. The area is better known now as the Blue Ridge Range with its thick green, forests, ferns, waterfalls, summer storms and creeping mist. Sitting to the East of Asheville is a smaller sister range of mountains, so lush and dark from a distance, that is aptly called the Black Mountain Range. To the west, straddling North Carolina and Tennessee sits the Great Smoky Mountains named for the blue mist, formed by tremendous amounts of water vapor often found hovering atop her peaks and along her valleys. The Cherokee Indians called these mountains Shaconage (shah-con-ah-jey), meaning place of blue smoke, aptly combining the dark color of the mountains with the white clouds and mist surrounding them. To the Southwest sits a half million acres of pristine woodlands, named the Nantahala Forest, named for the Cherokee word meaning "Land of the midday sun," and to Northeast sits the Pisgah Forest, established in 1915 when the Vanderbilt family sold wooded land to the federal government.

Today, local old-timers fondly recall the area's blue grass roots, and having a fiddle is still considered a requirement for any well-respected band. However, long before any foot stomping or clogging, moccasins of earlier native peoples softly walked the area. What became of them is not known, and their lives now just a whisper. Tens of thousands of years ago, during the last ice age, it is believed that a great variety of seeds from tall trees of the north had been absorbed in glaciers and as the glaciers melted those seeds were dropped in more southern climates. Places such as Western North Carolina, with nourishment from rain and river, provided rich soil and many of these seeds took root and ultimately thrived making the area home to nearly two thousand different species of trees, plants, and wildflowers.

The Paleo Indians were early arrivals to the area and with no permanent homes were classic hunters and gatherers. Hunting larger animals, they were followed by the Archaic Indians, who were more settled, and who hunted smaller animals including deer, moose and elk. Their culture gradually evolved into what is called the Woodland culture or tradition. The Woodland Indians built huge earthen mounds, preserved today as historical sites. These mounds are believed to have been used as burial grounds and had some sort of religious significance, with the most recognized mound in the area being Nikwasi in Franklin, North Carolina.

About 1,000 years ago a different civilization, the Mississippians, began to take hold. These people settled into larger villages, were more advanced in their cultural structure, and it is believed that these people greatly influenced the Cherokee and the Creek. The Cherokee are probably one of the most well-known Indian tribes, and based on their language, it is believed they are an offshoot of the Iroquois Nation from the New York area. Moving southward these people flourished and developed into the strongest and largest tribe in the Eastern part of the United States. Although the Cherokee did not believe in individual land ownership, the governing villages were in the upper part of South Carolina and along the present border of North Carolina and Tennessee, with the center of the Nation located in what is today, Swain County, North Carolina.

Sometime around 1770, Fort Davidson was built at the eastern edge of the Blue Ridge as a refuge for white settlers to fend off any attacks by the Cherokee. The fort was named for the Samuel Davidson family, generally accepted as the first white family in the area. Davidson was a colonel in the Revolutionary War, and like many veterans in the War for Independence, he received a land grant for his service. He, along with his wife and child, cleared land and built a cabin. When the family planted crops, it became clear to the nearby Cherokee that Samuel Davidson and his family intended to stay. Angry with such an encroachment, the Indians plotted against Davidson and one dark night they stole a bell from one of his horses and rang the bell from a nearby hilltop. Davidson, thinking one of his horses had wandered off, grabbed his gun in search of the animal. Instead of recovering his horse, he lost his life.

Davidson was ambushed, ultimately killed, and sadly scalped. His wife, hearing much of the commotion surrounding the attack, hid their child in a dirt room scooped out under the floor. While the Indians shouted from the woods outside, mother and child remained motionless until the Indians finally left. Later, after gathering a few belongings, she made it over the mountains and back to the fort ultimately named for her family. After relaying the events to other family members, Davidson's relatives traveled back to the cabin, found Samuel's body and gave him a proper burial. Bent on revenge, they found and killed Indians believed to have been part of the ambush, and as a further act of defiance, friends and relatives came back over the Blue Ridge and settled permanently on a site where the Bee Tree Creek joins the Swannanoa River. Such stories of expansion and encroachment, followed by unspeakable violence, are only well too known as part of the American story.

In 1792 the County of Buncombe was established, and was named for another Revolutionary War hero, Col. Edward Buncombe. Besides land grant holders, the area came to be populated with circuit riding preachers and missionaries. However, if Asheville has a founding father, it would be either John Burton or William Davidson. Davidson owned nearly 600,000 acres, also given to him for his service in the war, and his home and farm were established at Gum Spring on the French Broad River near the present-day gate to the Biltmore estate. Burton, meanwhile, was a land speculator, gristmill operator, and farmer, who purchased several hundred acres from Davidson and quickly went to work on making roadways. Based on old Cherokee trails, these roadways would become the present-day streets of Broadway and Biltmore Avenue. Next, he marked off one-half acre lots, selling his first lot for thirty shillings or approximately $320.00 in the day. English coins were still used in rural parts of America, including western North Carolina, until 1809 when North Carolina ordered the use of United States Currency.

Eventually the Burton town tract became the county seat. Legend has it that Burton influenced the vote of a William Morrison from Burke County by plying him with whiskey and by agreeing that the town would be called Morristown. True or not, nobody seemed to like the name, and just one year later it was changed to Asheville in honor of Samuel Ashe, a longtime lawyer who also served as governor of North Carolina from 1795 to 1798. Burton, who sold the last of his lots, moved on, but Davidson would remain in the area his entire life.

By 1830 the population of Asheville was 350 and by 1850 there were 640 souls, including 86 slaves and eight freed blacks. Like many parts of the country, slavery was tolerated but not particularly encouraged in many parts of North Carolina. Justification for such a brutal and immoral practice, found no place in the hearts of many

Americans. While others, like Zebulon Vance, were riddled with conflict. Born in 1830 in the northern part of Buncombe County, Vance would become an attorney and prominent landowner in the area. More importantly, he would serve in the United States Congress in the period leading up to the Civil War. His family had previously owned slaves, yet he had strong Union sympathies and argued for North Carolina to stay in the Union. Only after it became impossible for him to convince others to join him, he aligned himself with family and friends and relented to secession. He left congress, returned home, and raised a regiment from Asheville known as the Rough and Ready Guards. This regiment was regularly engaged and by the end of the war nearly all had been either killed or wounded.

When Vance was in Virginia with his regiment, he was called back to North Carolina to become governor, as he had won the popular vote in the Fall of 1862. He served as governor during a tumultuous time, and as the war ended with much of the South destroyed or thrown into chaos, North Carolina fared much better. In 1865, Vance, along with many other southern leaders, was arrested, taken into custody, and ultimately incarcerated at the old Capital prison. In July of that same year, he was paroled and returned home with nothing to his name. Stripped of everything, he settled in Charlotte with his family, and started his law practice again. He would return for a third term as governor, and returned to Washington D.C., not as a prisoner, but as a U.S. senator. Vance died in 1884 and just four years later the Vance Monument, a tall stone tower, was placed in the heart of downtown Asheville. Today, as the country still grapples with the stain of slavery, and the removal of historical artifacts occupies the current rage in big cities and college towns, the monument has not been torn down but instead is literally and figuratively wrapped in a black shroud awaiting its fate. Vance, who called Asheville the "Queen City of the Mountains," may not survive in statute form, but his story remains remarkable with or without spray paint.

By 1880 the Asheville population was over 2,500 and growing rapidly thanks, in part, to a novel titled *The Land of the Sky*. Written by Francis Fisher Tiernan, under the pseudonym Christian Reid, the story described in glowing terms the beautiful mountains surrounding Asheville. With railways slowly finding their way into southern mountain towns through tunnels and other miraculous engineering feats, Asheville found passenger trains full of summer visitors on her doorstep. Many of these early visitors, seeking a mild climate, were persons of wealth and privilege. In fact, known as a luxury destination for the rich, the Toxaway Inn, a hotel in Asheville, advertised for millionaires only and was served by four passenger cars daily. Soon others arrived looking for work at these facilities and in time they also needed housing and services. Fire departments, telegraph lines, an electrical plant, a hospital, and a baseball team called the *Moonshiners* represented the steady growth of a town into a small city.

Asheville not only became a destination for the rich, but it also became a place to find restoration especially for those that were ill. When the mayor of Asheville openly promoted the area as a health resort it did not take long for those with ailments to seek out the mountain town in search of fresh air and the mild climate. In the 1880s, health facilities began to take root, with one hospital being followed by another.

St. Josephs, which was founded in 1900 by the Sisters of Mercy, opened an eighteen-bed tuberculosis sanitorium. Physicians became known for treating tuberculosis and other lung conditions, so that at any given time thousands of people were being treated in this self-proclaimed health resort. However, not all who came to Asheville were there to seek a healthy make-over. Many, including industrialist Edwin George Carrier, stopped in Asheville en route to other southern destinations. Carrier, who was on his way to Florida from Michigan, saw a great opportunity in the area and moved his family permanently to Asheville in 1885. He bought up land west of the French Broad River, and with a successful lumber business in that state up north, he set about rebuilding the Sulphur Springs Resort. After reopening it as the Carrier Springs Hotel, he built a wooden dam to provide hydroelectric power for not only his hotel but also to provide power for a commercial streetcar. It would also power the first streetlights in Asheville. Carrier was not done yet, as his next construction project was a large steel bridge built across the French Broad River. This bridge, which would later come to be known as Carrier's bridge, led to expansion on the west side of the river, proving pivotal to further development of the area. Soon other bridges would follow.

George Willis Pack was not passing through town. Nor was he there for his own health. Learning of Asheville's reputation for health and restoration, he brought his ailing wife from Cleveland, Ohio and took up residence at the Swannanoa Hotel. Like others, who had come before him, he fell madly for the mountain town and took up permanent residence with his family. He gave generously to the community, and today, Pack Square, which is home of the temporarily covered statue of Zebulon Vance, serves as a reminder of the Pack family and all the former Ohioans did for Asheville.

Another prominent figure in Asheville in the 1800s was Franklin Coxe. Unlike Prack and Carrier, Coxe was a southerner, who had traveled north to attend school at the University of Pennsylvania. After graduating as an engineer, he worked with his brother in a family mine in Pennsylvania. However, when the Civil War broke out, he quickly enlisted as a private in Kershaw's brigade in the Butler's Guard of South Carolina Volunteers. What happened next can only be chalked up to the complexity of this unprecedented war. After fighting at the Battle of Bull Run, Coxe became aware that the United States government planned to confiscate private property including his family mines in Pennsylvania. Jefferson Davis, President of the Confederate States, released him from his military obligations allowing him to travel north to try to salvage the family business. Doing what many wealthy persons did at the time, he paid to have someone serve in his place. However, shortly after arriving in Pennsylvania, he joined the Union army. Ultimately, he paid for a substitute to take his place and so technically he served in both armies at the same time.

As if this is not odd enough, there is more to the story. Records seem to suggest, and Coxe appears to have been made aware, that not only did his substitutes fight against each other in battle, but both appear to have been killed. Perhaps this led to a complete disillusionment in the war and the confederacy as he moved to Paris, France and did not return to the United States until after the war. With businesses in both North Carolina and Pennsylvania, he later became the president of the Western North Carolina Railroad and found himself spending more and more time in Asheville. Eventually he purchased an area of land known as Battery Porter, renamed it Battery Park, and built his ornate Battery Park Hotel. Set on 22 acres this extravagant hotel would pave the way for a series of other unique and extraordinary hotels and homes in Asheville. One famous guest at the Battery Park Hotel was George Vanderbilt, who may very well have been impressed by what he saw.

CHAPTER 23

Sunset Mountain

Snuggled into an aptly named Sunset Mountain, with its distinctive red clay file roofs and granite rock, all with wonderful views of downtown Asheville, nearby Mountain Ranges and the French Broad River Valley, sits the Grove Park Inn. Stepping into the Great Hall of this Inn, being greeted by towering granite walls and columns with large oak furniture and an enormous fireplace, is like stepping into a postcard or magazine spread. Advertised at the turn of the 20th century as the finest hotel in the world, the Inn also promised its guests that it was "absolutely fireproof," was "open all year," and that "the altitude makes it cool in Summer." Also advertised prominently was the "five hundred feet of porch," referred to today as the Sunset Terrace. This outdoor terrace sits adjacent to the Great Hall, and being covered, offers spectacular (and dry) views to visitors and locals alike.

Like many famous Inns, the Grove Park Inn has had plenty of famous guests. The Inn has hosted Presidents: Franklin D. Roosevelt, Dwight Eisenhower, Woodrow Wilson, Herbert Hoover, William Howard Taft, Calvin Coolidge, Richard Nixon, George H.W. Bush, Barack Obama, and Donald Trump. Besides the 1918 camping party, other famous guests have included Eleanor Roosevelt, Charles Schwab, George Gershwin, John Denver, Will Rogers, Billy Graham and John D. Rockefeller. Actors including Sir Anthony Hopkins, William Shatner, Dan Aykroyd and Jeff Daniels are also known to have been visitors. Sir Daniel Day-Lewis was a guest of the Inn while filming *Last of the Mohicans*, much of which was filmed in Western North Carolina. Magician David Copperfield was a guest as was the great Harry Houdini, and basketball legend Michael Jordan has been a frequent visitor. Lastly, F. Scott Fitzgerald, who became a bit of a permanent resident at the Inn, at one point had his own room.

When the Vagabonds arrived at the Grove Park Inn on the evening of August 27, 1918, they had traveled approximately eighty miles from Jonesborough, Tennessee. Edison had held out hope of camping on Sunset Mountain as opposed to sleeping in the Inn and complained bitterly that he would have to change his clothes for the dining room. Whether the other campers put him up to it, or if he took it upon himself, Harvey Firestone made a last-minute pitch for staying at the Inn and at last Edison relented. So it was that at 8:30 PM the travelers were personally greeted by the cordial manager, F.L. Seely, and staff, who assured the campers that all their accommodations had been prepared. Edison, recently made agreeable to the stay, seemed again agitated as he lamented that his grip and wardrobe had not arrived so that he could not shave or put on a clean collar for dinner. His mood soon changed as a fine dinner was served in the dining room and after taking motion pictures with the party, Edison read until midnight, keeping everyone in the hotel up until he finally retired for the night.

Built five years earlier, the Inn was made for men like Ford, Edison and Firestone. In fact, a 1918 *New York Times* ad proclaimed, “If you are a Big Businessman and feel the need to rest after years of strain, you should come to the Grove Park Inn, Asheville, NC where rest is possible.” There was a belief that the men who patronized the Inn not only expected the finest amenities, but also peace and quiet. This belief was based mainly on the fact that the Inn was built by a like-minded businessman. Born on a small plantation in 1850, Edwin Wiley Grove, would become a father figure to modern Asheville. Striking out on his own when he was twenty-four, he became a clerk and pharmacist in a drug store in Paris, Tennessee and set about finding a formula or compound that would make him famous as a pharmacist. Within months he bought the drug store and renamed it Grove's Pharmacy.

The young Grove was not aimlessly mixing compounds, but instead was experimenting with making a tasteless chill tonic. As a young boy from Tennessee, he was keenly aware of malaria and the havoc it brought to those who had it. He was also aware that the only known remedy, quinine powder, had a horrible taste which made people reluctant to take or use it even when they should. Grove realized that if he could change that, it would make him a fortune. By 1878, Grove developed his first formula for suspending quinine in a liquid thereby making it relatively tasteless. He called it feberlin, but because of the high level of quinine, it had to be sold by prescription only. After additional experimentation he learned to further reduce the level of quinine, making it essentially an over the counter (non-prescription) remedy and to further enhance the taste by adding iron, lemon, and, of course, sugar. The result, Grove's Tasteless Chill Tonic, was an overnight sensation, and proved that the kid from Tennessee understood that a "spoonful of sugar helps the medicine go down." Although not a cure, it reduced the patient's symptoms of fever and chills and otherwise kept the malaria parasite in check. Soon it was a household name and, at one point in the 1890s, it even rivaled in sales another well-known Southern bottled drink: Coca-Cola.

It was not long until Grove's Pharmacy became Paris Medicine Company, moving from its original site to a larger manufacturing facility in St. Louis, Missouri where product could easily be shipped by rail to customers throughout the entire United States. The Groves tonic, with its famous trademark containing the face of a baby boy on the body of a plump pig and slogan "No Cure, No Pay," was one of the most recognized products of its time and made Edwin Grove a very rich man. However, money could not save Grove from unusual hardship, as his young wife, Mary Louise, died in 1884, and of his first four children, only one, Evelyn, survived infancy.

Grove continued to pursue new and different pharmaceuticals and created a cold tablet called Grove's Laxative Bromo Quinine. Later he commissioned The Parke-Davies Company (now a subsidiary of Pfizer) in Detroit, Michigan to produce the tablets and it was here that he met a promising young man by the name of Fred Seely, who would one day also become his son-in-law. Seely, who had attended the New York College of Pharmacy and who had been a clerk at Johnson & Johnson, had distinguished himself at Park-Davis by creating a machine that compressed tablets. This invention, along with his expertise, made him a perfect fit for Grove and the Paris Medicine Company. Grove must have also taken personally to Seely as it was not long thereafter that he introduced him to his daughter, Evelyn, and soon the two were married. Perhaps Grove was looking for an heir to his pharmaceutical company and saw a little of himself in the younger man. It was at, or about this time, that Grove had developed chronic insomnia and bronchitis and at the advice of his family physician in St. Louis had taken a trip to Asheville where he was advised to relax and seek out medical attention in one of Asheville's sanitariums. Although never fully cured of his ailments, Grove found Asheville a great escape from the steamy Midwest Summers of St. Louis and not only established a residence in North Carolina, but also set up a branch of his pharmaceutical company there. It was at this summer residence that Seely met his future wife.

Fred Seely's contribution to Grove's business proved to be substantial as his machine would form, count, and box tablets of non-liquid cold medicines making the Paris Medicine Company into one of the leading suppliers of cold remedies in the world. Meanwhile Grove began to accumulate real estate including heavily timbered land in and about Asheville and bought up lots on the north edge of town on Sunset Mountain. He established the E.W. Grove Park Company which would not only buy, sell and develop land for residential real estate, but also planned to own, build, erect, construct and manage hotel properties. Sometime around 1909 the idea of a resort hotel on Sunset Mountain began to take shape and Grove began to solicit architectural sketches for his new hotel. Grove wanted the hotel to look like a hotel from Yellowstone Park, but none of the designs submitted captured his fancy. In the end, it was a sketch from his son-in-law that caught his eye. Seely had basically taken the image of *The Old Faithful Lodge* in Yellowstone Park and replaced the inn of logs with native North Carolina boulders. What is somewhat astonishing is that Seely had little formal education in architecture and no previous experience in designing or sketching hotels, yet the original sketch is nearly identical to the hotel that sits on Sunset Mountain today.

The spot they picked to build the hotel was almost 2,500 feet above sea level and was designed to provide views of Asheville and the Western rim of the Blue Ridge Mountains. Seely took his drawings and designs to a certified architect, J.W. McKibben of Atlanta who served as the hotel's chief engineer. McKibben was joined by another man from Atlanta, J. Oscar Mills, who would serve as the construction engineer.

Successful building projects are often fascinating displays of engineering and perseverance, and the Grove Park Inn is no exception. Breaking ground in July of 1912, Seely and Grove had promised that the hotel would be open to the public by the following summer. This was a breathtaking, if not foolish, promise. Building a hotel of such magnitude on the side of a mountain would not be simple. Mills, the construction engineer, wasted no time by hiring four hundred men and by creating the best of all incentives: good pay. At one dollar a day for a ten-hour day, scores of workers, both old and young, were temporarily housed in a gigantic circus-like tent. Hauling granite stones up the side of a mountain is not an easy task, and mules were used to drag nearby boulders from neighboring mountains onto roads where they were then hoisted onto wagons. The wagons were then strung together to form what was dubbed the "automobile train" and were pulled up the mountain by three Packard trucks. Even with hauling up to forty tons of rock per trip, it was slow and tedious work. Many Italian stonemasons, who had worked two decades earlier on Vanderbilt's Biltmore estate, were put to work carefully arranging exposed uncut stones into place. Seely later recounted that the stones "were laid with the lichens and moss on them just as they were found." What these artisans created was six stories of rock walls, arranged neatly by the hands of men with the stones at the bottom often being more than four feet thick. Building the higher floors required the building of a crude elevator that was designed to lift huge buckets of wet heavy concrete and stone. The Inn has 5 concrete roofs, with the highest being over the Great Hall, and it was one of the largest continuous pour concrete roofs of the time.

By March of 1913 some of the work was being done throughout the night and the men were laying the very recognizable red roof-top tile shingles, meant to give the Inn an English thatch-like appearance. Meanwhile carpenters, plumbers, and stonemasons worked frantically inside on the Great Hall building a massive fireplace inspired, again, by the fireplace at the *Old Faithful Inn* with a unique twist as elevators were concealed within these giant structures. After the finishing touches were put into the guest rooms and throughout the Inn, Seely turned to a good friend, Elbert Hubbard, founder of Roycroft Shops located in East Aurora, New York who was known for making high quality furniture, metalware and lighting. For the opening, Roycroft built more than four-hundred oak chairs, created large corner servers, and provided an eight-foot-tall clock located just through the front doors. While handmade rugs were imported from France, a Mr. J.S. White of the White Furniture Company in Mebane, North Carolina reached out to Seely to provide amenities for the guest rooms including twelve hundred beds, dressers, tables and more chairs. Finding the products from the White to be of the greatest Carolina quality, they were also asked to make doors and the ornamental pieces throughout the Inn.

On Saturday, July 12, 1913, four hundred distinguished guests, including Secretary of State William Jennings Bryan, arrived at eight o'clock to attend the opening of the Grove Park Inn. The Secretary delivered a principal address to those in attendance and proclaimed that the hotel was "built for the ages," although the hotel was far from complete as there was no landscaping, the tile roof was not finished, and many guest rooms remained unfurnished. While Seely served as a toastmaster for the festivities, and Secretary Bryan as provider of the primary address, it was Edwin Grove himself that captured the night and the beginning of an age of austerity when stating, "A man never grows too old to build castles and dream dreams. Standing here in the midst of my friends and invited guests, I find a dream realized and a castle materialized." He also added that it helped that his son-in-law was "both an architect and a builder," and that the completion of the hotel in so short a time "seems almost beyond human endurance."

By the time our travelers descended upon Asheville, some five years after the opening, Seely had essentially leased the Grove Park Inn from his father-in-law (an arrangement that would one day lead to a strained relationship with Grove) and the Inn reflected his philosophy. There was no alcohol permitted at the Inn, even before prohibition, and smoking was strongly curtailed and discouraged. With these restrictions Ford and Edison were surely in agreement as neither smoked nor drank. The menu for the Inn also featured healthy food choices long before such choices became the modern norm they are today. One would assume that Edison and Ford enjoyed such healthy choices as both were known to have strong opinions about the benefits of certain diets, although Edison was well known to not always practice what he preached as he liked to snack and had more than a bit of a sweet tooth. The Inn also had a 10:30 PM curfew designed to ensure guests received much needed rest and relaxation. Edison clearly broke the suggested curfew, but if anyone complained it was not formally recorded.

CHAPTER 24

"I cannot possibly go any further."

The following morning, August 28th, the Vagabonds enjoyed a late breakfast at 10 AM, after sleeping in from their long travels and late-night merrymaking and hotel curfew breaking. After breakfast, Firestone and Ford took what had become one of their customary walks over to the adjacent golf links and then hiked up Sunset Mountain. Upon their return they met up with Thomas Edison and after some mutual concerns were expressed about John Burroughs and his obvious fatigue, it was decided that this might be a good time to leave their camping outfit. The aging writer had found it difficult to sleep from sheer exhaustion. Professor Deloach had an adjoining room with him, and when Burroughs came to his room the next morning, he told the professor, "DeLoach, I cannot possibly go any further on this trip. I am completely worn out, and I want you to help me in some honorable way to get the news to Ford that you are leaving and that I am going with you."

Burroughs, who was much older than everyone else, had been quite a trooper, but was clearly worn out and had decided on his own that this was a good point in the adventure to bid farewell. In his published impressions of the trip, the writer confessed that he had often been irritable, "but (his) companions were tolerant and gave little heed to the flitting moods of an octogenarian." In any event, it was decided by the party that Burroughs would take a passenger train home to his beloved Catskill Mountains. Seely, unaware of this afternoon decision, had been busy scouting out possible campsites for his famous guests and believed Chunn's Cove would provide a perfect setting. However, after the nature writer's decision to head home, all momentum was lost, and the remaining members decided they would turn north as well.

Like most goodbyes it was slow and hesitant, and after lunch the group took photos and motion pictures in front of the Inn to memorialize the final resting spot of the full party's 1918 road trip. It was not until 3 PM that they finally departed Asheville and perhaps to reflect the collective mood of the party they were greeted by a pouring rain. Before they left, the friends penned a letter to Seely on Grove Park Inn stationery:

> Dear Mr. Seely,
>
> After a ten days camping trip thru the mountains of West Virginia and your own "Land of the Sky," we felt when we arrived at the Grove Park Inn, the "Finest Resort Hotel in the world," that possibly we were not quite presentable enough to expect a welcome. We not only received the welcome but the warmest hospitality we have ever had extended to us. May you live long and be a blessing to many other travelers!
>
> John Burroughs, Thomas Edison,
> R.J.H. DeLouch, Harvey S. Firestone,
> Harvey S. Firestone, Jr., Henry Ford

While Burroughs was joined by Professor DeLoach, the remaining travelers departed West for Hickory, North Carolina in Harvey Junior's car with Edison in the front passenger seat and Harvey Sr. and Mr. Ford in the rear seats. This route would take them much further East for their Northern journey back home. On their way, they stopped at a hotel for supper in a little town called Marion. Apparently, the four went unrecognized and were waited upon by a rather grouchy waiter, who sported a toothpick in his mouth. Edison, perhaps equally worn out with the train-bound Burroughs, became confused when ordering his dinner as he could not hear what was being asked of him. In turn, the waiter became equally confused and a tad bit grouchier. Firestone diffused the situation by asking the waiter if he was ever known to smile, and although the waiter initially ignored the tire-maker, he ultimately smiled ear to ear. He was later rewarded by Edison who gave the man a dollar for his patience with him. Following the early supper, Harvey Jr., and Harvey, Sr. went in search of a telegraph office to send their congratulations to a family member and his bride but found the office to be closed. After asking around, they located someone in a nearby boarding house, who could deliver the telegrams.

On their way out of town, just as it was getting dark, a spring broke on their car. Ford again came to the rescue somehow fixing the damaged spring with a cord. Before reaching Hickory, a piloting party came out to meet the travelers and escort them into town. Firestone described eating "the usual amount of dust," but was thankful as in the dark, and without their guidance, they would never have found the hotel. The pared down party was able to secure two rooms at the Hotel Huffry, including a room with a bath for Edison and Ford and another room with a bath downstairs for the Firestones. The second room also had a kitchen on one side and an office on the other. For whatever reason, at three o'clock in the morning, a cleaning crew showed up to tidy up the nearby office. The elder Firestone, who had heard the ruckus for about half an hour, finally got up out of bed, and, in his nightshirt, went next door to ask if the cleaning could wait until later in the morning. Harvey was pleased when they agreed and returned to bed in hopes of finally getting some much-needed sleep only to hear the nearby kitchen begin to stir. The following morning the party had breakfast together and met a long-time agent for Ford, who had driven fifteen miles to see Henry Ford and his companions.

The next stop was due north of Charlotte in Statesville, North Carolina, where Ford believed a search for a more permanent solution to the fixed spring was warranted. However, he was unable to find a new spring in town, so Harvey Jr. telephoned ahead to a Winston-Salem Firestone branch where a new spring was located. Five miles out of town, Ford's concerns became well-founded as the make-shift spring gave way again. Ford, who took an hour to tinker with it, left the rest of the party with time to talk with nearby residents. Firestone met a "colored" family with eleven children, two of whom were married. The family, which left a favorable impression upon the tire-maker, told him they owned forty acres of land and rented an additional forty more.

After Ford had made the needed repairs, the group motored further down the road where they were met by a multitude of cars, perhaps six in total, that would escort them into Winston-Salem where they learned a dinner had been prepared for them. Again, Firestone, as a thanks for such hospitality, got out of the car and swapped places with a local resident who joined Ford in the back seat. Upon arrival in the Winston-Salem region, the party was taken to the Forsyth Country Club, where they visited many local citizens on a large club porch before a rather "formal" luncheon was served in the clubhouse. When the remaining vagabonds finally made it to Winston-Salem, another large reception awaited them at a local branch of the Ford Motor Company.

Following these festivities, and with their bellies full and a brand-new car spring, the party motored on towards Martinsville, Virginia. However, on the way, the road turned quite muddy, and the car got stuck. Ford and Edison believed the car should be jacked up and then backed out in some manner. "Father Firestone," who knew a thing or two about tires and traction, had much more faith in a team of mules, and managed to secure the animals from a nearby farmer. The party borrowed a chain from a woman, untying it from a tree where it tethered a cow. Thankfully, the mules easily pulled the car out of the mud and muck. During this escapade, Henry Ford had noticed that the woman, whose chain they had borrowed, had no teeth. He also expressed concerns to the other passengers about the welfare of her children, who appeared to be dealing with certain unknown health issues.

About this same time, a former Ford dealer, who had gotten word that Ford's car was stuck, had come down to the farm along with his family to see if he could lend a hand. He also wanted to finally meet his former boss. This provided the perfect opportunity for Henry Ford to ask the former dealer to help him out by making sure the woman got to a dentist and the children got to a doctor or hospital. It was agreed that the dealer would supervise these activities and would send the bill to Ford. Before departing, the automaker also slipped the woman twenty-five dollars.

Another large reception awaited the party in Martinsville. It seems the entire population had congregated at the Broad Street Hotel with many of the women dressed in all white. After eating inside the hotel, the party briefly attempted to wander about outside, but quickly reentered the hotel after it became obvious that the crowd would not allow them to move about freely. The one-time campers retired early. The following morning, on August 30th, another reception awaited them. It all was becoming a bit too much. On their way out of town, Firestone learned that Marshall Fields had a fabric mill nearby and convinced the other travelers to make a stop there to learn more. Of particular interest to Firestone and Ford was a new development that brought mountaineers down to the mill by furnishing them with nice homes for the rental of a dollar a month. Although Firestone described many of the workers as still looking "scrawny and poorly kept," the manager believed this would change in time as the mill was also providing better wages, along with furnishing schools, churches, and amusements. Little did he realize that such paternalistic endeavors were wrought with danger and were certain to back-fire.

The next stop was in Roanoke, Virginia and a stop at a Firestone agent where they inquired about lodging. Any idea of further camping was all but forgotten. Sato and Kline, along with the remnants of the camping convoy, were instructed to meet them at the hotel recommended by the agent. Later, while searching for a tube and gasoline, the auto ran out of gas and the famous travelers had to wait near the hotel until a wagon came by and gave them sufficient gas to get to the next filling station. Finally, while leaving Roanoke, they came upon a car whose driver wanted to pilot the tour out of the city. The weary passengers, who were no longer in any mood to be led to another possible reception, decided to pass the newcomers' car, whereupon a drag race ensued. For the next five miles, Harvey Jr. was encouraged by Ford and Firestone to not allow the other car to pass them. With a sporting blood, and much to the chagrin of Thomas Edison, the younger Firestone raced ahead of the other driver reaching speeds in excess of sixty-miles-an-hour.

When the racers reached the Natural Bridge later that afternoon, Mr. Ford, Mr. Firestone and his son paid a dollar each to see the natural wonder. Standing at 215 feet, the limestone gorge is carved out by Cedar Creek, creating a geological formation much like a cave or tunnel. Just south of Lexington, Virginia, the bridge was a sacred site of the Native American Monacan tribe, who believed it was the site of a major victory over the Powhatans centuries before the arrival of Europeans. The site is also one of the oldest tourist destinations in the United States and was visited by George Washington in 1750 as a young surveyor. In fact, many believe his initials are carved along one of the walls of the bridge. In 1774 Thomas Jefferson purchased 157 acres, including the Natural Bridge, from King George III of Great Britain for 20 shillings. It seems Jefferson always had a knack for making deals for great property at a great price—just ask the French. Describing it as "the most sublime of nature's works," Jefferson later built a two-room log cabin near the bridge which was used as a retreat. Apparently, unimpressed, worn out, or just not willing to part with a dollar, Edison stayed behind in the car. Of course, he was seventy-one years old, and perhaps the thought of a hike in unknown terrain was just too much for the great inventor.

It was about five o'clock when the Firestones and Ford went down and followed the trail under the bridge to a cave, the Lost River, and other points of interest. Two hours later the hikers emerged with a delegation from the nearby Natural Bridge Hotel, only to find Edison's car surrounded by other guests of the hotel. Ford and Edison wanted to get to Lexington right away, but after some local persuasion, it was decided they would stay for dinner. The Firestones convinced Edison that by staying for dinner they might avoid yet another crowd waiting for them in Lexington. However, there is some mention of the fact that there were "many good-looking young ladies" at the Natural Bridge Hotel, and one is left to wonder if the younger Firestone was the real reason the older members of the party relented. In any event, the proprietor furnished front rooms where they could wash up, and a band to escort them to the dining room. By all accounts, dinner was excellent.

After being given a royal treatment fit for visiting dignitaries, the four departed for the Castle Inn, located about a mile out of Lexington, Virginia. It was later, and darker, than initially anticipated, and the crew had a bit of difficulty in finding the Inn. Once they had located the place, and after they had been taken to their rooms, the four joined a welcoming party that had congregated on the front porch. Apparently, a rivalry developed between hostesses as each wanted the distinguished guests as their guests of honor. One woman, who was giving a dance party for her daughter, asked Firestone if he would bring his son. Trying to please everyone, the gentlemen essentially bounced back and forth between these dueling parties. At one point, Firestone tried to blend the parties into one, only to be politely reminded that this could not be done as one woman told him, "I'm not invited (to the other party)."

The next morning the travelers ordered breakfast at 7 AM. It was August 31st, 1918. When they finished eating, another reception was held in the lobby. After departing the Inn, the president of Washington & Lee University escorted the party through the nearby university, including a tour of the tomb of Robert E. Lee and Lee's office. Lee, who was President of Washington College from 1865 until his death in 1870 and for whom the university is now partially named, oversaw the construction of a chapel in 1867-1868. The chapel, now named Lee Chapel, is the final resting spot for the Confederate General. Lee's horse, Traveller, his beloved companion from West Virginia, who got a front row seat to much of the Civil War, is buried just outside the Chapel not far from his master's final resting place. The horse died a year after Lee. Ford, Edison, and the Firestones, would not have seen this grave as Traveller's remains were not moved there until 1971. Nor would they have seen the many coins and apples left by visitors to pay tribute to one of man's greatest friends: the horse. The stable where Traveller lived out his final days is directly connected to the Lee House on campus and traditionally stands with its doors left open to allow his spirit to wander freely. Our travelers may or may not have been made aware of this, but regardless might have felt his spirit.

It is also not known if the travelers stopped to visit Lexington's other college, Virginia Military Institute (VMI). If they did, they might have been told that it was founded in 1839 as America's first state military college, and that Abraham Lincoln referred to it as 'The West Point of the South." VMI has indeed lived up the nickname as it has produced more Army Generals than any other ROTC program in the United States. George Patton and George C. Marshall were alumni, and the school has had many famous professors including Thomas "Stonewall" Jackson who starting in 1851 taught Natural and Experimental Philosophy (physics) and artillery tactics. It is also not known if the travelers stopped to see the Confederate General's house just a few blocks away, or if they spent any additional time in the charming town of Lexington. Given their state of fatigue it seems unlikely.

At Staunton, Virginia, deep in the heart of the Shenandoah Valley and coincidentally the birthplace for President Wilson, the remaining vehicle with supplies and helpers who had wandered wayward from the more famous travelers, rejoined Ford, Edison and the Firestones. While in town the party stopped to purchase gas and a few items. The secretary of a local fair association asked Henry Ford if he would come to the local fair and speak as a political candidate. Ford, being good to his word, even if in another state completely, respectfully declined the invitation. After grabbing lunch, the travelers walked down a street to an Edison Store, where another large delegation had gathered to meet them. Twenty minutes later, the caravan departed northeast towards Winchester, Virginia for what would be one of their final stops together.

A steady rain greeted the party as they went into Winchester, requiring the party to stop at a garage to put the top up. The stop in town was short, and quite literally sweet, as Edison insisted on getting an ice-cream soda in a nearby store. From there they made one last stretch run to Hagerstown, Maryland, closely following a parallel route to the Appalachian trail that today is Interstate 81. The weary travelers wandered into Hagerstown around seven PM and managed to secure a few rooms at the Hamilton Hotel. Just over 100 years later, in 2020, after the hotel building had long become uninhabitable, renovation plans hit a serious roadblock when the building partially collapsed, but in 1918, it was considered the best hotel in town, and the Vagabonds were happy to dine there as well. Following dinner, Ford and Firestone made their usual post dinner walk-about through the streets of Hagerstown, and at some point, Firestone purchased a pair of wool socks. He was especially pleased with his purchase, telling his walking companion, who also happened to be the richest man in the world at the time, that the socks he purchased were well worth the fifty cents he paid for them as they normally cost two dollars. If Ford was shocked to learn that anyone would ever pay two dollars for a pair of wool socks, he never let on. When Ford and Firestone returned to the hotel following their walk, they found Edison sound asleep. That final night was described by Firestone as "happy" and "congenial," with plenty of talking about the many magical moments of the 1918 trip into the heart of Appalachia. Like most trips, everyone agreed they were happy to get home but also sad to see the trip come to an end.

The next morning, on September 1, 1918, so to avoid the usual attention, they stealthily drove several miles out of town, and there, along a now unknown road, they took pictures and motion pictures of what remained of their touring party. At noon Edison started for Orange, New Jersey, and Ford and Firestone, along with Harvey Jr., made their way towards Pittsburgh. Sato and Willmott followed in the Ford car.

CHAPTER 25

Fall Classics

On a late November night in Cleveland, Ohio on the "corner of Carnegie and Ontario," the Chicago Cubs defeated the Cleveland Indians to capture their first pennant since 1908, thus ending one of sports longest and most certainly talked about losing streaks. Trailing three games to one, the Cubs clawed back to even the series and did the improbable by winning a nail biting, extra inning, seventh and final game that sent the Northside of the Windy City into a frenzy and the Forest City into a shocked funk. For the neutral fan, the 2016 World Series was an instant classic. Twelve years earlier, the Boston Red Sox swept the St. Louis Cardinals to win the World Series ending their 86-year losing streak. It was hardly a classic, but more of a victory lap. Their improbable performance had come earlier against their dreaded rival, the New York Yankees. After losing the first three games and trailing in the ninth inning of game four in the American League Championship, the Boston Red Sox, who had gotten into the post season as a wild card, won four straight games to break the "Curse of the Bambino." Interestingly, Terry Francona was the manager for the Indians and the Red Sox finding himself on both sides of history in baseball lore.

These two beloved franchises met in the 1918 World Series with the Red Sox winning in six games. Not initially considered a classic Series, it is probably remembered more for the heartache that followed both teams into the 20th century. The Cubs would return to the World Series again in 1929, 1932, 1935, 1938 and 1945. For the seventy years that followed, the Cubs did not even get to the Fall Classic and many Cubs fans fully understood that this could be traced to a sports curse put on the team by William Sianis. Legend has it that Sianis, as the owner of the Billy Goat Tavern, had brought his pet goat *Murphy* to the 1945 World Series game at Wrigley Field but was asked to leave because the goat's odor was bothering other fans. An outraged Sianis, who apparently thought it perfectly normal to bring a goat to a baseball game, declared, "Them Cubs, they ain't gonna win no more." Poor *Murphy*, who was apparently being used as a publicity stunt, quite literally had nothing to say about this one way or the other and did not deserve to be a part of any curse. It is still not known if patrons of the tavern had ever complained about his odor, or if *Murphy* was even a Cubs fan. But, alas, a curse was born.

Red Sox fans are aware of sports curses, as well. They were a baseball powerhouse at the turn of the 20th century. Established in 1901, the Red Sox had won the World Series in 1903, 1912, 1915, 1916, and going into the 1918 World Series, they had a pretty darn good player. "Babe" Ruth, ultimately nicknamed the "The Bambino" and the "The Sultan of Swat," had been with the Red Sox since 1914. Later known more for belting home runs, The Bambino had led the American League in pitching in 1916 and pitched a shut-out in game one against the Cubs and won the 6th and deciding game of the 1918 Series. However, as every Bostonian knows, for some reason Red Sox owner Harry Frazee traded Babe Ruth to the New York Yankees for cash after the 1919 season. Once a Yankee, Babe Ruth would lead New York to four World Series titles while becoming a hitting machine. The slugging outfielder would lead the American League in home runs every year but two between 1919 and 1931, and along the way became synonymous with the sport itself. As for the Yankees, they would rack up 26 World Series Titles as the Red Sox and their fans became more and more suspicious. What had started out as an inexplicable business and baseball decision, was morphed into a curse. The curse of the Bambino.

In hindsight, the 1918 World Series was a classic matchup, but nobody would know it for decades to come. The Series would also be remembered for being played in early September as the World War had forced an early end to the season. To date, it is the only World Series played entirely in September. Many baseball fans, including some Cubs fans, might be shocked to learn the Chicago games were played at Comiskey Park as it was larger than Weeghman Park. The Cubs had shared Weeghman with the short-lived Federal League Chicago Whales (Chi-Feds). The Park, originally named after the lunch counter guru, Charles Weeghman, would later be expanded and renamed Wrigley field after the chewing gum magnet, William Wrigley, Jr. Although the Red Sox had played several prior World Series at Braves Field, the 1918 Title series was played at Fenway Park. Fenway, opened in 1912 and getting its name from the Boston neighborhood where it is located, has hosted 11 World Series with the Red Sox winning six of them and the Boston Braves winning one title.

Statistically it was a strange series. The Red Sox won four games on just 9 runs total, whereas the Cubs scored 10 runs but only managed to win two games. To date, it is the fewest runs scored by a winning team in World Series history. Neither team managed to hit a single home run which has only happened three times in World Series history (1906, 1907 & 1918) and which seems utterly improbable in today's game. As a feeling of nationalism swept the country during wartime, the 1918 Series marks the first known time *The Star-Spangled Banner* was performed in connection with a major sporting event. The anthem, which would later become the formal national anthem in 1931, was not played before the game but instead at the start of the 7th inning. As for *Take Me Out to the Ball Game,* it was not played for the delight of fans until the mid-1930s.

Life on the gridiron was equally odd in 1918, as football was clearly capsized by World War I and the flu pandemic. Many teams simply did not play that year, and those that did started later in the Fall and had shortened seasons. As for professional football, the Dayton Triangles defeated the Detroit Heralds to win the professional football championship. Originally organized as a football team in 1913, the Triangles were initially made up of graduates from St. Mary's College, now the University of Dayton. Three years later the team was reorganized to include employees from downtown Dayton factories including the Dayton Engineering Laboratories Company or Delco.

Named for their home field, Triangle Park, located at the confluence of the Great Miami and Stillwater rivers north of Dayton, the Triangles were quite successful going 9-1 in 1916 and 6-0 in 1917. In 1918, the team, like most other teams, lost players on account of their military service. However, given the industrial base of Southwest Ohio many other players stayed behind continuing their factory work which was equally important for the war effort thereby allowing the Triangles to keep a relatively strong squad on the field. In the end, the team went undefeated claiming what was at the time called the Ohio League Championship.

As for professional football, in its current form, America would have to wait another two years, when on September 17*th*, 1920, a group of men would meet at the Hupmobile (an automobile built between 1909 and 1939 by the Hupp Motor Car Company) showroom of Ralph Hay, who also just happened to own the hometown Canton football Bulldogs. The result of this meeting would be the birth of the National Football League (NFL) and would forever change Sunday afternoons in America. It would also make Canton, Ohio a bit of a mecca for thousands, if not millions, of football fans throughout the world.

Represented at the meeting were eleven franchises: The Akron Pros, Canton Bulldogs, Decatur Staleys, Chicago Cardinals, Cleveland Indians, Dayton Triangles, Hammond Pros, Massillon Tigers, Muncie Flyers, Rock Island Independents, and the Roosevelt Jeffersons. Originally called the American Professional Association for the first two seasons, the league was renamed the National Football League (NFL) for the 1922 season. Only two teams remain from that original fateful meeting in Canton as the Decatur Staleys would become the Chicago Bears and the Chicago Cardinals would later relocate to St. Louis and today are the Arizona Cardinals. Interesting to note, the Green Bay Packers, although formed in 1919 and being the oldest franchise in continuous operation with the same name and the same location, did not join the NFL until 1921.

The 1918 champs, the Dayton Triangles, never did reach the same level of greatness again and by the 1920s the mostly graduates and factory workers simply could not compete and were one of the worst teams in the league, and after operating many years as the Dallas Texans, the team folded. The Detroit Heralds did not fare well either as, for whatever reason, they were not even represented at the original Canton meeting..

Although professional football was in existence and growing in popularity, it clearly played second fiddle to College Football. In 1918 two teams are generally understood to have shared the National Championship. Before the BCS, playoffs, ESPN shows, talking heads and committees, and quite frankly not that long ago, this was not uncommon. This, in part, explains why so many college football stadiums boast multiple National Championships on their rings of honor. In a seriously truncated season, with depleted college rosters and abnormal amounts of starting freshman players, the Pittsburgh Panthers finished 4-1 and the Michigan Wolverines finished 5-0. Despite the Wolverines undefeated season, many, if not most, analysts put Pitt. at number 1. Their one loss came at the hands of the Cleveland Naval Reserves as in 1918 military training camps had their own football teams and were added to the schedule to add games and more competition.

The games also allowed those serving in the military to enjoy some time away from the war and all that comes with it. These military camp football teams were quite good as they were comprised of many college players and former players and often resembled what we might call "All

Star" teams. For instance, the Cleveland Naval Reserves had quarterback Gaylord "Pete" Stinchcomb, a Hall of Fame player for Ohio State and in the backfield was Richard Ducote, a star halfback from Auburn, and Georgia Tech's 1917 fullback, Judy Harlan. It is little wonder they were generally considered one of the best all-around football teams, military or otherwise.

On November 30*th*, 1918, Pittsburgh slugged it out with the Cleveland Naval Reserves, and after much controversy involving a referee, and what was later described by many as having a "broken watch," the Reserves kicked a game winning field goal as time expired and handed the Panthers their only loss, 10-9. This final game was a huge disappointment and was "Pop" Warner's first loss as head football coach of the Pittsburgh Panthers. However, as painful as this controversial loss might have been, it did not dampen the joy or negate the dominant performance against Georgia Tech. the week before.

When Georgia Tech played Pittsburgh at Forbes Field in Pittsburgh, Pennsylvania on November 23*rd* in 1918, it was the game of the year. Some 30,000 fans, along with well-known football men and sports writers from around the country, were in attendance to see two teams who had not lost any officially sanctioned game since 1914. Georgia Tech was coming off their National Championship season in 1917 and had been described by New York newspapers as "one of the truly great teams of all time." With a star-studded line up, the "Jump Shift" offense and John Heisman in his 19*th* year of coaching, the Tornado's 1917 team truly was a machine outscoring their opponents 491 to 17. Heisman later said it was the best team he ever coached and was the greatest team from the southern U.S. The backfield of Hill, Strupper, Guyan and freshman Judy Harlan, simply could not be stopped, and their defense was equally dominant holding opponents to less than three touchdowns the entire season. Pittsburgh's 1917 team was also a machine, but the teams would not meet until the following season. Apparently, Heisman challenged Warner to a game and although Warner thought it would have been a battle for the ages, it wasn't meant to be, and the teams had to wait until the following year for this much anticipated match-up.

Going into the 1918 game, Georgia Tech had been putting up huge numbers scoring over 100 points in three separate games. However, they were returning only 2 starters from the legendary 1917 team. Pitt, on the other hand, returned three of their starting backs: George "Tank" McLaren, halfback Katy Easterday, and quarterback Skip Gougler. However, it was the addition of freshman, Tom Davies, that gave the team an extra spark as he led the team in rushing, passing, receiving, and was also a good kicker and kick returner. The team was loaded with other consensus All Americans and many members of this Panther team are in the College Football Hall of Fame.

Like many highly anticipated matchups, the game itself did not live up to all the hype. Pitt completely shut down the "Jump Shift" offense of the Tornados and Georgia Tech had no answer for freshman Davies who returned 2 punts for touchdowns and who threw for 2 more in a convincing 32-0 blow-out. Oddly enough, Pitt only had 10 first downs in the entire game and Georgia Tech only had 4. But, as mentioned, all the big plays belonged to Davies. Although the teams are all but forgotten, the coaches remain household names. Warner, who coached Jim Thorpe at Carlisle and directed him towards Olympic greatness in track and field, would amass a record of 319 wins. An innovator of many modern blocking techniques, he also gave football the three point-stance, the trap run, the bootleg, the screen pass, and was one of the first to utilize a huddle to help players organize on the field.

Heisman, no stranger to innovation, allowed his center to toss the football back instead of rolling it or kicking it. He was also an early advocate for the legalization of the forward pass, and when you hear a quarterback say "hike," you can thank John Heisman. In his spare time, Heiman took to the stage as Shakespearean actor and was a founder of the first theatre group at Auburn. Warner, also a lover of the arts, was a painter in his spare time taking his imagination to brush and canvas. His *Pop Warner Little Scholars* program, started in Pennsylvania in 1929, continues to provide children with extracurricular activities to this day. Heisman, who later in life became the Director of the Downtown Athletic Club in Manhattan, began an award to honor the best football player east of Mississippi river. It was later changed to include any football player in the nation, and after his death in 1936, the trophy was renamed the Heisman Memorial Trophy. These two coaching legends, who battled for football supremacy in 1918, are both in the College Football Hall of Fame. These titans of the grid iron are gone but not forgotten.

CHAPTER 26

"Who won, who won?"

By the later days of Autumn, Germany slowly began to realize that the situation was hopeless. In fact, as early as September 28*th* the German Supreme Command informed Kaiser Wilhelm II, and the Imperial Chancellor-Count Georg Von Hertling, that he could no longer guarantee that the front would hold for a few more hours much less days. Quartermaster General Erich Ludendoff made it clear that he wanted an immediate ceasefire, and that Germany should consider accepting many, if not all, of the demands made by President Wilson in his Fourteen Points. One such demand, which allowed the German officers to deflect attention from a military victory to a political solution, would put Germany on a more democratic footing. On October 3*rd* Prince Maximillian of Baden was appointed Chancellor of Germany, and acting much like a Prime Minister, he replaced Von Hertling in what was clearly interpreted as a sign to negotiate an armistice.

Five days later German soldiers would encounter a 30-year-old railroad construction worker and logger, who was also a crack shot with a gun. Born in a two-room log cabin in Fentress County, Tennessee, near the Kentucky border, Alvin Cullum York, had a history of drinking and fighting. After a revival meeting in 1914, York put down the bottle, said goodbye to bar room brawls, picked up a bible, and became a fundamentalist Christian. In 1917 Alvin had received his draft notice. Anguishing as to what he should do, he later wrote, "My religion and my experience... told me not to go to war, and the memory of my ancestors told me to get my gun and go fight." York wanted to "be a good Christian and good American too." Having written on his draft card, "Don't want to fight," he was ultimately denied conscientious-objector status and was enlisted in the 82nd Infantry Division. Soon he found himself on active duty on the Western Front. His actions on October 8, 1918, during the Meuse-Argonne Offensive, would result in his receiving the Medal of Honor and becoming one of the most noticeable heroes during the war.

On October 7th York's unit received orders to relieve units of the 28th Infantry Division and to take Hill 223. By 6 AM the following morning, in a mix of rain and sleet, the Americans succeeded in taking the hill. Moving away from the hill, York's unit pressed forward to capture a narrow-gauge railroad. However, they soon came under bursts of German machine-gun fire from nearby hills. The American attack stalled, and they began to take heavy casualties. Essentially pinned down, York, who was a corporal and the company sharpshooter, was sent with 16 other soldiers under the command of Acting Sergeant Bernard Early to find a way to silence the German machine guns. As the soldiers worked their way through the fog that draped the brush and hilly terrain, German machine gunners continued their bursts of fire cutting down nine Americans including York's best friend Murray Savage. The remaining soldiers were left to face off against a much larger force.

What happened next is described in a journal York kept: "Those machine guns were spitting fire and cutting down the undergrowth all around me something awful ... I didn't have time to dodge behind a tree or dive into a brush, I didn't even have time to kneel or lie down... As soon as the machine guns opened fire on me, I began to exchange shots with them. In order to sight me or to swing their machine guns on me, the Germans had to show their heads above the trench, and every time I saw a head, I touched it off. All the time I kept yelling at them to come down. I didn't want to kill any more than I had to. But it was they or I. And I was giving them the best I had." Following York's lead, the remaining soldiers returned fire on the Germans, and within minutes 25 were dead. Twenty casualties are attributed to York alone. The German commander, believing he must be under attack from a much larger force, surrendered his garrison of 90 men. On their way back to friendly lines, York and his squad took more prisoners, and in the end captured a total of 132 men.

Throughout the month of October, the German government sent messages to the Americans seeking exact conditions for peace but were not yet ready to consider the Kaiser's abdication as part of a brokered peace deal in lieu of an outright surrender. Quartermaster Ludendoff, perhaps as an attempt to feign outrage at such a notion, demanded that the war resume until one side successfully charged over the other. However, the German soldiers were beyond their breaking point and for all practical purposes threatened to pick up and walk home. After a rash of desertions, Ludendoff was replaced by Wilhelm Groener and negotiations resumed only to be hampered by new demands made by the French, Italian, and British governments. Such demands included reparations, de-militarization of the Central Powers and newly drawn borders between countries.

On November 6th a delegation led by Matthias Erzberger, the Vice Chancellor of Germany, departed Berlin for France, and in a motorcade consisting of five cars, was escorted across the front line passing through miles of devastation in the war zone of Northern France. On the morning of November 8, 1918, he was taken to a secret destination aboard the French General and Supreme Allied Commander, Ferdinand Foch's private train parked on a railway in the forest of Compiegne. By most accounts, Foch appeared only twice during the next three days, first asking the German delegation what they sought, and to oversee the signing of the Armistice. When the Germans arrived, they were given a list of over 70 allied demands, and a 72-hour deadline. Any sliver of negotiating power they may have had was all but lost when on November 10th the delegation was handed newspapers from Paris with headlines announcing the Kaiser's abdication. Agreed to at 5 AM Paris Time on November 11, 1918, and signed shortly thereafter, the Armistice was to take effect six hours later at 11 AM.

Much has rightfully been made about the 11th hour of the 11th day of the 11th month in 1918. Afterall, the morning was both heartwarming and heart wrenching. Consider, for instance, the American fighting forces engaged at 5 AM on November 11th, with the 167th Field Artillery Brigade 92nd Division, being ordered to launch a final charge at 10:30 AM. Or US marines crossing the Meuse River in the final misty hours of the war. Elsewhere the 313th Division slogged through marsh and wetlands in a dense fog toward Ville-Devant-Chaumont. The advance was to be covered by the 311th Machine Gun Battalion, but with an impregnable fog the gunners had no idea where to direct their fire. At 10:44 AM, a runner caught up with the Brigade to report the Armistice had been signed. However, Brigadier General William Nicholson, who was commanding the Brigade, made the order, "There will be absolutely no let-up until 11 AM." Henry N. Gunther was from a predominantly German neighborhood in Baltimore, Maryland, was in his mid-20s, sported a mustache, and was among the ranks of the 313th. Like many of his brethren, he had arrived in France in July, before finding himself far from home in a foggy marshland on the morning of November 11th. With the 313th gathered below a ridge called the Cote Romagne, two German machine gun squads manned a roadblock and after sporadically firing towards the Americans all but stopped as the 11th hour neared. Suddenly Gunther rose and began to charge toward the German guns. The machine gunners waved him back, but Gunther kept advancing until the enemy reluctantly fired a quick burst. Gunther was struck in the temple and died instantly. His time of death was listed as 10:59 AM, making him officially the last American killed in the War.

Not everyone fought that final day. Colonel Thomas Gowenlock served as an intelligence officer in the American 1st Division and was on the front line that November morning and later wrote that he recalled his watch stating it was nine o'clock and with only two hours to go he drove over the Meuse River to see the finish. The shelling was heavy, and as Colonel Gowenlock walked down the road it only grew worse. It seemed like every battery in the world was trying to burn up its guns, much like the grand finale on a 4th of July fireworks show. The Colonel recalls looking at his watch when it turned 11, but the shelling continued for several more minutes. It was as if both sides were giving every bit of fight, they had left. While celebrations broke out throughout the world with dancing in the streets and the popping of champagne bottles, the mood for many on the front was different. Many tipped their hats, hugged those around them, or just wept. They spoke in hushed tones, fearful that they would be heard by the enemy and fired upon. Others built log fires for the first time in ages finally able to warm their hands and coffee. But, most of all, there was a deafening silence. J. Laurence Moffit described what he remembered some 85 years later: "All firing stopped. Complete silence. There wasn't a sound...." He also recalls taking off his helmet while standing upright for the first time in years. Private Anthony Pierro, who was guarding German prisoners in the Argonne Forest that morning, did recall that everyone was dancing in celebration of the war being over. When the dancing stopped, someone asked, "Who won? Who won?"

The following Spring, clusters of poppies again filled these same quiet fields in Belgium and France. Year after year they continued to flourish in Europe. However, it was an American woman, Miss Moina Michael, who helped create the red Flanders poppy as the modern-day symbol of Remembrance. Known later as "The Poppy Lady," Moina had been on duty at the YMCA War Secretaries headquarters in New York when in a few minutes of free time she came across John McCrae's poem in *Ladies Home Journal*, which was sometimes called *We Shall Not Sleep* and was better known as *In Flanders Field*. Her discovery, of this now famous poem, was just several months after Lieutenant-Colonel John McCrae had succumbed to pneumonia. Ms. Michael was transfixed by the poem, describing it later as a deeply spiritual experience. From that moment forward she elected to wear a red poppy as a symbol of remembrance of all who had perished, and later managed to find a small artificial silk poppy in a Wanamaker's Department Store. Soon she found herself passing them out to others. In the 1920s the American Legion adopted the poppy to commemorate American soldiers killed in World War I.

While poppies flourished in Europe following the war, so did anger and resentment especially among the losers of the "War to end All Wars." Adolf Hitler was one such person, and he would use the private carriage of the French General, Foch, as a symbol of revenge.

Following the war, Foch's private train, formally designated as CIWC #2419, was put back into regular service before being later attached to the French Presidential train. In the 1920s, this carriage, where the Armistice had been signed on that fateful morning in 1918, was an exhibit in Paris. In 1927 the carriage was placed in a building complex, named the Clairiere de l' Armistice, which had been constructed in a forest near the same spot the Armistice was signed. Outside of the building was a statue of Commander Foch and another statue depicting a German eagle impaled by a guard with the inscription: "Here on the 11*th* of November 1918 succumbed the criminal pride of the German empire...vanquished by the French people which it tried to enslave." It was here that the train car sat until a more ominous date with destiny.

On June 22, 1940, with a caravan of Nazi vehicles parked about the complex, Adolph Hitler demanded and received the surrender of France in the same train carriage: CIWC #2419. He had deliberately chosen the location, ordered the destruction of the site including the French statues three days later, and had the carriage itself hauled back to Berlin as a trophy of war where it was again made an exhibit. In 1945, as the allied forces advanced into Germany, the carriage trophy was removed to the town of Crawinkel. As the American armored columns entered the town, the

SS guarding it set the carriage ablaze and buried the charred remains. Following the Second Great War, the French forest site was rebuilt, and a replica of the carriage was rededicated on Armistice Day 1950. It seems that the train, much like the poppies, endures. Hopefully, for the sake of the world, it has found its final resting place.

While one war wound down, another continued to rage completely unabetted. Artillery blasts were replaced by a different type of explosion. During the summer, America had sent nearly one million soldiers across the Atlantic to fight a war in another continent. Now a different, but highly fatal, enemy had in return reached her shores. The story that followed was largely a tale of suffering, fear and death. However, it also represents a story of faith, countless heroic deeds and undeniable perseverance. Five days after Welch and company happened upon the pitiful scene at Camp Devens, marchers huddled and gathered in downtown Philadelphia to be part of the greatest parade ever organized by "The City of Brotherly Love."

The parade, which would stretch nearly two miles long, was a Liberty Loan parade designed to raise millions of dollars for the war effort. Several hundred thousand people, jammed along the parade route, shouted words of encouragement to the marching soldiers, bands, Boy Scouts and women's auxiliaries. By all initial accounts, the parade was a smashing success. Two days later, the epidemic was detected among the civilian population. Within a week, the city resembled Camp Devens. On October 1st, just three days after the parade, Spanish flu took the lives of one hundred seventeen people in a single day in Philadelphia. Some citizens, who woke up feeling fine, would grow ill in the early afternoon and succumb to the illness later that same evening. Others claimed to have watched people just collapse on the street or topple off a horse.

By October 3rd, the city banned all public meetings, closed all churches and schools, and prohibited public funerals. Headlines from local papers provide a horrifying glimpse into life in the crowded city during October. On October 9th, *Evening Public Ledger*, reported: **Influenza kills three in Family, Frank Connell, wife and daughter are buried in same grave.** The same story also described how a doctor and nurse (Dr. Edwin M. Smith and Miss Rose Cummings) at St. Joseph's Hospital had given their lives to minister to the stricken. On October 5th, another 254 souls perished followed by 289 the following day. The worst was yet to come. October 9th, saw a new record of 428 people dead from the virus. The following week the daily death toll doubled again. Philadelphia was soon on the verge of a structural and societal collapse. A sense of dread and terror permeated the city streets. Shortages of food were followed by shortages of medical supplies, doctors, nurses, and hospital rooms. Too many people needed medical help too quickly, overwhelming the medical system. Shortages soon came to the families of the dead. Gravediggers could not be found, and there were not enough caskets or mortuary space. Another October 9th headline from the *Evening Public Ledger*, reported: **Prisoners dig graves-Sent from Camden jail to help relieve funeral stress.** Many families were left to take matters into their own hands. Bodies were often being kept in houses or in nearby locations, and if caskets could not be made from household supplies, blankets were used to bury the dead. On October 12th, the *Evening Public Ledger* captured this heartbreaking situation, reporting: **Rabbi compelled to cart own son's body to grave**. The story described how the Rabbi was unable to procure an undertaker, so with the help of a friend he fashioned a coffin for his high school aged son and wheeled it to a nearby cemetery.

Heartbreak would soon be felt throughout America as the virus used every means possible to move across the country. Terror and dread came along as willing accomplices. Starting along the eastern coast, primarily north of Virginia, the virus turned west and south hitching a ride along every road, trail, boat, train, bridge, buggy and automobile it could find. Invisible to the naked eye, it traveled through cough, sneeze, perhaps handshake, and spoken word. This second wave of influenza was highly fatal, taking the lives of 195,000 Americans in October alone. However, it should be noted, that most people who got the virus felt better within a week and many never got sick at all. For those who did get sick, symptoms usually included fever and a cough, while others complained of throbbing headaches, excruciating earaches, and trouble breathing. Some claimed they lost their sense of taste and smell. The blood, sometimes spurting, from someone's nose, mouth, ears and around the eyes, terrified the healthy and sick alike. Many of the symptoms gave clues as to the virus being influenza, but this flu also brought another oddity. Influenza has always wreaked havoc on the weakest in a society, in part because pneumonia is most deadly for the old and vulnerable. The Spanish Flu killed indiscriminately, but, if anything, seemed to take specific aim at the young and strong with the average age of death being just 28 years old.

With a severe shortage of professional nurses, in part because a large number were previously deployed to military camps in the United States and abroad, the American Red Cross had dueling roles to play in the fall of 1918. The International Red Cross was founded in 1863, and the American Red Cross was founded in 1881 by Clara Barton. Barton, who was a hospital nurse during the American Civil War, set the precedent that the Red Cross would respond to natural disasters, in addition to war. When the United States entered World War I, the American Red Cross made it clear that it would do whatever it could to aid the ally cause. Not only did the Red Cross organize fifty base hospitals in France, but it had full responsibility to supply the military with tens of thousands of nurses.

On the home-front, the Red Cross soon was on the frontline of a natural disaster that swept from sea to shining sea. In 1918 some eight million Americans identified themselves as active supporters of the Red Cross, which meant roughly 8% of the entire population was mobilized to fight the war abroad and at home. With a national megaphone, the Red Cross issued an urgent call for volunteers. Tens of thousands, despite being petrified for their own safety, responded to the call.

CHAPTER 27

What an Ending!

After leaving Camp Devens, William Welch boarded a train for home. He was quite tired. It had been a long trip, and he was still haunted by the scenes from Devens. As the train rattled and rolled along the tracks that would take him to Baltimore, the doctor began to feel worse and worse. By the time he disembarked, he had a fever, a splitting headache, and a dry cough. The seventy-year-old doctor instinctively knew it was influenza, and since he sensed a trip to a hospital would only further burden local doctors and nurses, he went straight home and went to bed. He remained there for the next ten days. After he was able to get out of bed, he spent the next few weeks recuperating, and when at last a nephew came to visit, he gave him specific instructions to tell everyone that if anyone had symptoms of influenza to stay in bed "until the temperature has been normal for three days."

Besides the sage advice to stay home when sick, other parts of the country rolled out, and fumbled through, various forms of social distancing guidelines and lockdown mandates. The results were mixed, and a century later, evidence of the effectiveness of such measures is, at best, scant. Health officials in St. Louis immediately ordered closings and banned public gatherings, with initial success at lowering mortality rates. Of course, not having several hundred thousand people crammed together like sardines at a Liberty Loan parade clearly played an enormous role in "flattening the curve" in this midwestern city. However, the city was ultimately hit with later waves of the deadly virus.

As the pandemic marched towards the Rocky Mountains, many western Colorado towns had time to prepare for the onslaught. Silverton and Ouray were kept under complete lockdown, and much like a western movie with a gunfight about to happen, the towns appeared completely deserted. Every business remained shut and no one dared take a stroll down Main Street. Still, somehow, some way, the virus, much like a dreaded gunslinger dressed all in black, snuck into these towns in the dead of night. Every town, no matter how hard they tried, could not keep the virus at bay. That is, except one town. Gunnison, Colorado, was a small railroad town in 1918, and when word went out to shut things down, they took it seriously. Besides banning public gatherings, Gunnison posted lawmen to block all roads leading into or out of town. Train conductors warned passengers that no one was permitted on the platform in Gunnison even to stretch their legs. Tough times demand tough actions, and although Gunnison might have thrown civil rights through the swinging saloon doors, life in this rugged town very much continued to resemble a John Wayne western. It also managed to remain free of Spanish flu.

On October 22, 1918, a full-page newspaper ad declared *"Wear a mask and save your life."* The ad, placed by the mayor of San Francisco, along with the Red Cross, the Chamber of Commerce, and the Labor Council, further proclaimed that masks were "99% proof against influenza." If a screen could keep bugs off a front porch, surely a few layers of gauze would keep out flu bugs. In San Francisco, at the urging of the local health director, doctors, nurses, and Red Cross workers had worn masks since the beginning of the pandemic. On October 18*th* all store clerks were strongly encouraged to wear masks and all barbers were ordered to do so. A few days later, the city council voted unanimously

(15-0) that "every person appearing on the public streets, or in any public place...shall wear a mask or covering...over the nose and mouth, consisting of four-ply materials known as butter-cloth or fine mesh gauze." The law allowed for masks to be removed when eating but required the wearing of a mask in a home if more than two members of the family were present. After adopting his proposals, the local health director boldly declared, "If this plan is carried out, influenza here will be under control within a week."

Doctor Welch had also been an early convert to the idea of wearing a mask, declaring it "an important contribution in prevention of spray infections." Many of his esteemed colleagues were equally enamored with the flimsy solution, and when American cities began to see a decline in new cases and deaths, masks were seen as the only possible cause. Converts were made daily, and the masses came to believe that a mask would keep them safe. Why else would a doctor wear one? On November 1, 1918, Eugene C. Caley became the first man in Oakland, California to be arrested for not wearing a mask. "This is only the beginning" said the chief of police. According to the Oakland Tribune, the chief further elaborated, "We are going to enforce this mask ordinance if we have to pack the city jail with people. This epidemic is too serious to be taken as a joke, and men arrested...will find that it's no laughing matter when they face the police judges."

Of course, a virus is so tiny that is can easily pass-through cloth regardless of how tightly it is woven. True a mask might catch a droplet of water with virus hitching a ride to it. However, to be even slightly statistically effective the mask would have to be always worn, be made up of multiple layers, and tied firmly across the face. It would also need to be regularly replaced, or properly washed and dried between usage. Such requirements are difficult in a hospital setting, more difficult in a military setting, and nearly impossible for practical use in the general public. In the final days of 1918, nearly everyone wore a mask. They were useless. In the end, San Francisco, like most of the country, had done nothing to control the spread of the virus, and like the rest of the country their luck would soon run out. Two weeks after passing the mask ordinance, another wave of Spanish flu swept through the city.

While America masked up, scientists fanned out across the country, frantically searching for clues or answers on how the invasion might be stopped. One such scientist was Paul Lewis. Lewis, who a decade before had helped prove that a virus caused polio, turned in his Naval Uniform and immediately returned to his true home—the laboratory. His first hunch, which would ultimately be proven to be correct, was that the disease was influenza. What he did not know was how it could be prevented, cured or treated. What he also surmised is that this was a type of influenza unlike any seen before. When a new variant of influenza virus adopts itself to humans, it immediately is considered a pandemic threat, and given how easily it may be transmitted, it literally can exhaust the supply of susceptible hosts. This was happening throughout the Fall of 1918, even if no one fully understood it. Influenza and other viruses are now known to cause approximately 90% of all respiratory infections. Not surprisingly, pneumonia, which is really nothing more than an inflammation of the lungs with consolidation usually brought on by some invasion of a microorganism and the bodies defense thereof, often trailed the virus. However, again, at the time, no one fully understood this. Approximately 10 hours after an influenza virus attaches itself to a cell that cell will burst creating a "swarm" of between 100,000 and 1 million new influenza viruses. In this way, influenza moves at lightning speed and made it impossible for scientists or physicians to have any hope of catching up. Nonetheless, they tried.

H1N1 is the name now given to the 1918 influenza virus. Today, it is known to have found a home in swine. In 1918, as the pandemic raged on, there was no concern for a future swine flu, but instead all hands-on deck looked for an end to the immediate carnage. It seemed vaccines might offer some hope to end the misery. By 1918, science had successfully prevented a dozen or so diseases, and many believed a vaccine would lead a cavalry countercharge against the Spanish Flu. Research at the beginning of the twentieth century, in the form of serums, also looked promising in reducing the threat of pneumonia. Perhaps a reboot of sorts into these serums could help with treatment and lower the risk of death. Since most people who contracted the disease survived, it seemed rational to believe that their blood and serum held antibodies that might be used to cure the disease in others. Experiments, aimed at finding answers, broke out nearly as fast as the flu itself.

One of the first flu vaccines to gain any traction was created by Doctor Timothy Leary of Tufts Medical College, right outside of Boston. Others quickly followed, and soon batches of differing vaccines were being produced and distributed throughout the United States. Hundreds of vaccines were developed and rushed to market. Despite there being no provable immunologic value, many health officials, including those in San Francisco, encouraged mass inoculation efforts. Tens of thousands of citizens received a poke (or up to three pokes) of what was hoped to be "a real prophylactic against influenza." Doctors also did their part to help, and many took aim at what they knew could help. Since they had some knowledge that pneumonia was often caused by secondary bacterial infections, at least they could meet the virus on a more familiar battlefield. Surgeons developed techniques to drain pus and infection that had formed in the lungs, while doctors prescribed a host of medications and hospitals administered oxygen to those in need. Most importantly, doctors made heroic efforts to address the pain felt by their patients by prescribing everything from aspirin and codeine to morphine and even heroin. Unfortunately, antibiotics, as we now know them, were still decades away.

Almost everyone had a theory or idea about how to stop influenza. Some ideas were well meaning, while others were not. Doctors, on the fringe or simply desperate, recommended injecting metallic solutions, cupping, administering cocktail serums, and even bleeding. Newspapers were filled with advertisements, sometimes designed to look like news stories, of cures or preventive measures. Citizens were encouraged to wear garlic around their necks, and to keep their feet dry at all costs. While some homes kept every window open to circulate cold air, others kept every window shut hoping to keep hot air from escaping. Through it all, plenty of families, much like they still do today, applied healthy portions of Vicks VapoRub to family members and pets alike.

Still, wave after wave, the flu kept coming causing the head of the army's Division of Communicable Diseases to ponder on paper, "If the epidemic continues its mathematical rate of acceleration, civilization could easily... disappear from the face of the earth within a matter of a few weeks." However, by the end of November, the second seismic wave was largely over. This was followed by a slightly less horrific wave in mid-December. Ripples would continue for the next few years. During the entire fiasco, much like at the end of the war when the shelling finally halted, there was a silence. A strange and inexplicable silence. This silence lasted throughout the pandemic and came from one man. In a time when the country faced a national crisis and looked to her leaders for a path forward, or at least for words of encouragement to those afraid and suffering, President Wilson never uttered a single word about the pandemic in public. Equally astonishing is that he made no notes about influenza and rarely, if ever, mentioned it in his private conversations. It was as if America had only fought one war. It was as if the Commander in Chief could only wear one hat.

During a twelve-week period in the fall of 1918, over 5% of the entire human population on the planet had perished. Citizens of the world, much like the soldiers at the end of the war, slowly emerged from the trenches of their homes and neighborhoods. However, there was no corresponding moment to mark the end of this war unleashed by influenza. There was no official armistice, and there were no celebrations. The following spring, clusters of flowers, brought to life by a new sun and gentle showers, filled quiet fields stateside. The storm from the end of 1918, had been all but blown out to sea. Occasional thunder could be heard and when this would happen, every soul crossed their fingers, held their breath and dropped to their knees in prayer. But the same terrifying storm never came. Some experts now believe the worldwide death toll from Spanish flu to be somewhere between 50 to 100 million, with 675,000 Americans succumbing to the terrible disease.

Given the population of the United States was just over 100 million in 1918, this number would be more than 2 million deaths in the United States today. Put another way, it landed twice the wallop of Covid-19. Perhaps equally stunning is that the United States Public Health Service canvassing efforts in 1919 revealed that over one-quarter (over 25 million) of the entire population of the country had contracted the flu, while the United States Navy calculated that as many as 40% of naval personnel had the flu in 1918. American sailors and soldiers were hit especially hard. For every soldier who died in battle, 1.02 died from influenza, and the flu single-handedly caused the United States Army to lose a greater proportion of men since the days of the Civil War. Despite all the efforts made by experts and lay persons alike, nothing had come close to even slowing the virus. Scientists and physicians had recognized their colossal failure at anticipating the disease and finding ways to cure, treat or contain it. "Never again allow me to say that medical science is on the verge of conquering disease," was a common refrain from learned men. Disappointed in their shortcomings, scientists and researchers set out to make certain that nothing like this would ever happen again. However, as we all know, "those who do not remember the past are condemned to repeat it." Today we are painfully reminded that medical science remains far off from conquering disease.

The week before the ceasefire and the end of World War I, votes were tallied to determine the winner for the United States Senate race in Michigan between Henry Ford and republican Truman Handy Newberry. Newberry, a former Secretary of the Navy, had bludgeoned the industrialist-turned-democrat in the run up to the election with attacks on Ford's initial pacifism during the war and his helping his son avoid the draft. However, what was exponentially more damaging to the legacy of Henry Ford, was Newberry's hammering of Ford as an anti-Semite. The race was close, and after three days of counting, the final count showed

Newberry beating Ford by 7,567 votes. True to his word, Ford had run an old-fashioned campaign, making no personal appearance and spending virtually no money. Newberry, on the other hand, spent in excess of $175,000 to defeat Ford in the republican primary, and somewhere between $500,000 and $1 million to defeat Ford in the general election. Ten days before the election, two former U.S. presidents, William Howard Taft and Theodore Roosevelt, took Ford to task for his pacifism. Alas, the Peace Ship fiasco had sailed back into Ford's life to bite his backside.

Initially, Ford did not contest the election results. Bruised and battered, Henry Ford released a statement declaring he would not be "getting down in the ditch and throwing mud." However, with his patriotism questioned, he could not help but take a shot at Taft and Roosevelt, saying he would not behave like the two ex-Presidents who had "stopped making faces at each other long enough to get together and take a united wallop at (him)." Ford's statement in defeat went one step further, and, in doing so, made an argument for the political ages. Henry Ford expressed an appropriate distaste for the money his opponent had spent, cautioning, "If they would spend $176,000 to get one little nomination, they would spend $176 million to (sew up) the country. That is where the danger lies." After the election a groundswell of protest erupted among many citizens offended by Newberry's blatant spending practices, and when Newberry shrugged off calls from his own party to resign, an investigation was all but guaranteed. In truth Truman Newberry's Senate problems had begun even before the Michigan general election, when, on September 17*th*, a resolution was introduced in the Senate calling for an investigation into the Michigan primary. His spending on his own campaign was clearly in excess of the $3,750 limit imposed by Michigan law and the Federal Corrupt Practices Act. Ford, with the assistance of Harvey Firestone, hired a throng of private investigators to rummage the Michigan countryside for evidence of electoral fraud. Although the dirt they found could fill a dump truck, and a protracted fight lasting several years ensued, Henry Ford would never find himself a U.S. Senator representing the state of Michigan.

❧

On December 4, 1918, President Wilson sailed to Europe for peace talks and to promote his plan for a League of Nations, an international organization he envisioned to resolve future conflicts between nations. When he arrived in France on December 13*th*, he became the first U.S. President to travel to Europe while in office. Although he may have commented on Ford's Senate loss, he remained silent on the world's receding pandemic. Little did the President realize that he would soon face his own health crises.

❧

On September 5, 1918, months before the War ended and well before the breathtaking wave of Spanish Flu smashed against the American shoreline, John Burroughs wrote the following to Harvey Firestone from his home in Woodchuck Lodge in Roxbury, New York:

> Dear Mr. Firestone:
>
> I trust all went well with you and your party after you left the protecting care of De Louch and me. I did not quite cease grumbling and groaning till I got home, which was on Friday afternoon.
>
> Some allowance must be made for an octogenarian; he is a little baby and is entitled to a little indulgence on that score. I did get fearfully tired, but the few days in the green and sweet solitude have salved all my wounds, and I am thinking so well of the trip that I might try to write something about it.
>
> What beauties and wonders we saw! What glory of mountain tops and what summer ripeness and repose in the broad river valleys! How such a trip enhances one's knowledge of, and admiration for, his country!

What an impression of the mass and magnitude of a single state it gives one! How much more than a mere geographic division will West Virginia henceforth mean to us! Yes, and the Great Smoky Mountains-their smoke cannot blur the impression they made.

I wish I had the trip back up the Shenandoah Valley with you and Edison and Ford to look back upon, but I really was not then in a condition to have enjoyed it. I hope Harvey had a good time and that he has forgotten my seeming ungraciousness. His skill in driving the car, and his patience and forbearance with me and my contrary moods, I shall never forget. Your own serenity and good nature and spirit of helpfulness towards us all has an abiding place in my memory. You nearly spoiled us with luxuries, but your intentions were of the best.

The weather is fine, and we are hoping for nearly two months more of this salubrious climate.

Gratefully and sincerely yours,
John Burroughs

John Burroughs largely believed the trip had been a great success and that the campers had been fortunate in many ways—good weather, good company, good health, few delays, a world of wonderful scenery, and only enough bad roads to enhance an appreciation of the good ones. No serious accidents, and only one "hairbreadth escape"when a car full of young people, and going at high speed, came around a sharp turn on their side of the road. Apparently, the younger Firestone, while driving with his mother just a few weeks before the trip, had been forced off a bank by a reckless driver and had sustained minor injuries as a result of same. Such reckless driving, including the near escape along the journey south, caused Harvey Jr., to look back after the miscreants with what Burroughs described as "set teeth and clenched fists."

As a complete group, the Vagabonds traveled nearly 500 miles together, along dusty and often bumpy roads, from Pittsburgh to Asheville. For those that ventured from Asheville to Hagerstown, Maryland, they racked up another 450 miles together, resulting in nearly a one-thousand-mile journey. John Burroughs, who along with Professor DeLoach returned home by train, still managed to motor over 930 miles when including trips from New Jersey to New York and New Jersey to Pittsburgh. When factoring the journeys to and from the starting point of Pittsburgh and the ending point in Hagerstown, the remaining campers notched the following miles: Harvey Firestone (1,321); Thomas Edison (1,525); and Henry Ford (1,623).

Forty years later, long after 1918 was a distant memory, and when recalling his life and adventures, Professor DeLoach wrote that the impressions made upon him at the time of the camping trips were as vivid then as they were at the time, he took his last trip with the Vagabonds. He further recalled each person. Edison, he said, was not a technically scientific man, instead relying on a theory of investigation and learning through a trial-and-error method. He recalled Edison's expression: "There is no expedient to which man will not go to avoid the labor of thinking." When he endeavored to employ some college boys in any part of his work, Edison said he would always avoid those who knew too much. In other words, Edison never wanted to know what would and would not happen as that would show a closed mind. He wanted to employ persons who were willing to try anything, whether those who had tried it before had been successful or not. DeLoach recalled that Henry Ford had given the world a $5.00 a day minimum wage, and for this, many industrialists had considered him an outlaw. The professor further noted that Ford had unknowingly laid the foundation for major labor movements, whether he liked it or not. Ford had regularly discussed labor issues around the campfires, believing that if American industries would raise their standards, labor unions would not be needed. Ford also believed that nations could avoid war by raising their standards as well.

As for Firestone, DeLoach recalled his obsession in late night chats with the idea of providing a certain number of shares of the business to any helper who had been with him along the way. Firestone believed that if a man had a vested interest in a business with which he was connected, he would be a more loyal worker. DeLoach further recalled Harvey as a shrewd and efficient businessman, but also unselfish and philanthropic. One specific story stuck with DeLoach. Apparently, Firestone had grown disgusted with what he believed was an "over-organized office." The tire maker believed it allowed persons to avoid responsibility by claiming they had no specific knowledge of the area of concern. He called all his managers together, and said, "we are going to run this business and get rid of passing the buck." When Firestone asked those present to help him run the business, it was a turning point in his affairs. He saw for the first time that men realized that running a business was superior to holding a job. DeLoach believed Firestone had developed one of the soundest industries in existence. However, he saved his kindest words for John Burroughs.

When remembering John Burroughs, DeLoach wrote that he could not find any greater expression than the words expressed by Elbert Hubbard in his book, *Old John Burroughs*. He says, "John Burroughs is the most universal man I can name...He has no hate, no whim, no prejudice. He has no airs, and he believes in the rich, the poor, the learned, the ignorant. He believes in the wrongdoer, the fallen, the sick, the weak and the defenseless. He loves children, animals, birds, insects, trees and flowers. He is one who is afraid of no man, and of whom no man is afraid. He puts you at your ease—you could not be abashed before him. In his presence there is no temptation to deceive, to overstate, to understate, to be anything different from what you are. You could confess to this man, reveal your soul and tell the worst; and his only answer would be, 'I know! I know!' and tears of sympathy and love would run those heaven-blue eyes." DeLoach, in his own book, *Rambles with John Burroughs*, wrote in the introduction: "He gave me new eyes with which to see, new ears with which to hear, and a new heart with which to love God's great out-o'-doors." Burroughs had written himself, "I go to the woods without notebook but with a deep feeling in my heart that I shall see something new in the great world of nature. When I return home and try to express what I saw, I find that only the most important things come back to me and enable me to give expression to my observations."

DeLoach recalled his wonderful trips through the mountains and the valleys of New York, Pennsylvania, West Virginia, Virginia, Tennessee, and North Carolina in a Journal article entitled *In Camp with Four Great Americans*. He writes in 1959, "My ears were quickened by (Burroughs) remarkable wit and observations, and I only wish that I were able to pass along to my readers the fine spirit and breadth of view that I reaped from this wonderful association." The aging professor, and the last surviving member of the camping trips, further reflects that his impressions about these "four great Americans" are indelibly "pressed upon (his) mind and soul," and "as the years roll by and I approach the end of life, nothing helps keep me happier than thinking of the great days that I spent in the woods with them." His curiosity as to what they meant and what they stood for dwindled in the face of the great facts and meaning of life as they saw it. Their inspiration he found unbelievable, and in concluding his thoughts, DeLoach felt that "no one ever had the same opportunity that was given (him) to live intimately in camp with and enjoy the fellowship of these four great Americans." Realizing the golden opportunity, he had been given, he had vowed to live a richer life.

Besides camping supplies, the Vagabonds brought a wealth of creation with them. Thomas Edison not only brought a stack of newspapers, but also over 1,000 patents to his name, making him the most prolific inventor of all time. John Burroughs, although worn out from their travels, had not slowed with his pen as he had continued to write at an impressive pace including eight books published between 1910 and 1921. Henry Ford brought with him the Model T, the marvels of his factory at Highland Park, and the five-dollar workday. Harvey Firestone brought along recent victories at the Indianapolis Speedway including the first victory of a foreign built car. As a unit, they also brought with them a boatload of money. As a writer, Burroughs was not surprisingly the poorest of the lot, followed by Firestone who was worth a cool million. Thomas Edison was worth at least ten times that amount, and if adjusted for inflation he would have been worth in excess of $170 million today. Still, the richest of all, was Henry Ford. Although it is difficult to determine such things, some estimate his wealth today might approach $200 billion dollars. As one of the wealthiest Americans to ever live, his apparent disinterest in money remains a point of fascination for scholars and business experts alike.

The famous campers also brought a variety of life experiences. Ford and Edison brought slithers of formal education, whereas Firestone and Burroughs, considered more scholarly, brought more than a high school diploma. Edison, Burroughs and Firestone were all well-read. Ford, on the other hand, found little time for books. All the campers were or had been married. John Burroughs, as the eldest member, was a widower having lost his wife Ursula to colon cancer just the year before. The couple, who had been married for 60 years, had one son, Julian. Adopted by the couple in 1878, many have speculated that John Burroughs was the natural father of Julian. Thomas Edison shared the tragedy of losing a wife, as Mary Stilwell died when she was just 29 years old. She left behind their three children: Marion, Thomas, Jr., and William. Edison, initially left dazed and confused and with three small children, quickly remarried. His second wife, coincidently from Akron, Ohio, was Mina Miller. The couple, who by 1918 had been married for over thirty years, had three children of their own: Madeline, Charles and Theodore. Harvey Firestone would soon celebrate his being married twenty-three years to Isabelle Smith, and like Edison he too had six children: Harvey Jr., Leonard, Raymond, Roger and Elizabeth. Unfortunately, the Firestones had faced their own tragedy when their first born, Harry, had died several days after birth in 1897. Henry Ford had recently celebrated his 30th wedding anniversary to Clara Jane Bryant, and like John

Burroughs he had only one son, Edsel. Not surprisingly, the elder members of the group-Edison, Burroughs and Ford were all grandparents, with Henry Ford's grandson, named after his grandfather, just shy of celebrating his first birthday.

Every member of the camping party, regardless of age, brought with them a variety of life experiences, including damaged relationships, regrets, and a few skeletons. The trip provided a much-needed break from an unusually hectic time. Like much of the nation they followed the War, hoping for the best, but fearing the worst. Although they were relieved to learn about how the war was going in their early discussions in Pennsylvania with Commissioner Hurley, the group, like the entire nation, had no idea that victory was only several months away. As surprised as they might be with such a victory so close at hand, they would have been equally dumbfounded to learn, that immense devastation from an unknown flu virus awaited them upon their return home. They most likely passed this virus in their travels, but unlike the trucks of doughboys, or the lofty mountain tops and winding rivers, they never even saw it. These men also brought with them many glorious moments, strong friendships, pride, happiness, and, regardless of age, many hopes and dreams for themselves, their families and the nation. The roads they traveled, along with the people and places they encountered, share a story. Like the year 1918, these people and events, along with this trip, are now forever set in time, sharing a space with no other. However, a chance to get away, to enjoy friendships, to travel and explore, and to enjoy nature, we share together. It is not bound by time. In the end, their stories are part of our stories and *The Story*. May their trips spur us to go places, explore, and motivate us to look closely at life as it lurches by and tramps around. Everyone, now and then, needs a chance to breathe.

ONE YEAR LATER...

August 3, 1919

Car A, also referred to as the "kitchen cabinet car," was on a Ford chassis, and boasted a fully furnished kitchen and pantry, along with a water tank built below. The enamel and nickel finish glistened in the moonlit sky as the car gently swayed atop the evening waves on Lake Erie. On the running board was a large gasoline stove fed from the motor tank, and inside the car was a built-in icebox and beautifully crafted compartments designed to house foods needed for an extended camping trip. Harold Sato, seasoned driver and chef, dared not lean against the car to aide his balance even as the small waves caused his knees to slightly buckle. He knew the car had been tightly fitted, and as the designated driver for Car A, he knew full well it could attain a speed of forty miles per hour without even the slightest of rattles.

Car B, a Cadillac, was outfitted with camping gear as well. This car would be driven by Fred Loskowski, a muscular army veteran, recently returned home from the Great War. Loskowski was charged by Ford personnel with "making sure everything was OK and nobody bothered the Boss, nor the rest of them." His size and strength would come in handy when setting up the eight by ten tents, with sides that rolled up, flooring, and mosquito netting in front. He no doubt would also take charge when setting up the twenty-by-twenty dining tent, complete with a round table and Lazy Susan. Perhaps Sato might have snuck a lean against the Cadillac, but he dared not under the watchful eye of Loskowski.

Car C, a Ford touring car, would be driven by George Ebbing, who would double as the camp photographer. Earlier in the day this group of men had boarded a night boat in Detroit, Michigan bound for Buffalo, New York. Edward G. Kingsford, manager of the Ford Motor Company's holdings in Michigan's Upper Peninsula, had also accompanied Mr. Ford and his camping equipment across the Great Lake. Henry Ford, having just under a full year in "the off season" between trips, brought an entirely new group of vehicles and equipment. With the War finally behind him and his country, the automaker was able to devote more free time to preparing for this upcoming trip through New England that would cover some eleven hundred miles over eleven days. He enjoyed the work. It was a sublime distraction. With the Lazy Susan, he had already imagined how entertaining it would be to watch Mr. Edison spin a potato over to Mr. Burroughs at mealtime. He also wondered if he might convince his son Edsel, who was still busy on the home-front with a toddler, to join him on a future camping escapade. Anything to find some better connection with his son might also be sublime.

A few hours later, on a nearby shore, the Firestones arrived at the Detroit and Buffalo docks with the hope of meeting Ford, Kingsford, and the gang, as they disembarked upon arrival. Harvey Firestone was again a happy man. His eldest son, Harvey Jr., had agreed to join his father and friends for another round of vagabonding. Perhaps next year, or sometime soon, he might bring along one of his other children. His next oldest-Raymond was the logical choice, Firestone thought. The tiremaker also reflected upon his good fortune in securing a luxurious President's Stateroom, with a private deck. The father-son duo had made good use of the private deck on their ferry voyage from Cleveland to Buffalo the night before especially since the weather had been quite favorable.

The plans were loose, but after grabbing a meal, the general goal was to motor a six-car assembly from Buffalo to Syracuse where they might dine and sleep at the Onondaga Hotel. The following morning, they would travel the roughly one-hundred-and-fifty-mile span to the Capital of New York. Albany, much like Pittsburgh the year before, would be the starting line for this year's trip. It would be ground zero for assembling the gang. John Burroughs had celebrated his eighty-second birthday just several months before. This was not lost on anyone, which in part, is why a trip through New England seemed a perfect fit. It is also why Burroughs took a train from his nearby home in the Catskills, choosing to avoid any additional miles in an automobile. This time he intended to pace himself so that he might last for the entire adventure. The last member of the party, Thomas Edison, would drive his car from Orange, New Jersey, and hook up with everyone else once assembled in Albany. For whatever reason, the Wizard of Menlo Park would get off to a later than expected start.

However, these are stories from another year. They involve different places, with different histories and people to explore. They also belong to a different trip and might require a new box full of goodies from the Polsky Building.

Afterword

One day in June of 2018, several months after my father had passed away following his long and courageous battle with cancer, I found myself in West Park, New York searching for Slabsides. The secluded cabin, which once served as a writers' hut for John Burroughs, is a must see for any nature enthusiast and is a mecca for anyone who admired the man. Although I had access to the internet and my phone was fully charged, I still had found myself lost in trying to find the famous old cabin. At one point, my phone had assured me that I had "arrived," yet I was sitting in front of a local winery. Thankfully, the owner, who was apparently giving a bride-to-be and her parents a tour of what was going to surely be a beautiful reception, took the time to tell me I was not the first person looking for Slabsides who had showed up at his front door. He explained that the road was correct, but that it did not connect from my present location and that if I drove back the way I came, traveled further north, and then circled back, I would be able to find it. After several minutes of driving, and convincing myself I was lost on private property, I found a white banner across a small dirt road that read, "Welcome to John Burroughs' Backyard."

It was a clear summer day, but the sun was hidden behind the forest trees, as I approached a clearing that revealed the one time hang out of John Burroughs. Nestled atop a rocky patch of meadow sat Slabsides.

As I sat there completely alone in the woods, I was amazed at just how quiet it was and at first it was slightly unnerving. The cabin is amazingly well preserved and is clearly maintained by selfless and loving individuals, but as I wandered about this old writing retreat, a sense of melancholy swept over me. Yes, the cabin was still there, but long gone was her lovable owner and famous visitors. Now it seemed my father had finally joined them. A terrible question formed in my mind: "Is everything, at some point, finally forgotten?" Walking back through the still woods, fighting back my tears, I happened upon a wooden sign nailed to a tree with Burrough's words, "*If I were to name the three most precious resources of life. I should say books, friends, and nature; and the greatest of these, at least the most constant and always at hand, is nature.*" For the moment, the woods were still there. John Burroughs would approve, and so would my dad. It made me smile.

Acknowledgements

Lucky me. I'm surrounded by wonderful family and friends, who, through their love and encouragement, helped make this book possible. Thank you for your patience, your travels with me, and for letting me talk incessantly about all things 1918.

I would also like to thank my publishing partner, Libby Jordan. You introduced me to a whole new world, and without your expertise I'd still be stuck on third base. I would also like to thank Erin Mulligan for her beautiful rendition of the road trip taken by Thomas Edison, Henry Ford, John Burroughs and Harvey Firestone over a century ago.

The research for this writing would not have been possible without assistance from the following facilities: The University of Akron Archival Services; The Benson Ford Research Center; Rutgers University; Johns Hopkins University; The Henry Ford Museum & Greenfield Village; Thomas Edison National Historical Park; The Birthplace of Country Music Museum; Bridgestone Americas, Inc.; and the Ford Motor Company.

Lastly, I would like to thank the many places and people I encountered along my journey through Appalachia during the last few years. You are truly remarkable.

Another Author Note

Much of the information contained within these pages, is due to the hard work and research on those that walked these paths before I did. I marvel at their works, and it is my sincere hope that I have given them due credit. I also marvel at the amount of information available online. For good or bad, it has certainly made basic cursory research much simpler. One can now learn a great deal without ever leaving home.

As for the actual camping trip, I have relied upon notes kept by Harvey S. Firestone and his son, Harvey, Jr. The diaries and notes made during this trip were later written up as an overall account. Since there are several completed differing accounts, I have designated the first set as "Harvey S. Firestone notes," while the second set is simply designated as "Firestone notes." Furthermore, Harvey Jr.'s account is designated separately as "Harvey Jr. notes." Not surprisingly, John Burroughs, as the writer of the group, also kept a journal of sorts. His thoughts and descriptions of this trip were ultimately gathered in "A Strenuous Holiday," as part of a book titled *Under the Maples*, published in 1921. Firestone later privately published additional excerpts from Burrough's journal, along with selected photographs, in *Our Vacation Days of 1918.* This work, which was published in 1926 and after the death of John Burroughs, was given to the other surviving campers and close associates as a dedication to their friend. Unfortunately, there are no known existing notes from either Thomas Edison or Henry Ford. Lastly, I have also relied upon *There to Breathe the Beauty: The Camping Trips of Henry Ford, Thomas Edison, Harvey Firestone, and John Burroughs*, by Norman Brauer, published in 1995. Brauer's work, which inspired my title, also served as my compass throughout this process.

Many stories of Thomas Edison and Henry Ford have taken on a certain lore—known, or at least once known, by most everyone. However, the following works deserve specific mention. For Thomas Edison: *Edison-A Life of Invention*, by Paul Isreal; *Edison*, by Edmund Morris; and *The Wizard of Menlo Park-How Thomas Alva Edison Invented the Modern World*, by Randall Stross. For Henry Ford: *The People's Tycoon-Henry Ford and the American Century*, by Steven Watts and *Wheels for the World*, by Douglas Brinkley (a fellow Ohio State graduate). My copies of these excellent books are severely worn and filled with countless notes. Thank you, gentlemen.

For John Burroughs, lesser known than Ford and Edison, the works of Clara Barrus, including *Boy and Man*, and *Our Friend John Burroughs* were of great help. Furthermore, *The World of John Burroughs*, by Edward Kanze, needs specific mention as it gave me my first introduction to John Burroughs. I've been hooked ever since. As for Harvey Firestone, *Alfred Lief*, was the man. His works *Harvey Firestone* and *The Firestone Story* gave me a new appreciation for Firestone and Akron. When devouring my father's copy of *Harvey Firestone*, I found a paper note folded in the crease. After unfolding it, I recognized my grandfather's handwriting, which I had not seen in quite some time. It brought back many memories and was an added bonus to reading Lief's works cover-to-cover.

As previously stated, the year 1918 was dominated by World War I and the Spanish flu. *The First World War* by John Keegan was my primer to better understand the "war to end all wars" and introduced me to the Schlieffen Plan. I also need to mention *The Last of the Doughboys* by Richard Rubin as his interviews of the remaining surviving veterans of World War I provides an often-lacking human touch when thinking about war. Knowing that any discussion about the flu was well beyond my education as a lawyer, I turned to *The Great Influenza*, by John

Barry and *America's Forgotten Pandemic-The Influenza of 1918*, by Alfred Crosby. Having written much of this book during the Covid-19 pandemic, I was astonished by these works. Thankfully, such expertise exists, and was rightfully relied upon in a time of crises to give an anxious nation some historical perspective.

Much of my family hails from Appalachia, and more specifically, West Virginia. Getting things right about that region meant a great deal to me. The following works were key: *Appalachia, A History*, by John Alexander Williams; *A History of Appalachia*, by Richard Drake; *Ramp Hollow*, by Steven Stoll, *The United States of Appalachia*, by Jeff Biggers; *It Happened in West Virginia*, by Rick Steelhammer; and *West Virginia and the Civil War*, by Mark A. Snell. Hopefully, the family will approve and, for anyone else, pick up one of these books. As for camping and travel itself, I relied upon the following works to better paint America's relationship with taking time off: *Working at Play-A History of Vacations in the United States*, by Cindy S. Aron; *Heading Out-A History of American Camping*, by Terence Young; *Vagabonding*, by Rolf Potts; and *Under the Stars*, by Dan White. Lastly, four other sources need special mention. For the little girl from West Virginia-Katherine Johnson, I relied upon her own words in *Reaching for the Moon-The Autobiography of NASA Mathematician Katherine Johnson*. As for the "big bang of country music," besides relying on a wonderful tour of the *Birthplace of Country Music Museum,* I relied upon *The Bristol Sessions-Writings about the Big Bang of Country Music*, edited by Charles K. Wolfe and Ted Olson. For Asheville, and her fascinating history, I relied largely upon *Asheville-Mountain Majesty* by Lou Harshaw, and for the final spot that all four friends were together on the 1918 trip, I relied upon *Built for the Ages: A History of the Grove Park Inn* by Bruce E. Johnson. Of course, many other works and resources were relied upon and are more specifically set forth in the following notes.

Research Notes

A Gift from Polsky's

www.thedepartmentstoremuseum.org
www.waymarking.com/waymarks polskys department store akron ohio
https://natestweb.blogspot.com/2009/homes-of-rubber-barons-harvey-firestone
https://gardens.si.edu/collections/explore/ead_component/sova-aag-mar-ref1686
U.S. Decennial Census
Alfred Lief, *The Firestone Story. A History of the Firestone Tire and Rubber Company.*
Norman Brauer, *There to Breathe the Beauty-The Camping Trips of Henry Ford, Thomas Edison, Harvey Firestone, John Burroughs.*

Chapter 1. August 18, 1918

Harvey S. Firestone Notes, p. 1; Firestone Notes, pp. 1-3.
Brauer, *There to Breathe the Beauty-The Camping Trips of Henry Ford, Thomas Edison, Harvey Firestone, John Burroughs,* Preface IX, X, pp. 27-28, 30-31, 37-57, 63-64, 107.
John Burroughs and Harvey Firestone, *Our Vacation Days,* page unnumbered.
R.J.H. DeLoach, *Four Great Americans (In Camp With),* The Georgia Review, Vol. 13, No. 1 (Spring-1959), pp. 42, 44-46.
https://www.britannica.com/list/timeline-of-world-war-i.
https://www.history.com/this-day-in-history/romanov-family-executed
Ford's Nerves Reason for Trip, says Edison-With Noted Scientist Wizard Visits City on Way to Smoky Mountains, Pittsburgh Dispatch, August 18, 1918.
Electric Wizard Arrives in City; Silent as a Sphinx, Pittsburgh Post, August 18, 1918.

Edison, Ford, Burroughs and Hurley Off on Auto Trip, Philadelphia North American, August 19, 1918.

Chapter 2. Flivvers and Silent Movies

Harvey Firestone Notes, p. 1; Firestone Notes p. 3.
Deloach, *Four Great Americans,* The Georgia Review, p. 46.
Brauer, *There to Breathe the Beauty-The Camping Trips of Henry Ford, Thomas Edison, Harvey Firestone, John Burroughs*, pp. 15-19, 63-64.
Shifting Sands, 1918; *Tarzan the Apes*; *The Power and the Glory* (based on 1910 Novel-Grace MacGowen Cooke, 1918; *A Dog's Life*, 1918.
Jeff Biggers, *The United States of Appalachia-How Southern Mountaineers Brought Independence, Culture and Enlightenment to America*, pp. 150-153.
https://www.worldatlas.com/geography/us-states-ranked-by-statehood-date.
www.multipl.com/united-states-population/table/by-year
https://u.demog.berkeley.edu/~andrew/1918/figure2.html
http:/postalmuseum.si.edu/exhibition/fad-to-fundemantal-airmail-object-showcase-stamps-covers-o
American Statistical Association, New Series, No. 127, September 1919, pp. 412-439.
https://libraryguides.missouri.edu/prices-and-wages/1910-1919, pp. 68-281.
https://www.irs.gov/newsroom/historical-highlughts-of-the-irs; http://www.irs.gov.pub/irs, Ninety Years of Individual Income and Tax Statistics, 1916-2000, by Scott Hollenbeck and Keenan Kahr.
https://www.census.gov/topics/families-and-households/data/tables-1918
https://www.saturdayeveningpost.com/2018/02/brief-history-teenagers
https://www.theatlantic.com/business/archive/2016/02/america-in-1915.
https://www.worldbook.com/then-and-now/the-tallest-structure-in-the-world-1917-and-now
America's First Subway Opened in Boston 125 Years Ago on Sept. 1, The Boston Globe, Emily Sweeney, September 1, 2022.
https://www.history.com/...//new-yok-city-subway-opens
https://www.mlb.com/news/los-angelas-dodgers-team-name-history
https://www.encyclopedia.com/history/culture-magazines/1900s-birth-american-century
https://www.encylcopedia.com/history/culture-magazines/1900s-way-we-lived
https://deborahheal.com/snapshot-life-1918/, Deborah Heal, July 9, 2016.
https://www.goodhousekeeping.com/life/g5177/life-100-years-ago Caroline Picard, March 26, 2019.

https://vintagedancer.com/1900s/1918-fashion/

https://wwd.com/fashion-news/fashion-features/how-the-spanish-flu-of-1918-affected-fashion-1203646397/

https://www.history.com/topics/womens-history-the-fight-for-womens-suffrage

https://www.woemshistory.org/.../susan-b-anthony

https://www.wyomingtoday.org/theme-topics/collections/louisa-swain

Winton U. Soldberg, *Creating the Big Ten, Courage, Corruption, and Commercialization.*

Downton Abbey, Episode 5, Season 2.

https://www.history.com/news/first-restaurants

https://historyoffastfood.com/fast-food-history/timeline-of-fast-food

https://www.stories.hilton.com/hilton-history/hiltons-first-hilton

https://www.capecod.com/liefstyle/the-history-of-howard-johnsons-restaurant

https://traveltips.usatoday.com/history-holiday-inn-hotels

https://history.com/topics/us-states/interstate-highway-system

https://www.saferack.com/the-first-gas-station

https://worldhistory.us/american-history/cars-in-the-1920s-the-early-automobile

https://www.networks.h-net.org/timeline-federal-history. Society for History in the Federal Government.

https://www.defense.gov/news/features-stories/story/article/1779177/daylight-savings-time-once-known-as-war-time Katie Lange, March 8, 2019.

https://www.thesportsman.com/articles/when-the-spanish flu-brought-the-world-of-sport-to-a-halt-in-1918 Matthew Crist, March 17, 2020.

New York Times, February 16, 1918.

https://www.nhl.com/news/nhl-stanley-cup-champions-1918-1929

https://www.thethoroughbredracing.com/articles How American Racing Survived the 1918 Spanish Flu Pandemic, Mary Pitt, March 25, 2020.

https://www.tinpanalley.nyc/the-history

Richard Rubin, *The Last of the Doughboys-The Forgotten Generation and their Forgotten World War*, pp. 85-86, 95-96.

https://playback.fm/charts/top-100-songs/1918

Paul Israel, *Edison-A-Life-of-Invention*, pp. 440-443; 446-447; 450-452.

Edmund Morris, *Edison,* pp. 190, 198-199, 205, 208.

Harry N. Abams, *The World of John Burroughs,* pp. 77-79, 98, 102, 106-107, 126.

Clara Barrus, *Our Friend John Burroughs*, pp. 227-229, 236-239, 252-253.

Barrus, *Burroughs Boy and Man,* pp. 312-313, 331-336.

Steven Watts, *The People's Tycoon*, pp. 225, 236, 243-248.

Douglas Brinkley, *Wheels for the World*, pp. 190, 194-195, 206, 208-209, 212,

215, 217-219, 222, 226-231, 235.
Ford Nominated, Newberry Also, New York Times, August 28, 1918.
Lief, *The Firestone Story*, pp. 93-101, 135, 138.
Lief, *Harvey Firestone,* pp. 115-117, 147-155.
Paul Dickson and William D. Hickman; Bridgestone/Firestone, Inc., *Firestone. A Legend. A Century. A Celebration*, pp. 32-33.

Chapter 3. Wizardry & Stagecraft

Jill Jonnes, *Empires of Light-Edison, Tesla, Westinghouse and the Race to Electrify the World*, pp. 52, 54, 66.
Randall Stross, *The Wizard of Menlo Park*, pp. 3-9, 13, 15-21, 23-30, 36-37, 47, 81, 88, 98-101, 103.
Morris, *Edison,* pp. 3, 218, 361-366, 500-501, 503, 507-508, 511, 517, 520-541, 546-547, 549-551, 579-580, 583-588, 590-593, 598-601, 604-605, 607-608, 610-611, 615-619, 621-624, 628-630.
Israel, *Edison A Life of Invention*, pp. 1-10, 15-23, 25-28, 34, 40-42, 44-47, 50-54, 66-68, 74-75, 86-99, 110-115, 120, 122-124, 130-141.
Henry Ford, *Edison as I know Him,* Henry Ford., pp. 20, 24-25.
https://www.home.treasury.gov/.../financial-panic-of-1873.
https://www.worldwidetattoomuseum.com/oreilly/
The Papers of Thomas A. Edison, Baltimore Johns Hopkins University Press (1989-) containing Edison's reminiscences.
The Papers of Thomas A. Edison (digital edition); Rutgers University at https://edison.rutgers.edu. Specific documents available at https://edison.rutgers.edu/singledoc.htm
The True Story of Edison's Childhood and Boyhood, Michigan History Magazine 4 (1920).
The Deafness of Edison, Hearing International, February 9, 2013.
Edison's Trip and Inventions, New York Daily Graphic, August 28, 1878.

Chapter 4. Camp Hurley

Harvey Firestone Notes, pp. 1-4; Firestone notes, pp. 2-4.
Burroughs, *Our Vacation Days of 1918*, page unnumbered.
Brauer, *There to Breathe the Beauty-The Camping Trips of Henry Ford, Thomas Edison, Harvey Firestone, John Burroughs*, pp. 65-66.
DeLoach, The Georgia Review, *Four Great Americans,* pp. 42-51.
World-New York City, August 21, 1918.
Edison Takes a Vacation, Doylestown (Pa.) Democrat, August 21, 1918.

Uniontown (Pa.) Herald, *Edison, Hurley, Ford, Burroughs Praise War Work in the County,* August 20, 1918.
Philadelphia North American, *Edison, Ford, Burroughs & Hurley off on Auto Trip*, August 19, 1918.

Chapter 5. A Little "High Kicking"

Harvey S. Firestone notes pp. 2-4; Firestone notes pp. 4-7.
Brauer, *There to Breathe the Beauty-The Camping Trips of Henry Ford, Thomas Edison, Harvey Firestone, John Burroughs*, pp. 66, 67, 69.
Burroughs, *Our Vacation Days of 1918,* page unnumbered.
Connellsville (Pa.) Courier, *Henry Ford Demonstrates He is Not Afraid to Work; Repairs His Damaged Car,* August 21, 1918.
https://pbs.org/kenburns/horatios-drive/the-crew
https://www.thebaseandrange.com/story-behind-americas-first-roadtrip/ Charles Watkins.
https://nationalpurebreddogday.com/first-dog-to-drive-across-america July 22, 2016.
https://www.summitresort.com/history/
Pittsburgh Post-Gazette, *100-Year-Old Summit Hotel Gets a Face Lift*, June 1, 2007, Marylynne Pitz.
Ford, Edison and Burroughs show "Pep" by "High-Kicking," Fort Dodge (IA) Messenger, August 26, 1918.
Famous Old Friends have Jolly Vacation, Richmond Virginian, August 20, 1918.
https://www.nationalrdfoundation.org/the-national-road/history-of-the-road
https://www.nationalroad.org/history
https://nps.gov/people/albert-gallatin
https://www.nps.gov/places/the-mount-washington-tavern
https://www.nps.gov/fone/index.htm
Thomas Lewis, *For King and Country-George Washington-The Early Years,* pp. 151-157, 174-193.
James Thomas Flexner, *Washington-The Indispensable Man,* pp. 16-18, 24-27.
https://www.nps.gov/places/braddock-s-grave.htm
https://www.nps.gov/fone/braddocksgrave.htm
Five Wizards in the Wild, New York Times Weekend, undated.

Chapter 6. Wild and Wonderful

Rick Steelhammer, *It Happened in West Virginia*, Steelhammer, Preface IX, pp. 42-44, 58-62.
John Denver, *Almost Heaven West Virginia*, 1971.

West Virginia State Motto.
James McPherson, *Battle Cry of Freedom,* pp. 152-153, 201-233, 235, 298-299, 301, 303-304.
Mark A. Snell, *West Virginia and the Civil War-Mountaineers are Always Free,* pp. 18-19, 21-23, 45, 47-48, 50-53, 56-58, 82-84, 182.-

Chapter 7. A Painted Bunting

Burroughs, *Under the Maples-A Strenuous Holiday,* p. 47.
Burroughs, *Our Vacation Days of 1918,* p. unnumbered.
Harvey S. Firestone notes, pp. 5-7; Firestone Notes, pp. 8-9; Harvey Firestone, Jr. notes, p. 1.
Brauer, *There to Breathe the Beauty-The Camping Trips of Henry Ford, Thomas Edison, Harvey Firestone, John Burroughs,* pp. 67-68, 72.
Paul R. Ehrlich, *The Birders Handbook,* p. 351.
https://www.aba.org
https://www.nps/gov/articles/birding-for-beginners
https://lafeber.com/pet-birds/twitching-is-bird-watching-at-its-extreme/ By Matt Rowe, February 4, 2021.
https://www.thebirdgeek.com/birdwatching-slang
The Big Year, 20th Century Fox, October 14, 2011.
https://www.smithsonianmag.com/history/when-americas-titans-industry-and-innovation-went-roadtripping-together Shannon Wianecki, January 26, 2016.
https://www.thehenryford.org/collections
Friends, Families & Forays: Scenes from the Life and Times of Henry Ford, Ford, Richardson Bryan, pp. 44-48, published previously in *The Ford Legend,* Vol. VII, No. 2, 1998.
The Public Image of Henry Ford: An American Folk Hero and His Company, p. 56, David Lanier Lewis, Detroit: Wayne State University Press, 1976.
Ford Times, Volume 6, p. 289, 1912.
Henry Ford, *My Life & Work,* pp. 159-162.
Edison-Ford-Firestone Party in Winston-Salem, Charlotte Observer, August 30, 1918.

Chapter 8. "Knock-me-down-fever."

John M. Barry, *The Great Influenza-The Story of the Deadliest Pandemic in History,* pp. 14, 20, 25-26, 30-32, 36-37, 51-53, 56-57, 63, 65, 67, 69-72, 80, 82-84, 86-87, 91-93, 95-102, 123-124, 126-127, 135-136, 185-191, 265, 269.
Alfred Crosby, *America's Forgotten Pandemic-The Influenza of 1918,* pp. 3-12, 18-19, 319.

https://www.ancestry.com/corporate/blog/spanish-influenza-the-life-story-ofpatient-zero March 11, 2014.
https://www.origins.osu.edu/milestones/pandemic-flu-spanish-flu-1918-h1n1-ww1 Jim Harris.
https://www.smithsonianmag.com/history/journal-plague-year John Barry, November 2017.
htps://www.deeandrews.com/haskell-county-kansas
Burroughs, *Our Vacation Days of 1918,* p. unnumbered.
https://www.history.com/this-day-in-history/u-s-congress-passes-espionage-act
https://www.intelligence.gov/evolution-of-espionage/world-war-1/america-declares-war/espionage-act
https://www.history.com/this-day-in-history/u-s-congress-passes-sedition-act
https://www.history.com/news/1918-pandemic-spanish-flu-censorship
McPherson, *Battle Cry of Freedom,* pp. 287-290.
https://www.history.com/news/why-was-it-called-the-spanish-flu
https://www.medicalnewstoday.com/articles/323538
Santa Fe Monitor, February 14, 21 & 28, 1918.
Victor C. Vaughan, *A Doctor's Memories*, 1926, p. 383.
Simon Flexner and James T. Flexner, *William Henry Welch and the Heroic Age of American Medicine*, 1941, pp. 376-377.

Chapter 9. Watching Clouds

Edward Kanze, *The World of John Burroughs,* pp. 12, 15-18, 20-23, 27, 31, 35-46, 83, 98-99, 146.
Barrus, *John Burroughs Boy and Man,* pp. 12, 26-28, 35-37, 65-75, 82, 85-92, 152-155, 159-161, 166-167, 176-177, 182-185, 188, 191-199, 201-206, 209, 212-213, 215-217, 219-229, 232, 235-239, 243-246, 255, 260, 287.
Brauer, *There to Breathe the Beauty-The Camping Trips of Henry Ford, Thomas Edison, Harvey Firestone, John Burroughs,* pp. 14-16.
Barrus, *Our Friend John Burroughs,* pp. 47-48, 51-53, 55-61, 63-65, 73-81, 109, 162, 215-216.
Bill O'Reilly and Martin Dugard, *Killing Lincoln: The Shocking Assassination that Changed America Forever.*
Stephen M. Silverman, *The Catskills It's History and How it Changed America,* pp. 8-9.
McPherson, *Battle Cry of the Republic,* pp. 232-233.

Chapter 10. Founding Campers

Harvey S. Firestone notes, p. 7; Firestone notes, p. 9; Harvey Firestone, Jr., notes, p. 1.

Burroughs, *Under the Maples-A Strenuous Holiday,* p. 48.

Burroughs, *Our Vacation Days of 1918,* p. unnumbered.

https://cheatmountainclub.com

https://cheatmountainclub.com/history

Cindy S. Aron, *Working at Play-A History of Vacations in the United States,* pp. 158-161, 164-165.

Dan White, *Under the Stars,* pp. 3, 64-71, 73-78, 86-88, 110, 114, 203-206, 209, 331-332.

Terrance Young, *Heading Out-A History of American Camping,* pp. 3, 27-48, 50-53, 70-71, 74, 110-115, 211-212.

https://www.wiredforadventure.com/thomas-hiram-holding

https://www.smithsonianmag.com/innovation/briefhistory-rv Terrance Young, September 4, 2018.

https://www.foxnews.com/lifestyle/american-invented-motor-home Kerry J. Byrne, June 18, 2022.

Nathan Miller, *Theodore Roosevelt-A Life,* pp. 30-31, 36, 45-50, 166-167, 226, 316, 350.

Chapter 11. "Apalachen"

Burroughs, *Under the Maples,* p. 45, 48-49.

John Alexander Williams, *Appalachia A History,* pp. 8-9, 11-13, 19-20, 30-32, 37, 55-60, 68-69, 83-87, 148-153, 238, 247.

Richard B. Drake, *A History of Appalachia,* Introduction IX, X, pp. 22, 35, 40, 51, 54-55, 60-62, 65-67, 114-115, 146-151.

Biggers, *The United States of Appalachia,* Preface XV, pp. 138, 144, 146-150.

Steven Stoll, *Ramp Hollow-The Ordeal of Appalachia,* pp. 9-13, 23, 90-96, 98-100, 102-105, 118-125, 130-131, 136, 152-153, 165-168.

Edward O. Welles, *Into the Wilderness-William Bartram's Trail through Nature,* pp. 34-63.

Harvey S. Firestone notes, pp. 5-6; Firestone notes p. 8.

Robert Shogan, *The Battle of Blair Mountain-The Story of America's Largest Labor Uprising,* pp. 1-2, 6-7, 18, 20-26, 90-91, 157-158, 222.

John Alexander Williams, *West Virginia, A History,* p. 147.

https://www.history.com/this-day-in-history/mason-and-dixon-draw-a-line.

Chapter 12. A Time to Play

Brauer, *There to Breathe the Beauty-The Camping Trips of Henry Ford, Thomas Edison, Harvey Firestone, John Burroughs,* p. 73, 76-77.
Harvey S. Firestone notes, pp. 8, 10; Firestone notes, p. 11-12; Harvey Firestone, Jr., notes, p. 1.
Burroughs, *Under the Maples-A Strenuous Holiday,* p. 48.
DeLoach, *Four Great Americans,* p. 46-47.
Aron, *Working at Play-A History of Vacations in the United States.,* pp. 16-21, 23-29, 40, 48-49, 51, 66-71, 101, 127, 130, 132, 138-139, 142-145, 150-153, 156-161.
https://www.tophotsprings.com/united-states-hot-springs/
https://www.nps.gov/subjects/geology/hot-springs-htm
https://wvtourism.com/things-to-do/luxary-relaxation/natural-springs
https://www.roadsideamerica.com/story/32201
https://wvtourism.com/berkeley-springs-washington
https://www.berkeleysprings.com/GWarchives
https://www.onlyinyourstate.com/virginia/hot-springs-va Anna Strock, May 12, 2022.
https://www.cntraveler.com 15 Amazing Structures Originally Built for World's Fairs, Marisa Lascala, July 28, 2013.
Rolf Potts, *Vagabonding,* pp. 161-165, 168.

Chapter 13. Katherine

Brauer, *There to Breathe the Beauty-The Camping Trips of Henry Ford, Thomas Edison, Harvey Firestone, John Burroughs,* pp. 74, 76-78.
Harvey S. Firestone notes, pp. 9-11; Firestone notes, pp. 12-15; Harvey Firestone, Jr., pp. 2-3.
https://www.nasa.gov/content/katherine-johnson-biography
Katherine Johnson, *Reaching for the Moon,* pp. 2-4, 7-8, 29, 32, 35-36, 38, 61-67, 75, 77, 85, 89-91, 95, 101, 108, 111-14, 118, 125-126, 129, 133-134, 141, 145-146, 158-159, 166-168, 175, 175-177, 181, 201-204, 207-212, 240, 242.

Chapter 14. Shakespeare Reproduced

Brauer, *There to Breathe the Beauty-The Camping Trips of Henry Ford, Thomas Edison, Harvey Firestone, John Burroughs,* pp. 78-80.
Burroughs, *Under the Maples-A Strenuous Holiday,* pp. 49-52.
Burroughs, *Our Vacation Days of 1918,* p. unnumbered.
Harvey S. Firestone notes, pp. 11-13; Firestone notes, pp. 15-16; Harvey Firestone, Jr. notes, p. 3.

Ford, *Edison as I Know Him*, p. 56.

https://www.asce.org/about-civil-enginerring/history-and-heritage/notable-civil-engineers/john-loudon-mcadam

https://interestingengineering.com/cultue/john-loudon-mcadam-the-father-of-the-modern-road

Chapter 15. "You have it, keep at it."

Brinkley, *Wheels of the World,* pp. 4-10, 12, 15-17, 20-27, 31, 34-35, 38-40, 43-48, 50, 53-55, 60, 65-69, 72-73, 80-89, 100-103.

Steven Watts, *The People's Tycoon-Henry Ford and the American Century,* pp. 3-16, 23-30, 34-43, 45-49, 53-54, 57-60, 63-71, 73-88, 91-93, 95-100, 102, 107, 111-112.

https://hemmings.com/stories If not for the Chicago World's Fair 125 Years ago, the U.S. may not have become an auto building superpower, Daniel Strohl, August 28, 2018.

Ford, *Edison as I Know Him,* pp. 1-5, 37.

Ford Archives at the Benson Ford Research Center, Ford Museum & Greenfield Village, Dearborn, Michigan-containing written and oral reminiscences of Henry Ford and family.

Detroit Free Press, October 11, 1901.

Chapter 16. Birthplace

Brauer, *There to Breathe the Beauty-The Camping Trips of Henry Ford, Thomas Edison, Harvey Firestone, John Burroughs,* pp. 80-83.

Harvey S. Firestone notes, pp. 13-16; Firestone notes pp. 16-17.

Thos. A Edison, Henry Ford and Party Now Here, Asheville Citizen, August 28, 1918.

Edison-Ford Party Left City Yesterday, Asheville Citizen, August 29, 1918.

https://www.visitabingdonvirginia.com

https://www.abingdontavern.net/about-us/

https://www.themartha.com/history

https://bartertheatre.com/history

https://visitabingdonvirginia.com/landmarks/barter-theatre

Hidden History of Bristol-Stories from the State Line, V.N. "Bud" Phillips, p. 13.

https://www.bristoltn.org/History-of-Bristol

https://www.bristolhistoricalassociation.com/our-history

https://discoverbristol.org/visitors/discovery-bristol

https://discoverbristol.org/attractions/bristol-sign/

Burroughs, *Our Vacation Days of 1918,* p. unnumbered.

The Bristol Sessions, Writings About the Big Bang of Country Music, Edited by Charles K. Wolfe and Ted Olson, pp. 1-3, 7-12, 17-19, 20, 24, 31-53, 137-139, 257.
https://www.victorrecords.com/thegreateststoryeversold
https://www.countrymusichalloffame.org/artis/ralph-peer
https://www.pbs.org/wgbh/americanexperience/features/carterfamily-ralph-peer/

Chapter 17. Schlieffen's Plan

.https://www.archives.gov/exhibits/eyewitness-schwieger-diary Excerpt taken from official translation of Walter Schwieger's diary.
Diary of the German Captain who sank the *Lusitania*, University of California Press, Essay May 1, 1920.
The American Historical Review, vol. 41, no. 1 (Oct. 1935), pp. 54-73.
https://online.ucpress.edu/currenthistory/article-abstract/2/3/413/191027/the-warning-and-the-consequence University of California Press Volume 2, Issue 3, July 1915, The Warning and the Consequence.
https://poets.org/poet/john-mccrae
John Keegan, *The First World War,* pp. 16, 28-35, 48-51, 71-74, 77-78, 80-84, 87-93, 97-102, 109, 111-115, 123, 131, 135-137.
https://www.alphapublishing.com/worldwar1/schlieffen-plan/
https://www.history.com/news/was-germany-doomed-in-the-world-war-i-by-the-schlieffen-plan
Gerald Gliddon *The Spring Offensive 1918,* 1997.
https://www.history.com/this-day-in-history/german-assault-on-lieg-begins-first-battle-of-world-war-1
https://www.history.com/news/the-first-battle-of-the-marne-100-years-ago
https://www.washingtononline.com/world-war-i/race-to-the-sea-wwi Andrew Knighton, Guest Author, October 19, 2017.

Chapter 18. Before World War II

Candice Millard, *The River of Doubt: Theodore Roosevelt's Darkest Journey*, 2005.
The American Historical Review, Vol. 43. No. 4, Russell Buchanan (July 1938), pp. 775-790.
Keegan, *The First World War,* pp. 341-342, 350-353, 372-375, 407.
https://rmslusitania.info/primary-docs/too-proud-to-fight
Rubin, *The Last of the Doughboys,* pp. 29-30, 32-48.
Watts, *The People's Tycoon,* 228-235, 240.
Brinkley, *Wheels of the World,* pp. 193-200, 213.
https://www.kumc/school-of-medicine/academics/departments/history-and-

philosophy-of-medicine/archives/wwi/essays/military-medical-operations-america George Thompson.
https://www.fdmuseum.org/collection/online-exhibits/battle-of-cantingy
https://www.abmc.gov/Belleau-Wood
https://www.history.com/this-day-in-history/battle-of-belleau-wood-begins
https://www.historyonthenet.com/battle-belleau-wood
The Marines' Mythic Fight of Belleau Wood, David T. Zabecki, June 26, 2021.
https://www.history.com/this-day-in-history/quentin-roosevelt-killed
https://www.nps.gov/articles/captain-harry-truman
https://www.warfarehistorynetwork.com/patton-in-wwi
https://www.biography.com/militart-figures/douglas-macarthur
https://www.marshallfoundation.org/life-legacy
https://www.erwinrommel.info/first-world-war

Chapter 19. Harvey

The Legend of 1969: Mario Andretti's unlikely Indy 500 victory filled with Racing Lore, IndyStar, Jim Ayello, May 16, 2019.
https://www.americanhistory.si.edu/race-cars/brawner-ford-hawk-no-2-1969
50-Year Anniversary: Mario Andretti Savors his 1969 Indianapolis Victory, IndyStar, Peter Hughes, May 10, 2019.
Mario's Luckiest 500: Mario Andretti and as told by Marshall Pruett, Road & Track, May 21, 2019.
Purdue Marching Band is "Part of the Fabric of the 500," IndyStar, Jordan J. Wilson, May 27, 2016.
Firestone. A Legend. A Century. A Celebration., pp. 4-5, 7-9, 11-12, 87-102, 104-112, 128.
https://www.jimmy.org/jimmy-stewarts-biography
The Firestone commercials with Jimmy Stewart are still available for viewing thanks to YouTube™.
https://www.rubbernews.com/bridgestone-took-on-the-world-with-firestone-acquisition Roger Schreffler.
https://www.tirebusiness.com/news/when-rubber-hit-the-road-akron
Burroughs, *Under the Maples-A Strenuous Holiday,* p. 52.
Our Vacation Days of 1918, page unnumbered.
https://www.biggestuscities.com/city/akron-ohio
Lief, *The Firestone Story,* pp. 3, 4-6, 9-11.
Lief, *Harvey Firestone,* pp. 2-27, 36-48, 50-51, 67, 71-72.
Harvey S. Firestone and Samuel Crowther, *Men and Rubber-The Story of*

Business, pp. 14-17, 20-26, 31, 33, 37-39.
Notables Pay Mountains Visit, Nashville Banner, September 1, 1918

Chapter 20. Campfires and Storytelling

Harvey S. Firestone notes, pp. 18-20; Firestone notes, p. 18.
Brauer, *There to Breathe the Beauty-The Camping Trips of Henry Ford, Thomas Edison, Harvey Firestone, John Burroughs,* pp. 83, 86-88.
Burroughs, *Our Vacation Days of 1918,* page unnumbered.
Burroughs, *Under the Maples-A Strenuous Holiday,* p. 49.
Johnson City, Postcard History Series, pp. 6-9, 13
https://www.jonesborough.com
https://www.jonesborough.com/history
https://www.tennesseencyclopedia.net/entries/elihu-embree
H.W. Brands, *Andrew Jackson-His Life and Times,* pp. 24-30, 53-54, 107-110, 186, 263-283.
https://www.history.com/topics/war-of-1812/battle-of-new-orleans
https://www.nps.gov/jela/learn/historyculture/battle-of-new-orleans
https://www.nps.gov/articles/battle-of-new-orleans
https://www.history.com/topics/us-presidents/andrew-jackson
https://www.whitehouse.gov/.../andrew-jackson
https://www.jonesborough.com/locations/chester-inn-museum
Robert Morgan, *Boone, A Biography,* pp. 44-45, 48-55, 65-87, 88-125, 127-132, 136-137, 153-158, 163-164, 389-391.
https://www.biography.com/history-culture/daniel-boone
https://www.tennesseeencyclopedia.net/entries/daniel-boone
T.R. Fehrenbach, *Lone Star, A History of Texas,* pp. 205-215.
James Donovan, *The Blood of Heroes-The 13-Day Struggle for the Alamo-And the Sacrifice that Forged a Nation,* pp. 143-144, 149-153, 291-292.
https://tennesseeencyclopedia.net/entries/davy-crockett
https://www.tnstateparks.com/parks/david-crockett
https://www.smokymountains.com/articles/where-the-buffalo-roam
https://cherokeeregistry.com/journeys-of-james-needham-gabriel-arthur
https://www.tennesseeencyclopedia.net/entries/early-exploration
https://tennesseeencyclopedia.net/entries/state-of-franklin
https://www.smithsonianmag.com/smart-news/true-story-short-lived-sate-franklin
Kat Eschner, August 23, 2017.
https://daily.jstar.org/franklin-the-america-state-that-want
https://www.tipton-haynes.org

https://www.tennesseeencyclopedia.net/entries/john-sevier
https://www.northcarolina.org/encyclopedia/john-sevier
https://www.storytellingcenter.net
https://www.jonesboroughtn.org/residents/international-storytelling-center
Donald T. Williams, *Mere Humanity-G.K. Chesterton, C.S. Lewis, and J.R.R. Tolkien on the Human Condition,* p. 23.

Chapter 21. Unexpectedly Detained

Harvey S. Firestone notes, 20-26; Firestone notes p. 19.
Brauer, *There to Breathe the Beauty-The Camping Trips of Henry Ford, Thomas Edison, Harvey Firestone, John Burroughs,* pp. 88-93.
https://www.visitmadisoncounty.com/ww1-internment-camp-hot-springs
https://www.onlyinourstate.com/north-carolina/german-pow-camp-hot-springs
Most People in North Carolina Don't know about our Old German POW Camp, Robin Jarvis, April 17, 2018.
https://www.appalachian.net/2014/06/first-world-war-1-pow-arrive-at-hot-springs-nc
https://www.ncpedia.org/wwi-internment-camp
https://www.mhuedu/about/who-we-are/history-of-the-university
http://www.ncpedia.org/mars-hill-college
Acts 17:22
https://www.mhu.edu/news/rural-heritage-museum
Burroughs, *Our Vacation Days of 1918,* page unnumbered.
Thos. A Edison, Henry Ford and Party Now Here, Asheville Citizen, August 28, 1918.

Chapter 22. Land of the Sky

Lou Harshaw, *Asheville-Mountain Majesty,* pp. 3-7, 21-22, 27-28, 35, 43, 69-72, 89, 91, 95, 98, 106-109, 113-119, 120-122.
https://historicsites.nc.gov/history/zebulan-vance
https://www.ncenpedia.org/biography/vance-zebulan
https://exploreasheville.com/.../history
https://www.exploreasheville.com/architecture
https://www.ncepedia.org/biography/coxe-franklin

Chapter 23. Sunset Mountain

Bruce E. Johnson, *Built for the Ages-A History of the Grove Park Inn,* pp. 1-3, 4-8, 10-14, 16, 17, 18-20, 23, 26-27, 29, 35-37.
https://ncepdia.org/biography/seely-fred-loring

https://www.omnihotels.com/asheville-grove-park/property-details/history
https://www.tennesseeencyclopedia.net/entries/edwin-wiley-grove
Harvey S. Firestone notes, p. 26.
Thos. A Edison, Henry Ford and Party Now Here, Asheville Citizen, August 28, 1918.
Edison-Ford Party Left City Yesterday, Asheville Citizen, August 29, 1918.

Chapter 24. "I cannot possibly go any further."

Brauer, *There to Breathe the Beauty-The Camping Trips of Henry Ford, Thomas Edison, Harvey Firestone, John Burroughs,* 93-100.
Harvey S. Firestone notes, pp. 26-36.
Ford and Edison Jaunt Thru on Gasless Sunday, Hagerstown Mail, September 1-2, 1918.
https://virginiahistory.org/learn/history-virginias-natural-bridge-so-beautiful-arch
https://worldhistory.us/american-history/robert-e-lee-president-of-washington-college
https://www.battlefield.org/visit/heritage-sites/lee-chapel-and-museum
https://encyclopediavirginia.org/entries/lee-chapel
https://www.vmi.edu/.../stonewall-jackson-at-vmi
https://www.battlefields.org/visit/heritage-sites/stonewall-jackson-houe
https://www.edu/museums-and-archives/jackson-house-museum
https://heraldmailmedia.com/story/news/local Julie E. Greene, November 25, 2020.

Chapter 25. Fall Classics

Tom Hamilton, a radio play-by-play announcer for the Cleveland Indians and the Cleveland Guardians, regularly uses the phrase "On the corner of Carnegie and Ontario" to describe the home field location of Cleveland's baseball park. Although I might be biased, Hamilton is one of the all-time great radio announcers.
https://www.baseball-refrence-com/postseason/2016_ws
https://www.mlb.com/news/cubs-indians-world-series
https://www.baseball-reference-com/postseason/1918/_ws
https://www.chicagotribune.com/sports/ct-wrigley 1918 World Series Started the U.S. Love Affair with the National Anthem, Don Babwa, July 3, 2017.
https://www.mlb.com/news/chicago-cubs-history
https://www.cbssports.com/mlb/news/cubs-curse
https://www.mlb.com/news/curse-of-the-bambino
https://www.history.com/news/curse-of-the-bambino-ruth-red-sox-broken

https://www.bostonmagazine.com/news/2017/10/26 Renae Reints, October 26, 2017.
https://www.daytontriangles.com
https://www.daytondailynews.com/news/local/things-you-should-know-about-the-dayton-triagles-the-team-that-started-the-NFL
https://profootballarhives.com/1918
https://www.nfl.com/100/original-towns
https://www.sports-reference-com/cfb/years/1918
https://www.si.com/college/tmg/tony-barnhart/spanish-flu The Pandemic and College Football: A Look Back at the 1918 Season, Tony Barnhart, May 2, 2020.
https://tiptop25.com/champ1918
https://pittnews.com/article/160077/sports/pandemic-panthers-reliving-pitts-1918-national-championship-amid-the-spanish-flu Griffon Floyd, September 15, 2020.
https://www.heisman.com/articles/heisman-history
https://www.britannica.com/biography/John-Heisman
https://www.britannica.com/biography/Pop-Warner
https://www.smithsonianmag.com/history/the-early-history-of-football's-forward-pass Jim Morrison, December 28, 2010.

Chapter 26. "Who won, who won?"

Keegan, *The First World War,* pp. 412-420.
Rubin, *The Last of the Doughboys,* p. 26, 76.
https://www.britannica.com/biography/Alvin-Cullum-York
https://www.history.com/this-day-in-history/us-soldier-alvin-york-displays-heroics-at-argonne
https://www.americanheritage.com/american-hero-sargeant-york
https://origins.osu.edu/milestones/wwi-armistice-centennial-armistice-november-11-1918-worldwar-surrender Julie M. Powell.
https://www.history.com/this-day-in-history/world-war-i-ends
https://www.history.com/news/world-ar-i-armistice-last-american-death
https://militaryhistorynow.com/2018/10/16/the-last-to-fall-world-war-one-final-casualties
https://eyewitnesstohistory.com/armistice
https://harpers.org/archive/2018/11/the-ghosts-of-versailles Kevin Balger.
https://www.news.uga.edu/poppy-lady-moina-michael
https://www.georgiaencyclopedia.org/aricles/history-archeology/moina-belle-michael-1869-1944

https://armistice-museum.com/the-armistice-carriage
https://www.history.com.uk/article/the-compegne-wagon-one-train-carriage-two-peace-treaties

Chapter 27. What an Ending!

Crosby, *America's Forgotten Pandemic-The Influenza of 1918,* pp. 70-87, 91, 95, 100-113, 298-299.
Barry, *The Great Influenza,* pp. 111, 128-130, 200-201, 203, 209, 220-227, 257-259, 307-308, 345-346, 352-353, 355-356, 358-359, 370, 374-375, 397, 402-403
Robert John Hadfield, *Virus 1918-Spanish Influenza, the words of people who lived it,* pp. 24-25, 40-41, 76.
https://www.redcross.org/about-us/who-we-are/history
https://www.history.com/news/1918-spanish-flu-mask-wearing-resistance Becky Little, May 6, 2020.
https://www.seatlletimes.com/nation-world/everyone-wore-a-mask-during-the-1918-pandenic-they-were-useless Elizabeth McGraw, April 2, 2020.
https://www.cdc.gov/flu/pandemic-resources/1918-pandemic
https://www.dailysignal.com/2020/04/15/woodrow-wilson-strange-silence-on-flu-epidemic-during-great-war Eric Felton, April 2, 2020.
Watts, *The People's Tycoon,* pp. 243, 248.
Brinkley, *Wheels for the World*, pp. 228-230, 233-234.
https://www.senate.gov/about/powers-procedures/expulsion/102TrumanNewberry-expulsion
https://www.history.com/news/who-was-the-first-U.S.-president-to-travel-abroad-while-in-office
Letters from John Burroughs, 1918.
Our Vacation Days of 1918, pages unnumbered.
DeLoach, *Four Great Americans,* pp. 48-51.
Brauer, *There to Breathe the Beauty-The Camping Trips of Henry Ford, Thomas Edison, Harvey Firestone, John Burroughs,* pp. 107-109.

Selected Bibliography

Adkins, Leonard M. *West Virginia-An Explorer's Guide*. The Countryman Press, 2011.

Allen, Hugh. *Rubber's Hometown*. Stratford House, 1949.

Aron, Cindy S. *Working at Play-A History of Vacations in the United States*. Oxford Press, 1999.

Bailey, Rebecca J. *Matewan-Before the Massacre. Politics, Coal, and the Roots of Conflict in a West Virginia Mining Community*. West Virginia University Press, 2008.

Barrus, Clara. *John Burroughs-Boy and Man*. Doubleday, Page & Company, 1920.

------, Clara. *Our Friend John Burroughs*. Houghton Mifflin Company, 1914.

Barry, John M. *The Great Influenza-The Story of the Deadliest Pandemic in History*. Penguin Books, 2004, 2009.

Biggers, Jeff. *The United States of Appalachia-How Southern Mountaineers Brought Independence, Culture and Enlightenment to America*. Counterpoint Press, 2006.

Brands, H.W. *Andrew Jackson-His Life and Times*. Anchor Books, 2005.

Brauer, Norman. *There to Breathe the Beauty-The Camping Trips of Henry Ford, Thomas Edison, Harvey Firestone, John Burroughs*. Norman Brauer Publications, 1995.

Brinkley, Douglas. *Wheels for the World-Henry Ford, His Company, and a Century of Progress*. Penguin Books, 2003.

Burroughs, John. *Under the Maples*, 1921.

Crockett, Davy. *King of the Wild Frontier: An Autobiography by Davy Crockett*, Dover Publications, 1836, 2010.

Crosby, Alfred W. *America's Forgotten Pandemic-The Influenza of 1918*. Cambridge University Press, 2003.

Dickson, Paul. Hickman, William D. Bridgestone/Firestone, Inc. *Firestone. A Legend. A Century. A Celebration*. Forbes Custom Publishing, 2003.

Donovan, James. *The Blood of Heroes-The 13 Day Struggle for the Alamo and the Sacrifice that Forged a Nation*. Back Bay Books, 2012.

Drake, Richard B. *A History of Appalachia*. The University Press of Kentucky, 2001.

Ehrlich, Paul R., Dobkin, David S., Wheye, Darryl. *The Birder's Handbook-A Field Guide to the National History of North American Birds*. Simon & Schuster, 1988.

Fehrenbach, T.R. *Lone Star-A History of Texas and the Texans*. Da Capo Press, 1968, 2000.

Firestone, Harvey S., Crowther, Samuel. *Men and Rubber-The Story of Business*. Doubleday, Page & Company, 1926.

Flexner, James Thomas. *Washington-The Indispensable Man*, Back Bay Books, 1969.

Ford, Henry. Crowther, Samuel. *Edison as I Know Him*. 1930.

-------, Henry. *My Life & Work-An Autobiography of Henry Ford*, 1922.

Hadfield, Robert John. *Virus 1918-Spanish Influenza, the word of the people who lived it*. Thick and Mystic Media, LLC., 2020.

Harshaw, Lou. *Asheville-Mountain Majesty*. Bright Mountain Books, Inc., 2007.

Israel, Paul. *Edison-A Life of Invention*. John Wiley & Sons, 1998.

Johnson, Bruce E. *Built for the Ages-A History of the Grove Park Inn*. The Grove Park Inn and Country Club, 1991.

Johnson, Katherine. *Reaching for the Moon-An Autobiography of NASA Mathematician, Katherine Johnson*. Atheneum Books, 2019.

Jonnes, Jill *Empires of Light-Edison, Tesla, Westinghouse and the Race to Electrify the World*. Random House, Inc., 2004.

Kanze, Edward. *The World of John Burroughs*. Harry N. Abrams, Inc., Publishers, 1993.

Keegan, John *The First World War*. Vintage Books, 1998.

Lamott, Anne. *Bird by bird-Some Instruction on Writing and Life*. Anchor Books, 1994.

Lewis, Thomas A. *for King and Country-George Washington-The Early Years*. John Wiley & Sons, Inc., 1993.

Lief, Alfred. *Harvey Firestone-Fee Man of Enterprise*. McGraw-Hill Book Company, Inc., 1951.

------, Alfred. *The Firestone Story. A History of the Firestone Tire & Rubber Company*. Whittlesey House, McGraw-Hill Book Company, Inc., 1951.

McPherson, James. *Battle Cry of Freedom-The Civil War Era*. Oxford University Press, 1988.

Miller, Nathan. *Theodore Roosevelt-A Life*. William Morrow and Company, Inc., 1992.

Morgan, Robert. *Boone-A Bibliography*. Algonquin Books of Chapel Hill, 2007.

Morris, Edmund. *Edison*. Random House, Inc., 2020.

Phillips, V.N. *Hidden History of Bristol-Stories from the State Line*. The History Press, 2010.

Potts, Rolf. *Vagabonding-An Uncommon Guide to the Art of Long-Term World Travel*. Ballentine Books, 2002.

Roberts, L. Thomas. *Johnson City-Postcard History Series.* Arcadia Publishing, 2008.

Rubin, Richard. *The Last of the Doughboys-The Forgotten Generation and Their Forgotten World War*. First Mariner Books, 2014.

Shaffer, Marquerite S. *See America-First Tourism and National Identity, 1880-1940.* Smithsonian Institution, 2001.

Shogan, Robert. *The Battle of Blair Mountain-The Story of America's Largest Labor Uprising*. Basic Books, 2004.

Silverman, Stephen M., Silver, Raphael D. *The Catskills-It's History and How it Changed America*. Alfred A. Knopf, 2015.

Snell, Mark A. *West Virginia and the Civil War-Mountaineers are always Free.* The History Press, 2011.

Steelhammer, Rick. *It Happened in West-Virginia-Remarkable Events that Shaped History*. Morris Book Publishing, 2013.

Stoll, Steven. *Ramp Hollow-The Ordeal of Appalachia*. Hill and Wang, 2017.

Stross, Randall. *The Wizard of Menlo Park-How Thomas Alva Edison Invented the Modern World*. Three River Press, 2007.

Watts, Steven. *The People's Tycoon-Henry Ford and the American Century*. Vintage Book, 2006.

Welles, Edward O., Jr. *William Bartram's Trail Through Nature. Into the Wilderness*. National Geographic Society, 1978.

White, Dan. *Under the Stars-How America Fell in Love with Camping*. Henry Hill and Company, LLC., 2016.

Williams, Donald T. *Mere Humanity-G.K. Chesterton, C.S. Lewis and J.R.R. Tolkien on the Human Condition*. Broadman & Holman Publishers, 2006.

Williams, John Alexander. *Appalachia-A History*. The University of North Carolina Press, 2002.

------, John Alexander. *West Virginia-A History*. West Virginia University Press, 2001.

Wolfe, Charles K., Olson, Ted. *The Bristol Sessions-*Writings *About the Big Bang of Country Music-Contributions to Southern Appalachian Studies, 12.* McFarland & Company, Inc., Publishers, 2005.

Wood, Donald F. *RVs & Campers 1900-2000. An Illustrated History*. Iconografix, 2002.

Young, Terence. *Heading Out-A History of American Camping*. Cornell University, 2017.

Archives and Locations

Abingdon, Virginia
Akron, Ohio
Asheville, North Carolina
Barter Theatre, Abingdon, Virginia
Bartow, West Virginia
Benson Ford Research center, Dearborn, Michigan
Beverly, West Virginia
Birthplace of Country Music Museum, Bristol, Virginia
Bluefield, West Virginia
Bluff City, Tennessee
Bolar Springs, Virginia
Braddock Grave, Farmington, Pennsylvania
Bristol, Tennessee
Bristol, Virginia
Burroughs Memorial Field, Roxbury, New York
Cheat Mountain Club, Durbin, West Virginia
Chester Inn Museum, Jonesborough, Tennessee
Columbiana, Ohio
Connellsville, Pennsylvania
Dearborn, Michigan
Durbin, West Virginia
Edison and Ford Winter estates, Fort Myers, Florida
Elizabethton, Tennessee
Elkins, West Virginia

Fair Lane-Home of Clara & Henry Ford, Dearborn Michigan
(closed to public for restoration)
Farmington, Pennsylvania
Fort Myers, Florida
Fort Necessity National Battlefield and Museum, Farmington, Pennsylvania
Greenville, Tennessee
Greensburg, Pennsylvania
Hagerstown, Maryland
Hansonville, Virginia
Hickory, North Carolina
Hot Springs, North Carolina
Hot Springs, Virginia
International Storytelling Center, Jonesborough, Tennessee
Jackson (Stonewall) House Museum, Lexington, Virginia
Johnson City, Tennessee
Jonesborough, Tennessee
Jonesborough-Washington County History-Museum, Jonesborough, Tennessee
Keysers Ridge, Maryland
Lead Mine, West Virginia
Lebanon, Virginia
Lexington, Virginia
Marion, North Carolina
Mars Hill, North Carolina
Mars Hill University, Mars Hill, North Carolina
Martinsville, Virginia
Milan, Ohio
Mocksville, North Carolina
Mt. Washington Tavern Museum, Farmington, Pennsylvania
Narrows, Virginia
Natural Bridge State Park, Natural Bridge, Virginia
Newport, Tennessee
Parsons, West Virginia
Pittsburgh, Pennsylvania
Poughkeepsie, New York
Princeton, West Virginia
Roanoke, Virginia
Roxbury, New York

Rural Heritage Museum, Mars Hill University, Mars Hills, North Carolina
Slabsides and the John Burroughs Nature Sanctuary, West Park, New York
Statesville, North Carolina
Staunton, Virginia
Sweet Springs, West Virginia
Tazewell, Virginia
The Greenbrier, White Sulphur Springs, West Virginia
The Henry Ford Museum & Greenfield Village, Dearborn, Michigan
The Historic Summit Inn, Hopwood, Pennsylvania
The Martha Washington Inn & Spa, Abingdon, Virginia
The Omni Grove Park Inn, Asheville, North Carolina
The Tavern, Abingdon, Virginia
Thomas Edison National Historic Park, West Orange, New Jersey
Tipton-Haynes State Historic Site, Johnson City, Tennessee
Uniontown, Pennsylvania
University of Akron, Akron, Ohio
Virginia Military Institute, Lexington, Virginia
Warm Springs, Virginia
Washington & Lee University (University Chapel), Lexington, Virginia
Weaverville, North Carolina
West Orange, New York
West Park, New York
White Sulphur Springs, West Virginia
Winchester, Virginia
Winston-Salem, North Carolina
Woodchuck Lodge, Roxbury, New York

www.ingramcontent.com/pod-product-compliance
Lightning Source LLC
LaVergne TN
LVHW010633110826
845149LV00014B/2837

* 9 7 9 8 9 8 8 4 9 5 7 0 3 *